THE CONSTITUTIONAL SYSTEMS OF THE INDEPENDENT CENTRAL ASIAN STATES

This book undertakes the first comparative constitutional analysis of the Kyrgyz Republic and Republics of Kazakhstan, Turkmenistan, Uzbekistan and Tajikistan in their cultural, historical, political, economic and social context. The first chapter provides a general overview of the diverse and dynamic constitutional landscape across the region. A second chapter examines the Soviet constitutional system in depth as the womb of the Central Asian States. A third chapter completes the general picture by examining the constitutional influences of the 'new world order' of globalisation, neo-liberalism and good governance into which the five states were thrust. The remaining five chapters look in turn at the constitutional context of presidents and governments, parliaments and elections, courts and rights, society and economy, and culture and identity. The enquiry probes the regional patterns of neo-Sovietism, plebiscitary elections, weak courts and parliaments, crony capitalism and constraints on association, as well as the counter-tendencies that strengthen democracy, rights protection and pluralism. It reveals the Central Asian experience to be emblematic of the principal issues and tensions facing contemporary constitutional systems everywhere.

Pictorial Narrative

The Independent Central Asian Republics: *Mythical Frontiers.*

The Romanov Imperial crown on double-headed eagle, to the left, and Soviet Union's sickle and hammer with red star, to the right, converge on a yurt etched with the year 1991. This part of the composition refers to the continuous Russian political dominance from the 19th century up to 1991 when the Central Asian Republics achieved independence. Over the yurt, the crescent moon with rising star symbolises Islam, the common religion of the Republics.

To the right Tamerlane(*), the iconic founder of the Timurid Empire, recalls the medieval Turco-Persian splendour of the 'heart of the world.' Tajikistan's flag forms part of Tamerlane's crown—a blazing sun radiates from Kyrgyzstan's flag and envelopes his left arm. Adjoining the yurt is Norman Foster's Pyramid of Peace and Accord in Astana (capital of Kazakstan). Uzbekistan's flag occupies the other side of the pyramid. Kazakstan's flag is stretched across the bottom right corner. Turkmenistan's flag is spread in front of the pyramid. The composition concludes with a solitary swordsman and his white horse(**) under a starry night—capturing the nomadic past of the steppes and the spirit of adventure.

Putachad
Artist

* From forensic facial reconstruction of Tamerlane, from his tomb in Uzbekistan, by Gerasimov.

** Inspired by a Soviet poster 'we cannot dispense with the horse', Russian and Uzbek, Tashkent 1933, Mardjani.

Constitutional Systems of the World
General Editors: Peter Leyland, Andrew Harding and Benjamin L Berger
Associate Editors: Grégoire Webber and Rosalind Dixon

In the era of globalisation, issues of constitutional law and good governance are being seen increasingly as vital issues in all types of society. Since the end of the Cold War, there have been dramatic developments in democratic and legal reform, and post-conflict societies are also in the throes of reconstructing their governance systems. Even societies already firmly based on constitutional governance and the rule of law have undergone constitutional change and experimentation with new forms of governance; and their constitutional systems are increasingly subjected to comparative analysis and transplantation. Constitutional texts for practically every country in the world are now easily available on the internet. However, texts which enable one to understand the true context, purposes, interpretation and incidents of a constitutional system are much harder to locate, and are often extremely detailed and descriptive. This series seeks to provide scholars and students with accessible introductions to the constitutional systems of the world, supplying both a road map for the novice and, at the same time, a deeper understanding of the key historical, political and legal events which have shaped the constitutional landscape of each country. Each book in this series deals with a single country, or a group of countries with a common constitutional history, and each author is an expert in their field.

Published volumes

The Constitution of the United Kingdom; The Constitution of the United States; The Constitution of Vietnam; The Constitution of South Africa; The Constitution of Japan; The Constitution of Germany; The Constitution of Finland; The Constitution of Australia; The Constitution of the Republic of Austria; The Constitution of the Russian Federation; The Constitutional System of Thailand; The Constitution of Malaysia; The Constitution of China; The Constitution of Indonesia; The Constitution of France; The Constitution of Spain; The Constitution of Mexico; The Constitution of Israel; The Constitutional Systems of the Commonwealth Caribbean; The Constitution of Canada; The Constitution of Singapore; The Constitution of Belgium; The Constitution of Taiwan; The Constitution of Romania

Link to series website
http://www.hartpub.co.uk/series/csw

The Constitutional Systems of the Independent Central Asian States

A Contextual Analysis

Scott Newton

• HART •

OXFORD • LONDON • NEW YORK • NEW DELHI • SYDNEY

HART PUBLISHING
Bloomsbury Publishing Plc
Kemp House, Chawley Park, Cumnor Hill, Oxford, OX2 9PH, UK

HART PUBLISHING, the Hart/Stag logo, BLOOMSBURY and the Diana logo are trademarks of Bloomsbury Publishing Plc

First published in hardback, 2017
Paperback edition, 2018

A catalogue record for this book is available from the British Library.

Library of Congress Cataloging-in-Publication Data

Names: Newton, Scott, (law teacher), author.

Title: The constitutional systems of the independent Central Asian states : a contextual analysis / Scott Newton.

Description: Oxford ; Portland, Oregon : Hart Publishing, 2017. | Series: Constitutional systems of the world | Includes bibliographical references and index.

Identifi ers: LCCN 2016046229 (print) | LCCN 2016046772 (ebook) | ISBN 9781849462501 (pbk. : alk. paper) | ISBN 9781509909469 (Epub)

Subjects: LCSH: Constitutional law—Former Soviet republics. | Commonwealth of Independent States. | Former Soviet republics—Politics and government. | Constitutional law—Asia, Central.

Classifi cation: LCC KLA2070 .N53 2017 (print) | LCC KLA2070 (ebook) | DDC 342.58—dc23

LC record available at https://lccn.loc.gov/2016046229

ISBN: HB: 978-1-78043-157-4
PB: 978-1-50992-845-3
ePDF: 978-1-78043-157-6
ePub: 978-1-78043-157-7

Typeset by Compuscript Ltd, Shannon

To find out more about our authors and books visit www.hartpublishing.co.uk. Here you will find extracts, author information, details of forthcoming events and the option to sign up for our newsletters.

For Victoria and Sylvan, wife and son, companions throughout, with love and gratitude.

Contents

Introduction

First Principles: Constitutional Orders, Constitutional Functions, Constitutional Processes – Methodology and Schools of Thought – Plan of the Work

THE PRESENT VOLUME is a comparative study of the constitutional systems of several states in a common region. These are the former Soviet republics of what has variously been known as Central, Middle, or Inner Asia—a region notable, perhaps before anything else, for the historical obscurity into which it appeared to slip (and the fascination it has thereby exercised) after the decline of the Timurid Empire in the fifteenth century.[1] It remained largely insulated and isolated from the shaping forces of modern constitutionalism even as it was incorporated into the Romanov Empire over the course of the nineteenth century.[2] When constitutionalism did come to Central Asia, it came in its distinct Bolshevik variant, when the region was organised in the 1920s and 1930s as five among 15 constituent polities of a federal state, the Union of Soviet Socialist Republics. In consequence its perennial obscurity and fascination were perpetuated and enhanced for a further seven decades.[3]

[1] For general historical/cultural surveys of the region, reflecting its abiding mystique for Europeans see R Grousset, *Empire of the Steppes* (New Brunswick NJ, Rutgers University Press, 1971); C Thubron, *The Lost Heart of Asia* (London, Vintage, 2004); S Soucek, A History of Inner Asia (Cambridge, Cambridge University Press, 2000).

[2] For accounts of the incidents of the Russian annexation of the region and the background Anglo-Russian rivalry, see P Hopkirk, *The Great Game: On Secret Service in High Asia* (Oxford, Oxford University Press, 1991); F Burnaby, *A Ride to Khiva: Travels and Adventures in Central Asia* (New York, Cosimo, 2007).

[3] See F Maclean, *Eastern Approaches* (London, Penguin, 2006) for a rare outside glimpse in the 1930s into the then recently constituted and largely inaccessible Soviet Central Asian republics.

The Central Asian states present a particularly compelling episode in constitutional history, and a unique comparative laboratory of constitutional development, unedifying as the contemporary results might strike a sceptical observer. Like Commonwealth African states, they all became sovereign jurisdictions at a particular historical conjuncture (although of course in the one case that is a matter of more than a decade, in the other of a month, December 1991), as inheritors of a parent constitutional tradition, which they then proceed to modify and adapt, in parallel but revealingly divergent ways. The filial threads binding the Central Asian states to Russian/Soviet constitutional thought and practice are perhaps more fraught than those binding Nigeria, Kenya and other sub-Saharan former crown colonies to British constitutionalism. The decolonisation analogy between Central Asia and Africa will be examined at length in due course.

Kazakhstan, Uzbekistan and their sister jurisdictions acquired sovereignty in the wake of an unprecedented systemic collapse, which definitively discredited the general state socialist and particular Soviet project which had constituted them in the first place. Like Minerva they had sprung forth fully formed, but at a singularly propitious moment. For 1989 and its aftermath were not merely a fin-de-siècle springtime of nations, by analogy to the revolutionary year of 1848,[4] but of constitutions and constitutionalism. By the time of communism's collapse, constitutionalism in the form of world or global constitutionalism had become an authoritative, indeed normative, international discourse, integral to the putative 'New World Order' and the foretold 'End of History'.

But the demands of global economic integration, together with the now-unchallenged institutional supremacy of Western industrial democracies, exercised paradoxical effects. They appeared to enhance the significance of constitutionalism for the new post-socialist states but also to delimit the field of choice among constitutional architectures ex ante. Of all the Soviet Socialist Republics (SSRs) which comprised the Union, the Central Asian five were perhaps the most exposed to the contrary winds blowing across the twentieth century. Almost entirely Soviet artefacts, they were devoid of any pre-revolutionary political coherence, much less an antecedent modern legal tradition which might furnish constitutional resources (unlike, say, Russia or Georgia). They might therefore be supposed to have been just as much

[4] M Howard, 'The Springtime of Nations' (1990) 69 (1) *Foreign Affairs* 17, 18.

at the mercy of the (ostensibly) oecumenical New World Order at the close of the twentieth century as at the mercy of the partisan Bolshevik order at its start.

The evolution of Central Asian constitutionalism has been complex and contradictory, as this volume will elaborate. The simultaneous push from the repudiation of the Soviet past and pull of the embrace of the globalised present did not simply catapult Central Asia into the constitutional future—at least into any predictable or prefigured one. Neither the repudiation nor the embrace was as wholehearted as might have seemed at the time. After 20 years, the contemporary Central Asian constitutional systems exhibit something old (Turko-Persian-Islamic culture), something new (original ideas and devices), something borrowed (from world constitutionalism), something blue—or in this case red (derived from Soviet experience, ie path-dependent). The resulting hybrid manages to be dynastic/patrimonial, makeshift, liberal-democratic and neo-Soviet, all at once, and owes something to both Madison and Stalin—among other constitutional architects.

The five post-Soviet Central Asian constitutions are all to a significant degree instrumentalist. They were drafted by and in the interests of the ruling SSR elites. With the exception of Kyrgyzstan and Tajikistan, the serving Soviet Republican party secretaries succeeded to the office of President of the independent republics. The constitution drafters had little use for a 'veil of ignorance' (a speculative device in political theory intended to ensure a just political order by preventing parties' awareness of one another's interests and advantages from influencing their original choice in designing institutions);[5] they had their eyes on the main chance. The constitutional narrative of Central Asia presented here will no doubt strike some readers as more properly a matter of politics, or even journalism, than jurisprudence—an absorbing and still unfolding story, with plot twists and turns, and ironies and surprises aplenty. The politics of 'constitutional moments' should, in the view of some, be high-minded and principled as befits 'higher lawmaking'[6] but the politics of the Central Asian constitutional moments have fallen far short of such an ideal. Perhaps, though, they serve as a sobering and salutary counter-example, a reminder that constitutional politics are as much political as constitutional.

[5] J Rawls, *A Theory of Justice* (Cambridge MA, Harvard University Press, 1999).

[6] B Ackerman, *We the People: Transformations, Volume 2* (Cambridge MA, Harvard University Press, 2000) 266–94.

Notwithstanding their putative status as transitional or provisional, the five Central Asian constitutions all presented themselves as assured and definitive exercises in constitutional design. Constitutions must inevitably function as comprehensive legal-institutional charters, even when announcing themselves as interim or temporary.[7] Once they had adopted formal constitutions, the Central Asian states were in effect 'committed to launch', and followed out a constitutional trajectory. However, that trajectory has been erratic not ballistic or linear, with multiple swerves in the form of constitutional amendments—and for Kazakhstan and Kyrgyzstan, new constitutions. These serial amendments (or constitutions) do not merely reflect a learning or 'debugging' process, as might be anticipated for new states negotiating simultaneous economic and political transition (from plan to market, and isolation to integration, and from Soviet rule to something sui generis). They are also very much a reaction to interim events—from civil war in Tajikistan to parliamentary defiance in Kazakhstan and successive revolutions in Kyrgyzstan. They present a striking rebuke to the common error of supposing that constitutional systems, like self-determination, are a one-off matter. Constitutionalism has been in ferment in the region for two decades.

Now, though, almost two and a half decades on, a comparative constitutional analyst confronting the Central Asian systems cannot purport to evaluate constitutional design prospectively, in the manner of commentators on draft documents or provisions. Rather, they must inspect functional (or dysfunctional) constitutional machinery in operation. Central Asian constitutionalism has moved out of the realm of R&D and into that of consumer testing. And herewith a caveat: the temptation to harsh and hasty judgement, even derision, must be resisted. Certainly the circumstance that the Central Asian states are widely and not without warrant regarded as the most residually (or resurgently) Soviet of all former SSRs,[8] and indeed as some of the very

[7] *cf* the South African constitution of 1993, H Klug, *The Constitution of South Africa: A Contextual Analysis* (Oxford, Hart Publishing, 2010).

[8] J Heathershaw, 'New Great Game or Same Old Ideas? Neo-Sovietism and the International Politics of Imagining "Central Asia"' in D Dusseault (ed), *The CIS: Form or Substance?* (Cambridge, Cambridge University Press, 2007) 237–68, 237 (regional ideology of neo-Sovietism).

most repressive polities on the planet,[9] sharpens the challenge facing this enquiry. Doing justice to rather than simply dissing or dismissing the constitutions of the Central Asian states is no easy matter, but the intention here over eight chapters is to write on them rather than write them off.

FIRST PRINCIPLES: CONSTITUTIONAL ORDERS, CONSTITUTIONAL FUNCTIONS, CONSTITUTIONAL PROCESSES

Constitutional system or order. Although the five written constitutions will serve as the magnetic North of the analytic navigation here, to which our discussion will be by default orientated, the 'constitution outside the constitution'[10] (sub-constitutional legal norms effectively doing constitutional work) and the 'material constitution'[11] (the actual configuration of political and economic power in a society which produces the formal constitution) will be critical coordinates throughout. As evident in the title, this volume looks beyond the constitutional text to the *constitutional systems or orders* of the Central Asian states: all those aspects of the normative order, whether canonically constitutional or not (indeed whether formalised or not) that perform one or more constitutional roles.[12] A constitutional order need not mean 'constitutional government' in a praiseworthy sense, since a constitutional order can just as readily constrict political space by foreclosing deliberation and contestation.

[9] Freedom House has assigned Turkmenistan and Uzbekistan a score of 1 or 0 on its 1–40 index of political liberties in seven and ten, respectively, out of the last 13 annual evaluations and single digit scores on its 1–60 index of civil liberty for both in all 13. Only Kyrgyzstan merits the designation 'partly free'. Freedom House, Freedom in the World 2014, Comparative and Historical Data, available at www.freedomhouse.org/report-types/freedom-world#.VAhl-PmwLMo (accessed 6 November 2015).

[10] EA Young, 'The Constitution Outside the Constitution' (2007–08) 117 *Yale Law Journal* 408, 411.

[11] A Negri, 'The Material Constitution' in A Negri, *Books for Burning: Between Civil War and Democracy in 1970s Italy* (London, Verso, 2005) 180–81.

[12] M Tushnet, *The New Constitutional Order* (Princeton NJ, Princeton University Press, 2003) 1.

Constitutional functions, roles and criteria. Every scholar has their cherished set of defining constitutional functions, according them variable weight or ranking, for example, structuring, meta-normative (process-policing), rights-protecting, legitimising, aspirational (developmental), transitional (systemic change-regulating), social-redistributive, difference-accommodating (pluralist), identarian, economic, instrumentalist. There are also expansive and restrictive definitions of the term 'constitution' itself. The Anglo-American concept of specified limits to government has been distinguished from the continental concept of 'plan of government': is a given constitution superior to the rest of the normative order or does it simply collapse into it? One classic and illustrative definition posited the following comprehensive criteria for a genuine constitution: constitutive of a legal system, stable, written, superior, justiciable, entrenched and expressive of a common ideology.[13]

A constitution serving as an instrument of, not a constraint on, the governors has been argued to be merely a façade or a sham constitution.[14] While the Central Asian constitutions are not sham in any facile sense, they are instrumentalist. Though many of the enumerated possible constitutional functions and roles will be examined and evaluated here for the Central Asian cases, the reader is warned that instrumentalism will loom large. The use of general constitutional forms to prosecute very particular interests is especially likely to afflict constitutional systems like all those considered here that are: 1) young (not long established, therefore fragile or insecure and temporally close to the interests which design them); 2) transitional (following the sudden collapse and discrediting of a prior societal system); and 3) path-dependent (bearing the very particular legacy of a constitutional tradition notoriously subject to instrumentalisation).

Constitutional processes. Constitutions as legal texts could well be imagined to be less significant than the processes they set in motion: of interpretation and elaboration, of institutional evolution, of

[13] J Raz, 'On the Authority and Interpretation of Constitutions: Some Preliminaries' in L Alexander (ed), *Constitutionalism: Philosophical Foundations* (Cambridge, Cambridge University Press, 1998) 152–54.

[14] G Sartori, 'Constitutionalism: A Preliminary Discussion' (1962) 56 *The American Political Science Review* 853 (restricting the term 'constitutionalism' to cases of valid guarantees and enforceable limitations).

democratisation. Compelling drafting language—pregnant and artful textual provisions (eg the South African Constitution of 1996)[15]—can facilitate a ramifying jurisprudence. Thus, US constitutionalism might be said to owe much to the felicitous formulations of the text, which have beseeched continual interpretive labour. The Central Asian constitutions qua texts, readers should be forewarned, are not stellar examples of the modern genre; they present no great novelty or compelling departure. These are not notably imaginative documents. Unsurprisingly, neither has Central Asian constitutional jurisprudence covered itself with glory in its two decades of development. The states have largely foreclosed the kind of judicial autonomy and unrestricted institutional breathing space essential for constitutional imagination and insight to flourish, and correlatively for component institutions to develop and mature. Constitutional jurisprudence has been largely stunted across the states and constitutionalism has not become generally embedded in legal and political culture in a dynamic manner (with the notable exception of Kyrgyzstan and to a lesser degree Kazakhstan). In consequence, constitutional logic and argument have only in a restricted and qualified sense become part of broader processes of democratic deliberation and collective self-understanding. It is hard to detect evidence anywhere in the Central Asian cases of 'constitutional patriotism',[16] by which constitutionalism is stitched into the fabric of national life and traditions, defining not just reflecting national culture. Nor is it any easier to discover Central Asian examples of an evolving and dynamic 'constitutional identity',[17] which would take root in the particularities of collective history and experience.

METHODOLOGY AND SCHOOLS OF THOUGHT

The analysis developed at length below draws on four principal schools of analysis/bodies of literature:

[15] Klug (n 7).

[16] J Habermas, 'The Postnational Constellation and the Future of Democracy' in J Habermas, *The Postnational Constellation* (Cambridge MA, MIT Press, 2001) 56–112, 76.

[17] G Jacobsohn, 'Constitutional Identity' (2006) 68 *The Review of Politics* 361, 363.

Critical Constitutionalism

The Central Asian constitutional experience has also unfolded in a period of bold advances in critical constitutional theory and thought. Not only do the five constitutions furnish an intriguing comparative design laboratory, but also a tough empirical terrain to road-test the theoretical instruments of a new generation of constitutional scholars.[18] The Central Asian systems allow one to observe some of the standing tensions of constitutional theory—between limited government (guarantees) and plan of government (as among other identified functions of constitutions), between constitutional order and written instrument (or material and formal constitution), between constitutionalism and democracy, between norm (meta-norm) and exception. Constitutional constraints might sound farcical in the land of sultanistic presidents, when extensions of presidential term by special referendum or one-off waivers of term limits by constitutional amendment are a recurrent feature and 'First President' is a special status, distinct from that of President.[19] Constitutional protection of human rights might seem a grim joke where torture, telephone justice, targeted extra-judicial killings and even mass state violence are not simply faint historical echoes.[20] But to a critical constitutional analysis, even such flat-out examples of constitutional self-cancelling or hypocrisy shed light on the nature of modern constitutionalism and merit sustained, serious attention.

[18] For an example see N Sultany, 'The State of Progressive Constitutional Theory: The Paradox of Constitutional Democracy and the Project of Political Justification' (2012) 47 *Harvard Civil Rights–Civil Liberties* 371 (discursive analysis and critique of the competing major schools of constitutional thought regarding the counter-majoritarian problem) or D Kennedy, *A Critique of Adjudication: Fin De Siècle* (Cambridge MA, Harvard University Press, 1997) (exposition of elaborate ideological underpinnings of adjudicative rationality and their systematic disguise and 'translation' in judicial decisions).

[19] See eg Kaz Law 20.07.2000. (References to the five constitutions currently in force are designated in footnotes by three-letter abbreviations—Uzb, Kaz, Kyr, Taj, Tkm—and article number; earlier versions by year; references to subsidiary legislation by abbreviation, type of enactment and date; see Table of Authorities.)

[20] See eg Human Rights Watch, 'Bullets Were Falling Like Rain: The Andijan Massacre, May 13, 2005', available at www.hrw.org/sites/default/files/reports/uzbekistan0605.pdf (accessed 6 November 2015).

World Constitutionalism/Transition/ROL/Democratisation

The term 'world constitutionalism' has been proposed to capture the development of plural traditions of constitutional jurisprudence in the post-war world, a trend held to have accelerated dramatically post-Cold War.[21] The states emerging from the collapse of socialism, the Central Asian states among them, were carried on the crest of a constitutionalist wave. The Central Asian states together with the rest of the former socialist Bloc were subsumed under the dominant 'transition' paradigm, which encompassed the embrace of market economies, the practice of good governance, rule-of-law (ROL) reform and democratisation.[22] In this connection, the notion of an ideal constitutional design and an ideal set of political and economic institutions, borrowed from the best available models but suitably simplified and adapted, had begun to gain traction.[23] Democratisation had been grounded in human rights in the form of the 'emerging right to democratic governance', constructed in stages from the rights to self-determination, political expression and participation in free and fair elections.[24]

Bilateral and multilateral development agencies and institutions played a critical role as enforcers of emerging democratisation/ROL standards and promoters of correlative reforms in the region. Beyond undertaking specific programmatic interventions in the Central Asian states, the development agencies both produced and sponsored studies, served as a recurrent object of the scholarly attentions of others, and influenced the conceptual and political terms of debate. It is simply impossible to chart the course of constitutionalism in Central Asia over the last two decades without critically examining both the claims of the

[21] B Ackerman, 'The Rise of World Constitutionalism' (1997) 83 *Virginia Law Review* 771.

[22] See discussion in ch 3 for a definition and analysis of the transition paradigm.

[23] See J De Lisle, 'Lex Americana? United States Legal Assistance, American Legal Models and Legal Change in the Post-communist World and Beyond' (1999) 20 *University of Pennsylvania Journal of International Economic Law* 179; S Marks, 'Guarding the Gates With Two Faces: International Law and Political Reconstruction' (1998) 6 *Indiana Journal of Global Legal Studies* 457, 464–65 (promotion for transition states of formalistic, elections-focused concept of democracy without substantive institutional transformation).

[24] T Franck, 'The Emerging Right to Democratic Governance' (1992) 86 *American Journal of International Law* 46.

democratisation/ROL literature and the uses to which it has been put in donor interventions.

Native Constitutional Discourse

The venerable and rich Russian legal discourse remains conceptually native to many post-Soviet Central Asian jurists, whatever their professional vernacular. Like its sister civilian traditions in France or Germany it is formalist and as a general matter eschews extra- or meta-juridical perspectives such as public policy, law and economics, legal realist or critical legal analysis, socio-legal studies and legal anthropology. The body of constitutional commentary and analysis in Central Asia tends to be expository and doctrinal, as well as politically acceptable and inoffensive, given the very narrow limits of permissible critique of the regimes in place and their legitimising constitutional orders. It is nonetheless important for this study to attend to the constitutional discourse of Central Asian jurists (as well as their Russian colleagues), both for its independent analytic force and for its role in constructing and articulating constitutional ideology.

Central Asia Studies

Central Asia studies, formerly the province of a handful of scattered specialists and a subdivision of either oriental (for an older generation) or Soviet (for a younger generation) studies,[25] has flowered as a self-standing academic discourse and discipline in its own right, shaped and informed by a wide range of contemporary social-scientific and critical methods and approaches. A rich literature (as well as specialised journals and research/scholarly networks)[26] has grown up over the last two decades developing, exploring and analysing a broad array of regionally

[25] Hélène Carrère d'Encausse, René Grousset and Peter Hopkirk, to name three very disparate Central Asianists of a former day.

[26] Among them *Central Asia Survey, The Central Asia-Caucasus Analyst,* Cambridge Central Asia Forum, SOAS Centre for Contemporary Central Asia and the Caucasus, Johns Hopkins Central Asia-Caucasus Institute, European Society for Central Asia Studies.

distinctive or inflected themes and paradigms: neo-patrimonialism and the political salience of clientilistic, affective and extra-institutional ties; the High Politics of resource extraction/distribution and counter-terror in the post 9/11 era (irresistibly though imprecisely termed the New Great Game); nation-building and the political construction of identity (language, culture, citizenship and ethnicity in historical and contemporary context); democratisation/good governance; conflict studies and post-conflict transition; and development, market transition and global economic integration (globalisation). Such studies have deployed in the process the full complement of contemporary critiques, including post-coloniality, discourse, gender and national/international political economy. The present work seeks both to bring constitutional law into the Central Asia studies fold, and to employ the rich new literature to illuminate specifically legal and constitutional problems and issues.

PLAN OF THE WORK

This enquiry, in keeping with the spirit of the series, is a selective comparative analysis: an examination of the most salient themes and issues which a comparison of the five constitutional orders is likely to suggest, in light of the first principles and the methodology set out above.

Chapter one offers an overview of the main constitutional features of each of the jurisdictions at present, a contemporary snapshot, together with a brief sketch of relevant extra-constitutional context and an identification of the main constitutional events and trends of the two decades elapsed since independence. All the principal issues and themes to be examined in later chapters are outlined here.

Chapter two undertakes a comprehensive characterisation and analysis of the main aspects of the constitutional order of the USSR, the matrix in which those of the five states examined here all originated. As the reader will rapidly grasp, the view put forward here is that of all former SSRs, the particular constitutional predicament of the 'stans is least possible to fathom without a thorough grounding in the system that produced them in the first place. The depth of treatment here is warranted moreover to counter the prevalent view that the significance of the Soviet colossus has receded with its shadow.

Chapter three looks at the moment of emergence of the five independent states and canvasses the range of factors, influences and contingent developments which congenitally marked and shaped their constitutional orders. Among these are the circumstances of the dissolution of the Union, the centrality of sovereignty, the impatience and insistence of global market forces, and the tutelage, expectations and pressures of a public international community with an ideologically blinkered concept of 'transition.'

Chapters four and five look sequentially at the balance of power and governing responsibilities as between executive and legislative organs, both as conceived by the designers and stewards of the constitutional orders, and as they proceeded to play out once the institutions were functioning. In particular, chapter four seeks to explain how presidentialism acquired constitutionally grounded extraordinary powers across the region—sooner or later, gradually or precipitously, progressively or transiently—but came to lose them in Kyrgyzstan, uniquely. Chapter five explores the correlative question of how and why parliamentarianism (along with any remote hope for limited government) was strangled in the cradle in Turkmenistan and Uzbekistan by the consolidation of super-presidentialism,[27] why it was developmentally stunted in Kazakhstan and Tajikistan, and how it managed to overcome significant interim adversity and enjoy the reasonable prospect of reaching maturity in Kyrgyzstan.

Chapter six tracks the chequered fortunes of the court systems, their organisation, development and struggles for constitutional majority. It addresses the plight of rights and the general failure everywhere of Central Asian judiciaries to assert their constitutional role and keep their end up: they have not effectively policed constitutional boundaries either between states and citizens (the protection of individual rights) or between the structures of authority themselves. Here too, the challenge is to account for divergence across the five jurisdictions.

Chapter seven takes up the constitutional regulation of economic life for the five states but in an unusually broad perspective. It probes the 'constitution of economic transition' as well as the constitutional force of civil codification. Picking up on themes from chapter three, it considers as well the constraints on constitutional architecture imposed

[27] A constitutional system in which the president wields grossly disproportionate albeit less-than-total power over all other branches. JT Ishiyama and R Kennedy, 'Superpresidentialism and Political Party Development in Russia, Ukraine, Armenia and Kyrgyzstan' (2001) 53 *Europe-Asia Studies* 1177.

by the demands of global integration and international economic law, in the context of the diverse development strategies and the underlying political economy rationales among the states. At the end, it analyses privatisation and the constitutional configuration of market and state (private and public power), assessing the pivotal significance of cronyism, corruption and patronage networks for the constitutional orders.

Finally, chapter eight treats perhaps the knottiest of constitutional questions facing the young republics, the place of culture and identity, for it was the peculiar juridification of culture under the Soviet policy of developmental ethnonationalism that created the five polities and societies, as well as their constituent identities, in the first place. It examines the constitutional dimensions of cultural, social and religious pluralism: citizenship, equality, identity, autonomy and participation in public life.

FURTHER READING

Clientelism, Clans and Corruption

Radnitz S, *Weapons of the Wealthy: Predatory Regimes and Elite-led Protests in Central Asia* (Ithaca NY, Cornell University Press, 2012).

Resource Extraction and Counter-terror

Hiro D, *Inside Central Asia: A Political and Cultural History of Uzbekistan, Turkmenistan, Kazakhstan, Kyrgyzstan, Tajikistan, Turkey, and Iran* (London, Duckworth Overlook, 2013).

Kleveman L, *The New Great Game: Blood and Oil in Central Asia* (New York, Grove Press, 2004).

Rashid A, *Taliban: Militant Islam, Oil and Fundamentalism in Central Asia* (New Haven CT, Yale University Press, 2010).

Nation-building, History and Identity

Dave B, *Kazakhstan—Ethnicity, Language and Power* (Abingdon and New York, Routledge, 2008).

Edgar AL, *Tribal Nation: The Making of Soviet Turkmenistan* (Princeton NJ, Princeton University Press, 2006).

Martin T, *The Affirmative Action Empire: Nations and Nationalism in the Soviet Union, 1923–1939* (London and Ithaca NY, Cornell University Press, 2001).

Politics and Conflict

Heathershaw J, *Post-conflict Tajikistan: The Politics of Peacebuilding and the Emergence of Legitimate Order* (London, Routledge, 2009).

Peyrouse S, *Turkmenistan: Strategies of Power, Dilemmas of Development* (Armonk NY, ME Sharpe, 2012).

Olcott MB, *Kazakhstan: Unfulfilled Promise*, Revised Edition (Washington, Carnegie Endowment for Peace, 2010).

——, *Tajikistan's Difficult Development Path* (Washington, Carnegie Endowment for Peace, 2012).

Development, Market Transition and Globalisation

Gleason G, *Markets and Politics in Central Asia (Economies in Transition to the Market)* (London, Routledge, 2013).

Jones Luong P and Weinthal E, *Oil Is Not a Curse* (Cambridge Studies in Comparative Politics (Cambridge, Cambridge University Press, 2011).

Kandiyoti D, 'The Cry for Land: Agrarian Reform, Gender and Land Rights in Uzbekistan' (2003) 3 *Journal of Agrarian Change* 225.

1

Constitutional Overview

Lie of the 'Stans

Uzbekistan (Constitutional Background, Constitutional Essentials, Constitutional Vicissitudes) – Turkmenistan (Constitutional Background, Constitutional Essentials, Constitutional Vicissitudes) – Tajikistan (Constitutional Background, Constitutional Essentials, Constitutional Vicissitudes) – Kazakhstan (Constitutional Background, Constitutional Essentials, Constitutional Vicissitudes) – Kyrgyzstan (Constitutional Background, Constitutional Essentials, Constitutional Vicissitudes)

THE READER WHO is confronted with not one but five distinct constitutions in as many jurisdictions, all likely still unfamiliar enough to challenge his or her knowledge of geography, might find useful here at the outset a brief potted biography of each state and its constitution. The Republic of Kazakhstan, the Republic of Tajikistan, the Kyrgyz Republic, the Republic of Uzbekistan and the Republic of Turkmenistan all declared themselves independent states and claimed the status of subjects of international law in December 1991.[1] But while they may have only at that moment

[1] All five republics simultaneously became members of the UN in early 1992, thus belatedly joining two former fellow SSRs, Ukraine and Belarus, which oddly enough had been founding UN members, having joined on 24 October 1945, the same day as the USSR itself. Stalin had contrived this form of limited international recognition for the two European (Slavic) SSRs to increase the representation of socialist states in the new world organisation.

impinged on the world's consciousness as new sovereignties, they were all in fact national successor states to pre-existing subnational republics, as evident in their very names. Before December 1991, they were known officially as the Kazakh Soviet Socialist Republic (SSR), the Tajik SSR, the Kyrgyz SSR, the Uzbek SSR and the Turkmen SSR, and informally as (Soviet) Kazakhstan, Tajikistan, Kyrgyzstan (or Kyrgyzia), Uzbekistan and Turkmenistan. The constitutional history and legacy of the Central Asian SSRs are treated for the most part in chapter two, apart from a detailed analysis of the constitutional significance of ethno-territoriality and nationality, which is deferred until chapter eight.

As constituent Soviet republics, they each possessed a comprehensive armature of governing institutions: a Republican Soviet or Parliament, a Republican Council of Ministers or Executive and a Republican Judiciary—Supreme Court and lesser courts. They also were equipped with a battery of other Republican cultural, social and administrative institutions, not to mention a formal Republican party organisation and a scheme of local government and administrative territorial subdivisions. Two of the five—Tajikistan and Uzbekistan—further boasted an internal federal organisation of autonomous, sub-republican units, one for each, Gorno-Badakhsan and Karakalpakstan respectively. Every Central Asian SSR also possessed a formal written constitution, which, as suitably and separately amended, served them all for the initial period of independence until they adopted new constitutions—Turkmenistan and Uzbekistan over the course of 1992, Kyrgyzstan and Kazakhstan in 1993, and Tajikistan in 1994.

The five Central Asian states were thus emphatically not conjured into being at this juncture or created ex nihilo. Much like former colonial states, at the moment of independence they had long since been established as political-territorial entities. Unlike colonial jurisdictions however, the SSRs all enjoyed formal sovereignty and a formal constitution as well. So the first thing to understand when one surveys the constitutional histories of the Central Asian states is that well before independence they had been *comprehensively constituted in the formal sense of the term* –at independence they were already structured, regulated and fully kitted out institutionally as specified by a foundational written document, pursuant to which public authority was ostensibly exercised.

UZBEKISTAN

Constitutional Background: History, Context, Characteristics

From ancient times the most urbanised and central patch of Central Asia, Transoxiana or the Land beyond the Oxus, Uzbekistan (the name, as that of the other states, is a Soviet contrivance) was the site of its grandest architectural monuments and centre of both its Persian and Turkic cultural traditions. On its territory was the seat of the last native imperial (Timurid) dynasty in the fourteenth century, as well as of the last two pre-modern khanates (Kokand and Khiva) and emirate (Bokhara). The Russian conquest of that territory, by General MG Chernaiev, the 'Lion of Tashkent', was completed by 1875. It was annexed to the Romanov Empire as the central provinces (Syr-Darya, Samarkand and Fergana) of the General Governorate of Turkestan; the remaining provinces encompassed what are now Tajikistan, Turkmenistan, Kyrgyzstan and southern Kazakhstan. The khanates were dissolved, but the emirate was left as self-governing until after the 1917 Revolution. Tsarist Turkestan consisted of garrison provinces, with a thin Russian settlement and a thin penetration of Russian customs and norms. Things only got 'thick' once the Bolsheviks had consolidated their authority, reorganised the jurisdictions and launched their comprehensive emancipation project in the early 1920s.

Uzbekistan along with Kazakhstan is one of the two significant regional powers. Nearly twice as populous, it falls short of Kazakhstan's resource abundance and ethnic diversity. It lacks as well any democratic opening, having remained stonily and austerely authoritarian from the outset. Like Turkmenistan, although in a less extreme manner, Uzbekistan under the leadership of its autocratic president has embraced a nationalist ideology that stresses enduring unity and integrity; both those claims are difficult to square with the historical and demographic facts. It has consolidated the region's second most controlled political system and a correspondingly pliant constitutional order. Uzbekistan has figured prominently in the politics and strategic policy of counter-terror, extending its welcome to the US military after 9/11 only to rescind it four years later after international condemnation of the 2005 slaughter by government forces of 800 protestors kettled in a public square in Andijon.[2] It has proved a difficult, at times truculent and defiant, prospect for international engagement.

Uzbekistan was the site of the USSR's plantation economy, the vast agricultural extension project to support cotton mono-cropping, which generated prodigious yields accompanied by equally prodigious environmental destruction and corruption.[3] This project, from the mid-1950s to the end of the USSR, involved vast hydraulic engineering works to divert the waters of the Syr Darya and Amu Darya rivers (the Jaxertes and Oxus of ancient geography) to irrigate the cotton crops, and vast quantities of pesticides to protect them. The effects were to desiccate the Aral Sea, once the world's fourth largest inland body of water, and to trigger runaway ecological degradation across its watershed for millions of hectares. This disaster has impacted all the Central Asian states, but Uzbekistan most extensively.

Uzbekistan, unlike its neighbours, has carried over from Soviet days significant aspects of the statist organisation and direction of its cotton-based economy. It has also retained the preponderance of its inherited public assets in state ownership or ultimate control while enabling a private sector, umbilically joined to state officials, to thrive in other respects. Uzbekistan also inherited a large contingent of Soviet forces and the headquarters of the Turkestan military district, covering Central Asia, and boasts the region's largest standing military. The Uzbek security and police services are also exceptionally well-organised, powerful and omnipresent. Uzbekistan has gained notoriety for its draconian repression of any dissent or independent political activity, most infamously for the Andijon massacre. While the pattern of Uzbek human rights violations has been readily sensationalised in the media,[4] many other concerning developments in post-Soviet Uzbekistan have

[2] Human Rights Watch, 'Bullets Were Falling Like Rain: The Andijan Massacre, May 13, 2005', available at www.hrw.org/sites/default/files/reports/uzbekistan0605.pdf, accessed 6 November 2015.

[3] D Kandiyoti, *Agrarian Reform, Gender and Land Rights in Uzbekistan*, UNRISD 2002, available at www.unrisd.org/80256B3C005BCCF9/(httpAuxPages)/C2919AC1CD7B5379C1256CCA00369D07/$file/kandiyoti(sml).pdf, accessed 5 February 2016, 3.

[4] See generally C Murray, *Murder in Samarkand: A British Ambassador's Controversial Defiance of Tyranny in the War on Terror* (Edinburgh and London, Mainstream Publishing, 2007) (lurid but veracious account of Uzbek human rights violations).

remained in the background, such as the impact of state-set crop prices on rural livelihoods[5] or controlled exchange rate on traders and the discriminatory impact of language and schooling policies on the large Tajik minority.

Constitutional Essentials: Formal Structure of Government and System of Rights

The Uzbek Constitution[6] consists of 128 articles, organised under 26 chapters in six sections: General Principle; Basic Rights, Freedoms, and Duties; Society and Personality; Administrative Territorial and State Structure; Organisation of State Authority; and Amendment Procedures. The fifth section on state authority contains chapters each for Parliament, President, Cabinet, Local Government, Judiciary, Elections, Procuracy, Finance and Defence/Security. Of the five constitutions, it is the most elaborately structured and subdivided, though of modest length, just exceeding 7,000 words. It provides for a presidential system with an independent mandate and sweeping powers. The president nominates for consideration and confirmation by the parliament or Oliy Majilis, and removes from office, the prime minister, and confirms the Cabinet of Ministers. The president also nominates judges of the three apex courts and appoints and discharges all other judges and the provincial *hokims* (governors)[7] as well as the General Procurator, the head of the National Bank and other senior officials. The president is empowered to arrest or rescind the acts of government officials at central and local levels, and to issue decrees with mandatory force across the entire territory of the Republic.[8] The president is elected by direct universal suffrage for a term of seven years.[9] The Oliy Majlis is bicameral, consisting of a lower house, the Legislative Chamber and an upper house, the Senate. The 150 deputies of the Legislative Chamber are elected on the basis of territorial constituencies in accord

[5] See Kandiyoti (n 3).
[6] 08.12.1992 Constitution (hereinafter 'Uzb').
[7] Uzb 93.
[8] Uzb 94.
[9] Uzb 90.

with subsidiary legislation.[10] Six senators are elected from each territorial subdivision (provinces, the city of Tashkent and the Republic of Karakalpakstan) by the deputies of the respective local representative bodies (not directly elected), and an additional 16 are appointed by the president from among eminent persons.[11] The term of office for deputies of both chambers is five years.

Local government is in the form of councils elected directly but headed by a *hokim* (governor). The *hokim* at the provincial (oblast) level is appointed by and answerable to the president; the *hokim* at sub-provincial levels is appointed by and answerable to the provincial *hokim*. At the most local levels, neighbourhood or *mahalla* committees have been institutionalised as 'organs of self-government'. These traditional structures of authority were tolerated and used but not recognised by the Uzbek SSR but they have become formal tools of the Republic of Uzbekistan.[12] Uzbekistan has carried over its Soviet-era federalism: the Constitution has established Karakalpakstan as an Autonomous Republic (the term for a federal subdivision subordinate to a Union SSR and inherited in this case from the Uzbek SSR), with its own constitution and organs of government.[13]

Judicial authority is tripartite with three apex courts: Supreme Court, Supreme Arbitration Court and Constitutional Court. The Constitutional Court determines the constitutionality of laws, resolutions of the Oliy Majlis, presidential decrees, resolutions of central and local government and international treaties, and also gives authoritative interpretations of norms of the Constitution and statutes.[14] The General Procuracy has supervisory responsibility for the 'strict and uniform execution of all laws'.[15] A comprehensive catalogue of rights

[10] Uzb Law 12.12.2002.

[11] Uzb 77.

[12] Uzb 105, Uzb Law 02.09.1993. See T Dadabaev, 'Changing Nature of the Mahalla: Outcomes of the Project' (2006) 15 *RICAS Newsletter* 5, 8, available at www.ricas.ioc.u-tokyo.ac.jp/pub/pdf/nl015.pdf, accessed 4 February 2016; Human Rights Watch, 'Uzbekistan, From House to House: Abuses by Mahalla Committees' (2003), available at www.hrw.org/sites/default/files/reports/uzbekistan0903full.pdf, accessed 4 February 2016. See also discussion in ch 8.

[13] Uzb 70–75.

[14] Uzb 109.

[15] Uzb 118.

is enumerated in three chapters, Personal Rights,[16] Political Rights[17] and Social and Economic Rights;[18] these are balanced by Citizens' Duties.[19]

As in the other four states, the 'constitution outside the constitution', even in the strictly formal sense (setting aside issues of application, practice and informal or customary norms) is extensive. The principal designated Constitutional Laws include those on the Legislative Chamber, on the Senate, on Increasing the Role of Political Parties, on Results of the Referendum and Fundamental Principles of the Organisation of State Authority.[20] Other legislation carrying clear constitutional charge and part of the formal constitutional order would include the civil and criminal codes (substantive and procedural codes), the Laws on the Constitutional Court, Media, and Religious Organisations and the Constitution of Karakalpakstan.[21]

Constitutional Vicissitudes: Amendments, Elections/Referenda 1991–2014

Uzbekistan's first constitution was adopted on 8 December 1992 and took effect immediately, but pursuant to it, the sitting Supreme Soviet exercised parliamentary authority until the first elections to the Oliy Majilis two years later. The new body assumed authority only in 1995. Subsequent parliamentary elections were held at the expiry of the first mandated five-year term in 1999. Following a national referendum in January 2002, two constitutional amendments were approved, 1) introducing a second, upper chamber (the Senate) and 2) extending the presidential term-in-office from five to seven years. The number

16 Uzb 23–31.

17 Uzb 32–35.

18 Uzb 36–42.

19 Uzb 47–52.

20 Uzb 12.02.2002 Constitutional Law (Legislative chamber), 12.02.2002 Constitutional Law (Senate), 11.04.2007 Constitutional Law, 04.04.2002 Constitutional Law.

21 Uzb Criminal Code 22.09.1994, Criminal Procedure Code 22.09.1994, Criminal Enforcement Code 25.04.1997, Civil Code I 21.12.1995, Civil Code II 29.08.1996, Civil Procedure Code 30.08.1997, Law 30.08.1995 (Constitutional court), 26.12.1997 (mass media), 14.06.1991 (religious organisations), Constitution 09.04.1993 (Karakalpakstan).

of deputies to the Legislative Chamber was reduced to 120. Elections to the bicameral legislature have been held at due five-year intervals in December 2004, 2009, and most recently in December 2014. Presidential elections have been held in 2000 (on the basis of the five-year term deemed to have commenced when the Constitution came into effect in 1995), in 2007 (on the basis of the extension of term to seven years pursuant to the 2002 amendments and referendum), and most recently in January 2015 upon the expiry of the previous term.[22]

The adoption of the Constitutional Law of 4 April 2007 on political parties was intended to mark something of a democratic demarche and led to a further set of constitutional amendments (adopted by statute, not referendum) in 2011. These augment formal governmental and parliamentary authority at the expense of presidential, by (inter alia) transferring to the prime minister the power to appoint and direct the Cabinet of Ministers, by granting the prevailing parliamentary party the power to nominate the prime minister, and by providing a procedure for the Legislative Chamber to conduct a no-confidence vote.[23] But these formal changes have not affected the real distribution of power. Uzbekistan has not relentlessly ratcheted up the constitutional mechanism in the noisy, blatant manner of Turkmenistan, but has instead discreetly but inexorably consolidated its own brand of presidential absolutism. The Andijon events of 2005, in the wake of which the state barred any media access and successfully frustrated demands for an international inquiry, were in fact a glaring exception (in publicity and scale) to the shadowy, background operation of the 'repressive state apparatus'. Although Uzbekistan's police state is not elaborated in the constitutional black-letter provisions, it is grounded in the constitutional system, as discussed in chapter four.

The Uzbek state regarded Andijon as a dangerous and intolerable armed challenge to state authority. It readily categorised as terrorism the actions of the elements of the crowd who had earlier stormed a prison to free a group of local businessmen arrested for alleged Islamic extremism. But in so doing it exploited the general international

[22] www.osce.org/odihr/elections/uzbekistan/165876?download=true, accessed 6 November 2015.

[23] Uzb 98.

discourse and policy of counter-terrorism and the particular 'discourse of danger' respecting Central Asia[24] (not to mention its strategic alliance with Western governments). These international trends have greatly strengthened the hand of Uzbek hardliners and emboldened the forces of repression—the security state-within-a-state (see discussion of its Soviet roots in the next chapter). The threat from regional jihadists is certainly not imagined[25] but the reflexively brutal response has been to some extent fortuitously legitimised by the War on Terror.

TURKMENISTAN

Constitutional Background: History, Context, Characteristics

Turkmenistan, a largely desert expanse endowed with extraordinary hydrocarbon reserves like its sister-republics on the Caspian littoral (Kazakhstan, Azerbaijan), was the latest subdued and least politically unified territory in the Tsarist conquest and annexation of the region. It was home to the several nomadic and only loosely organised Turkmen tribes, whose self-appointed Bolshevik tutors organised their economic, social and political life along socialist lines and sought to forge among them a common sense of nationhood, notwithstanding a history of strong tribal identity and intertribal hostility. Tsarist rule had left social structures intact but Soviet authorities forcibly sedentarised the Turkmen and brought to an abrupt end their nomadic pastoral traditions over the course of mass collectivisation in the 1930s.[26] Turkmenistan was next after Uzbekistan in Moscow's Central Asian imperial plantation economy; its cotton production was similarly an artefact of massive centrally organised and implemented hydraulic intervention.

After independence Turkmenistan achieved a singular notoriety for its bizarre developmental trajectory, a Central Asian twist on a

[24] J Heathershaw and N Megoran, 'Contesting Danger: A New Agenda for Policy and Scholarship on Central Asia' (2011) 87 *International Affairs* 589, 589–91.

[25] See generally A Rashid, *Jihad: The Rise of Militant Islam in Central Asia* (London, Penguin, 2002) and A Rashid, *Taliban: Militant Islam, Oil and Fundamentalism in Central Asia* (New Haven CT, Yale University Press, 2010).

[26] A Edgar, *Tribal Nation: The Making of Soviet Turkmenistan* (Princeton NJ, Princeton University Press, 2006) 167–220.

dystopic fantasy—a cross between Orwell's *1984* and Terry Gilliam's film *Brazil.* The SSR Party Secretary, Saparamurat Niyazov, emerged upon independence as an over-the-top self-orientalising despot, ruling with near-absolute power until his death in 2006 as Turkmenbashi, 'Father of all Turkmen', and enforcing a cult of personality to make Stalin blush. Emblematic of Niyazov's unbridled megalomania was the Pharaonic-scale, revolving and round-the-clock verse-declaiming sculpture of the *Ruhnama* in the centre of Ashghabat. The *Ruhnama*[27] is the autobiographical 'book of wisdom' and ersatz national scripture he penned (with its five sections, Turkmen, Turkmen's Path, Turkmen Nation, Turkmen State and Spiritual World of the Turkmen) and made compulsory study for all schoolchildren and adults. From among the *embarras de richesses* of other incidents of Niyazov's self-glorification, such as his portrait on all banknotes, or the official renaming of January as 'Turkmenbashi' and April as 'Gurbansoltan' (his mother), every commentator had their cherished favourites.[28]

Apart from its signature ostentatious sultanism, independent Turkmenistan has distinguished itself by providing virtually free utilities and housing, while simultaneously frustrating/disabling individual initiative and entrepreneurialism as well as social protection (drastically curtailing social support and downsizing the health and education provision by mass sackings and curtailment of services). The local reception of Turkmenbashi's system has been complex, involving appropriation and subversion by those on whom it was imposed, in a manner analogous to the local/peripheral reception of the preceding Soviet system.[29] On the international plane, Turkmenistan has pursued a managed isolationism, having adopted 'positive neutrality', ostensibly on the Swiss

[27] S Turkmenbashy (Niyazov), *Rukhnama: Reflections on the Spiritual Values of the Turkmen* (Turkmenistan, Ashgabat, 2005).

[28] D Hiro, *Inside Central Asia: A Political and Cultural History of Uzbekistan, Turkmenistan, Kazakhstan, Kyrgyzstan, Tajikistan, Turkey, and Iran* (London, Duckworth Overlook, 2013) 20–25; S Peyrouse, *Turkmenistan: Strategies of Power, Dilemmas of Development* (Armonk NY, ME Sharpe, 2012) 82–84; SN Cummings, *Understanding Central Asia: Politics and Contested Transformations* (Abingdon and New York, Routledge, 2012) 57.

[29] A Bohr, *Turkmenistan: Power, Politics, and Petro-Authoritarianism* (London, Chatham House, 2016); Peyrouse (n 28) 108–31.

model, as a central constitutional principle. Having navigated over its first two decades the turbulent waters of pipeline diplomacy (successfully negotiating with, and playing off against one another, China, Russia, the US and Iran), greenfield exploitation, the fluctuating prices of commodities and non-paying customers (recalcitrant Russia notably accumulated staggering gas arrears), Turkmenistan has earned vast revenues and accumulated commensurate wealth—little of which has trickled down to its tiny population (five million), who have been deliberately 'underdeveloped'. Improbably, the passing of Turkmenbashi has left his monuments and his system alike intact.[30]

It is certainly sobering that such an egregious recapitulation of interwar European dictatorship could be constitutionally clothed at the century's end. Nonetheless, the perverse fascination exercised on everyone by the spectacle of post-Soviet Turkmenistan should be resisted: it obscures the functionality of the system in a globalised context. 'Positive neutrality' (which did not prevent Niyazov from assisting in the 9/11 aftermath by permitting coalition overflights and in other ways) and one-man decision-making have facilitated Turkmenistan's interrelated economic and strategic global integration. Much as Roosevelt is reported to have remarked of the comparative ease of negotiating with Stalin,[31] who was unencumbered by Parliament or Congress, Niyazov was the 'whole works', for diplomats (whether Russian, US, Iranian or Chinese) and multinationals alike (he was referred to as 'Mr 33 per cent').[32] Turkmenistan's constitutional order, however repugnant in its internal manifestations, was welcome in its external. 'World constitutionalism', it would appear, rather fails to appreciate the political economy of tyranny in this strategic frontier of a new world order that is both resource-hungry and terror-obsessed.

[30] 'A horse, a horse … Turkmenistan president honours himself with statue', the *Guardian* 25 May 2015, available at www.theguardian.com/world/2015/may/25/horse-turkmenistan-president-statute-berdymukhamedov, accessed 16 June 2016.

[31] R McIntyre, *Twelve Years With Roosevelt* (London, Putnam, 1948) 171.

[32] MB Olcott, *Central Asia's Second Chance* (Washington, Carnegie Endowment for Peace, 2005) 101.

Constitutional Essentials: Formal Structure of Government and System of Rights 2014

The compact and compendious Turkmen Constitution,[33] consisting of 117 articles in eight sections (Fundamentals of Constitutional Structure; Citizen and Human Rights, Freedoms, and Duties; System of Governance; Local Self-Government; Electoral System; Judiciary; Procuracy; Concluding Provisions), is by a significant margin the briefest (less than 5,000 words) of the five constitutions and is characterised by terse formulations without elaboration. It was last amended in 2008 after the death of Niyazov. It provides[34] for a democratic, law-based and secular state embracing a presidential form of government and enjoying 'permanent neutrality', as recognised in a cited UN General Assembly Resolution.[35] The state language is Turkmen, and no official provision is made for any other language, save that all citizens have the right to use their native tongue.[36] Turkmenistan has a pure presidential system, without a prime minister, the president serving as head of government and acting through a directly subordinate Cabinet of Ministers. The president, elected on a separate mandate for a five-year term is 'head of state and the executive, the guarantee of state independence and the status of neutrality.'[37] Presidential powers include appointment and dismissal with agreement of the parliament, the unicameral Mejlis, of the Chair of the Supreme Court, the General Procurator and the Ministers of Internal Affairs and Justice (*Adalat*);[38] otherwise the Cabinet is subject to direct formation and appointment by the president.[39] The president forms the State Security Council[40] and the Elections Commission[41] and exercises legislative authority as

[33] 18.05.1992 Constitution (hereinafter 'Tkm').

[34] Tkm 1.

[35] UN General Assembly Resolution 50/80. See generally L Anceschi, *Turkmenistan's Foreign Policy: Positive Neutrality and the Consolidation of the Turkmen Regime* (Central Asia Research Forum 13) (London, Routledge, 2008).

[36] Tkm 14.

[37] Tkm 50.

[38] Tkm 54(12).

[39] Tkm 73.

[40] Tkm 54(4).

[41] Tkm 54(8).

well, via the promulgation of decrees and order binding across the entire national territory.[42]

The right of legislative initiative is vested in the president, Mejlis deputies, the Cabinet and the Supreme Court Chair.[43] The Mejlis is composed of 125 deputies, elected to five-year terms on the basis of territorial constituencies of rough parity of electors.[44] The General Procuracy, beyond its prosecutorial functions, has supervisory responsibility for the legality of investigations[45] as well as general supervisory responsibility for the 'strict and uniform execution' of all laws, acts of the president and Cabinet and Mejlis resolutions.[46] The judiciary is organised and regulated by subsidiary legislation,[47] as a unified system, with three chambers (civil, criminal, commercial or arbitration).[48] Alone among the five states, Turkmenistan lacks a Constitutional Court. Civil, political, economic and social rights are elaborated comprehensively.[49] Norms of constitutional import include constitutional laws, substantive and procedural criminal and civil codes and subsidiary legislation, including inter alia the Laws on the President, Courts, the Mejlis, Mass Media, Religious Organisations and Normative Acts.[50]

Constitutional Vicissitudes: Amendments, Elections/Referenda 1991–2014

Adopted in 18 May 1992, less than six months after independence, and the first of the five, the Turkmen Constitution already clearly exhibited the hallmarks of an 'own road', though surely not the sole

[42] Tkm 5.
[43] Tkm 65.
[44] Tkm 60.
[45] Tkm 111.
[46] Tkm 110.
[47] Tkm 15.8.2009 Law.
[48] Tkm 109.
[49] Tkm 18–47.
[50] Tkm Constitutional Law 12.12.1995 (permanent neutrality), 21.05.2011 Law (President), 15.8.2009 Law (courts), 09.01.2009 Law (Mejlis), 22.12.2012 Law (media), 21.10.1993 Law (religious organisations), Law 07.12.2005 (normative acts), 12.07.1997 Criminal Code, 18.04.2009 Criminal Procedure Code, 17.07.1998 Civil Code.

self-declared anomaly in modern constitutional history.[51] Turkmenistan can be understood to have carried on the Bolshevik tradition of constitutional experimentation and innovation (or sheer audacity), discussed in chapter two, but with transparent instrumentalism and in a sceptical world environment. The chief novelty of the first constitution was the *Halk Malslahty* (People's Council), established in its original form as a supreme representative organ of *people's* power,[52] distinct from (and lexically prior to) the three branches of government, which wielded supreme *state* power. In its original form, the Halk Maslahaty was a consultative organ consisting of the senior-most state officials from all branches (President, Chairs of Supreme and Supreme Economic Court, General Procurator, Cabinet of Ministers), as well as all the Mejlis deputies and the heads of local government and specially elected representatives, *halk wekilleri* from each district (*etrap*), who were outnumbered by the ex officio members.[53] Its remit was limited to highest matters of state (constitutional amendments, referenda, state and administrative boundaries, declaration of war, inter alia) and it was to be convened no less than once a year by the president.[54]

The 1999 amendments, adopted by the Mejlis (a 2/3 vote of the Mejlis was sufficient to amend per article 115), vastly enhanced the power of the Halk Maslahaty at the expense of that same Mejlis. The Halk Maslahaty could now amend the Constitution directly[55] (rather than to advise and consider, as before), which it proceeded to do forthwith in granting the sitting president 'the exclusive right to exercise the powers of head of state without term limits', as well as exercise comprehensive control over the electoral process. Its stature was enhanced in 2003 to a co-equal fourth branch of state power[56] and it was granted

[51] The Constitution of the Democratic People's Republic of North Korea provides in its preamble: 'The DPRK Socialist Constitution is a Kim Il Sung constitution which legally embodies Comrade Kim Il Sung's Juche state construction ideology and achievements.'

[52] Tkm 1992 (unamended) 45.

[53] Tkm 1992 48.

[54] Tkm 50, 48.

[55] Tkm 1999 art 113.

[56] Tkm 2003 4, 'State authority is divided among the halk maslahats, legislative, executive, and judicial powers, which shall act independently, balancing one another.' In the 1992 version, art 4 only made reference to the three conventional branches of government.

inter alia the power to dissolve the Mejlis and local councils, the power to call elections at all levels and appoint the electoral commission and a quasi-judicial power to pronounce unspecified actions treasonous and persons traitors.[57] The Cabinet, the Mejlis, the General Procuracy and the Supreme Court were all required to report to it annually. Subsidiary legislation in 2005, annulled two years later, established Halk Maslahaty at regional and local levels.[58]

The sequel of the attempted coup in 2002 perfectly demonstrates the constitutional order's 'prime directive': before all else to safeguard and immunise the ruling power by forestalling ex ante and eliminating ex post any threat or challenge. Niyazov's former foreign minister Shikhmuradov, who had earlier broken with him spectacularly and launched a bitter denunciation from self-exile, apparently returned secretly to Ashghabat and organised a (botched) ambush of Niyazov's motorcade. In the aftermath not only were Shikhmuradov and associates apprehended (and forced to make humiliating public confessions), and the Uzbek ambassador implicated, but an ever-widening dragnet engulfed hundreds of ostensible suspects. The whole scenario seems to have been lifted straight from the 1934 Kirov affair (when Stalin launched a purge via the investigation into the mysterious assassination, almost certainly at his personal instructions, of the Leningrad party chief), even down to the persecution of family members, numbers of whom were evicted and expelled from Ashgabat.[59] The 2003 amendments, and particularly the treason sub-article for the Halk Maslahaty, clearly seem to represent the constitutional assimilation of these events. The 2008 amendments after Niyazov's death were brought in to excise the more unsightly constitutional carbuncles but have left largely intact the physiognomy of the Niyazov state. The national Halk Maslahaty has been effectively constitutionally 'disappeared', and the institution relegated to a single brief article in the chapter on local

[57] Tkm 2003 47, 48(4), 48(2), 48(9).

[58] Tkm Law 25.10.2005 (invalidated); Const Law 26.09.2008 (abolishing the Halk Maslahaty). See discussion in ch 8 on local governance.

[59] See E Decaux, 'OSCE Rapporteur's Report on Turkmenistan' 12 March 2003, available at www.osce.org/odihr/18372, accessed 9 February 2016.

government,[60] while the Mejlis has had restored to it its proper breadth of legislative authority.

Presidential elections were held in 1990 when the office was first established for the Turkmen 1990, and again post-independence in 1992 when Niyazov was elected unopposed. A referendum called by the Halk Maslahty in 1994 extended his term without an election for five years. Upon the basis of the 1999 amendments, as just noted, he was made president for life. After his death in late 2006, in elections held in early 2007, Acting President Kurbanguly Berdymukhamedov, Deputy Prime Minister and former Minister of Health (and previously the late Turkmenbashi's dentist, the capacity in which he first came to prominence, as well as being practically a presidential body double)[61] prevailed. Berdymukhamedov was re-elected in 2012, from among a field of exclusively Democratic Party of Turkmenistan (DPT) candidates (as in 2007). Elections to the Mejlis have been held in 1994 (only one of 50 seats was contested), 1999, 2004, 2008 and 2012. Seats have only ever been contested by the DPT, the reconstituted Communist Party of Turkmenistan, the only such registered, although citizens enjoy a formal right to form political parties.[62] The post-Niyazov changes in the political system appear to have re-normalised Turkmenistan in the regional mould of a centralised authority dividing the political spoils with satellite and subordinate, but locally powerful, authorities—a shift from one-man sultanism to a more dispersed (and regionally familiar) neo-patrimonialism may be observed.[63]

The series of constitutional amendments before 2008 closely tracked and reflected the development of an idiosyncratic and erratic despotic regime. If the USSR Constitution in the perestroika reforms under Gorbachev, as discussed below in chapter two, was progressively sanitised and civilised, Turkmenistan's constitutional evolution (until

[60] Tkm 79, Constitutional Law 26.09.2008 (invalidating the Constitutional Law 15.08.2003). Powers and organisation of the local halk maslahats are as elaborated in subsidiary legislation.

[61] Hiro (n 28) 20.

[62] Tkm 28. The devil generally residing in the subsidiary legislative and regulatory details, no-one has ever managed (or dared) successfully to register another party.

[63] See N Kunysz, 'From Sultanism to Neopatrimonialism? Regionalism Within Turkmenistan' (2012) 31 *Central Asian Survey* 1.

recently) was in the opposite direction. Turkmenistan exemplifies in particularly stark form a Central Asian pattern—progressive constitutional stringency in the direction of consolidation of an existing configuration of power, making for a trademark constitutional 'shamelessness' in the context of punctilious formalism. Indeed, the Turkmen Constitution itself has served as a kind of theatre for the staging of the rituals of dictatorship.

An enduring, formally extra-constitutional feature of the Niyazov era which was in fact fundamental to the constitutional order was the Turkmenistan National Revival Movement, Galkynysh,[64] a master public association which coordinated the DPT with the other official, sectoral public associations, the Trade Union, the Women's Union, the Youth Union and the Veteran's Union. This comprehensive state puppetry of ostensibly self-organised bodies, a perfect specimen of a counterfeit public sphere, if anything, represents an intensification of the state colonisation of civil society characteristic of the Soviet constitutional order and examined in chapter two.

KAZAKHSTAN

Constitutional Background: History, Context, Characteristics

Kazakhstan, by far the largest (ninth in area in the world, with a land mass greater than Western Europe), most diverse and developmentally successful new Central Asian sovereignty, resists stereotyping as yet another regional tinpot autocracy, and presents particular challenges to an analysis such as this in its contradictions and complexities. It manages to be authoritarian and managed but not notably repressive or dictatorial, to be prosperous but patchily so, to be sophisticated but still recognisably Soviet, and to concentrate authority at the centre but accommodate regional power structures. In Soviet times, Kazakhstan functioned in part as a quarantine zone of exile and experimentation (economic and military). Its northern and western stretches were the sites of a notorious section of the Gulag, a misbegotten campaign to

[64] Const Law 15.08.2003 art 2; J Šír, '*Halk Maslahaty* in the Context of the Constitutional Evolution of Post-Soviet Turkmenistan' (2005) 6 *Perspectives on European Politics and Society* 321, 327.

plant the steppe in wheat (Khrushchev's 'virgin lands'), the dumping ground of exiled unreliable populations (Volga Germans, Chechens, Koreans, Meskhetian Turks, Poles), an open-air nuclear testing ground (the Polygon, near Semipalatinsk), and the showcase staging platform of the Soviet space effort (Baikonur).

Occupying the vast steppelands between the southern Urals and the Altai, Kazakhstan has both geographically and historically enjoyed a much tighter connection to Russia than its sister Central Asian republics.[65] 'Central Asia and Kazakhstan' was the standard Soviet designation for the region, emphasising the distinctiveness of Kazakhstan. The Kazakh nomads accepted the protection of the Imperial Crown in the eighteenth century, and large numbers of Russian settlers moved south. If Kazakhstan as something of a European frontier has typically been regarded as to a degree historically Russified (in language, culture and mindset),[66] rather than simply Sovietised (as its sister 'stans),[67] its constitutional trajectory since 1991 also recalls Russia's. Less dramatically than its northern neighbour, and with fewer plot twists, Kazakhstan too is the protagonist of its own constitutional coming-of-age story, and does supply some modest narrative élan. Unfortunately, the really interesting bits came very early on, for, like Russia, Kazakhstan replaced its first, presidentialist constitution after a legislative–executive confrontation and crisis (though without artillery) with a second, super-presidentialist one.[68] If the second Russian Republic[69] has counted three presidents in its 20 years (albeit with the prospect of an indefinite alternation between numbers 2 and 3) and tolerated a limited but shrinking degree of openness (while imposing ineffective constraints on rulers),[70] Kazakhstan's

[65] MB Olcott, *The Kazakhs* (Stanford CA, Hoover Institution Press, 1995) 28–82 (Russian rule, settlement and cultural impact).

[66] B Dave, *Kazakhstan—Ethnicity, Language and Power* (Abingdon and New York, Routledge, 2008) 50–54 (primacy of Russian language).

[67] It was coercively sedentarised and collectivised, contemporaneously with the events in the Ukraine, and with a similarly devastating death toll. Olcott (n 65) 176–87.

[68] JT Ishiyama and R Kennedy, 'Superpresidentialism and Political Party Development in Russia, Ukraine, Armenia and Kyrgyzstan' (2001) 53 *Europe-Asia Studies* 1177.

[69] R Sharlet, 'Transitional Constitutionalism: Politics and Law in the Second Russian Republic' (1995–96) 14 *Wisconsin International Law Journal* 495, 495.

[70] J Henderson, *Constitution of the Russian Federation* (Oxford, Hart Publishing, 2011) 255–59.

successor constitutional system, from 1995 onwards, has progressively and severely constricted the space for political contestation, and entrenched the regime of its first and only president.

Kazakhstan has also stood out regionally as a significant international actor in its own right, and increasingly as a capital-exporter as well as importer, rather than as a largely passive object of strategic or investment calculation on the part of other international powers, whether states or multinational corporations (MNCs). Kazakhstan has taken a lead role in international and regional organisations, having been the only Central Asian state to assume the presidency of the OSCE (Organisation for Security and Co-operation in Europe, the principal East–West intergovernmental security and development organisation). It has maintained consistently cordial and beneficial relations with the US, the EU, China and Russia, all at once and no mean feat.[71] Eschewing the default (and facile) 'nation-building' ideology of neighbouring states, Kazakhstan's Nazarbayev has employed a distinctly more nuanced and outwardly orientated developmentalism[72] as the template for his political project, all the while securing his ultimate control. Indicative of Kazakhstan's regionally unique positioning is its progressive education policy, encompassing accelerated modernisation at home and state-funded higher education abroad. To insist on applying the habitual metric of 'democratisation' is to miss the salient features of Kazakshtan's constitutional development.

Constitutional Essentials: Formal Structure of Government and System of Rights 2014

Consisting of 98 articles arranged in nine sections (General Provisions; Person and Citizen; President; Parliament; Government; Constitutional

[71] MB Olcott, *Kazakhstan: Unfulfilled Promise*, Revised Edition (Washington, Carnegie Endowment for Peace, 2010) 275–88.

[72] Nazarbaev's vision is elaborated in successive strategic plans *Kazakhstan 2030,* announced in 1997, and replaced in 2014 by *Kazakhstan 2050. Kazakhstan 2030*, available at www.kostanay.gov.kz/eng/strategija_kazahstan_2030.html, accessed 6 November 2015; *Kazakhstan 2050*, available at www.strategy2050.kz/en/, accessed 6 November 2015; Olcott (n 71) 272–73; D Matthews, 'Kazakhstan goes West, but only so far' *Times Higher Education*, 8 March 2012, available at www.timeshighereducation.co.uk/419261.article, accessed 6 November 2015.

Court; Courts and Justice; Local Administration and Self-government; Concluding and Transitional Provisions), Kazakhstan's Constitution[73] is as vast as its territory: coming in at over 11,000 words it is characterised by comprehensive and elaborate textual regulation. It was adopted in 1995, replacing the inaugural Constitution of two years earlier, and last amended in 2011. Kazakhstan has embraced an emphatically presidential system. State and private ownership are both recognised; land, subsurface and other resources are in state ownership, article 6; land (but not other resources) may be in private ownership, as provided by subsidiary legislation. Kazakh is established as state language, but Russian as an 'official language' is given parity.[74] A very broad catalogue of civil and political and social and economic rights is elaborated and judicial guarantees are further specified. Notable among constitutionally guaranteed rights are those to a minimum wage and pension, social security on specified grounds (old age, disability), and to free medical assistance.[75] Principal constitutional laws include those on the Government, Elections, the First President, the President, the Constitutional Council, State Independence, the Judicial System and the Status of Judges, and Parliament and the Status of its Deputies. Many other legislative acts would qualify as fundamental aspects of the formal constitutional order, including the criminal and civil substantive and procedural codes, and the Laws on Normative Acts, Religious Organisations, Mass Media and others.[76]

The president is the 'symbol and guarantee of the unity of the people and state power, the inviolability of the Constitution' and 'facilitates the functioning in concert of all branches of government', thus enjoying a supreme constitutional status over and beyond executive, legislature and judiciary.[77] The term is five years, subject to a two-term

[73] 30.08.1995 Constitution (hereinafter 'Kaz').

[74] Kaz 7.

[75] Kaz 28–29.

[76] Kaz Constitutional Laws 16.10.1995 (Parliament and deputies), 18.12.1995 (Government), 26.12.1995 (President), 20.07.2000 (First President), 28.09.1995 (elections), (25.12.2000 (judiciary), 16.12.1991 (independence); Civil Code (General Part) 13.12.1997, (Special Part) 01.07.1999; Civil Procedure Code 13.07.1999; Criminal Procedure Code 27.12.1994, Criminal Code 16.07.1997; Laws 24.03.1998 (normative acts), 23.07.1999 (media), 11.10.2011 (religious activity).

[77] Kaz 40.

limit,[78] although pre-term presidential elections may be designated by the president. Exclusive presidential powers of appointment and dismissal extend to the prime minister (upon agreement of the Majilis), the Ministers of Foreign Affairs, Internal Affairs, Defence, Justice and the provincial Akims (governors). The president also appoints, with the consent of the Senate, the General Procurator, the Chair of the National Bank and the Chair of the Committee of National Security.[79] The president determines the structure of government, forms the Security Council, the Supreme Judicial Council and the Assembly of the People. He forms and disbands the central executive organs of the Republic, as well as the bodies subordinate to the president. The president further has the right to suspend or rescind the acts of central and local government, and to issue binding decrees and resolutions (ie to legislate directly).[80] Beyond the provision regulating the office in general, there is a separate constitutional law in Kazakhstan applying exclusively to the sitting (first) president.[81] Pursuant to it, the constitutional two-term limit is not applicable to the First President.

Parliament consists of a lower house, the Majlis, composed of 107 deputies, 98 of whom are elected on the basis of territorial constituencies and nine by the Assembly of the People, serving five-year terms; and an upper house, the Senate, consisting of two Senators from each province (and the major and capital cities), and 15 Senators appointed by the president, serving six-year terms, with half the elected Senators subject to re-election every three years.[82] Supermajorities of 2/3 of both chambers are required to override a presidential veto of ordinary legislation, and 3/4 a veto of constitutional legislation.[83]

The Kazakhstani judiciary is a unitary system, with the Supreme Court at its apex. There is no separate Economic Court; there are separate civil and criminal collegia at Provincial and Supreme Courts. Judges are appointed permanently; chairs for a term of five years. The Higher

[78] Kaz 42.
[79] Kaz 44.
[80] Kaz 45.
[81] Kaz Law 20.07.2000.
[82] Kaz 50–51.
[83] Kaz 54.

Judicial Council, separately regulated by constitutional law[84] and consisting of the Chairs of the Constitutional Council and Supreme Court, the General Prosecutor, the Minister of Justice, Senators, judges and other persons to be appointed by the President of the Republic, recommends the appointment and discharge of Supreme Court justices and provincial (*oblast'*) chairs and judges; a lesser body, the Qualification Commission, performs similar functions for district judges. The Procuracy enjoys both broad supervisory as well as prosecutorial powers. It is responsible for supervising the 'strict and uniform execution' of laws, presidential decrees and other legal normative acts, as well as the legality of investigative operations. It can challenge laws and other legal normative acts contradicting the Constitution.[85]

The Constitutional Council (treated under a separate constitutional chapter from the Judiciary), consisting of seven members serving six-year terms, has the power of judicial review of constitutionality of legislation before entry-into-force and only upon the application of the president, the Chairs of the Majlis and the Senate, no less than one-fifth of parliamentary deputies, or the prime minister.[86] Where a court considers that a law or normative act abridges human or citizens' rights, it is obliged to make application for a determination by the Council.[87] Presidential objections to Council resolutions require a 2/3 vote to be overridden.[88] Local government is in the form of elected *maslikhat*s (councils), at provincial (oblast') and district level, but the presidentially appointed *Akim*s direct the work of the *maslikhat*s. The Assembly of the People, though referenced in the Constitution, is separately chartered and regulated.[89] It is a consultative body with a remit to facilitate inter-ethnic relations and promote national unity consisting of members drawn from civil society and ethno-cultural organisations. It has the right to elect nine Majlis deputies.

[84] Kaz Constitutional Law 25.12.2000.
[85] Kaz 83.
[86] Kaz 72.
[87] Kaz 78.
[88] Kaz 73.
[89] Kaz Law 20.10.2008.

Constitutional Vicissitudes: Amendments, Elections/Referenda 1991–2014

Kazakhstan's initial 1993 Constitution was law of the land for little more than two years. It granted significant powers to the Supreme Soviet (as it continued to be known), and left the precise delineation of appointment and other powers unclear as between executive and legislature, scope for manoeuvre which was promptly exploited by the unlucky thirteenth convocation of the Kazakhstan Supreme Soviet. The first parliamentary elections were held in 1994 but the results were invalidated in an unexpected decision by the previously quiescent Constitutional Court, in the wake of a presidential–parliamentary stand-off over the demanded recall of the prime minister.[90] During its brief 11-month life, the thirteenth Supreme Soviet had overridden presidential vetoes and generally proved itself a formidable force—much as its Russian counterpart had done. The president lost no time in dissolving the Supreme Soviet after affirmation on (his own) appeal of the Constitutional Court decision (with the Cromwellian touch of dismissing the deputies in person and immediately depriving them of any state privileges), revoked all its acts and ruled by decree until a new, reliably presidentialist constitution was drafted and adopted by referendum several months later.

Nazarbaev had shelled his legislature into submission every bit as definitively as his Russian Federation colleague, but by constitutional coup alone. The formally independent Constitutional Court was replaced with a much more pliant and weaker Council (borrowed from the French Constitution) in the new 1995 dispensation. Elections to the new bicameral and now constitutionally so-designated 'Parliament'

[90] The case itself was brought by an unsuccessful candidate, T Kviatkovskaia who claimed that the districting by the Central Elections Commission was unconstitutional on the grounds of grossly unequal representation (numbers of voters). 06.03.1995 Ruling, Constitutional Court. See Olcott (n 71) 109–12 for an account of the political context. The plaintiff's subsequent career successfully standing for a seat on the presidential party ticket suggests a comparison to L Timashuk, the Kremlin cardiologist whose accusation of malpractice in the treatment of Leningrad party chief Zhdanov set in motion the investigation and prosecution of the Doctors' Plot in Stalin's final years. J Brent and V Naumov, *Stalin's Last Crime: The Doctors' Plot* (London, John Murray, 2003) 13–53.

took place at the end of 1995, and again in 1999 and 2003 (for the Majilis), per constitutional requirements. Principal amendments to the Constitution have only been brought in twice, in 1998 and 2007[91] (the exceptionally complex amendment process allows the president to bypass the requirement for a referendum at his discretion, in lieu of adoption by Parliament).[92] Following the 2007 amendments, the president called early Majilis elections for 2007; the last set of elections took place on schedule in 2012.

Immediately following the 1995 dissolution of the Supreme Soviet, Nazarbaev called a referendum extending his term until 2000. The first presidential elections under the 1995 Constitution were in fact held in 1999, following the adoption of constitutional amendments in late 1998 that extended the presidential term to seven years. Elections were next held in 2005 rather than 2006 following a Constitutional Council decision. In 2011, the Majilis authorised (by a bill amending the Constitution) a referendum to extend the president's term in office until 2020 (when he would be 80). Like Caesar refusing the crown offered by Marc Antony, Nazarbaev referred the bill unsigned to the Constitutional Council, which ruled it unconstitutional,[93] whereupon he called pre-term elections for later that year (which he won handily).[94] Nazarbaev won the most recent presidential elections in 2015, also called pre-term, with 97.7 per cent of the votes.[95]

TAJIKISTAN

Constitutional Background: History, Context, Characteristics

Tajikistan, not blessed with resources apart from topographic relief (useful for hydropower generation) and a left-over Soviet aluminium smelter (a major facility, by far the largest percentage of Tajikistan's

[91] Kaz Laws 07.10.1998, 21.05.2007.

[92] Kaz 91.

[93] Constitutional Council Ruling 31.01.2011.

[94] 16.06.2011 OSCE Final Report Republic of Kazakhstan Early Presidential Election 3 April 2011.

[95] 29.07.2015 OSCE Final Report Republic of Kazakhstan Early Presidential Election 26 April 2015.

industrial production and largest source of its foreign reserve),[96] has always been the least coherent of the Central Asian republics. Something of a rump jurisdiction, it was devised by Stalin to accommodate scattered and heterogeneous Persian-speakers, reconstituted as bearers of a novel Tajik ethnicity, after the principal historical Persian centres in the region (Bokhara and Samarkand) had been incorporated in Uzbekistan. Beyond its still largely agricultural economy (principally cotton, though only a tiny portion of the terrain is arable) and its smelter, Tajikistan is notable as a drugs and weapons corridor, unsurprising in view of its 1,344-kilometre border with Afghanistan, and as a source of migrant labour. Close to a million Tajiks, a staggering portion of the population, work abroad, overwhelmingly in Russia, whose remittances are an indispensable prop to the economy (notwithstanding which Tajikistan has the lowest GDP of all former Soviet republics).

The Tajik SSR's complex history of uneven economic development even in a compact geographic compass, directed labour migration and resettlement of Pamiris and others, and concentration of Republican authority in a small northern elite,[97] led to regionalism, organised in a particularly complex manner along socio-political, ethnic and religious lines (with a lately-acquired Islamist dimension). Its late Soviet-era divisions and discrete, precipitated interests[98] might have been a blessing had they not proved the worst of curses and led to war. They gave Tajikistan congenital politics and pluralism (dramatically unlike Uzbekistan and Turkmenistan), which might conceivably have been channelled into democratic, contestatory politics by (among other things) a suitable constitutional conduit.

Instead, widespread popular mobilisation in the wake of the collapse of the Union and resentment against the leadership degenerated rapidly

[96] MB Olcott, *Tajikistan's Difficult Development Path* (Washington, Carnegie Endowment for Peace, 2012) 177. It also earned the Government's London solicitors the highest fees ever paid over in UK litigation to date when a dispute with the smelter at its centre made its way through the High Court in 2005–07. M Murphy, 'Tajikistan case set to test fee records' *Financial Times*, 30 April 2008. The convoluted proceedings shed light on the obscure and complex power politics of contemporary Tajikistan involving the president, assorted domestic officials and business interests, the Russians and European companies. Olcott 82–216.

[97] J Heathershaw, *Post-conflict Tajikistan: The Politics of Peacebuilding and the Emergence of Legitimate Order* (London, Routledge, 2009) 20–24.

[98] ibid. 24–26.

into all-out, exceptionally brutal violence. Tajikistan suffered perhaps the most catastrophic civil conflict of the wars of the socialist succession in the 1990s, sustaining as many as 100,000 dead out of a population of five million, most in a brief period in 1993 in a context of ferocious local warlords and hideous civilian massacres, and many times that number of casualties.[99] An internationally mediated peace process resulted in an internationally guaranteed peace agreement,[100] the constitutional reform and power-sharing provisions of which appeared to create an opportunity for institutionalised pluralism—an opportunity unfortunately squandered in the event, as post-war Tajikistan reverted to super-presidentialist regional type, and authoritarian executive control was re-established and consolidated.

Constitutional Essentials: Formal Structure of Government and System of Rights 2014

Consisting of 100 articles in ten chapters (Fundamentals of Constitutional Structure; Human and Citizen Rights, Freedoms and Fundamental Duties; Parliament (Majlisi Oli), President, Government, Local Authority, Gorno-Badakshan Autonomous Province, Court, Procuracy, Amendment Procedure) the Tajik Constitution[101] rivals only the Turkmen in brevity (just over 6,000 words) and terse formulation; it was last amended in 2003. Gorno-Badakshan is recognised as an autonomous province, regulated by a constitutional law, with its own Majlis of People's Deputies.[102] Tajik is the state language; Russian the language of 'international relations'.[103] The form of government is presidential, with very broad appointment and dismissal powers (Prime Minister and Cabinet of Ministers, local government chairs at all levels (chairs of regional, town, district majilis of people's deputies), General Procurator, Head of National Bank), and possesses decree-making authority.

[99] ibid. 27–30.
[100] 27.06.1997 General Agreement.
[101] Constitution 06.11.1994 (hereinafter 'Taj').
[102] Taj 81–83.
[103] Taj 3.

The president also nominates, for election by the Majlisi Milli, the chairs and justices of the apex courts, and appoints and dismisses all other judges upon the proposal of the Council of Justice (the judicial administrative body, constitutionally established by the president but regulated by separate legislation).[104] Additionally, the president is vested with the authority to issue binding decrees and orders.[105] The Majlisi Milli (the National Assembly) and the Majlisi Namoyandagon (the Assembly of Representatives) comprise the bicameral Majilisi Oli. Of the 63 deputies to the Majlisi Namoyandagon, 22 are elected from party lists on the basis of proportional representation, 41 from territorial constituencies on a greater-than-50 per cent majority basis, to five-year terms. Of the 33 members of the Majlisi Milli, 25 are elected by local councils, and eight appointed by the president.[106] Legislative initiative is reserved to the two chambers of the Majlisi Oli, the president, Government and the Majlis of Gorno-Badakshan.[107]

The judiciary is quadripartite and consists of three apex courts, Constitutional, Supreme and Supreme Economic, as well as a Military Court and subordinate lower courts.[108] The term of office is ten years. The Constitutional Court, composed of seven members, including one from Gorno-Badakshan, commands the power of judicial review of all laws and regulations of state authorities, including the Supreme Court and Supreme Economic Court.[109] The Procuracy has separate constitutional status and is accountable to the president and Majlisi Milli; it has supervisory authority over the 'strict and uniform execution of all laws'.[110] Principal constitutional laws include those on the Procuracy, Local Bodies of State Authority, Gorno-Badakhsan Autonomous Province, on Courts, on the Majlisi Oli, on the Constitutional Court, on Citizenship, on Presidential Elections, on the Majlisi Oli Elections

[104] Taj 69.
[105] Taj 70.
[106] Taj 49, Taj Con Law 19.04.2000, Con Law 10.12.1999.
[107] Taj 58.
[108] Taj 84.
[109] Taj 80.
[110] Taj 93–94.

and on the Government.[111] Other legislation of constitutional import includes the substantive and procedural civil and criminal codes, as well as other codes and subsidiary legislation.[112]

Constitutional Vicissitudes: Amendments, Elections/Referenda 1991–2014

Tajikistan's precipitous descent into maximally violent civil conflict delayed adoption of its constitution until 6 November 1994, three years after independence and last of the five. In the initial post-independence chaos, the former deputy Republican Party Secretary who had been elected president in 1990 was forced to resign. The post of President was then abolished by amendment to the Tajik SSR Constitution, and the parliamentary Speaker Rahmonov (since de-Russified to Rahmon) became head of government. The post of President was restored with the adoption of the 1994 Constitution, which was substantially amended pursuant to the Peace Accords of 1999, and then again four years later.[113]

The National Reconciliation Commission, consisting of 26 members each of the Government and the United Tajik Opposition (UTO), drafted the amendments, without direct international participation. They were accepted after a delay by the president, approved by the Majils, and submitted for referendum by the electorate. The amendments included the rewording of article 28 so as to permit the formation of parties on a religious basis (an absolutely fundamental point, as the unconstitutionality of the Islamic Renaissance Party, the leading force of the UTO, had been a casus belli), an extension of the presidential term from five to seven years but subject to a two-term limit,[114]

[111] Taj Const Laws 21.07.1994 (Presidential elections), 03.11.199 (Constitutional court), 04.11.1995 (citizenship), 10.12.1999 (Majlisi Oli elections), 19.04.2000 (Majlisi Oli), 12.05.2001 (Government), 06.08.2001 (courts), 17.05.2004 (local authorities), 25.07.2005 (Procuracy), 30.07.2007 (Gorno-Badakhshan).

[112] Taj Civil Code I 30.06.1999, Civil Code II 11.12.1999, Civil Procedure Code 06.08.2001, Economic Procedure Code 05.01.2008, Criminal Code 21.05.1998, Criminal Procedure Code 03.12.2009, Criminal Penalty Enforcement Code 05.01.2008, Administrative Violations Code of 31.12.2008, Law 08.12.2003 (normative acts).

[113] Taj Constitutional amendments 22.0.2003, Resolution 30.10.1999.

[114] Taj 85.

the addition of an upper house, Majlisi Milli to create a bicameral legislature, the introduction of proportional representation (PR) for a portion of the legislative seats in the Majlis Namoyandogan (lower house), and an augmented list of presidential powers.[115]

The core of the accord however was a power-sharing arrangement between the Government and the UTO pursuant to which the UTO was to receive 30 per cent of state posts at central (and local) levels, with a designated distribution of ministerial portfolios.[116] However, unlike consociational arrangements where the constitutional order, in the context of the political culture, has been able to stabilise and accommodate ongoing power-sharing among (ethnically) distinct constituencies,[117] Tajikistan's gambit was doomed to failure given the preservation of a unitary, centralised presidential system, notwithstanding the constitutional shift to partial PR. Following the 1999 amendments and the failure fully to implement the allotment of government posts, the UTO swiftly lost momentum and was largely co-opted and incorporated in the progressive consolidation of presidentialist rule. Further amendments in 2003 inter alia extended the presidential term limit from two to three terms, strengthened certain judicial guarantees, and qualified article 28 by requiring that the structure and activity of political parties 'conform to democratic norms'. Elections to both houses of the now bicameral Majlisi Oli were held in 2000 under the new system, and again in 2005, 2010 and 2015 at the end of the constitutionally mandated period. Presidential elections have been held in 1994, 1999 (on the basis of the five-year term), 2006 and 2013 (on the basis of the amended seven-year term), returning Rahmon to office at each instance.

[115] Taj 69.

[116] General Agreement 27.06.1997, Annex II (Protocol on Political Issues, 18 May 1997) 3.

[117] A Lijphart, 'Constitutional Design for Divided Societies' (2004) 13(2) *Journal of Democracy* 96, 97: '[T]he successful establishment of democratic government in divided societies requires two key elements: power sharing and group autonomy. Power sharing denotes the participation of representatives of all significant communal groups in political decision making, especially at the executive level; group autonomy means that these groups have authority to run their own internal affairs, especially in the areas of education and culture.'

KYRGYZSTAN

Constitutional Background: History, Context, Characteristics

Kyrgyzstan, land of yurts[118] and very much the USSR's homegrown 'third world', with a small, resource-poor economy subsidised in significant degree from Moscow, had much dimmer prospects than its neighbours for state sovereignty. Like Tajikistan, it is riven and segmented by mountains, and notwithstanding its modest extent, exhibits striking cultural and economic disparities (and political differentiation) between the more urbanised though still residually pastoral, russophone north, and the largely agrarian Kyrgyz- and Uzbek-speaking Fergana Valley in the south. The Fergana, parcelled among Tajikistan, Kyrgyzstan and Uzbekistan in a particularly rococo exercise of Stalin's jurisdictional delineation, with arabesques and curlicues of interstate boundaries (including a pair of Uzbek extraterritorial islands inside Kyrgyzstan), and a motley of populations, has proved an inter-ethnic tinderbox (see the discussion in chapter eight).

Kyrgyzstan made an early bid as democracy's Central Asian poster child, having elected a dark horse academician and physicist, Oskar Akaev over the Republican Party Secretary as President in the twilight year of the Kyrgyz SSR. Apart from its serial reversals of presidential and constitutional fortune, Kyrgyzstan can claim fame for its Canadian-mined Kumtor gold deposits (its showcase foreign investment resource project) and its contentious hosting of rival US and Russian military bases (the US Manas Airbase, critical to Afghanistan operations and a lucrative source of rental income, was vacated in 2014). Like Tajikistan, Kyrgyzstan has also gained notoriety for gun- and drugs-running and human-trafficking, owing to its geographic situation.

In its first post-Soviet years, it became a privileged beneficiary of international assistance, something of a development darling, and welcomed an array of multilateral and bilateral donor programming and technical advisors, in everything from infrastructure to democratisation/civil society and legal and judicial reform. If Turkmenistan shifted furthest and quickest of the five in the direction of singular despotism, Kyrgyzstan marked out a constitutional place for itself at

[118] The Kyrgyz flag depicts the stylised cross-axis of the tent poles at the top of a yurt (*tunduk*), forming the smokehole at the centre.

the other end of the spectrum with a regionally unmatched pluralism and openness. It rapidly developed the most boisterous and outspoken media in the region, but the auroral pluralism and civic and legislative autonomy gave way in the glare of day to executive aggrandisement of power, legal and extra-legal diminution of political space, and endemic corruption and dynastic cronyism (compounded in Kyrgyzstan's case by the reach of prison-based organised criminal structures into the very heart of government).[119] Like its bordering high-relief sibling, Tajikistan, Kyrgyzstan appeared by the middle of its second decade to have reverted to regional type, having dashed its early constitutional promise and trod the well-worn neo-Soviet Silk Road of constitutionalising authoritarian structures of rule.

Astonishingly, it proceeded over its next decade to reclaim its status as the great regional anomaly, becoming the only state to oust its president, indeed two presidents in succession, and accomplish the momentous shift from super-presidentialism to a (modified) Westminster system. In 2005, Kyrgyzstan followed Georgia and Ukraine into the headlines, earning Central Asia its only 'colour [perhaps better, floral] revolution', the Tulip, when mass demonstrations in Bishkek following grievances in the south drove President Akaev from office and brought in a southerner, Kurmanbek Bakiev, on a specific promise of constitutional reform. Five years on, after first surviving a determined parliamentary onslaught which forced him to deliver at least partially on that promise, but then eclipsing his predecessor in brazen larceny, familial favouritism and intimidation, Bakiev was himself driven from office in a strikingly similar scenario, though this time with considerable bloodshed. An interim government supervised the preparation of the long-sought new constitution, which was adopted later that year and paved the way for new presidential and parliamentary elections in 2011.

2010 may have been a constitutional *annus mirabilis*, but it was a social *annus horribilis*. Just two months after Bakiev's departure (and not unconnected with it), organised pogroms targeting ethnic Uzbeks swept across Osh and Jalalabad in the Fergana Valley. The Kyrgyz Fergana had witnessed similar inter-ethnic clashes 20 years before,

[119] International Crisis Group (ICG), 'Kyrgyzstan's Prison Nightmare', Asia Report No 118, 16 August 2006.

in the *fin de Union* moment, but the scale this time was without precedent, with 900 deaths. The fractious politics[120] which had thwarted the authoritarian centralisation so characteristic of post-Soviet Central Asian constitutional orders and forced the untimely resignation of two successive presidents exhibited a very dark side as well.

Constitutional Essentials: Formal Structure of Government and System of Rights 2014

The current Kyrgyz Constitution[121] of 114 articles in nine sections (Fundamentals of Constitutional Structure; Human and Citizen Rights and Freedoms; President; Legislature; Executive; Judiciary; Other State Organs; Local Self-Government; Amendment Procedure) is the wordiest after the Kazakh (over 10,000) and commensurately detailed in its textual regulation. It was adopted by a national referendum in 2010, replacing the (multiply amended) 1993 Constitution, which had last itself been amended by referendum as a 'New Edition' in 2007. The incomparably multi-adjectival Kyrgyz state is not only 'sovereign, democratic, law-based, secular, and unitary', but 'social' as well.[122] Interestingly, the Constitution omits to characterise the form of government, which by a conventional classification would clearly be mixed presidential-parliamentary (semi-presidential), though with the balance shifted toward the latter. In provisions relating to the basis of power,[123] mention of the unicameral Jogorku Kenesh always precedes that of the president. Kyrgyz is the state language; Russian is an official language.[124]

The president is elected for a six-year term on the basis of a 50 per cent majority in a two-round voting system. Presidential powers are severely curtailed in comparison with any of the other republics,

[120] S Radnitz, *Weapons of the Wealthy: Predatory Regimes and Elite-led Protests in Central Asia* (Ithaca NY, Cornell University Press, 2012) 131–66 argues persuasively that the Tulip Revolution in 2005 demonstrated the capacity of rival local elite politicians to recruit, organise and mobilise client networks.

[121] Constitution 27.06.2010 (hereinafter 'Kyr').

[122] Kyr 1.

[123] Kyr 2–4.

[124] Kyr 10.

and principally involve appointment and dismissal with consent of the Jogorku Kenesh of the Prosecutor General and the Members of the Government with defence and security portfolios,[125] signature or rejection of laws (subject to a supermajority requirement of two thirds for override of a presidential veto by the Jogorku Kenesh), and, upon recommendation of the Council for the Selection of Judges, submission to the Jogorku Kenesh of candidates for appointment to (or incumbents for dismissal from) judicial posts of the Supreme and ordinary courts. The president formally appoints, but cannot reject, the prime minister selected by the Jogorku Kenesh.[126]

The Jogorku Kenesh consists of 120 deputies, elected entirely on a proportional representation basis for five years, with a 5 per cent threshold and a cap of 65 seats for a party in any election.[127] Crucially, the majority faction or coalition of factions proposes the prime minister.[128] The members of the Government are the prime minister, deputy prime minister, ministers and chairs of state committees;[129] sitting deputies cannot serve in these posts.[130] The Jogorku Kenesh has the power to impeach and dismiss the president on the basis of a criminal charge.[131] Legislative initiative is vested in an aggregate of 10,000 voters (popular initiative), Jogorku Kenesh deputies and the Government. Uniquely among the five states, the president has no right of legislative initiative, nor any decree-making authority.[132]

The Judiciary is a unified system, with one apex Supreme Court consisting of four chambers (civil, criminal, economic, constitutional), and is fully self-administered, by the Council of Judges elected by the general Congress of Judges. The Council on the Selection of Judges is responsible for recruitment and dismissal; its membership includes both judges and civil society representatives and is one third appointed by each of the Council of Judges, the parliamentary majority and the parliamentary opposition (a wholly unique and innovative procedure

[125] Kyr 64(4).
[126] Kyr 84(5).
[127] Kur 70.
[128] Kyr 84.
[129] Kyr 83.
[130] Kyr Law 18.06.2012.
[131] Kyr 67.
[132] Kyr 79.

among the Central Asian republics). The Constitutional Chamber of the Supreme Court has the power of judicial review of the constitutionality of all laws and other legal normative acts;[133] standing to challenge the constitutionality of laws and other legal normative acts before the Chamber is unrestricted.[134] The General Procuracy has responsibility for criminal prosecution and for the representation of the state or the citizen in court in cases specified by law (as well as responsibility for the observance of the law by investigative bodies). It has general supervisory responsibility for the 'strict and uniform' execution of the law by central and local executive authorities and officials.[135]

An exhaustive catalogue of civil and political as well as economic, social rights is set forth.[136] The Kyrgyz Constitution, uniquely among the five, contains a special article elaborating non-derogable rights and prohibitions: rights to humane treatment of those deprived of liberty, to request lessening or pardon of a punishment, to appeal, to freedom of thought and opinion, to freedom of conscience and religious conviction, to freedom to determine and indicate ethnic affiliation, to compensation for harmed caused by unlawful state action, to judicial defence, to free primary and secondary education, of citizens to return to Kyrgyzstan; and prohibitions on the death penalty, torture, ill-treatment, involuntary medical experimentation, slavery, human trafficking, child labour, criminal prosecution for libel and slander, deprivation of freedom for breach of civil-legal obligations liability, coerced expression of religious or other convictions, coerced participation in peaceful assembly, forced identification/indication of one's ethnic affiliation and arbitrary deprivation of dwelling.[137]

Principal constitutional laws include those on the Status of Judges, the Constitutional Chamber of the Supreme Court, and Elections of the President and Deputies of the Jogorku Kenesh and the Government. As in the case of the other four states, a host of subsidiary legislation regulates constitutional matters and should be considered

[133] Kyr 97(6).
[134] Kyr 97(7).
[135] Kyr 104.
[136] Kyr 21–49.
[137] Kyr 20.

a critical component of the formal constitutional order, including the substantive and procedural civil and criminal codes, the Laws on Normative Legal Acts, Media and Religious Belief.[138]

Constitutional Vicissitudes: Amendments, Elections/Referenda 1991–2014

Kyrgyzstan adopted its first constitution on 5 May 1993, a year and a half after independence. It provided for a mixed system, with significant powers vested in the bicameral Jogorku Kenesh (Legislative Assembly and Assembly of People's Representatives), as well as a robust presidency. Its history of subsequent amendment is riveting. Unlike the dismal parade of retrogressive amendments elsewhere in the region, the Kyrgyz amendments betoken constitutional politics itself, a politics of constitutional design, rather than the constitutional foreclosure of politics. Unlike sister jurisdictions, Kyrgyzstan's constitution-in-force has always required constitutional amendments to be approved in referenda.[139] In 1996, amendments so approved and a further set of amendments two years later included legalisation of private ownership in land, restructuring of seats in Kyrgyzstan's bicameral parliament including a shift to party lists and one national electoral district, change in the Government's fiscal decision-making abilities, greater freedom for the media, and limiting the immunity of deputies in parliament.[140]

In 2003, further amendments were approved, marking a step backward, a decided shift in the balance of parliamentary/presidential power toward super-presidentialism, with augmented presidential authority, the replacement of a bicameral with unicameral Jogorku Kenesh and a concomitant diminution of parliamentary powers and numbers (reduction in deputies to 75 from 105 and restoration of

[138] Const Laws 18.06.2012 (Government), 02.06.2011 (election of the President), 09.07.2008 (judges), Civil Code I 08.05.1996, Civil Code II 05.01.1998, Civil Procedure Code 29.12.1999, Criminal Code 01.10.1997, Criminal procedure Code 30.06.1999, Criminal Enforcement Code 11.11.1999, Administrative violations Code 04.08.1998, Law 20.07.2009 (normative acts).

[139] Kyr 1993 96, Kyr 2010 114.

[140] Kyr Law 16.02.1996, Kyr Law 21.10.1998.

single-member mandates). At the same time they reduced the remit of the Constitutional Court respecting the constitutionality of state enactments but enlarged it respecting political parties and social and religious organisations.

The crisis which led to the resignation and flight of Akaev in 2005 was constitutional, set in motion by disputed first elections to the unicameral parliament. Deputies pressed for constitutional reform under the new president, seeking a redistribution of power from presidency to the Jogorku Kenesh, to roll back the super-presidentialst tide of the preceding decade, but Bakiev resisted. By late 2006, three constitutional drafts were circulating, and the Kyrgyz Government applied to the Venice Commission of the Council of Europe for consultation.[141] At the end of the year, amidst mass demonstrations organised to force the issue, a standoff between Bakiev and the Jogorku Kenesh over competing drafts saw two constitutions adopted in quick concession (a compromise mixed system and a restored presidentialist system), neither submitted for referendum.[142]

Ultimately, in yet another referendum the following year (the fourth in the 15 years since the 1993 entry-into-force of the Constitution), a New Edition Constitution was approved, and this time shifted the balance of power back in the direction of parliament, but not as decisively as the first of the two constitutions of the previous year.[143] The most significant changes included the replacement of territorial constituencies with party list-based proportional representation, in conjunction with an increase in the number of deputies from 75 to 90, and formation of the Government by the party with most seats. However at the same time, the election of heads of local government was replaced with presidential appointment. In what does a new or replacement constitution consist? How should it be distinguished from an amended New Edition, or for that matter from a serially amended Original Edition?

[141] Venice Commission Opinion 42/2005, Comments 383/2006.

[142] Kyr Laws 09.11.2006, 15.01.2007. The period from late 2006 to late 2007 saw nearly as many Kyrgyz constitutions as AD 69 (the 'year of the four emperors') saw Roman emperors.

[143] Kyr Law 23.10.2007.

The old chestnut comes to mind of the visiting constitutional scholar who, upon enquiring in a prestigious London legal booksellers whether he might purchase a copy of his home country's Constitution, is advised, 'I'm terribly sorry, sir, we don't stock periodicals.'

Three years on, in 2010, the parliamentary faction finally triumphed, and an entirely new constitution, firmly establishing the only quasi-parliamentary system in the region, was approved by referendum number five. Indeed, the first decade of the twenty-first century in Kyrgyzstan recalls the middle decades of the seventeenth in England as an epic struggle for parliamentary supremacy, as constitutional reform itself became, however improbably, the premier theatre of politics. Just how it came about that Kyrgyzstan threaded its tortuous way to a twenty-first-century doctrine of 'President-in-Parliament,' and what implications for contemporary constitutionalism it might carry are compelling questions which must await detailed exploration until chapter five below.

Central Asian elections, as can be glimpsed from the brief summaries in this chapter (and will be scrutinised at length in another section of chapter five), have typically proved to be centrally orchestrated exercises in mass mobilisation with foregone outcomes rather than motivated exercises of the franchise with contingent outcomes. Against this background, Kyrgyz elections stand out for their levels of contestation as for their undeniable constitutional import—as well as their kaleidoscopic changes in frame. Presidential elections have been held in 1990 under the (amended) Kyrgyz SSR Constitution, in 1995 for the first time under the 1993 Constitution, in 2000, and then again in 2005 (early, for the first time) and most recently in 2011. The regularity of the elections (save for 2009) disguises the circumstance that of the last three, two (2005 and 2011) occurred in the wake of the forced resignation of the sitting president. Parliamentary elections have been held at deceptively regular intervals, but on the basis of wild oscillations of parliamentary structure and electoral basis: 1995 (unicameral, single-member constituencies), 2000 (bicameral, proportional representation for the lower house), 2005 (unicameral, single-member constituencies), 2007 (unicameral, more seats, proportional representation) and 2010 (unicameral, yet more seats, proportional representation). As noted above, this merry whirl has been accompanied at each turn by constitutional referenda (1996, 1998, 2003, 2005, 2007 and 2010).

FURTHER READING

General

SN Cummings, *Understanding Central Asia: Politics and Contested Transformations* (Abingdon and New York, Routledge, 2012).

G Gleason, *Markets and Politics in Central Asia: Structural Reform and Political Change* (London, Routledge, 2013).

D Hiro, *Inside Central Asia: A Political and Cultural History of Uzbekistan, Turkmenistan, Kazakhstan, Kyrgyzstan, Tajikistan, Turkey, and Iran* (London, Duckworth Overlook, 2013).

P Jones Luong, *Institutional Change and Political Continuity in Post-Soviet Central Asia: Power, Perceptions, and Pacts* (Cambridge, Cambridge University Press, 2002).

O Roy, *The New Central Asia: The Creation of Nations* (London, IB Tauris, 2000).

Uzbekistan

C Murray, *Murder in Samarkand: A British Ambassador's Controversial Defiance of Tyranny in the War on Terror* (Edinburgh and London, Mainstream Publishing, 2007).

Turkmenistan

A Bohr, *Turkmenistan: Power, Politics and Petro-Authoritarianism* (London, Chatham House, 2016).

AL Edgar, *Tribal Nation: The Making of Soviet Turkmenistan* (Princeton NJ, Princeton University Press, 2006).

S Peyrouse, *Turkmenistan: Strategies of Power, Dilemmas of Development* (Armonk NY, ME Sharpe, 2012).

Kazakhstan

B Dave, *Kazakhstan—Ethnicity, Language and Power* (Abingdon and New York, Routledge, 2008).

MB Olcott, *The Kazakhs* (Stanford CA, Hoover Institution Press, 1995).

MB Olcott, *Kazakhstan: Unfulfilled Promise*, Revised Edition (Washington, Carnegie Endowment for Peace, 2010).

Tajikistan

J Heathershaw, *Post-conflict Tajikistan: The Politics of Peacebuilding and the Emergence of Legitimate Order* (London, Routledge, 2009).

MB Olcott, *Tajikistan's Difficult Development Path* (Washington, Carnegie Endowment for Peace, 2012).

Kyrgyzstan

S Radnitz, *Weapons of the Wealthy: Predatory Regimes and Elite-led Protests in Central Asia* (Ithaca NY, Cornell University Press, 2012).

2

Red Origins

Doing Justice to Soviet Constitutionalism

Soviet Constitutional Order – Soviet Authority (CPSU) – Soviet Federalism and Nationalities Regulation – Soviet Government – Soviet Planning and Ownership – Soviet Social Regulation and Protection – Soviet Rights Protection – Soviet Ideology – Soviet Local Variation – Soviet Constitutional Order and the Soviet Constitution – Soviet Constitutional Problems and Solutions

BEFORE DOING ANYTHING else, and with apologies to readers looking for local colour rather than a pervading scarlet, this volume must address Soviet constitutionalism. For the Bolsheviks, once governing, asserting state power and not contesting it, proved ardent constitutionalists—perhaps fittingly, given their self-understanding as architects of a new societal dispensation.[1] What they ultimately designed and built—not all at once, since the Soviet constitutional order was a complex and developing one[2]—was something

[1] They were less enthusiastic regarding constituent processes, at least not those under their complete control, as witnessed by Lenin's dissolution of the Constituent Assembly after one day in session in January 1918.

[2] The 1924 Constitution was amended four times, the 1936 (Stalin) Constitution was amended 43 times between 1936 and 1977, ie on average more than once a year. In keeping with Soviet practice, the amendments were made to the body of the text, rather than supplementing it. The 1977 (Brezhnev) Constitution was amended five times over its 13-year life.

altogether extraordinary in the annals of constitutionalism, however now discredited or in its day derided. The Central Asian states have thus derived their constitutional traditions not so much from a supremely tyrannical or 'totalitarian' source (though that characterisation is not wholly groundless) as from one of the very few examples of radically novel, comprehensive constitutional experimentation in history.

The successive constitutions of the USSR have been an irresistible object of scorn and the favourite exemplar of a sham constitution.[3] Indeed, the recurrent caricature would style them a fig-leaf for absolutism rather than a frame for constitutionalism, a pretext for a prerogative state sooner than a text for a limited state. Far from realising the revolutionary ideals of equality and freedom from domination, Soviet constitutionalism appears to betray and negate them. Yet it is perhaps too easy to suppose that revolutionary zeal and energy long endure and prevail in the face of the inertia of consolidated structure and rules. The initially plastic or provisional Soviet constitutional order cured as it matured, and eventually grew brittle—the forms and the institutions had their revenge on those who fashioned them when the Union spectacularly came undone in 1991. This was particularly the case for the forms and institutions of Soviet federalism (and the complementary regulation of ethnic identity in the form of nationalities), which were of paramount constitutional significance for the Central Asian successor states. But in any case the relevant, non-prejudicial question for this enquiry is not 'Was the Soviet Constitution a fraud?' but 'What was the nature of the Soviet constitutional order?' Only then can the implications of a transition from that order to a post-Soviet order in the Central Asian cases be assessed and analysed.

SOVIET CONSTITUTIONAL ORDER

The Soviet constitutional order was sui generis. While many distinct historical tributaries flowed into it, their confluence yielded a novel mode

[3] G Sartori, 'Constitutionalism: A Preliminary Discussion' (1962) 56 *The American Political Science Review* 853; R Sakwa, 'The Struggle for the Constitution in Russia and the Triumph of Ethical Individualism' (1996) 48 *Studies in East European Thought* 115. See also J Henderson, *Constitution of the Russian Federation* (Oxford, Hart Publishing, 2011) 35–38.

of state and societal organisation. It exhibited a never-before conceived arrangement of federalism, consisting in nested ethno-linguistic autonomies and juridical nationalities. It adopted a novel form of ultimate political authority, the Communist Party of the Soviet Union (CPSU)). It embraced a unique organisation of the economy, planning and exclusive public ownership. It devised a conciliar system of government of central, republican and local Soviets. It entrenched an unprecedentedly broad scheme of social welfare and regulation, encompassing comprehensive provision of social goods and control over associational and personal life. Finally, it was grounded in a radically innovative ideology, multinational Marxism-Leninism.

In Soviet terminology the term of art was 'state law,' and its capacious ambit fairly corresponds to the notion put forward here of 'constitutional order':

> The significance of Soviet state law is defined by its position as the leading branch in the system of Soviet law. The substance of Soviet state law is conditioned by the tasks and functions of our state, its socialist nature and activity. The institutions and norms of Soviet state law express and reinforce the principles and forms of:
>
> 1) the societal system (dictatorship of the working class, union of the working class and labouring peasants, the leading position of the Communist party in Soviet society and state, the rule of the socialist system of the economy and socialist ownership of the means of production, personal ownership of citizens, principles of socialist planning, principles of socialist labour);
> 2) the state system (national basis of the Soviet state, organisation of Soviet federalism and autonomy, the sovereign rights of the USSR and the Union republics, the state-legal mutual relations of the Union of SSRs and the Union republics, the administrative-territorial system of the USSR);
> 3) the organisation of state authority (system of state organs, their legal position, the forms of mutual relations and the legal terms of their activity);
> 4) Soviet democracy (the legal foundations of Soviet citizenship, the realisation of people's authority and people's rule [democracy] in all spheres of state life of the USSR).[4]

[4] SM Ravin, 'Gosudarstvennoe pravo' in OS Ioffe (ed) *40 let sovetskogo prava, 1917–1957, Period of the Building of Socialism, Volume 1* (Leningrad, Izdatel'stvo Len-

SOVIET AUTHORITY (CPSU)

The USSR was the first 'Party state', and the CPSU a novel political institution and constitutional force. Soviet authority—*Sovetskaia vlast'*—was a misnomer,[5] since the authority of the Soviets (councils or legislative organs) was de facto derivative, though formally original, in the Soviet system. *Sovietskaia vlast'* was in substance *partinnaia vlast'*—Party authority. The role of the CPSU in the Soviet constitutional order was restricted to little more than a constitutional mention *en passant* until 1977, when its overwhelming—literally transcendent—constitutional significance was formalised.

> Article 6. The leading and guiding force of the Soviet society and the nucleus of its political system, of all state organisations and public organisations, is the Communist Party of the Soviet Union. The CPSU exists for the people and serves the people.
>
> The Communist Party, armed with Marxism-Leninism, determines the general perspectives of the development of society and the course of the home and foreign policy of the USSR, directs the great constructive work of the Soviet people, and imparts a planned, systematic and theoretically substantiated character to their struggle for the victory of communism.

Capturing just what was constitutionally novel about the CPSU is not as straightforward as might appear, for the role of any modern political party is in fact always constitutional whether or not it is formalised—parties are integral to any constitutional order and cannot therefore be said to be 'extra-constitutional.' The Bolshevik party (first the 'All-Union Communist Party (Bolsheviks)', then renamed the CPSU) monopolised public authority indefinitely and remained unaccountable to any other institution or to the citizenry, for that matter. It is not for all that, as observers have been tempted to insist, an entirely gross anomaly or unrecognisable perversion. It did not differ from the modern political party, and indeed was modern in an exemplary fashion,

ingradskogo universiteta, 1957) [Равин, С.М., 'Государственное право,' Иоффе О.С, отв. ред., 40 лет советского права, 1917–57: Период строительства социализма. т. 1] 76.

[5] Indeed, 'Union of Soviet Socialist Republics', like 'Holy Roman Empire', is liable to the charge of serial misnomer: imperial not federal, party-ruled not conciliar, state-capitalist not socialist, and monarchical not republican.

insofar as it grafted its own internal organisation and programme onto the formally constitutional structures of public authority: all parties do that when they assume power (whether legitimately following elections or otherwise) and become governments. Indeed the Westminster usage of 'Shadow Cabinet' precisely captures the way in which (parliamentary) party organisations can track or 'shadow' public offices and institutions. Parties either rule or prepare to rule.

Where the CPSU did blaze a trail was in performing this shadowing function in a uniquely unremitting and comprehensive manner, since its structures, dominated at the apex by the Politburo, were the real sources of decision-making by public authority *at all times*. That is, the CPSU did not merge or 'disappear' into government, taking on the colouration of public office as a kind of camouflage, but the Party retained entirely its own complex internal articulation even as it governed, directing government institutions and instructing administrative personnel at all levels from ministers to clerks in a sort of pervasive puppetry (hence the deeper significance of party state, the party apparatus as controlling and paralleling or duplicating state offices and functions). And unlike parties in multi-party systems, of course, its purchase on power was indefinite and uncontested.

All of which is to suggest that the CPSU rules and procedures, the constitution of the Party itself[6] (again, like the charter and internal procedures and rules of any modern party, eg the Labour Party Rule Book in the UK, of which the first chapter is the party constitution),[7] was a fundamental part of the Soviet constitutional order, and indeed arguably of greater weight than the Constitution itself. It thus becomes a semantic or ideological point whether the CPSU was supra-, extra-, or para-constitutional.[8] To a critically minded observer, the structure

[6] The party charter (ustav), regularly amended and issued in new editions, regulated membership and qualifications, responsibilities and functions, structure and governance, and discipline. See USSR 31.10.1961 Resolution. Many Party norms were a result of usages, ie customary rather than formal Party law. JA Getty, *Origins of the Great Purges: The Soviet Communist Party Reconsidered, 1933–1938* (Cambridge, Cambridge University Press, 1987) 10–37 analyses the relation between formal norms and actual Party practice in the 1930s.

[7] www.labourlist.org/wp-content/uploads/2013/04/Rule-Book-2013.pdf, accessed 6 November 2015.

[8] Commentators typically define the Party's constitutional basis narrowly, eg M Nicholson, 'The New Soviet Constitution: A Political Analysis' (1978) 34(1) *The*

and functions of the CPSU were constitutional, pure and simple, even in a formal sense.

The CPSU thus functioned as the guarantor or guardian of the constitutional order, poised to intervene not just in a crisis or a state of exception (as the armed forces of some states, eg Turkey or Egypt, understand their role), but routinely and incessantly. But the principle of the exception overriding the norm (or the general sponginess of the normative ground) was a general feature of the Soviet constitutional order and was by no means confined to the CPSU alone. Other institutions, most notably and notoriously the security apparatus (the 'Organs', in Soviet shorthand, referring to the Cheka, OGPU, NKVD and KGB in succession), but also including other designated officials (economic, military, investigative, law enforcement, etc), enjoyed the power to act in spite of, or contrary to, applicable constitutional norms.

Indeed, the USSR bids fair to be regarded as police state as much as Party state, and the security forces constituted what can defensibly be styled a 'state-within-a-state,' in the sense that they functioned according to a *lex specialis*, a distinct set of ground norms, which were supplemental (and superior) to express constitutional norms, rather than subordinate to them. In other words, the Organs had their own 'constitution', in the form of chartering and enabling legislation (the basis for their issuance of subsidiary regulations and orders) and indeed their own constitutional order, characterised not only by ministerial enforcement and judicial systems, but a penal system, an economy (the industrial system of the camps), and health and welfare systems as well, even orphanages (for children of enemies of the people).[9] Of course, from the point of view developed here, the existence of states-within-a-state, their possibility to begin with, was a fundamental

World Today 14–20, 17: 'Thus the Party has been "constitutionalized" only to a certain extent; there is, as before, no mechanism in the Constitution to constrain its power.'

[9] See O Mozokhin, *Right of Repression: Extrajudicial Powers of the Organs of State Security 1918–1953* (Moscow, Kuchkovo polie, 2006) [Мозохин, Олег, Право на репрессии. Внесудебные полномочия органов государственной безопасности, Москва: Кучково поле 2006] for a comprehensive analysis of the long series of such acts from the founding of the Cheka in 1917. See A Applebaum, *Gulag: A History of the Soviet Camps* (London, Penguin, 2004) for a comprehensive account of the NKVD's carceral empire.

part of the Soviet constitutional order. The internal circuitry of power of the Soviet state was wired in parallel as well as in series. This is to some degree true of all national security states, even of all elaborate contemporary administrative states in more conventional constitutional orders, which contain powerful agencies, such as revenue authorities or security services, that operate with very considerable autonomy and specially relaxed constraint.

The balance of norm and exception in the Soviet constitutional order should not be seen as categorically distinct, particularly in a post-9/11 world. The current fascination with states of emergency or exception captures a profound paradox of twentieth-century constitutionalism, first and most memorably articulated by Carl Schmitt: 'the sovereign is he who decides the state of exception.'[10] From such a standpoint, of course, the CPSU was sovereign in the Soviet constitutional order since it could (routinely, and not just in an emergency) 'decide the exception.' Thus the USSR for most of its life existed in something like an undeclared semi-permanent state of exception. But it was only the first and most extreme (or paranoid) national security state, and all modern constitutional systems must reckon with a shadowy constitutional borderland of relaxed or suspended limits. The idea of self-limitation underlying traditional constitutionalism becomes in the light of this analysis famously unstable, in something like an infinite regress paradox (*quis custodiet ipsos custodes?*).

Many democratic constitutional states provide for a suspension of otherwise applicable norms or guarantees and the assumption of broadened executive powers in the event of an emergency.[11] Perhaps ironically, the mature Soviet constitutional order did not make explicit provision for any such emergency powers. There might earlier have been a 'dictatorship of the proletariat' (frequently invoked though not formalised as an emergency regime), but there was no legal basis in the USSR for a temporary constitutional dictatorship as such. The fundamental constitutional problem posed by 'states of exception',

[10] C Schmitt, *Political Theology: Four Chapters on the Concept of Sovereignty* (Chicago and London, University of Chicago Press, 1985) 6.

[11] G Agamben, *State of Exception* (Chicago, University of Chicago Press, 2005) 11–22.

how to understand the normatively regulated suspension of norms never confronted the USSR as such, since the boundary between norm and exception was not even purportedly regulated normatively but was itself subject to Party judgement and discretion.

But the CPSU more even than guarantor or guardian was closer to something like the instantiation (even personification) and author of the constitutional order itself. The real anomaly here goes to the heart of a separation of powers issue more fundamental than the customary one among government branches: the separation between the *pouvoir constituant* (constituent power, ie the people or ground of authority) and the *pouvoir constitué* (constituted power, state authority or government), a separation which enables the act of constitution itself and so is a condition of possibility for constitutional government in the first place. The CPSU in the Soviet scheme was in effect not just supreme constitutional authority, but the real *pouvoir constituant.* As such, it remained actively engaged throughout the 70-year life of the country, and the *pouvoir constitué* might have seemed commensurately contingent and unstable

The rigid requirement of ideological conformity and support for the official constitutionalist line (amounting to a kind of scholarly cheer-leading—not by any means unique to the Soviet system) prevented any real critical Soviet constitutional analysis of the place of the Party until Gorbachev posed the challenge of a *pravovoe gosudarstvo*, or law-based state. At least until very late in the life of the USSR, this instrumentalisation of the constitutional order to serve the needs and priorities of the party authorities, while never exactly proclaimed or celebrated (after the promulgation of 'socialist legality'), was understood as justified and not perceived (or capable of being identified even if perceived) as a constitutional 'problem' meriting analysis and exegesis (say, like the countermajoritarian problem in US constitutional law). The declaratory because non-justiciable or enforceable requirement in Article 6 that party organisations 'function within the framework of the Constitution of the USSR,' was a belated attempt to normalise and subordinate party functions in the face of a perceived constitutional anomaly, more something in the nature of a regulative ideal than an enforceable standard. It presented the same fundamental 'sovereign paradox': the guarantor could not continue to 'decide the exception' and be bound by the norm.

SOVIET FEDERALISM AND NATIONALITIES REGULATION

The Bolsheviks pioneered the world's first comprehensively and formally multinational federation. The Soviet constitutional order was expressly designed to make a socialist virtue of an imperialist necessity, and globally (politically, socially, economically and culturally) to transform, rather than reverse or undo, the result of four centuries of relentless Muscovite territorial aggrandisement. The Romanov dynasty had forged the most extensive overland colonial empire of any European power, altogether sui generis in its make-up, encompassing as it did the largest and most diverse assortment of non-European (and some European) subordinate peoples in geographic contiguity with a dominant European (Slavic) nation. From the seventeenth century onwards the Tsars had expanded their state eastwards across Siberia, from the eighteenth southwestward across the Kazakh steppe and the Caucasus, and finally in the nineteenth century southeastward across Middle or Inner Asia.

Their Bolshevik successors, fervent anti-imperialists now masters of a boundless imperial expanse, over their first decade and a half of *Sovietskaia vlast'* devised an audacious scheme, not merely for regulating but for *fostering* nationalism among their subject peoples and harnessing it to the project of building a communist society. Lenin championed self-determination for 'undeveloped' nations in a socialist context and proposed a federal structure; and Stalin worked out the full implementation, thus completing the project of 'self-determination in one country'. They devised a constitutional framework for cultural or ethnolinguistic pluralism which has never been matched in its complexity (or its unintended consequences). No other constitutional order has ever essayed a comparable juridification and institutionalisation of ethnicity ('nationality' in Soviet parlance), on a scale and of an order of complexity that eluded the imagination and the resources of any colonial power. To this improbable scheme, an unacknowledged and mostly unlamented monument to the twentieth-century constitutional imagination, all five Central Asian states, unlike any other post-Soviet sister jurisdictions (and arguably, unlike any other jurisdictions full stop), owe their very existence, their territories and their collective identities.

The Soviet federal scheme consisted of a series of four nested autonomous jurisdictions or autonomies: constituent Union republics

(Articles 76–80), autonomous republics (Articles 82–83), autonomous provinces (*oblast*) (Articles 86–87) and autonomous areas (*okrug*) (Article 88). These enjoyed respectively decreasing degrees of formal self-government: the republics possessed their own constitution and the Union republic the attribute of sovereignty. The ethno-territorial scheme was reflected at the centre as well, in the upper chamber of the Supreme Soviet. The Soviet of Nationalities was composed 32 deputies from each Union Republic, 11 deputies from each Autonomous Republic, five deputies from each Autonomous Region, and one deputy from each Autonomous Area (Article 110).

To what territorial entity an included Soviet national or ethnic group was assigned (and whether it was assigned one at all) was a function of a complex formula accounting for its demographics, its level of development and its 'political' valence (as perceived by the authorities). Smaller, 'undeveloped' (backward or non-European) peoples were assigned lesser autonomies (autonomous regions and areas, occasionally autonomous republics, particularly within the Russian Soviet Federated Soviet Republic (RSFSR), the vastly disproportionate Russian Republic). The Central Asian peoples were a conundrum because, albeit non-European, they were relatively numerous and also possessed (at least in part) lengthy and sophisticated pre-European written traditions. The untidy alignment of demographics and territory which has challenged nationalists and irredentists was no less vexing for the Soviets, and the ethno-territorial scheme they devised was inevitably imperfect—autonomies included both titular nationals (eg Kyrgyz in the Kyrgyz SSR, Tatars in the Tatar ASSR) and non-titular nationals (members of a native minority either possessing or lacking an included lesser autonomy, eg Karakalpaks in Uzbekistan, or Pamiris in Tajikistan), as well as settler/exiled nationalities (eg Russians or Germans). The 'national delimitation', as this process came to be characterised in Soviet terminology, of the Central Asian republics over a decade and a half was particularly cartographically mangled.[12]

Soviet constitutional multinationalism was expressly conceived and carried out in a developmentalist framework. The Soviet Union was

[12] See A Farrant, 'Mission Impossible: The Politico-geographic Engineering of Soviet Central Asia's Republican Boundaries' (2006) 25 *Central Asian Survey* 61 and ch 8 below.

the first developmental state, in that it pursued a policy of accelerated industrialisation and forced modernisation on the basis of massive state investments and corresponding comprehensive directive—indeed maximally coercive—policies, imposed across the whole population (much like later examples of statist developmentalism in the post-war and post-colonial world). Of course it inflected development in a specifically socialist way—not simply from traditional agrarianism to industrial modernity, but from exploitation to socialism to communism. But the Soviet constitutional order was developmentalist in another, more radical and innovative sense, for it was premised on overcoming uneven geographic development[13] within its very borders. That is, the Union was to be not only self-developing, but cross-developing: the more developed parts (European centre, the Soviet metropole) were to assist the less developed parts (non-European periphery) to achieve economic, social and *civilisational* parity.[14] The Second World of Soviet socialism contained its own, internal First and Third Worlds, and this disparity was of implicit constitutional importance.[15] In practice, the underdeveloped parts of the Union, Central Asia prominently, received financial and in-kind subsidies of all sorts, in the context of top-down industrialisation and economic development policies. These policies of course cut both ways, favouring but also exposing: if the peripheral republics were beneficiaries of development, they were simultaneously targets of resource extraction and labour exploitation.

Ethno-territorial federalism was complemented by the classification of all Soviet citizens by official nationality—of which there were at the demise of the USSR officially 93 indigenous nationalities[16] (the number had been gradually revised downward from over 200 in the mid-1920s, the height of Stalinist 'ethnophilia').[17] The Constitution itself speaks

[13] D Harvey, *Spaces of Global Capitalism: Towards a Theory of Uneven Geographical Development* (London, Verso, 2006) 70–75.

[14] See generally T Martin, *The Affirmative Action Empire: Nations and Nationalism in the Soviet Union, 1923–1939* (London and Ithaca NY, Cornell University Press, 2001).

[15] '[T]he all-around development and drawing together of all the nations and ethnicities (*narodnosti*) of the USSR' USSR 19, 36; '[S]tate plans for economic and social development, with due account of the sectoral and territorial principles' 16.

[16] USSR 25.02.1988 Dictionaries of nationalities and languages.

[17] Martin (n 14) 409–10.

only of the equality of citizens of 'different races and nationalities' (Article 36), leaving any elaboration and regulation to subsidiary legislation. Nationalities were not merely identified and tabulated, in a process subject to on-going revision[18] in which Soviet ethnography and politics played equal parts, they were recognised as a legal status for individuals (with election rules for those of mixed parentage)—the basis for both positive and negative discrimination.[19] Nationalities policies ranged from educational preferment and indigenisation ('*korenizatsiia*', recruitment of 'native cadres' to replace ethnic Russians or others in prominent institutional, political and economic posts in peripheral places)[20] to mass deportation of politically unreliable or problematic populations[21] (like Volga Germans, Meshketian Turks, Greeks, Chechens, Poles and Koreans, many of whom were sent to Central Asia, further diversifying the demographic mix there). Particularistic legislation and regulations abounded, from the official classification of peoples in censuses to determination/adjustment of the status or territory of autonomies to decrees on orthography and language.[22]

Thus the Soviet constitutional order was not merely federal, it was constitutively pluri-cultural and multi-national. Other constitutional orders have adopted ethno-territorial or linguistic federalism (India, notably), or have recognised sub-state cultural (and less frequently political) autonomy (eg so-called Indian Country, tribal reservations and land in the US), or have assigned juridical status to ethnicity, descent or cultural affiliation (eg affirmative action for disadvantaged minorities), but none has so effectively combined all three and made the principle of cultural difference so integral a part of the formal constitutional foundation, or so pervasively institutionalised it. Once the Soviet constitutional order had fashioned the appropriate die (and

[18] Reflected in the periodic censuses: USSR 1988 Dictionaries of nationalities and languages, USSR 1959 Dictionaries of nationalities and languages.

[19] R Brubaker, 'Nationhood and the National Question in the Soviet Union and Post-Soviet Eurasia: An Institutionalist Account' (1994) 23(1) *Theory and Society* 47, 53; Y Slezkine, 'The USSR as a Communal Apartment, or How a Socialist State Promoted Ethnic Particularism' (1994) 53 *Slavic Review* 414, 444–55.

[20] Martin (n 14) 125–81.

[21] ibid. 311–43.

[22] Slezkine (n 19) 427–29 (census categories); Martin (n 14) 31–75 (assignment and status of autonomies), and 182–207 (language and orthography).

determined the developmental, ie cultural, hierarchy) for the cognisable forms of cultural identity, it could stamp out nationalities and territorial autonomies almost at will (within constraints imposed by cultural and demographic reality and geography). In consequence, the constitutions of the autonomies were but variations on a theme, as indeed were the flags and insignia, all incorporating hammer and sickle but with other regionally or culturally distinct symbols, designs, decorations and colour schemes. Any picture of the VDNKh, the permanent Exhibition of People's Economic Achievements, the great theme park or world's fair of Soviet multinationalism built in 1950s Moscow, demonstrates this sameness-in-difference with its myriad national pavilions.

The particular configuration of the federal order undergirding the USSR was thus massively overdetermined: simultaneously constitutional (elaborately and innovatively, not merely employing but refining such devices of twentieth-century constitutional statecraft as federalism and devolved authority), imperial (rationalising and entrenching the domination of a European nation over an array of non-European others), developmental (coercively imposing a particular socialist version of modernity—Eurocentric but avowedly progressive—across an entire population, with differential impact, most transformative for pre-industrial, agrarian and pastoral ways of life characteristic of Central Asia) and instrumental (enabling the ruling political institution at the centre, the CPSU, to exercise control over the periphery).

Soviet federalism was typically derided by Western commentators as sham, since the autonomies remained wholly subordinate to central authority, and indeed were set up in the first place to suit the ideological and practical needs of the centre. The Soviet nationalities scheme was similarly suspect, a Procrustean effort liable to invidious application and abuse. But these fully institutionalised forms of life—juridically fixed vessels for identity, channels for career advancement and vehicles for political and social activity—were fully internalised by Soviet citizens. They were available in the ripeness of time for the mobilisation of unapproved, 'anti-Soviet' nationalist claims, grievances, aspirations and agendas. In Central Asia (as elsewhere in the Soviet periphery), they not only established the political boundaries, they institutionalised the spaces within them and constructed the identities of the inhabitants. They set terms to Central Asian collective and subjective life which endure, and which find their place in all of the post-Soviet Central Asian constitutional orders.

SOVIET GOVERNMENT

The mature formal structure of Soviet government was in some ways the most pedestrian and least patentable aspect of the entire constitutional order, apart from the novelty of the names (Congress of Councils [Soviets] for 'parliament', or People's Commissariat for 'ministry'): fairly standard provision for legislative, executive and judicial authorities, their powers, organisation and terms of office (selection and duration), so-called agencies of state power (so-called from 1936 onwards, as distinguished from agencies of state administration). The initial Bolshevik 1917 call to arms, 'All power to the soviets!' purportedly envisaged a novel decentralised mode of governance, through spontaneously organised workplace councils, exercising commensurate authority, and in turn electing councils of greater authority. The councils—soviets—confronted the Bolsheviks as *faits accomplis*, which they cannily colonised for their own purposes. The soviets were swiftly bolshevised and governmentalised, reconfigured as conventional legislative bodies, as far as their nominal functions were concerned, at local, republican and Union levels.

In the 1924 Constitution, which preserved in form something of the original bottom-up conciliar concept, soviets organised at the city and provincial levels (local government) elected delegates to the Union-level bicameral Congress of Soviets (Articles 9 and 10). Republican Soviets were organised for each Republic (Article 64). In the 1936 Constitution, the two chambers of the now-renamed Union-level Supreme Soviet and the unicameral republican Supreme Soviet were directly elected (Articles 34 and 35), with analogous provisions for Autonomous Republics (Article 89) and for all other Soviet jurisdictions (local government, Article 94). The 1977 Constitution recharacterised, but did not substantively alter, the scheme in a manner recalling something of the original conciliar concept, elaborating (Article 89) a coordinate system of people's councils, all elected by direct suffrage at all levels:

> The Soviets of People's Deputies, i.e. the Supreme Soviet of the USSR, the Supreme Soviets of Union Republics, the Supreme Soviets of Autonomous Republics, the Soviets of People's Deputies of Territories and Regions, the Soviets of People's Deputies of Autonomous Regions and Autonomous Areas, and the Soviets of People's Deputies of districts, cities, city districts, settlements and villages shall constitute a single system of bodies of state authority.

Candidates for elections to the Soviets were famously pre-selected.[23] Voters were thus not presented with a choice among candidates, although they were presented with a choice to approve the pre-selected candidate or not. Strictly speaking, all Soviet elections were thus in effect plebiscites, referenda of persons not questions, rather than staged or mock elections (as they have often been ridiculed): not an absence of choice but a choice the terms of which had been determined beforehand. This essential, albeit not formalised, plebiscitary character of the Soviet constitutional order will be important to bear in mind when one is surveying the formal devices in Central Asian constitutional systems to ensure plural rather than binary choice in the expression of collective will (as indeed also in surveying the adoption of those systems themselves by constitutional referenda).

In the USSR, from local to Union level, executive authority was formally subordinate to parliamentary authority (local executive–administrative bodies before the local soviets, the Council of Ministers before the Presidium of the Supreme Soviet).[24] Thus as a technical matter the USSR was a parliamentary, not a presidential, state.[25] In practice, the deputies to the soviets were as much constrained in their collective decision-making as the general electorate, carrying the plebiscitary or ratification principle into parliament itself, and the ministers themselves were effectively instructed by the highest party authorities (the Central Committee and the Political Bureau). In such a turbo-instrumentalised and executory constitutional order, where even the formally executive organs were non-autonomous, the non-executive organs were especially weak and undeveloped institutionally. The judiciary was in consequence the most supine and subordinate aspect of the Soviet structure of government. Courts did of course exercise properly judicial functions (again within the constraints of a party state, taking instructions in

[23] Henderson (n 3) 40.

[24] USSR 99, 129.

[25] Less than one year before dissolution of the Union, a constitutional amendment created the Presidency of the USSR, elected by separate mandate, and with power to appoint the cabinet of ministers (as well as other customary presidential powers), 26.12.1990 Law; Henderson (n 3) 52–53. The Union republics (SSRs), including all five Central Asian republics, had similarly established presidencies in the penultimate year of 1990.

ruling in 'political' cases, ie those in which the Party took an interest)[26] in civil, criminal, economic[27] and administrative proceedings, but they had nothing whatsoever to do with government as such, or policing the constitutional governing processes. The Constitution was non-justiciable: its meaning and application could not be challenged in court or interpreted by courts, which were thereby excluded from playing any role in Soviet constitutionalism until its last year.[28]

A very wide zone of administrative discretion characterised the Soviet order. In the Soviet universe, the vast administrative bureaucracy actually set and continually revised the terms of collective existence. If the alphabet soup of federal agencies is a significant part of 'the constitution outside the constitution' for the New Deal state in the US, or the quagmire of 'quangos' for the New Labour state in the UK, then the vast planning, party and managerial bureaucracies were their greatly augmented counterparts in the Soviet state. The agencies of state administration were not themselves subject to any codified norms (like the US Administrative Procedure Act). Additionally, the Soviet system of government included anomalous institutions such as the Procuracy. Peter the Great's 'Eye of the State' was Soviet *avant la lettre* and so recommended itself to the Bolsheviks: an omnipotent instrument of state vigilance combining properly justice functions—criminal investigation and prosecution, state representation in civil and administrative proceedings, victim representation—with a much broader set of 'general supervisory functions,' including *protest*, the ability to challenge the legality of any administrative, legislative or judicial act or decision.

SOVIET PLANNING AND OWNERSHIP

The USSR constitutional order asserted its radical departure from all pre-existing such orders in placing socialist ownership and the public monopoly on the means of production almost at its head.

[26] H Berman, *Justice in the U.S.S.R.: An Interpretation of Soviet Law* (Cambridge MA, Harvard University Press, 1963) 270–71.

[27] Economic disputes between the state enterprises were reserved to a special system of economic tribunals, State Arbitration, USSR 163.

[28] Henderson (n 3) 200–03.

> The foundation of the economic system of the USSR is socialist ownership of the means of production in the form of state property (belonging to all the people), and collective farm-and-co-operative property. … Socialist ownership also embraces the property of trade unions and other public organisations which they require to carry out their purposes under these rules.[29]

This constitutional privileging of public ownership might have scandalised bourgeois states of the day, but what is really striking in the Soviet case is the foregrounding to begin with of the normative basis for the property regime (the 'material constitution'), which is typically part of background rules, having either been secured through common law (in Anglo-American jurisdictions), or separately by statute (in code jurisdictions).[30] The Soviet constitutional order formalised the material or economic constitution.

The distinction between plan and market is often seems to be treated as polar rather than as points on a spectrum.[31] But the Soviet economic order, though it combined and developed them in a novel way, *from a legal standpoint* consisted of thoroughly familiar elements: civil legal concepts of subjects, objects and relations of ownership, on the one hand, and sovereign regulatory authority, on the other. After Lenin's fateful expedient of recodification to underpin the New Economic Policy (NEP) in 1922, civil law remained the standing predicate of the Soviet organisation of the economy: state enterprises were ultimately granted civil legal personality and capacity, and entered into enforce-

[29] ibid. 10. Chapter 2, Arts 10–18 are devoted to the Economic System, which follows the Political System (Chapter 1), but comes ahead of Social Development and Culture (Chapter 3), Defence of the Motherland (Chapter 4), Foreign Policy (Chapter 5), Citizenship of the USSR and Rights, Freedoms and Duties of Citizens (Chapter 6).

[30] The legal realists amply demonstrated the constitutional force of background property and contract rules. D Kennedy, 'The Stakes of Law, or Hale and Foucault!' (1991) 15 *Legal Studies Forum* 327, 328–30.

[31] See eg World Bank, *World Development Report 1996: From Plan to Market*, available online at www-wds.worldbank.org/external/default/WDSContentServer/IW3P/IB/2013/02/27/000425962_20130227162239/Rendered/PDF/158920REPLACEMENT0WDR01996.pdf, accessed 6 November 2015.

able contractual relations with one another.[32] Ownership was redefined to distinguish socialist (state and collective/co-operative) from personal (rather than 'private', a term that offended socialist sensibilities) ownership.[33]

The *raison d'être* of the Bolshevik Revolution was the replacement of an exploitative property order, to 'expropriate the expropriators'. Expropriation (nationalisation) is a one-off, however, not a new property regime; as Trotsky subsequently was pithily to observe, 'A revolution in the forms of ownership does not solve the problems of socialism but raises them.'[34] It was Stalin who worked out the solution in the form of the command–administrative economic system, which was enabled by a singular assemblage of legal institutions which can legitimately be appreciated as the Soviet Economic Constitution. At its heart was the normative basis for the planning apparatus, reflected in myriad planning acts and directives, but nowhere codified and only constitutionally anchored in the slender textual moorings in Articles 11 (principle of planning), 68 and 70 (planning function of Council of Ministers and inclusion of GosPlan, State Planning Committee) of the 1936 Constitution, and the rather more elaborate Article 16 of the 1977 Constitution.[35]

These few brief constitutional provisions undergirded a breathtaking scope of state monopoly and control, unprecedented in economic or legal history. The basic unit of the industrial economic regime was the state enterprise and of the agricultural economic regime, the collective farm. As a result, in the Soviet constitutional order, the state did not regulate the economy; it constituted the economy in the first place and

[32] Berman (n 26) 110–13. In the first codification, civil codes were adopted for each of the constituent Republics beginning in 1922 with the RSFSR. These were replaced in the second 1962–63 codification with a new set, conforming to Union-level principles of civil legislation.

[33] Elaborated respectively in USSR 11–13.

[34] LD Trotsky, *The Revolution Betrayed: What is the Soviet Union and Where is it Going?* (1937), ch 2, available online at www.marxists.org/archive/trotsky/1936/revbet, accessed 6 November 2015.

[35] It was a source of consternation to some Soviet jurists that economic law was never codified, as civil law had been at the outset, and they agitated, repeatedly but ultimately unsuccessfully, for the adoption of an economic code. Berman (n 26) 108–09.

then conducted its operation. The Soviet constitutional order thus did not accommodate, or supply the enabling conditions for, a market, but *personated* one, creating and controlling the operative units of commerce and business.[36] Oddly enough for an order which so valorised labour, it placed management in supreme control of its production system. The Soviet normative framework for economic decision-making (both routine and investment) grounded in these provisions makes it the ultimate employer- or business-orientated model.

'Planning', in the sense of the macro- and micro- determination and direction of production, distribution and consumption of all manner of goods and services, was not confined to the economic sphere alone. Even though the State Planning Committee (GosPlan) and the vast planning bureaucracy were formally chartered with the planning of material production alone,[37] everything from novels and symphonies to ethnic identity was effectively subject to the logic and practice of planning. The ubiquity of the planning principle in the organisation of Soviet society meant that the constitutional order was singularly and comprehensively directive—it was not a meta-frame for collective, autonomous decision-making (will expression) at multiple levels, it was a vast encompassing scheme of heteronomous decision-making (will imposition) itself. Not 'a machine that would go of itself',[38] but a machine demanding the untiring efforts of a multitude of operators, united under a single command. Soviet communism was the most ambitious, audacious, meticulously thought-through and resolutely carried-out political project in history.

SOVIET SOCIAL REGULATION AND PROTECTION

The constitutional order for a union of *socialist* republics was necessarily emphatically and essentially *social* in character, but in a sense wider than

[36] Save for a small residual zone of permitted personal agricultural and artisanal production, USSR 13.

[37] Berman (n 26) 101–08.

[38] James Russell Lowell's characterisation of the popular belief in a perfectly self-executing, 'automatic' US Constitution. M Kammen, *A Machine that Would Go of Itself: The Constitution in American Culture* (New Brunswick NJ, Transaction Publishers, 2006) 17.

the customary usage of 'social state'. The fundamental social compromise of twentieth-century industrial states positions the state as redistributor of the joint social product of capital and labour and mediator between their respective claims. In the USSR, the state itself assumed the rights and functions of capital and labour both, and therefore engaged in a kind of self-mediation and self-redistribution. Cradle-to-grave insurance and benefits, both universal and means-tested, meant that social protection in the Soviet scheme was defined in broad terms.

> Article 24. In the USSR, state systems of health protection, social security, trade and public catering, communal services and amenities, and public utilities, operate and are being extended.[39]

Social protection was tightly linked to the economic system, in that the hub of social benefits distribution and services provision was the workplace: the enterprise or the collective farm. Notwithstanding that social protection was a central constitutional guarantee; it was effected in a thoroughly decentralised manner. Though this scheme was formalised in subsidiary legislation and regulations, it should nonetheless be deemed an integral part of the Soviet constitutional order as defined here. Further, this very linkage between access to services and work should be appreciated as itself constitutional, reflecting the overall labour-centric organisation of Soviet collective life. Moreover, the USSR was really a 'societal state', in that its constitutional order encompassed comprehensive regulation of social relations as well as comprehensive provision of social goods, and thus combined the characteristics of a welfare state and a disciplinary state—a simultaneously 'maternal' and 'paternal' public authority. Indeed, provision and regulation were the obverse and reverse of one social coin. Yet welfare systems even in a democratic context are commonly critiqued as incorporating a disciplinary dimension, in that they foster clientilistic attitudes and relationships.[40] Any 'social state' disciplines as it provides, a circumstance militating against the attribution of any categorical anomaly to the Soviet case.

[39] USSR 1977 24.

[40] M Foucault, *Discipline and Punish: The Birth of the Prison* (London, Penguin, 1991) 135–41; C Offe, *Contradictions of the Welfare State* (Cambridge MA, MIT Press, 1984) 154–57; W Scheuerman, *Between the Norm and the Exception: The Frankfurt School and the Rule of Law* (Cambridge MA, MIT Press, 1987) 286–87.

The USSR Constitution valorised labour above all else,[41] deeming it in proper Marxist fashion the source of all value, and endowing it with an array of constitutional privileges and protections (including participation in factory, political and economic affairs to rights to work, a 41-hour week, rest and leisure).[42] Of course in its practices and norms (one-person management, regulation of trade unions, imposition of labour discipline) the USSR had an equal claim to be regarded a managers' as a workers' state. But the core of the Soviet regulation of labour and its preeminent significance was located in the Republican labour codes, which beyond meticulously elaborating the terms and conditions of employment, dispute procedures, discipline and the like, also elaborated the array of social insurance and incidental benefits. The SSR labour codes elaborated comprehensive rights to a guaranteed state wage commensurate with the quantity and quality of expended labour, rest, limited work day and week, annual paid vacation, health and safe conditions, free initial and continuing professional training, association and trade unions, participation in the management of production, social security, state social insurance for old age, illness and disability. They also regulated female and child labour, collective bargaining and agreements, and dispute resolution and imposed duties including labour discipline and fulfilment of work norms.[43] The Soviet state enterprise was integral to the social as well as the economic order and multiply referenced in the Constitution. It served as custodian of discretionary development and social funds and as support hub for comprehensive social services, from sanatoria and sports facilities to clinics, crèches, libraries, training centres, schools, refectories and social halls.[44]

The social organisation was the established form for Soviet citizens to organise and pursue some common aim on an (ostensibly) voluntary basis, but even its laconic constitutional treatment amply demonstrates its function as an instrument of state purpose.

41 1977 USSR 14.

42 1977 USSR 8, 40, 41.

43 See eg Kaz SSR Labour Code 1971.

44 USSR State enterprise regulations 04.10.1965.

> Article 7. Trade unions, the All-Union Leninist Young Communist League co-operatives, and other public organisations, participate, in accordance with the aims laid down in their rules, in managing state and public affairs, and in deciding political, economic, and social and cultural matters
>
> Article 24. The state encourages co-operatives and other public organisations to provide all types of services for the population. It encourages the development of mass physical culture and sport.
>
> Article 26. In accordance with society's needs, the state provides for planned development of science and the training of scientific personnel and organises introduction of the results of research in the economy and other spheres of life.
>
> Article 27. The state concerns itself with protecting, augmenting and making extensive use of society's cultural wealth for the moral and aesthetic education of the Soviet people, for raising their cultural level.
>
> In the USSR development of the professional, amateur and folk arts is encouraged in every way.[45]

Citizens' associational life and activity ('civil society') was thoroughly conditioned and constrained to the very extent it was enabled in the first place. Similarly, scientific research and cultural performance and production were 'public', that is, state-organised, -sponsored and -directed. No sanctioned area of organised collective life remained outside the regulation of the constitutional order, or the available legal form of the organisation or cooperative. However, as discussed below, in some instances, notably Central Asia, surviving customary forms of social organisation were tolerated in a kind of grey zone, neither recognised nor suppressed.

The Soviet constitutional order thus expressly structured social space in a singularly comprehensive fashion, to the twin ends of support and control or direction. The successor Central Asian systems may have eliminated the anomalous express constitutional regulation, but they have retained a very significant degree of state presence in social space, effected through sub-constitutional legislation, as discussed in chapter seven. Their welfare dimensions have admittedly become vestigial in the context of the shift to the market, providing only supplementary and conditional (means-tested) social support. But their control

[45] USSR 1977 7, 24, 26, 27.

dimensions if no longer total remain significant: all systems, though to varying extent, have perpetuated state registration and regulation of social associations, especially onerous for those of a religious or political nature. In Turkmenistan, the continuing exceptional degree of state control over associational life is only intelligible as a carryover of unreformed Soviet patterns and practices.

SOVIET RIGHTS PROTECTION

There can have been few constitutional orders in history at once so stridently righteous and so cavalier about the substance of rights and the procedure for their enforcement. Soviet collectivism did not disregard individual rights but it did effectively subordinate them, both through hedging them with duties and qualifying their exercise. The Constitution was non-justiciable, so in no case did a Soviet court have occasion to protect or enforce any from among the catalogue of rights,[46] or to assess the constitutionality of state action or enactment as such. Nonetheless, the Procuracy supplied a comprehensive scheme for protesting (challenging) the 'illegality' (non-conformity with applicable statutes or other normative legal acts) of any action or enactment of any state official or body, including judicial decisions.[47] It could act on its own initiative or upon the application of a citizen. This constant check on the legality of official acts was the default rights enforcement system, but was selective and vulnerable to political interference. Much of course depended on the probity and integrity of the procurators, as anywhere.

Thus the received picture of Soviet rights enforcement as non-existent and Soviet rule as utterly arbitrary does not stand up to examination. The Procuracy, though, was not tasked with vindicating individual rights, but with policing the system at a macro-institutional level. Certainly, in the post-terror period, an understanding was widely shared of the permissible bounds of official action even if goalposts did shift (and with the standing exception of security and perceived threats to Soviet authority). Indeed, the recognition of the scope and staggering 'illegality' of the terror, following Khrushchev's 1956 denunciation and

[46] USSR 1977 Chapter 7, 39–59.
[47] USSR 1977 164.

the ensuing thaw, resulting in the provision of a rehabilitation procedure for victims and relatives, revealed some degree of self-correction on the part of the system, even if the generalisation of that procedure had to await Gorbachev and perestroika.[48] The rights of the accused, as opposed to the rights of the citizen at liberty, were rather a different matter. The extremely high conviction rates were a function of an inquisitorial system without procedural or practical equality of arms, with a generally passive and acquiescent judiciary.[49] The Soviet culture of rights remained singularly weak, and the procedural mechanisms for their assertion by citizens and their enforcement by courts were conspicuously undeveloped. These structural defects were carried over into the successor Central Asian systems and have continued to afflict them, to varying degrees.

SOVIET IDEOLOGY

Integral to the Soviet constitutional order was a highly elaborated and complexly rationalised ideology. Unlike the implicit or coded ideology of liberal constitutional systems (privileging property and private right, eg), Soviet ideology was explicit and doctrinal, resembling more a confessional scriptural tradition than a civic religion. The Leninist turn on Marxism and the subsequent Stalinist turn on Leninism placed the constitutional order on a simultaneously (and dialectically related) universalistic (socialist) and particularistic (ethno-nationalist) basis, and imparted to it a developmentalist, if not millenarian, thrust. For unlike merely aspirational constitutions,[50] the Soviet constitutional order was calibrated and then continually readjusted for an inevitable (because historically determined) societal transformation, but one the duration and pacing of which could not be precisely determined in advance. The Soviet constitutional order was thus in some ultimate sense only

[48] USSR Decree 13.08.1990.

[49] See E Huskey, 'The Politics of the Soviet Criminal Process: Expanding the Right to Counsel' (1986) 34 *American Journal of Comparative Law* 93.

[50] KL Scheppele, 'Aspirational and Aversive Constitutionalism: The Case for Studying Cross-constitutional Influence Through Negative Models' (2003) 1 *International Journal of Constitutional Law* 296.

ever provisional, in a perpetual state of becoming, because communism always remained to be achieved, and could not be immediately secured. The ideology of no prior constitutional order carried this particular sort of teleological charge or future-orientation. The Soviet Constitution was in fact the original specimen, at least in an ideological register, both of 'aspirational' and 'transitional' constitutionalism. Its supercharged and pervasive ideological character has posed a challenge to the Central Asian constitutional systems which have struggled to find a serviceable substitute.

SOVIET LOCAL VARIATION

Despite the fractal geometry of the Soviet constitutional order, replicating at ever-finer levels of jurisdiction (the graded series of autonomies and local government) precisely the same institutional contours as the Union itself, it never achieved anything remotely approaching perfect isomorphy. Such a vast and heterogeneous Eurasian space, one sixth of the land surface of the globe, necessarily exhibited a fair bit of local and regional variation, in spite of the homogenising and regularising aims of the Bolshevik Unionists. Local Soviet institutions had particular impact on still traditionally organised, small-scale Central Asian societies, implementing, administering or facilitating social policies under the global banner of Soviet modernisation, from women's emancipation and general literacy to sedentarisation and collectivisation. The collective farm (*kollektivnoe khoziastvo, kolkhoz*) was in the Soviet constitutional order as a whole the primary authority and functional governance institution in rural areas (though formally figuring in the Constitution only insofar as its ownership rights were set forth (Article 12), and its role in the provision of economic and social entitlements for agricultural workers was defined, co-ordinate with that of state enterprises for industrial and urban workers (Articles 41 and 43)). In the overwhelmingly rural Central Asian SSRs, it assumed particularly pivotal significance.[51]

Reciprocally, the formal framework for local government and the local economy were annealed in the ovens of prevailing conditions

[51] The Central Asian *kolkhoz* 'functioned as a global collectivity: it took care of work, administrative identity, the sharing out of incomes and public works

and customs. Central Asia is perhaps the supreme example of the local inflection, adaptation, assimilation and hybridisation of imposed Soviet forms. Soviet Central Asia was Soviet precisely in the same degree as it was 'Central Asian' (itself a Soviet construct and coinage). Primordial traditions and embedded cultural values and practices did not just persist in some subterranean fashion. Rather, Soviet institutions themselves were shaped across complex, contingent processes of local negotiation and reception, in which 'subaltern agency' necessarily asserted itself.[52]

In Central Asia, existing affective networks based on clan and lineage ties, particularly in the recently nomadic or tribal societies of Kyrgyzstan, Kazakhstan and Turkmenistan, as well as existing and emergent patron–client systems grafted themselves onto party and state structures, resulting in a complex Sovietised neo-patrimonialism.

> A neopatrimonial regime provides loyalty and submission to a ruler by means of both formal and informal mechanisms, some of which may be found in well-established democratic systems. Neopatrimonial regimes are based not only on patriarchal values and norms, but on rationally driven exchange of services, when a patron buys the loyalty of a client in exchange for protection of client's [sic] interests.[53]

Patrimonialism was by no means confined to Central Asia, since connections and 'blat' were as an essential mode of the functioning of the Soviet economic system generally,[54] but it took on distinct regional characteristics in Central Asia. Although such networks are by definition informal and extra-legal, therefore *a fortiori* extra-constitutional

(irrigation, etc): O Roy, *The New Central Asia: The Creation of Nations* (London, IB Tauris, 2000) 88.

[52] Kandiyoti takes note of 'a degree of capture of Soviet institutions and of possibilities of maneuvering within them in the framework of local networks of obligation and clientelism': D Kandiyoti, 'The Cry for Land: Agrarian Reform, Gender and Land Rights in Uzbekistan.' (2003) 3 *Journal of Agrarian Change* 225, 293.

[53] A Ilkhamov, 'Neopatrimonialism, Interest Groups and Patronage Networks: The Impasses of the Governance System in Uzbekistan' (2007) 26 *Central Asian Survey* 65, 66.

[54] AV Ledeneva, *Russia's Economy of Favours: Blat, Networking and Informal Exchange* (Cambridge, Cambridge University Press, 1998) 11–38 (phenomenology of forms and uses of blat in Soviet life as subversion/circumvention /manipulation of prescribed rules).

in the strict sense, they can be understood as forming part of the functioning or application of the constitutional order in the wider sense. They supplied the universal lubricant for the administrative machinery and worked through (produced their effects via) formal rules and institutions, thereby conditioning in critical ways the circulation of power and claims to resources. (Obviously, the same points could be made about consolidated democratic constitutional orders, from the US to Italy, since the rigour of any constitutionally premised proceduralism is inevitably softened and humanised in its application.) The Soviet constitutional order might have been designed to serve as a privileged instrument of the CPSU, but it was simultaneously available to be instrumentalised for other purposes and by other interests—from clans to black market profiteers to '*vori v zakone*' or thieves-in-law, the organised crime syndicate based in the prison system—all of whom enjoyed complex interpenetrating relations with official structures.

Existing (pre-European) forms of organised, collective life in the Central Asian SSRs also underwent this differential, negotiated Sovietisation process, and notably Islamic institutions, both ecclesiastical (mosque, clergy, madrasah) and lay (in particular village governance/social institutions, eg mahallas). Central Asian Islam presented the Soviet constitutional order with a significant challenge, since Islam permeated collective life throughout the region and formed a defining part of the very cultural rhizome. It could not be ignored, inasmuch as no collective form of life could well be left untouched by the Soviet Marxist-Leninist-Stalinist dispensation, particularly one so pervasive and authoritative, and therefore potentially threatening. But neither could it have been simply repressed, in the way that Russian orthodoxy was during periodic surges of anti-clericalism, without delegitimising the Soviet cultural nationalist project in particular and *Sovietskaia vlast'* in general. Rather, its ecclesiastical dimension was 'assimilated' and comprehensively regulated, organised through approved official channels of individual as well as collective expression. Clerical Islam was Sovietised; the principal institutions serving this purpose were the Spiritual Directorates of Muslims (DUM, *духовное управление мусульман, dukhovnoe upravlenie mussul'man*).[55] Its lay or community dimension, in the form of

[55] Y Ro'I, *Islam in the Soviet Union: From the Second World War to Perestroika* (London, C. Hurst, 2000) 104–08; Roy (n 51) 52–54.

solidarity structures (mahallas) and functionaries (mullahs), was tolerated unofficially, and achieved a kind of symbiosis with imposed Soviet structures. In particular, the *kolkhoz* represented the territorialisation and recomposition of local tribal/ethnic solidarity groupings throughout rural Central Asia, particularly where nomadic populations had been forcibly sedentarised in the course of collectivisation.[56]

CONSTITUTIONAL ORDER AND THE CONSTITUTION

What then did the USSR Constitution itself have to do with this many-sided constitutional order? In light of the constitutional functions posited earlier,[57] it fulfilled the chartering (plan of government), declaratory/ideological and legitimising functions but its meta-normative function, the constraining or binding action, was weak or non-existent. It was conceived as non-constraining; otherwise it would not have withstood the Marxian critique of constitutionalism as speciously universal and meta-political in the first place, when always only class-bound and partisan. The Soviet Constitution was manifestly not simply sham or deceptive, however, as in the facile received view, but rather reflective, in good Marxist fashion. It gilded the lily of a party state—hence its non-justiciability, as well as its supplementarity and non-supremacy. The thought of the political class respecting fundamental Soviet institutions continually evolved. Its refinement, revision and elaboration required to be memorialised and operationalised, and changes of a significant enough quality or magnitude would eventually find themselves reflected in the Constitution. Soviet constitutionalism can perhaps best be construed as a 'General Line', an authoritative restatement of policy on state law, and is the proper analogue in Soviet terms of the processes found elsewhere in academic discourse and jurisprudence.

The Constitution was never intended to serve as any sort of opening up or frame for politics (which was only ever the politics of 'democratic centralism,' ie intra-party, and, for high politics, intra-politburo) nor even as a housing or containment vessel for politics. That is why the Soviet constitutional *process*, like the Soviet political process, was not

[56] Roy (n 51) 86–94.
[57] Introduction to this volume.

conditioned by the Constitution itself. The material constitution of the USSR was the constantly proliferating set of general norms, both in terms of formal legislation and in terms of party directives (which insofar as they were promulgated and circulated in written form were also formal). The paper Constitution represented at best an ex-post formalisation and restatement, and existed precisely to suture any gap between formal and material—which is of course was as impossible for the Soviet Constitution as for any other sort.

Soviet constitutionalism in its mature form came to present a striking composite of (hyper) formalism and (sweeping) instrumentalism, and any account of it has to do justice to both. While there endured some significant degree of institutional stability across the life of the USSR in the chief features and contours of the constitutional order, set forth above, it was a function of path-dependence and institutional inertia rather than entrenchment. The cumulative mass of normative legal acts across all spheres of the regulation of Soviet society was never remotely tamed, systematised or codified. The USSR lacked a law on normative legal acts (adopted in most post-Soviet jurisdictions), establishing a clear classification and hierarchy of acts that establish, modify, suspend or rescind a legal norm (including statutes, ministerial regulations, orders, decrees, enactments, decisions and sundry other sorts).[58] Part of the impetus behind the 1977 constitutional reform process set in motion by Brezhnev was to retrieve the Constitution from its vitrine and operationalise it, plumb it directly into the pipework of the general normative system (without going so far as to make it justiciable), thus addressing the embarrassment or offence it presented to Soviet formalist sensibilities, and bring it into closer conformity with the existing constitutional order (hence, eg, the expanded constitutional treatment of the CPSU).

It was not until the twilight of the USSR, however, that the problems of the constitutional order itself, as opposed to the Constitution, were grasped, identified, analysed and discussed openly in all their cumulative enormity. The last leader of the Party, like the first a jurist, attempted in perestroika nothing short of a Reformation of the standing constitutional order, for which *pravovoe gosudarstvo*, a law-based state, was the

[58] Henderson (n 3) 5–6.

rallying cry.[59] Three principal foci of this Lutheran ambition may be discerned: 1) the redress of the gross imbalance between individual rights and the power and prerogative of the state (a variant of a Diceyan rule of law); 2) the subordination of the agencies of state administration to the agencies of state power and the latter's concomitant actual exercise of state power in lieu of obedience to external (CPSU) instructions (something like the institution of Weberian formal-legal rationality); and 3) the reorganisation of the Union along properly federal (as opposed to instrumentalist pseudo-federal) lines. Perestroika of course failed to realise the project of a Soviet *pravovoe gosudarstvo,* Soviet limited government, bequeathing that dream to the successor states (which, it saddens one to note, have had little use for it). But it bears remembering that the independent sovereign Central Asian states (along with their sister ex-SSRs) arose out of the course of the first and only thorough-going reform of the Soviet constitutional order. They were products of the reform process itself, not of its failure.

SOVIET CONSTITUTIONAL PROBLEMS AND SOLUTIONS

The titanic and shambolic Soviet constitutional order, equal parts grandeur and grandiosity, monument and makeshift, was a very tough act to follow for its orphaned Central Asian creations. It could as little be roundly repudiated by them as simply forgotten, although in the minds of many Western (particularly American) constitutional therapists in the early nineties, it might as well have been a 'bad relationship', to be as rapidly as possible got over or recovered from.

It has become customary for analyses of Central Asia (as indeed the former Soviet Union in general) to invoke 'Soviet legacies' as

[59] See generally VP Kazimirchuk, MM Slavin and BN Toropin (eds), *The Socialist Law-based State: Problems and Discussions* (Moscow, IGiP AN SSSR Press, 1989) [Казимирчук ВП, Славин ММ, Топорнин БН (Отв ред), *Социалистическое правовое государство Проблемы и суждения*, Изд-во ИГиП АН СССР]; K Beninger, 'Administrative Law and the Socialist Law-based State' (1989) 6 *Pravovedieniie* 66, 68 [Бенингер, К, 'Административное право и социалистическое правовое государство', *Правоведение* 6, 66–68 (1989)]; Iu M Baturin and RZ Livshits, *The Socialist Law-based State: From Idea to Realisation Politico-legal Perspective* (Moscow, Nauka, 1989) [Батурин ЮМ, Лившиц РЗ, *Социалистическое правовое государство: от идеи к осуществлению, Политико-правовой взгляд*, Москва: Наука 1989].

encumbering successor states. Legacies sometimes serve as a convenient shorthand for everything which makes either democratic true-believers or devout free-marketeers queasy about the new Central Asia, but chiefly seem to refer to the obstinate persistence of Soviet political and administrative culture, attitudes and reflexes, after the demise of Soviet ideology.[60] More suitable for a comparative contextual analysis than lamentations over vague 'legacies,' like a mentalité overhang, would be a consideration, in light of the constitutional portrait just limned, of the particular, specifically *constitutional* challenges and burdens presented to the successor states. For the nascent Central Asian orders, the USSR had posed, framed and to a large extent predetermined the response to, a set of fundamental constitutional problems. How the five independent republics addressed these challenges forms the core of the analysis in this book, elaborated in chapters four to eight.

The problem of order (the vacant guarantor). The Soviet constitutional order lacked internal mechanisms for stabilisation and reinforcement, apart from the force of institutional habits and patterns and the growth of agency interests or bureaucratic fiefs (which should by no means be discounted), and depended on the external prop of the Party, its guarantor and source of order. Once that prop had been kicked away with the collapse of the Union and the dissolution of the central party structures, the Central Asian states had not only to fashion a replacement constitutional order, but to find a replacement constitutional authority or guarantor. The prospects of an internal constitutional authority spontaneously developing in the short term, even under favourable enabling conditions, were remote.

Of course a constitutional order worthy of the name might be supposed to be self-guaranteeing, notwithstanding that constitutional history is rife with examples of this external guarantor or guardian role. (It is not always a vanguard party; in some cases the military has assumed this function.) So Central Asian states might have taken the

[60] Legacy talk is ubiquitous in the literature, understandably, eg MB Olcott, *Kazakhstan: Unfulfilled Promise*, Revised Edition (Washington, Carnegie Endowment for Peace, 2010) 16 ('legacy of Soviet-era understandings of nationalism'); SN Cummings, *Understanding Central Asia: Politics and Contested Transformations* (Abingdon and New York, Routledge, 2012) 71 (legacy of formal institutions).

bold step of ceasing to search for a guarantor and dispensing with one altogether—that is, accepting the full stakes of the constitutional wager. But the USSR's adoption of a unique political institution to serve both as ultimate guarantor/guardian and proximate director of the constitutional system was fateful. The Central Asian states, as any successor states would have been, were predisposed to see their constitutional predicament in these inherited terms. This likelihood was further massively enhanced because the interim state authorities across Central Asia were necessarily the Republican Party elites: the regime in the peripheral Soviet Union, unlike in Russia itself, had not been deposed, only decapitated, and was therefore bodily intact. It was all but sealed by the chaotic and precipitous end of the Union, which plunged all successor states into an immediate cauldron of uncertainty and instability, depriving them suddenly of central resources and making the problem of order paramount. The Party itself was no longer available to carry on this institutional role, but new presidential institutions were ready to assume it.

The problem of instrumentalism. The Soviet Constitution was only ever a very loose cage for the Soviet constitutional order. It structured government, certainly, but it did not effectively limit it, nor was it intended or designed to do so. Rather, it was instrumental to the elites exercising state power. The (impossible) challenge presented by the Soviet constitutional order for its Central Asian successors was to resist the siren call of instrumentalism, to reconceptualise the very function of a constitutional order—from one that closed political space and secured decision-making to the standing leadership to one that opened that space and released decision-making to much broader potential constituencies and sets of power-holders.

The problem of separation of powers. The separation of powers is a particularly knotty and problematic aspect of the transition from Soviet-style constitutionalism.[61] The Soviet constitutional order in practice exhibited a marked interpenetration or promiscuity of powers: legislative, executive and judicial authorities were not autonomous, all being subordinate to an effective 'fourth branch', an organising power standing beyond them. Thus the real problem of 'separation of powers' is

[61] R Teitel, 'Post-Communist Constitutionalism: A Transitional Perspective' (1994) 26 *Columbia Human Rights Law Review* 167,176–79.

that the 'agencies of state power', the formal powers themselves, executive, legislative and judicial branches, actually had very little to do with the way state power was exercised in the USSR. They were insufficiently separated inter se because the formal governmental system itself was not separated from the CPSU and was not autonomous.

Functional separation of powers is a function of an internal, self-regulating scheme of ordering, and would actually frustrate or obstruct an external scheme, such as the Soviet, for which separation of powers served as pure administrative convenience or formalist device of governance. The Soviet constitutional order never developed any Madisonian dispersal of state authority, nor any mechanisms of cross-constraint (apart from inter-agency rivalry and competition for resources), which would have been counter-productive, as well as ideologically problematic in view of the professed unity of the working class. Executive authority was unchecked and imbalanced, save by the occult play of bureaucratic interests, court politics and the hold of party traditions of collective leadership ('democratic centralism').

The problem of the 'deep state'. Eighteenth-century separation of powers issues are greatly compounded by twentieth-century concentrated knots of administrative power, the 'deep state' or 'states within a state'. Any contemporary administrative bureaucracy represents a conundrum for constitutional regulation[62]—as of course do the security and enforcement services. The overblown administrative apparatus, the 'agencies of state administration', are the primary interface between government and governed in any society—the 'agencies of state power' are remote and faceless. Benefits clerks or immigration judges or police constables impinge far more directly on ordinary lives than do ministers and MPs. Yet a far greater amount of constitutional parchment is typically occupied with the latter than the former. The Soviet constitutional order, as shown above, gave *chinovniki*, government officials, very great latitude and members of the security services and police virtually free reign. The Soviet 'deep state', represented by the substantively though

[62] 'The attempt to satisfy a universe of legal claims couples with the need for extensive regulatory activities to generate a massive administrative apparatus that takes over many of the activities once more directly managed by elected legislators', Scheuerman (n 40) 237 (discussing Kirchheimer's critique of Western welfare bureaucracies).

not formally most powerful 'agents of state administration' in the constitutional order, was likely to survive as a core component of any new constitutional order in Central Asia.

The problems of ideology, identity, legitimacy. The Soviet constitutional order drew on at least three principal sources of legitimacy: the over-arching ideology of Marxism-Leninism, developmentally inflected nationalism (ethnicity, as defined for socialist purposes) and (notional) popular consent expressed through periodic elections (democracy). The irrevocable loss of the first confronted the Central Asian republics with a 'legitimation crisis' at birth, and the need and occasion to adapt the remaining two to new purposes and circumstances. One could venture an over-arching fourth, the great common ordeal of the Soviet twentieth century, the cumulative succession of privation, upheaval, terror and mass violence, culminating in the staggering devastation of the Great Patriotic War, across which not the 'New Soviet Man' but a simultaneously proud and bitter Soviet 'constitutional identity' was forged.[63]

As a (singular) constitutional theory, Soviet-style Marxism was inimitable. It subordinated the formalism of constitutional logic and arrangements to the materialism of class relations, the supremacy of the working class and the vanguard role of the Party in administering and institutionalising that supremacy. It did all of that and moreover accommodated and instrumentalised the force of national identity. It was thus potent, resonant and elaborately rationalised in a way that posed a very high bar for any of the ersatz contenders for its status in Central Asian (and post-Soviet) constitutional discourse generally. Of nationalism, managed democracy, consumerism, natural resource baronialism, or Asian-style developmentalism, none has come remotely close to commanding the force and coherence of Soviet ideology.

Still nationalism was the odds-on favourite. Territorially based cultivated ethno-nationalism had served as the unlikely reinforcement of cosmopolitan socialism in the strange Soviet scheme. When the latter was thoroughly repudiated, the former remained available and eminently serviceable for the new Central Asian political class. It had been tailor-made for Soviet dependent Republican sovereignty and it proved ideal for post-Soviet independent Republican sovereignty,

[63] G Jacobsohn, 'Constitutional Identity' (2006) 68 *The Review of Politics* 361.

virtually ensuring ethnicity and language as default candidates for the organisation of collective political identity in the new states. The juridified essentialism of the Soviet model thus rather loaded the constitutional dice for the Central Asia states in favour of ethno-nationalist rather than civic-republican polities (although Central Asian nationalist ideology has been differentially formulated, from the hard, mono-ethnic style of eg *uzbekchilik* [Uzbekness][64] to the softer multi-ethnic Kazakh *primus inter pares* variant). Soviet constitutionalism had long gone its own anachronistic path to constitutional pluralism. It had eschewed or ignored the possibilities post-modern constitutionalism had in the meanwhile developed to accommodate heterogeneous and dynamic (not static or essential) identities.[65]

Similarly, Soviet formal-democratic validation, again in its distinctive local permutation of plebiscitary, managed elections, also remained serviceable and available. For the Central Asian constitutional orders, democratic legitimisation was inevitably going to prove something of a challenge, owing to the rise of international democratisation standards (an aspect of world constitutionalism) and the presence of international monitoring bodies. Times had changed and Soviet show or staged elections, the counterpart of show trials—formal exercises in the ratification of a pre-ordained decision, whether by voters or triers of fact—had become unfashionably old-school. 'Political technology', the term of art for the media-savvy manipulation and management of elections in post-Soviet space so as to ensure outcomes, proved a refinement of inherited techniques.[66] For the Central Asian states, the political technology not just for elections but for collective identity had been massively pre-developed, perfected over the decades of Soviet rule. They inherited an entire apparatus of communications (propaganda, media, school curricula and textbooks) and juridical (citizenship, language status) techniques. All that was required was to tweak it a bit and bring it up to date. Moreover, managed democratic contestation

[64] See ch 8.

[65] See J Tully, *Strange Multiplicity: Constitutionalism in an Age of Diversity* (Cambridge, Cambridge University Press, 1995) 183–212; S Tierney, *Constitutional Law and National Pluralism* (Oxford, Oxford University Press, 2004) (variety of constitutional means for accommodation of sub-state nationalism).

[66] A Wilson, *Virtual Politics: Faking Democracy in the Post-Soviet World* (New Haven CT, Yale University, 2005) 38–40.

and managed national identity formation had become default props of authoritarian post-colonial constitutional orders, and those had not benefitted from the comprehensive Soviet apprenticeship.

The problem of property (capital). Once the Soviet constitutional order took the fateful step of formalising the material constitution, and foregrounding the great legal innovation of socialist property and the state monopoly on the means of production, the die was cast for any successor order. If the USSR and SSR constitutions had avowed the categorical privilege of a socialist property regime, then the post-Soviet constitutions were constrained (or determined) in reaction to avow that of a private property regime.[67] The regulation of property (and of the economy more generally) was destined to emerge as a constitutional problem in Central Asia even if the constitutional solution was inadequate and failed to address the division of the Soviet spoils (privatisation). The Central Asian constitutional systems all have accommodated—indeed enabled—the transformation of party states into crony capital (and clan capital) states, as elaborated in chapter seven.

The problem of sovereignty. The Soviet republics were all born sovereign, thanks to the revenge of Soviet federal constitutional law. But their congenital sovereignty was literally paper-thin: they were endowed with all the indicia and institutions of formal sovereignty (legislature, executive, judiciary), without a shadow of substantive sovereignty. While sovereignty for the newly independent 'stans along with other peripheral SSRs was thus straightforward as a legal matter, it was a formidable challenge as a practical and governance matter, with (initially) a significant prospect of failure. Though the Soviet Union had come undone, its vast centre, the Russian Federation, remained intact, exerting an overwhelming gravitational force—political, economic, strategic—on the successor states, like Jupiter on its moons. Asymmetric diecast Soviet federalism burdened the new constitutional orders with an excessive pre-occupation with *gosudarstvennost'* (государственность—statehood, really 'stateness') and control over population, resources and borders.

[67] In the views of some a very good thing. See CR Sunstein, 'On Property and Constitutionalism' (1992–93) 14 *Cardozo Law Review* 907.

FURTHER READING

VV Aspaturian, 'The Theory and Practice of Soviet Federalism' (1950) 12(1) *Journal of Politics* 20.

HJ Berman, 'The Spirit of Soviet Law' (1948) 23 *Washington Law Review & State Bar Journal* 152, 166.

——, 'Soviet Law and Government' (1958) 21 *Modern Law Review* 19, 26.

——, *Justice in the U.S.S.R.: An Interpretation of Soviet Law* (Cambridge MA, Harvard University Press, 1963).

T Martin, *The Affirmative Action Empire: Nations and Nationalism in the Soviet Union, 1923–1939* (London and Ithaca NY, Cornell University Press, 2001).

S Newton, *Law and the Making of the Soviet World: The Red Demiurge* (Abingdon, Routledge, 2015).

OS Ioffe and PB Maggs, *The Soviet Economic System: A Legal Analysis* (Boulder CO, Westview Press, 1987).

PG Roeder, 'Soviet Federalism and Ethnic Mobilization' (1991) 43(2) *World Politics* 196.

R Schlesinger, *Soviet Legal Theory: Its Social Background and Development* (London, Kegan Paul, Trench, Trubner, 1945).

Y Slezkine, 'The USSR as a Communal Apartment, or How a Socialist State Promoted Ethnic Particularism' (1994) 53 *Slavic Review* 414.

RG Suny and T Martin, *A State of Nations: Empire and Nation-making in the Age of Lenin and Stalin* (Oxford, Oxford University Press, 2001).

AY Vyshinsky, *The Law of the Soviet State* (New York, Macmillan, 1948).

3

Natal Chart

Constituent Influences and Processes

The Post-Soviet Moment and the Exigency of Sovereignty – The Constituent Process and the Texts Themselves – Property, the Market and Welfare – Culture and Constitution – Transition Tutelage: Good Governance, Rule of Law, Democratisation – Conclusion

ALTHOUGH THE SOVIET constitutional tradition bore down ponderously on the new Central Asian states, it was just one among diverse factors shaping the new constitutions. Gauging the full range of influences and making sense of the emergence of the Central Asian systems, their similarities and differences as well as their subsequent trajectories, means casting a proper natal chart. Following first is an examination of the demands of sovereignty, then a look at the constituent processes and the constitutional texts. The chapter next analyses in turn the force of marketisation, the significance of cultural influences and the role of international transition discourse and practice.

THE POST-SOVIET MOMENT AND THE EXIGENCY OF SOVEREIGNTY

From a constitutional perspective, December 1991 was not a moment of the liberation of constituent imagination or energies; it was a moment of rupture and crisis. Following upon the Belavezha Accords[1] (not attended by any of the Central Asian leaders, though Nazarbaev had been invited) that set in motion the legal dissolution of the Union, the Central Asian republics together with the other SSRs were cut off at one stroke from central resources. These resources were not just material, but political and legal-constitutional as well. Cast adrift, the Soviet 'stans were left to their own constitutional devices. In perestroika reform energies had been channelled from the centre outwards, and met with divided reaction in Central Asia as elsewhere in the periphery: nascent social forces and emergent elites welcomed them and vested bureaucratic and party interests resisted them or instrumentalised them to maintain power.[2] The Central Asian republics, despite having made formal declarations of sovereignty like other peripheral republics at the time, had little interest in independence or the substitution of a weak commonwealth for a superpower Union.[3] Their inherited SSR constitutions became by default the basic legal framework for the five suddenly independent states; but the constitutional challenges were formidable.

In late Soviet times, as the nature of the Union was actively debated and discussed, the crux of the issue rapidly became one of sovereignty or the organisation and configuration of sovereignties in a multi-sovereign polity. The driving force behind sovereignty appeared to be the reassertion of nationalism in non-canonical, heretical forms. The revenge of Soviet multi-nationalism was now at hand as the collective political identities so meticulously cultivated and managed by Soviet authorities for their multiple national wards escaped control. The fundamental animating question of twilight constitutionalism was the state of the Union itself: the apportionment, dimensions, entailments

[1] 21.12.1991 Accord.

[2] SN Cummings, *Understanding Central Asia: Politics and Contested Transformations* (Abingdon and New York, Routledge, 2012) 55–56; for accounts of perestroika popular discontents and elite manoeuvrings see D Hiro, *Inside Central Asia: A Political and Cultural History of Uzbekistan, Turkmenistan, Kazakhstan, Kyrgyzstan, Tajikistan, Turkey, and Iran* (London, Duckworth Overlook, 2013) at Kindle 2503–2694 (Uzbekistan), and Kindle 4743–4900 (Kazakhstan).

[3] Kazakhstan has the dubious distinction of having been the very last Union Republic formally to declare independence and quit the Union.

and relations of sovereignty, for both federal centre and autonomies ('autonomy' is the generic term used in the scholarly literature to refer to the Soviet federal components at all levels).

Nothwithstanding the fact that pursuant to their own constitutions and the common Union Constitution, the constituent SSRs already enjoyed formal sovereignty, 1989 to 1990 witnessed a cascade of sovereignty declarations by all 15.[4] The import of these declarations varied: for some (the Baltics, Georgia), they were a salvo in a campaign for independence, and were followed in due course by independence declarations; for others, like the Central Asian five, they were salve to subaltern nationalist sentiment, and an elite claim to devolved political authority, 'home rule'. But it was the assertion of sovereignty by the RSFSR, and the strategic motivations behind it, which sounded the death knell for the Union. Because of the grossly asymmetric stature of the RSFSR in the USSR, it was never a titular Russian Republic, in the manner of the other SSRs—it was the rather the federated heart of the union, important as an envelope for sub-republican autonomies but not an 'autonomy' itself, just as Russian nationality was generic not specific like all others.[5] Only the Russian Federated Republic's institutions of governance (which had been historically less developed than those of the peripheral republics because they had no 'national' significance)

[4] Latvian SSR 28.07.1989, Estonian SSR 16.11.1989, Lithuanian SSR 18.04.1989, Azerbaijan SSR 23.09.1989, RSFSR 12.06.1990, Uzbek SSR 20.06.1990, Bielorussian SSR 27.07.1990, Georgian SSR 26.05.1990, Moldavian SS 23.06.1990, Ukrainian SSR 16.07.1990, Turkmen SSR 22.08.1990, Armenian SSR 24.08.1990, Tajik SSR 24.08.1990, Kazakh SSR 25.08.1990, Kyrgyz SSR 15.12.1990. The 'parade of sovereignties' was also joined by the lesser autonomies, eg Abkhaz ASSR 25.08.1990, Bashkir ASSR 11.10.1990. The Baltics, Georgia and Azerbaijan adopted independence declarations prior to the August 1990 failed coup. Only the independence of the three Baltic republics was recognised by the USSR prior to its break-up in December 1991. 06.09.1991 Resolutions.

[5] Y Slezkine, 'The USSR as a Communal Apartment, or How a Socialist State Promoted Ethnic Particularism' (1994) 53 *Slavic Review* 414, 434–35; T Martin, 'An Affirmative Action Empire: The Soviet Union as the Highest Form of Imperialism' in RG Suny and T Martin (eds), *A State of Nations: Empire and Nation-making in the Age of Lenin and Stalin* (Oxford, Oxford University Press, 2001) 67–90, 80; R Brubaker, 'Nationhood and the National Question in the Soviet Union and Post-Soviet Eurasia: An Institutionalist Account' (1994) 23(1) *Theory and Society* 47, 51–52.

were in a position to sap and then usurp the central Union governance functions. And that is precisely how Boris Yeltsin sought to instrumentalise them, in his bid to challenge the Kremlin for central control.[6]

If the *assertion* of sovereignty before Union collapse was perhaps less fraught for the Central Asian SSRs than for others, the *anxieties* of sovereignty after collapse were greater. They were all Soviet constructs without any tradition of modern sovereignty except as received and administered through *Sovetskaia vlast'*. *Gosudarstvennost'* was the paramount concern of the newly independent republican leaderships in each of the Central Asian states.[7] Securing effective sovereignty was one of the main motors of Central Asian constitutional discourse, thinking and strategy, following on from the place it had commanded in late Soviet constitutional thought.

Owing to this overriding constitutional imperative, the first generation Central Asian constitutions served a distinct political function and sounded in a different tonal register from the constitutions of the Central European states which emerged from the wreckage of the Bloc. Apart from the component units of the federal states of Czechoslovakia and Yugoslavia which became independent, the Central European cases were all historic polities of some duration, however much their national territories had shifted over the vicissitudes of twentieth-century post-imperial and post-bellum resizing (Hungary, Romania, Poland). With the collapse of communism, they were reasserting a historical sovereignty, whereas the Central Asian states were proclaiming their sovereignty before the world for the very first time.

The end of perestroika and exigency of sovereignty did not however augur well for Central Asian constitutionalism, contrary to received opinion. Commentators typically have celebrated the collapse of the Union together with its constitutional reform processes as unshackling the successor states to attack more substantive reform. In fact, the end of the USSR set serious constitutional reform *back* in the Central Asian states, whatever it did in Russia and elsewhere, and arguably doomed

[6] P Reddaway and D Glinski, *The Tragedy of Russia's Reforms: Market Bolshevism Against Democracy* (Washington, US Institute of Peace, 2001) 31–33.

[7] See Cummings (n 2) 57–62 for a parsing of the sovereignty question facing the Central Asian states into internal (authority over domestic space) and external (international status and stature) dimensions.

it altogether. *Pravovoe gosudarstvo* never resonated with the peripheral leaderships as it had with the centre, and they were relieved to let slip the promise and peril of the late Soviet constitutional moment. If reform seeking actually limited government and enforceable rights protection had been an important driver of perestroika at the centre, it had a very different significance in the periphery. Indeed, the relaxation of control by the Union authorities in late-perestroika and its fateful consequences served as a kind of political morality tale and disinclined the Central Asian authorities to decentralise or disperse their own latterly acquired state power. For the Central Asian elites carrying the neo-natal states on their backs, the disintegration of the Soviet constitutional order did not liberate them to repudiate Soviet authority but rather to recuperate it in a more reliable and stable local form. Their urgent need was not limited government but strong government, effective state authority as a bulwark against disintegration and chaos: the terrifying spectacle of Tajikistan immediately to hand served as a sobering and salutary object lesson.

THE CONSTITUENT PROCESS AND THE TEXTS THEMSELVES

Both as respects the drafting and the contents of their constitutions, the Central Asian states continued what the SSRs had launched, in the process diverting onto so many single-ended sidings the grand trunk of the Soviet constitutional reform process.[8] The new draft Treaty of Union circulated in June 1991 was to serve as the basis for thoroughgoing reform of the Constitution of the USSR and its probable replacement, as well as contemporaneous reform of the constitutions of the Union republics. The Central Asian states arose when the Union reform process eventuated not in a new generation of Union and Republican constitutions but rather in the dissolution of the Union and its conversion to a loose (and feeble) 'Commonwealth of Independent States' (CIS) in December 1991. The new states thus did not find themselves suddenly faced with a constituent emergency. Rather they began

[8] J Henderson, *Constitution of the Russian Federation* (Oxford, Hart Publishing, 2011) 48–57 chronicles the salient constitutional developments in the ferment of 1988–91.

independent life with a constitutional reform process well advanced and long underway, the significance of which was now transformed. Indeed, it was the acceleration of Soviet constitutional reform itself that unexpectedly calved the 'stans.

If there was ever a moment when multiple avenues were open,[9] it was late-Soviet and not post-Soviet. The opportunities for substantive reform in the direction of a *pravovoe gosudarstvo*, a constitutionalism of constraint and limitation, diminished markedly with the dissolution of the Union, as priorities, calculations, aims and expectations all shifted tectonically in Central Asia. Nonetheless, the first generation Central Asian constitutions represented to a variable extent the modification and redirection of the perestroika constitutional reform processes, and were much more reasonable qua first adopted than subsequently amended. The secular constitutional shift across the region in the direction of progressive executive aggrandisement and super-presidentialism was largely a function of further constitutional revision. The Central Asian constitutions all grew more problematic and neo-Soviet the more they departed from the late Soviet templates from which they ultimately derived. The dissolution of the USSR might not have been the 'greatest geopolitical catastrophe of the century', as Putin styled it,[10] but it was a constitutional disaster for the Central Asian republics.

New SSR constitutions were in preparation in late perestroika.[11] Those might well have made more credible and functional frameworks for democracy than the independent constitutions proved to be. New constitutions of Union republics could not have contravened basic rights of the Union, as these were contemplated to be enshrined in

[9] B Ackerman, *We the People: Transformations, Volume 2* (Cambridge MA, Harvard University Press, 2000).

[10] I Novikova, 'Vladimir Putin: Collapse of the Soviet Union was the greatest geopolitical catastrophe of the century' *Pravda*, 25 April 2005, available at www.pravda.ru/politics/authority/kremlin/25-04-2005/50878-poslanie-0/, accessed 9 September 2016 [Новикова Инна 'Владимир Путин: Крушение Советского Союза было крупнейшей геополитической катастрофой века,'*Правда* 25.04.2005]. Nor was Putin's phrase simple hyperbole, Reddaway and Glinski (n 6) 2.

[11] See A Imomov, 'Development of the Conception of the Constitution of a Sovereign Republic (on the Basis of the Experience of Tajikistan)' (1991) 11 *Sovietskoie gosudarstvo i pravo* 11, 18 [Имомов, Ашурбой 'Развитие концепции конституции суверенной республики (на опыте Таджикистана), *Советское государство и право*, № 11, 1991].

and secured by a new Union constitution. Further, notwithstanding the centripetal forces and the drive towards sovereignty, the force of Union imperatives would have continued to be felt. Even though tight harmonisation was not in view and not especially sought, the liberalising impetus and energies released by perestroika would have continued to exert their effects Union-wide. A provision embodying something along the lines of the US Fourteenth Amendment[12] would have ensured that the rights elaborated in the Union Constitution provided a floor for the Union republics which they could not diminish or vitiate.

Constituent processes for the five new states, Ashghabat and Tashkent 1992, Bishkek and Almaty 1993 and Dushanbe 1994, did not exactly recapitulate Philadelphia 1787. But perhaps extended, impassioned deliberations followed by an attentive and informed public are too lofty a standard, even supposing they did correspond to the actual goings-on at the US Constitutional Convention. In the present age of constitutional expertise, drafting is generally down to experts and draftspersons, not educated laypeople and citizen-thinkers. Any modern exercise in constitution-making has been elite in the sense of technocratic, even if the result is democratically adopted after the fact. The French Constitution of 1958 was just as susceptible to the charge of elitism (and instrumentalism)[13] as any first generation Central Asian constitution. Those responsible for producing the five constitutional drafts were doing a commissioned job, under considerable time and political pressure. They were (mostly) journeymen, part-time constitutionalists, serving their political masters—not Olympian framers.

In each of the five cases, the sitting Supreme Soviets functioned as constituent assemblies as they had already been doing for the drafting of the planned but aborted new Union Republican constitutions. The work appears to have followed the standardised Soviet legislative drafting protocol: the appointment of a working group or drafting commission from relevant agencies of ministries, the preparation of an initial

[12] 'No State shall make or enforce any law which shall abridge the privileges or immunities of citizens of the United States; nor shall any State deprive any person of life, liberty, or property, without due process of law; nor deny to any person within its jurisdiction the equal protection of the laws.' Section 1. That post-Civil War provision extended basic rights protection against infringement by state rather than solely federal authorities as previously.

[13] S Boyron, *The Constitution of France: A Contextual Analysis* (Oxford, Hart Publishing, 2013) 29–42.

concept (*konsepstia*), laying out the broad parameters and approaches, the preparation and circulation of iterative drafts for comments and revision, and the submission to the Soviet for a series of hearings, with further revision on the basis of the latter. Constitutional working groups were distinguished by a broader commission membership, the consultation of foreign models, and at least a formal opportunity for public discussion and consultation.[14] They appear to have continued the work already commenced rather than to have been reconvened post-independence.

Efforts at broader public consultation and participation were undeniably a feature of late-Soviet Union-level constitutional reform, and were mounted to varying degrees in the parallel processes in the Central Asian SSRs and then in their independent successor states (even Turkmenistan).[15] But they ran up against powerful socio-political limitations. Soviet constitutional institutions (agencies of State power, the soviets and the judiciary, and agencies of State administration, the Cabinet of Ministers and others), together with the rules and procedures (election rules and decision rules, terms of office, etc) had been matters generally beyond the ken and even curiosity of the governed. Any political decision-making, let alone the founding or constituent sort, had been the exclusive prerogative and affair of the narrow Soviet political class. The opacity and irrelevance of the formal Soviet constitutional order for citizens had been a plain fact of political life. Constitutional reform under perestroika aimed to render it transparent and immediate, and *glasnost'* was intended to and did in fact spur public debate about it. But

[14] The level of participation and consultation varied. Some drafting groups did receive or request international consultation and did canvas a range of local views (particularly on issues such as citizenship and language). S Kanter, 'Constitution Making in Kazakhstan' (1993) 5 *International Legal Perspectives* 65; J Anderson, 'Constitutional Development in Central Asia' (1997) 16(3) *Central Asian Survey* 301; B Ryskozha, 'The 1993 Constitution infringing his powers displeased only Nursultan Nazarbayev', Radio Azzatyq, 29 January 2009 (interview with Serikbolsyn Abdil'din, former Speaker of the Supreme Soviet), available at www.rus.azattyq.org/content/article/1376014.html, accessed 8 November 2015 [Рыскожа, Болат 'Конституция 1993 года, ущемляющая его полномочия, не понравилась только Нурсултану Назарбаеву' Радио Азаттык 20.01.2009] (Kazakhstan).

[15] J Anderson, 'Constitutional Development in Central Asia' (1997) 16(3) *Central Asian Survey* 301, 302–11.

perestroika could not magic a complacent and apathetic public into a self-conscious *pouvoir constituant*.

Public debate about the post-independence constitutional order certainly featured in Kazakhstan and Kyrgyzstan. Against the odds, the lively press discussions during the four-month consultation periods in both suggest that (some) citizens took decided views on the power balance between executive and legislature. Limited government was in demand and for a brief moment in prospect. Kyrgyzstan's fateful and fitful shift towards eventual parliamentary rule was charted early on when three alternative constitutional drafts circulated in 1992 and the selection of a parliamentary form of government was an immediate post-independence possibility.[16]

On the other side of the ledger, the overnight collapse and delegitimation of the Soviet order did not suddenly inspire general belief in or legitimise the succeeding order, the new set of rules, procedures and institutions. If anything, particularly with the follow-on metamorphosis of presidents into super-presidents, it vindicated the prevailing constitutional apathy, which was never likely to give way to sustained, passionate constitutional engagement. With some qualifications Central Asian constituent processes were neither broadly socialised nor politicised in the sense of exposure to contestation and a breadth of views and interests—emphatically not outside the two 'K' states (Kazakhstan and Kyrgyzstan). Rather, they were elite and technocratic, preceding politics rather than emerging from politics.

In sum, the five first generation constitutions were untimely ripped from the Soviet womb, not brought to term over the course of the contemplated perestroika reform process. Thus, while all looking like the genuine article, they suffered to varying extents from the same legitimation deficit as the Brezhnev-era Union and Republican constitutions. None of them was submitted for referendum; they were all adopted by the sitting Supreme Soviets. The constituent process was usurped or pre-empted either immediately after perestroika (for Turkmenistan and Uzbekistan) or after a brief further interval (for the others), in a reversion to Soviet type, to whatever extent the content was novel. The resulting constitutions have all been imposed, ab initio or by

[16] ibid. 303.

subsequent amendment, by the governors on the prospective governed, rather than by the governed on the prospective governors.

Granted that the constituent processes were circumscribed, what about the contents, the general plan and organisation and the formulation of individual provisions? Did these five new states look beyond their inherited Soviet horizons for models? What did they borrow? At the time the five constitutions were drafted, there was a growing literature on theoretical constitutional design, as well as on comparative analysis of existing constitutions and on constitutional borrowing.[17] Although specific evidence is lacking, the members of the various Central Asian constituent committees or working groups appear not to have enjoyed the leisure, the wherewithal or the inclination to consult the available scholarship or to undertake a systematic survey of institutional design possibilities, both those realised in particular existing constitutional orders and those speculatively proposed. In any case, the *travaux preparatoires* (the preparatory drafts and related documents) have not been made available.

The contents themselves, which will be analysed in considerable detail in the chapters following, were in no way remarkable. For all the attention and concern focused on the new post-Soviet states, and all the general fuss over constitutionalism post-1989, the new Central Asian constitutional arrangements exhibited little ingenuity or novelty, with the exception of the Turkmenistan Constitution with its disquieting anomalies.[18] They were anaemic insofar as they sought to reappropriate and deploy a tradition of constitutional formalism just at the point where it had been subject to unprecedentedly searching and trenchant critique. Their textual qualities were formulaic and anachronistic: they gave a very poor accounting of fin-de-siècle constitutionalist thought. If the US Constitution is anomalous as a surviving archaic form, which however much amended retains its eighteenth-century

[17] Constitutional borrowing is a function of political choices. See L Epstein and J Knight, 'Constitutional Borrowing and Nonborrowing' (2003) 1 *International Journal of Constitutional Law* 196; S Newton, 'Transplantation and Transition: Legality and Legitimacy in the Kazakhstani Legislative Process' in M Kurkchiyan and D Galligan (eds), *Law and Informal Practices: The Post-communist Experience* (Oxford, Oxford University Press, 2003) 151–70.

[18] See ch 1.

contours and configuration (the horseshoe crab among modern constitutions),[19] then the post-Soviet Central Asian constitutions, far from uniquely, demonstrated very little interim evolution in constitutional theory or design.

Perhaps this circumstance was only to be expected. The constituent process was inevitably a reconstituent process, a redaction and revision of an existing text, and *a reworking and repurposing of existing institutions.* Constitution-as-reconstitution was a widely shared condition at the time. The stunning seismic collapse of the Bloc set off an extraordinary tsunami of roughly contemporaneous refoundations and reconstitutions, moving 'from Stettin in the Baltic to Trieste in the Adriatic'… and on east to the Pacific and south to the Caspian and the Pamirs. In the USSR (as in the other federal states of the Bloc, Yugoslavia and Czechoslovakia) the reconstitution accompanied a constitutional disintegration as well, as federal states came apart along constitutional lines, and formally subordinate jurisdictions (republics or states) achieved independence and international recognition. But the Central Asian states confronted the refoundation in a very special sense, since they had never before existed as modern state jurisdictions.

The familiar look and feel of the first generation constitutions to any Soviet jurist, notwithstanding the exotic names, is a function of the shared legal ground and context. The constitutions all speak the same legal language, even when the official text is in the national tongue (and it has invariably been back-translated from Russian, which was the universal language of legal drafting). All the Central Asian systems carried over the entire Soviet-derived Russian legal system—its categories, concepts, vocabulary and logic. But this was a matter not just of the carryover from the perestroika moment of a constitutional idiom, but of *an entire complement of functioning constitutional institutions*: legislature, judiciary and executive. In not a single case was an existing major governing institution dissolved or dismantled, only renamed and reorganised. This institutional continuity is apt to be overlooked. In any Central Asian Supreme Court or General Procuracy, the obligatory

[19] Klug examines the ways in which US constitutional provisions have served as both negative and positive examples (model and anti-model) for other jurisdictions. H Klug, 'Model and Anti-model: The United States Constitution and the "Rise of World Constitutionalism"' (2000) *Wisconsin Law Review* 597.

portrait gallery of past chief justices or general procurators extends from the period of the SSR in an unbroken line to the present. If the five 'stans were born on to the world stage in late 1991, they had gestated for most of the preceding 70 years inside the USSR. To this long period of foetal constitutional development they all owe their institutional limbs and organs.

The five constitutions were all drafted 'in proud isolation'—unlike, for example, the civil codes of all the states except Turkmenistan, which were based on a CIS Model Civil Code drafted in 1994.[20] The possibilities for useful constitutional cross-fertilisation would arguably have been much greater had the Union held; just prior to its dissolution an Inter-Republican Scientific Consultative Committee had been established under the Institute of State and Law of the Academy of Sciences, which promised to serve as a key constitution-making resource.[21] Still, the five initial constitutions, though not derived from a common model in a strict sense, exhibited striking family resemblances. They all embraced a presidential system,[22] with a president elected by separate mandate and enjoying wide powers including the appointment of government (prime and line ministers).[23] Kazakhstan, Uzbekistan and Tajikistan carried over the inherited unicameral Supreme Soviet; all subsequently introduced upper chambers, respectively in 1995, 1999 and 2004. Kyrgyzstan added a second chamber in 1998 but

[20] 29.10.1994 Model civil code for states-members of the Commonwealth of Independent States (Part 1) [Модельный Гражданский кодекс от 29.10.1994 для государств—участников Содружества Независимых Государств (часть первая)], available at www.iacis.ru/upload/iblock/e0e/model_gk.pdf, accessed 8 November 2015; MS Korableva, 'A Comparative Study of the Protection of Civil Rights: The Civil Codes of CIS Countries' (2002–03) 28 *Review of Central and East European Law* 167, 168. The Model Code was prepared under the auspices of a Russian research institute, with the participation of prominent civilists from former Soviet republics, including the Central Asian states, as well as senior Dutch civilist technical advisors, and adopted by the Inter-Parliamentary Assembly for the Commonwealth of Independent States.

[21] Imomov (n 11).

[22] As the USSR had done in the last set of constitutional amendments in 1990. Henderson (n 8) 52–55.

[23] All five had previously established presidencies in each case prior to the break-up of the union by laws and amendments to the 1978 republican constitutions. Tkm Law 11.10.1990, Kaz Law 24.04.1990, Uzb Law 24.03.1990, Kyr Law 24.10.1990, Taj Law 29.11.1990.

subsequently abolished it and restored unicameralism in 2007. The lower or general chamber was placed on a population-equalised geographic district basis (separate constituency, as the Republican soviets had been). Turkmenistan has remained steadfastly unicameral but did something characteristically idiosyncratic with its 'supercameral' Halk Malashaty, as noted above in chapter one and discussed in depth in chapter five following. All the new legislatures were suitably renamed from the Persian or Turkic.[24]

All five constitutions retained the standard SSR judiciary consisting of a Supreme Court and a separate Supreme Arbitration (Economic) Court, as well military and lesser courts. With the exception of Turkmenistan, they also created a Constitutional Court charged with judicial review, which would be replaced by a French-style Constitutional Council in Kazakhstan in 1995, and absorbed as a Constitutional Chamber into the Supreme Court in Kyrgyzstan in 2010. They all retained the Russian/Soviet institution of the General Procuracy as a distinct state body, typically with its own constitutional chapter.[25] They all retained the administrative subdivisions of the SSRs to which they succeeded (subject to subsequent reorganisation). Uzbekistan and Tajikistan, which as SSRs each contained an autonomous unit, respectively the Karakalpak Autonomous Republic and the Gorno-Badakhshan Autonomous Area, carried them intact into the independent constitutional order. All five constitutions enumerated extensive catalogues of civil and political rights, influenced by the language of the International Covenant on Civil and Political Rights (ICCPR), as well as economic and social rights (to work, health care and pensions), in conjunction

[24] In Kyrgyzstan the initially unicameral Jogorku Kenesh (divided after five years into a lower Legislative Assembly and an upper Assembly of People's Representatives, but unified again thereafter into a single Jogorku Kenesh), in Kazkakhstan, the initially unicameral Majilis (supplemented after an interim period of several years by an upper house, the Senate), in Uzbekistan the initially unicameral Oliy Majlis (joined by the Senate in 2002), in Tajikistan, the initially unicameral Majilisi Oli (split in 2000 into the Majlisi Milli, the National Assembly and the Majlisi Namoyandagon, the Assembly of Representatives), and in Turkmenistan the unicameral Mejilis (National Assembly) and the now-defunct Halk Maslahaty (People's Council, which as discussed had a separate status as supralegislative supreme organ of state).

[25] Tkm 1992 110, Kyr 1993 78, Kaz 1993 106–108, Taj 1994 93–97, Uzb 1992 118–121.

with duties (either generally, as in Turkmenistan, or elaborated in a separate section, as in Uzbekistan).[26]

Making the Central Asian constitutions was in fact more than a simple post-Soviet decanting of vintage Soviet wine, but the continuities are as striking as the discontinuities—and they were reinforced and grew more prominent with time. From a textual though not contextual standpoint, these are manifestly not 'transitional constitutions', in the sense of an avowedly interim arrangement subject to later refinement or modification.[27] They presented themselves as finished products, not works-in-progress. Some might contend they were transitional only in the unfortunate sense that they were an early stage in the consolidation of authoritarian governance—examples of regressive not progressive 'transitional constitutionalism.'

The Central Asian constitutional texts suggest that the 'rise of world constitutionalism' is an extensive not an intensive trend. Constitutions might be proliferating, but constitutional design is not necessarily thereby growing more sophisticated or innovative in practice. World constitutionalism remains a banner or bandwagon. Indeed, when it comes to basic institutional design of systems of government, there continue to be dismayingly few real options on offer, mostly variants of three: parliamentary, presidential and mixed.[28] The range of particular examples of these broad categories of course varies considerably. Contemporary constitutions have combined a variety of electoral rules and constituency-bases (proportional representation, first-past-the-post, weighted voting), on the one hand, and selected from among

[26] Uzb 47–52 (chapter 11).

[27] R Teitel, 'Post-Communist Constitutionalism: A Transitional Perspective' (1994) 26 *Columbia Human Rights Law Review* 167 (transitional constitutions as a kind of jury-rig while underway, pending the resolution via further constitutional deliberation or jurisprudence of contentious separation-of-powers issues). See H Klug, *The Constitution of South Africa: A Contextual Analysis* (Oxford, Hart Publishing, 2010) 32–43 for a detailed account of one such arrangement, the South Africa 1993 Interim Constitution.

[28] 'Study shows that the range of existing constitutional frameworks in the world's long-standing democracies is narrower than one would think. With one exception (Switzerland), every existing democracy today is either presidential …, parliamentary …, or a semipresidential hybrid of the two.' A Stepan and C Skach, 'Constitutional Frameworks and Democratic Consolidation: Parliamentarianism Versus Presidentialism' (1993) 46(4) *World Politics* 1, 2–3.

an array of developed constitutional devices for the constraint and allocation of power (separation of powers, judicial review, federalism, etc), on the other. However, while the world's constitutional systems exhibit multiple permutations, Actually Existing Constitutionalism, like Actually Existing Socialism in its day, offers a restricted field of choice compared to the theoretical possibilities.

PROPERTY, THE MARKET AND WELFARE

For Central Asia, as fundamental a marker of post-Soviet emancipation as the repudiation of a quasi-colonial party state was the rejection of the command-administrative economy. In the circumstances, a market economy was universally understood to require a constitutional grounding. But the move away from planning and state ownership was not as categorical as the abandonment of *Sovietskaia vlast*; the emergent Central Asian leaderships were less disposed than their Russian counterpart to embrace 'shock therapy', the Western policy prescription for overnight privatisation and deregulation.[29] They adopted a cautious approach to the pace and manner of marketisation and global integration. The initial constitutions convey a certain hesitancy, effectively hedging economic policy options.

The five states became independent just at the moment that the global normative framework for economic integration—the constitution of globalisation, so to speak—was in the process of being assembled under the rubric of 'international economic law'. All save Turkmenistan commenced World Trade Organization (WTO)/General Agreement on Tariffs and Trade (GATT) accession negotiations within the first few years of independence; Kyrgyzstan (1996) and Tajikistan (2013) have acceded, Uzbekistan and Kazakhstan continue negotiations. Kazakhstan, Turkmenistan, Uzbekistan and Kyrgyzstan became members of the International Bank for Reconstruction and Development ((IBRD), the World Bank) and the International Monetary Fund (IMF) in 1992, Tajikistan the following year. All five also became members of the European and Asian Development Banks (EBRD and

[29] J Sachs, 'Shock Therapy in Poland: Perspectives of Five Years', *The Tanner Lectures on Human Values, Volume 16*, University of Utah, 1995.

ADB). But while the pressures to liberalise closed economies might have been circumambient, the Central Asian elites were not about to abandon either control over economic decision-making (and state assets) or social commitments. Post-Soviet the first generation constitutions of Central Asia assuredly were; post-socialist less so.

Thus, while all the first generation constitutions enable private ownership of the means of production, they do not privilege it, and indeed they place it on a par with state ownership, recognising in effect that private property is not the natural or originary form and state property is not the artificial and derivative form. Uzbekistan's Constitution provides (Uzb 53):

> The economy of Uzbekistan, evolving towards market relations, is based on various forms of ownership. The state shall guarantee freedom of economic activity, entrepreneurship and labour with due regard for the priority of consumers' rights, as well as equality and legal protection of all forms of ownership
>
> Private property, along with the other types of property, shall be inviolable and protected by the state

Notable scholarly voices recommended expressly constitutionalising a liberal economic order in the particular post-socialist circumstances, entrenching robust protection for private property rights and freedom of contract.[30] But they did not extend such concern to the distribution and assignment of rights in the first place, a curious omission. Any set of property rules must by definition exert particular further distributional effects on the basis of an initial distribution of assets, or more properly, rights to assets.[31] Across post-Soviet space, the process of privatisation itself, the grand divestiture and allocation of state property, exercised profound and far-reaching effects on equality and welfare in

[30] 'A dramatic legal and cultural shift, creating a belief in private property and a respect for markets, is indispensable. It is therefore surprising but true that the case for a strongly negative constitution, protecting market arrangements, is under current conditions powerful in Eastern Europe, even if it is ambiguous in the West.' CR Sunstein, 'On Property and Constitutionalism' (1992–93) 14 *Cardozo Law Review* 907, 922.

[31] D Kennedy, 'The Stakes of Law, or Hale and Foucault!' (1991) 15 *Legal Studies Forum* 327.

the emerging societies. If the Central Asian constitutions waffled on the liberal economic order point, they wholly failed (as have most post-socialist constitutions) to address or regulate the disposition of inherited state assets. There was no constitutional clue that at independence societal wealth in the 'stans was maximally concentrated in the state and that its distribution or reassignment was a looming political task with profound social consequences—that the initial dealing of the deck might be of vastly greater moment than the rules of the card game.[32]

If anything, in the post-collapse circumstances of general dislocation and widespread impoverishment that disproportionately afflicted the largely rural Central Asian economies, the new constitutions might have been counselled to entrench robust social protection ahead of property protection. Although they reflexively carried over much of the social rights catalogues from their Soviet predecessors, they made no attempt to buttress them or ensure their realisation. Merely declaratory social rights allowed the ascendant elites to bask serenely in the prevailing neo-liberal sunshine without fear for power or purse. Ironically, whereas Soviet social guarantees though not formally justiciable had been substantively secured, the position under the new constitutions was effectively reversed. Nor did the constitutions attempt to gauge, much less reckon with or consult, social interests after the collapse of the USSR or to envisage any sort of constitutionally premised balancing of nascent social groups at the dawn of Central Asian capitalism (the poor, agricultural and industrial workers, managers and businesspeople, capitalists and investors). These economic and social dimensions of the Central Asian systems will be analysed at length in chapter seven.

CULTURE AND CONSTITUTION

Constitutions as charters for national communities are typically held to cast an eye backwards and forwards: retrospectively to reflect (or incorporate anew) national culture and traditions, and prospectively to

[32] The relation between the one-off distribution of state assets and the legal framework for private trade in assets generally (property and contract) will be examined in ch 5.

project a future civic identity.[33] In the Central Asian case as elsewhere the nation-building rulers have posited culture as the ground of constitutionalism. But culture in the Central Asian case is a particularly loaded concept. The way culture has come to constitutionalism in Central Asia is impossible to separate from Soviet mediation; antecedent cultural forms have long been refracted through the Soviet lens. The constitutional texts do not reveal any primordial (pre- or extra-constitutional) cultural influence or determination or carry any cultural DNA.

Any attempt to apply the paradigms of constitutional patriotism or identity[34] to the Central Asian cases must do so in the *long durée* and commence the enquiry in 1917 and not 1991. For it was in a sense the imposed or constructed Soviet constitutional (ethno-territorial-republican) identity which in multiple ways had shaped the development of Central Asian national or cultural identity to begin with. Soviet federalism (really, the whole Soviet constitutional order for culture discussed in the previous chapter, consisting of ethno-territorial federalism, juridical nationalities and Marxist-Leninist-Stalinist developmentalism) operated in a paradoxical way to reverse the logical order of emergence of constitutional out of pre-constitutional (cultural, ethnic, primordial) identities.[35] It was the peculiar Soviet constitutive reification of culture and nation in the first place that generated distinct Uzbek, Kazakh, Tajik, Turkmen and Kyrgyz collective identities, so conferring on them both objective and subjective reality. Here, improbably, constitutions produced ethnic nations not just national communities, making them *constitutional artefacts*—perhaps a unique case for comparative constitutionalists. The pre-constitutional factors[36] are here in some measure always already constitutional, that is, Soviet-constitutional, and the relevant pre-Soviet factors are therefore 'Soviet pre-Soviet' factors.

Though the place of cultural or 'primordial' identity in the Central Asian constitutive moment was uniquely fraught, there is little evidence

[33] See M Rosenfeld, 'Modern Constitutionalism as Interplay Between Identity and Diversity: An Introduction' (1993) 14 *Cardozo Law Review* 497 for a comparative survey of scholarly views on the relationship between constitutions and identity.

[34] G Jacobsohn, 'Constitutional Identity' (2006) 68 *The Review of Politics* 361.

[35] Rosenfeld (n 33).

[36] M Rosenfeld, 'The Problem of "Identity" in Constitution-making and Constitutional Reform' (2005) Benjamin N. Cardozo School of Law Jacob Burns Institute for Advanced Legal Studies Working Paper No 143, 14–16

of culture, either in a primordial or inherited Soviet conceptualisation, in the texts themselves. It is difficult to discover features of the original generation of constitutions which could defensibly be characterised as indigenous (pre-Soviet or pre-modern, which are effectively synonymous here), drawing on an authentic autochthonous tradition or institution. All five constitutions used the term 'people' or 'nation' (*narod*) as a general rule to refer to people of the entire state, rather than the titular nation, and constitutionalised the equality of all minorities, though the Turkmen and Kyrgyz constitutions separately make mention of the Turkmen and Kyrgyz nation. In all cases the titular language was made the state language; the status of Russian and the other minority languages varied across the constitutions. The preambular recitals invoke 'our ancestors testament that we live in unity, peace and accord' only for Turkmenistan and Kyrgyzstan (identical formula); for Kazakhstan and Uzbekistan, a reference to historical statehood, and for Tajikistan, no mention of Tajik antiquity. The names of the legislatures, and of local authorities are typically indigenised for all five constitutions, but the Uzbek and Kazakh Senates acknowledge the abiding constitutional prestige of the Roman Republic. There are, as noted above in chapter two, in the Kyrgyz, Uzbek and Turkmen cases organs of local self-administration, which formalise existing social associations.

Only in the case of Turkmenistan was there any apparent intent to put forward a culturally distinct 'national' institution itself, the *Halk Maslahaty*. The Turkmen *maslahats* were traditional structures of governance in Turkmen society, village or tribal associations with authority commensurate with the size of the unit, as elsewhere in the region. Their (ideologically asserted) status as a collective inheritance of the Turkmen people is set forth in the *Ruhnama*.[37] As discussed in chapter one, such a body exercising formal authority at the level of a modern state was of course wholly unprecedented. The 1992 Constitution contained other culturalist anomalies, such as the imposition of an ethnic as well as an age restriction on eligibility for the presidency. Article 55 required that the president be a citizen of Turkmenistan 'from among the number of the Turkmen'. That requirement has subsequently been abolished. In the Turkmen political context, these avowedly

[37] J Šír, '*Halk Maslahaty* in the Context of the Constitutional Evolution of Post-Soviet Turkmenistan' (2005) 6 *Perspectives on European Politics and Society* 321.

culturalist constitutional innovations strike the observer as calculated and 'self-orientalising'.

The question inevitably arises of Islam and its putative constituent influence on, and general significance in, constitutional development in Central Asia. The five constitutions were in no discernible manner Islamic, nor did they exhibit any Islamic features. The widely entertained expectation that Central Asia, once shot of the Soviet yoke, would undergo a simultaneous spiritual and national renaissance itself failed to reckon with the degree to which Central Asian religious identity as well as national identity were shaped in the same Soviet forge.[38] The constitutions declared the respective states secular (saving Uzbekistan, which did not employ the term)[39] and made no provision for establishment or special recognition. The inherited Soviet prohibition of polygamy was carried over unchanged.

All of the constitutions provide for freedom of conscience and worship, and for religious organisations. None accords any special place to or even constitutionally mentions any aspect of Islamic belief or attach any particular status to Muslims. At a sub-constitutional level, however, as elaborated and analysed in chapter eight below, the independent states carried over the inherited Soviet approach to the regulation of religious organisations and activities, usually elaborated in a Law on Religious Organisations, and including the recognition of official clerical bodies. The Soviet Central Asian Spiritual Directorate of Muslims (DUM) or *Muftiat* was fragmented along national lines, and each of the five states established its own, national *Muftiat*.

Finally, apart from the place of national culture in the Central Asian constitutions is the place of specifically legal culture. Both the continuing role and place of the Russian legal tradition and the power and prestige of Russian legal language and conceptual vocabulary swamp any 'indigenous' factors. So for that matter do the prestige and pull of European constitutional ideals, values and standards. Central Asia is at least arguably caught on the horns of its version of the Slavophile-Westerniser dilemma so recurrent a feature of Russian reform and indeed self-understanding:[40] should it look west to Europe or east for

[38] See discussion above in ch 2.
[39] Tkm 1992 1, 11; Taj 1994 1, 100; Kyr 1992 1; Kaz 1993 1.
[40] Henderson (n 8) 31.

a culturally distinct model? Europeanisation as a conceivable Central Asian project, including as a critical component constitutionalism—not as a metaphysical ideal but a practical institutional project in the age of the *Acquis communautaire*—cannot be dismissed as culturally wrong-headed or inappropriate.

TRANSITION TUTELAGE: GOOD GOVERNANCE, RULE OF LAW, DEMOCRATISATION

At the moment the Central Asian states made their entirely unexpected debut in late 1991 before the international community, the receiving line lost no time in slotting them into the transition paradigm, which it had in the meanwhile devised for and applied to the Central European states that had left the socialist fold two years before. Transition, as it came to be canonically formulated entailed (at least) a double shift, along the economic axis from plan to market, and along the political axis from authoritarian to democratic rule (parallel processes of liberalisation and democratisation).

Three allied discourses and their applied schools-of-analysis-cum-projects-of-intervention fed into the general transition paradigm. *Good governance* had grown up in the development context as rubric for reforming and scaling back bloated, corrupt and inefficient state administration in the context of the neo-liberal critique of statism in the 1980s. *Rule of law* (ROL), a further refinement of that general critique, was a 1990s reformulation of 1960s 'law and development' on the basis of a neo-Weberian theory of the indispensability of a stable, enforceable, and comprehensive private law framework to a market economy.[41] Like good governance, although initially prescribed

[41] For the scope of the phenomenon, see generally T Carrothers, 'The Rule of Law Revival' (1998) 77 *Foreign Affairs* 95; for the relation of ROL to law and development see DM Trubek, 'The "Rule of Law" in Development Assistance: Past, Present, and Future' in DM Trubek and A Santos (eds), *The New Law and Economic Development: A Critical Appraisal* (Cambridge, Cambridge University Press, 2006); S Newton, 'The Dialectics of Law and Development' in DM Trubek and A Santos (eds), *The New Law and Economic Development: A Critical Appraisal* (Cambridge: Cambridge University Press, 2006) 95–173. For a comprehensive *Ideologiekritik* of governance and ROL see respectively J Gathii, 'Retelling Good Governance Narratives

for third world (developing) cases, it proved all the more apt for even more egregiously statist second world (socialist) cases, once they were eligible for therapeutic attention. ROL and good governance were both inflected in a predominantly economic register as chiefly technical challenges of incentive structures, institutional design and rule calibration,[42] all in service of the goal of smooth integration into the global market economy. Against this view it may be contended that nothing is more political or less technical than the 'economic', especially in the former Land of the Soviets.[43] *Democratisation* had been the focus of the original political science transition theory, proposed to explain the transitions from authoritarian rule in the '70s in the Latin American cone and Southern Europe. It proved felicitously applicable as well to the transitions from 'totalitarian' rule at the turn of the '90s in Central Europe and Eurasia.[44]

The transition paradigm was premised on a posited trajectory between clearly understood and identifiable start- and end-points. These discourses were authoritatively promulgated to support and justify a broad range of tutelary policies by key multilateral and bilateral actors with a development remit, including the development banks (the World Bank, Asian Development Bank and European Bank for Reconstruction and Development all developed significant loan portfolios in Central Asia), the UN Development Project (typically the co-ordinator of all UN programmes and activities in the Central Asian states), the Organisation for Security and Cooperation in Europe, the European

on Africa's Economic and Political Predicaments: Continuities and Discontinuities in Legal Outcomes Between Markets and States' (2000) 45 *Villanova Law Review* 971 and J Ngugi, 'Policing Neo-liberal Reforms: The Rule of Law as an Enabling and Restrictive Discourse' (2005) 26 *University of Pennsylvania Journal of International Economic Law* 513.

[42] I Shihata, 'Governance and the Role of Law in Economic Development' in A Seidman, RB Seidman and T Walde (eds), *Making Development Work: Legislative Reform for Institutional Transformation and Good Governance* (Amsterdam, Kluwer Law International, 1999) xviii–xxi.

[43] Newton (n 17).

[44] See G O'Donnell and PC Schmitter (eds), *Transitions from Authoritarian Rule, Volume 1; Southern Europe: Prospects for Democracy, Volume 2; Latin America: Prospects for Democracy, Volume 3; Comparative Perspectives: Prospects for Democracy, Volume 4; Tentative Conclusions about Uncertain Democracies: Prospects for Democracy* (Baltimore MD, Johns Hopkins University Press, 1986).

Union, the major bilateral development donors and their agencies (US, UK, Netherlands, Japan, Germany, France, Canada, Switzerland, coordinating their financing through the Development Assistance Committee (DAC), of the Organisation for Economic Cooperation and Democracy (OECD)), and other donors such as the Soros Foundation, as well as the major human rights NGOs. These agencies and organisations came to play a role as international midwives, or at least would-be governesses and tutors, of the new Central Asian states.

Under the transition umbrella, and along its various ribs—ROL, governance and democratisation—an extraordinary surfeit of international donor-funded 'technical assistance' programming was organised and delivered to the Central Asian states (as virtually everywhere across post-socialist space): everything from the reorganisation of health care to the seeding of civil society organisations, from the reform of state administration to the drafting of commercial laws and the training of judges).[45] Democratisation was articulated in a positivist manner, and rested on a tripod of human rights protection and advocacy, elections monitoring and civil society support—all points of ready leveraging of resources, all programmatically feasible, and all results-orientated and measurable (points of favour in development agencies). Constitutionalism as such was not part of the original package—donors as a rule did not flog unsolicited constitutional reform assistance, for obvious reasons of basic diplomatic etiquette, though they did routinely critique constitutional provisions and amendments. Constitutionalism can

[45] Notable particular programmes were those pursuant to the US Freedom Support Act under the USAID Central Asia regional mission's offices of democratic and market transition, programming under the UK Know-How Fund, World Bank projects in specifically legal and judicial, as well as economic, reform, and the EU TACIS programme (Technical Aid to the Commonwealth of Independent States. See, eg, Newton (n 17); Department for International Development, UK (1998) Support for Transition Countries: A New Strategy; World Bank (1999), Project appraisal document on a proposed loan in the amount of US$16.5 million equivalent to the Republic of Kazakhstan for a legal reform project, available at www-wds.worldbank.org/external/default/WDSContentServer/WDSP/IB/1999/09/14/000094946_99051205330031/Rendered/PDF/multi_page.pdf, accessed 8 November 2015; European Commission, 'The Tacis Programme Annual Report 1995', Brussels, 22 July 1996 Com (96) 345 final, available at www. eur-lex.europa.eu/legal-content/EN/TXT/PDF/?uri=CELEX:51996DC0345&rid=7, accessed 8 November 2015.

nonetheless be understood as the backbone in particular of the sundry democratisation programmes, though also self-evidently a predicate of the more economically inflected parallel projects of good governance and ROL. Many projects had constitutional implications (eg local government reform, anti-corruption and civil society support), while others directly addressed the failure to enforce constitutionally guaranteed rights or sought to build parliamentary or judicial capacity. Indeed, democratisation in general has been something of a proxy or (perhaps Trojan horse) for predicate constitutional reform.

At the time the first generation constitutions were adopted—across the two years following the Belavezha Accords—there was very little in the way of co-ordinated multilateral assistance and support. Central Asia presented the West and the international community with something of a policy puzzle, initially, and once the public international legal formalities (recognition, admission to the UN, accession to multilateral instruments) were dispatched, and until coherent multilateral strategic and development assistance policies were forthcoming and formulated (eg the EU partnership cooperation agreements (PCAs), the 'stans were left on the back burner. At the formative moment of Central Asian constitution-making, there was little international guidance on offer, respecting choice of constitutional provisions, approaches, and even basic conceptions. No technical assistance project appears to have been essayed in constitutionalism or constitutional drafting as such. Nonetheless, although democratisation/human rights programmes were deployed only after the constitutions were *faits accomplis*, they undeniably have made Central Asian authorities and citizenries aware of the consequences of those choices to begin with. And whatever their conceptual and political errors and their practical failings, they have provided the occasion for continuously shining a public spotlight on constitutional issues and processes in Central Asia, and forcing public authority on the defensive.

Thus the holding of the Central Asian states to the emergent standards of world constitutionalism was more a matter of ongoing critique and analysis than of consultation and advice ab initio. This may in fact have represented a recognition on the part of donors that the constitutional framework was less important in its design details, save where these were particularly egregious or obnoxious (extension of term limits, consolidation of executive power, appointments, elections and so on), than in its general functioning as constraint on rather than instrument of the exercise of state authority, that is, as conducive to the growth of a culture of constitutionalism. The amount of constitutional pressure and attention brought to bear over the years in Central Asia, by concerned outsiders and insiders alike, nonetheless strikes the observer as in inverse relation to the responsiveness of state authorities. With the notable exception of Kyrgyzstan, Central Asian state actors have not seemed particularly disposed to real engagement and dialogue on constitutional matters, and have hardly availed themselves of the rich constitutional resources put at their disposal by donors.

There is in fact a spectrum. Some states, notably Kazakhstan, have for the most part benignly tolerated or hosted international monitoring and evaluation, as well as gratis technical assistance projects, but have not sought it (Kazakhstan notably withdrew from World Bank-financed institutional reform projects after deciding it would no longer wish to incur debts for these purposes, when if necessary they could be funded from the state budget). Uzbekistan and Turkmenistan have been perhaps the most sceptical, if not disdainful, of international constitutional expertise, particularly insofar as it has assumed the form of human rights scrutiny, but even they have struck postures of co-operation and compliance. Two states have received very extensive constitutional support, for disparate reasons. Kyrgyzstan has sought it and welcomed it. Tajikistan has been the object of an intense internationally sponsored conflict-resolution process. (See the discussion in the last section of chapter five.) But the role of foreign (international) constitutional experts should not be assumed to be indispensable, or even desirable or necessarily benign. Even established or famous constitutionalists in established or famous constitutional democracies might not be the *fons et origo* of constitutional wisdom and expertise. Indeed from the perspective of critical constitutionalism, one might commend the value of consulting the radical critics of established or famous constitutional orders.

The most prominent multilateral actor in the constitutional history of Central Asia has been the Organisation for Security and Co-operation in Europe (OSCE). (The Council of Europe has also played a modest supporting role, chiefly with respect to Kyrgyzstan.) The larval Commission on Security and Co-operation in Europe (CSCE), the loosely structured and non-institutionalised body created by the Helsinki Accords, metamorphosed into the OSCE, in a process which commenced at the Paris Summit of 1990. That summit rededicated and repurposed the body for a post-Cold War environment and created the institutional framework for pan-European co-operation across a broad political, economic and social agenda, a year before the collapse of the Soviet Union. From this point forwards, the original commitments to the 'human dimension' of security as part of the basic East–West compromise, encompassing human rights and democracy, were made much more prominent and became the focus of concerted technical assistance and resource allocation. The OSCE moved into the Central Asian arena in the mid-1990s, establishing field missions in each of the states (first in Tajikistan in 1993, in pursuit of conflict resolution), co-ordinating a variety of programming.

The 'constitutional' remit of the OSCE arises out of the 1990 CSCE Copenhagen Documents—the closest any international instrument comes to establishing general constitutional standards, outside the human rights treaties which arguably aspire to a kind of international constitutional law of rights protection. However, additional instruments, such as the 1993 Paris Principles and 1985 Basic Principles on the Independence of the Judiciary, have clear constitutional implications. The Copenhagen Document sets out specific commitments respecting separation of powers, political contestation, free and fair elections and rights protection. These have served as the basis for the OSCE's ongoing projects and programmes, ranging from legislative analysis and law reform to police training and counter-trafficking, under its Human Dimension responsibilities, chiefly channelled through is Office of Democracy and International Human Rights (ODIHR),[46] as well as its systematic (parliamentary and presidential) elections monitoring (all states but Turkmenistan).

OSCE has had a difficult and troubled course, at both ends of its geographic stretch (its primary theatres of operations have been the Balkans, on the one hand, and the post-Soviet periphery, on the other). Its Human Dimension agenda in Central Asia has triggered a fair amount of resentment over time, on the part of its intended beneficiaries and their Russian patron, as unwarranted interference and a biased distribution of resources and concerns (mostly forcefully

[46] See its website at www.osce.org/odihr, also OSCE 2005 Human Dimension Commitments.

expressed in the 2004 'Astana Appeal' signed by all states in the region save Turkmenistan, as well as Armenia, Belarus, Russia and Ukraine).[47] OSCE/ODIHR has enjoyed varying degrees of receptivity to its presence and activities, with Turkmenistan at one end of the spectrum and Kyrgyzstan at the other. Nonetheless, it has been seen throughout as a critical forum and institutional vehicle, as witness Kazakhstan's determined and ultimately successful pursuit of the organisation's annual Chairmanship-in-Office (C-i-O), in 2010.

On the international stage, Central Asian as all post-Soviet constitutionalism had a completely different objective and motivation to classic Soviet constitutionalism. As discussed at length in chapter two, that was in a sense an attempt to wrest a whole school of political thought from the capitalist West and redeem it by transposing it into a classless context, reinventing it for socialism. Soviet constitutionalism, like Soviet law, was the purer, uncompromised and untainted form of the bourgeois counterpart. The Stalin Constitution of 1936 had nothing to prove—it asserted its superiority over, not its common membership in, the community of modern ('bourgeois') constitutional states. If Soviet constitutionalism remained as standing challenge to Western constitutionalism, post-Soviet constitutionalism has sought from the outset to assimilate to it. If the USSR wore its constitution as a badge of difference and defiance, the Central Asian states donned theirs as identity badges for admission to the counsels of power and the councils of intergovernmental deliberation and decision. But this is no mere act of disguise, whether clumsy or clever, an attempt to gate-crash or 'pass' in international society. The very 'prestige effect' of world constitutionalism is rather itself to blame, and more particularly in the context of a legitimising discourse of universal standards of governance, democracy and ROL. Certainly one of the chief incentives for Central Asian states in adopting state-of-the-art, democratic constitutions was their general prestige and status as indicia of full international citizenship. The sovereignty imperative meshed with at least the formal requirements of membership in good standing in the international community.

But beyond prestige, recognition and a textual anchor for their fragile sovereignty, to the extent the Central Asian states sought substantive

[47] 2004 Astana Appeal.

international legitimacy for their constitutional orders, they faced a high bar. In addition to the 'soft law' of governance, democratisation and ROL discourse discussed earlier, international hard law had come indirectly to regulate the organisation of public authority. Democracy itself had become a human rights norm, as reflected in the 'right to democratic governance'.[48] Even in the absence of internationally specified norms for constitutional provisions themselves, the constitutional dimensions of that right were manifest. The structural and institutional enabling conditions for democratic governance could only be constitutional. The rise of world constitutionalism and the emergence of universal democracy standards in practice seemed to entail that institutions of governance everywhere converge on the political and economic forms of Euro-Atlantic industrial society, 'the West'. The constitutional orders of emerging states like the Central Asian five were duly expected to present some credible version of 'free market democracy'.

By hoisting constitutional banners so gaily and proudly in this new era, the five 'stans assumed a significant burden of exposure. Their constitutionalism would undergo relentless scrutiny and evaluation, whatever indulgence they might initially be accorded. As orphans of the Soviet state now under a kind of international tutelage or wardship, they would grow up subject to the periodic inspections and progress reports of their constitutional elders. The US Department of State annual human rights reports and the OSCE election monitoring reports are two eminent examples of this general tendency. This evaluative mode has permeated engagement with Central Asia by the institutionalised international community, with some significant exceptions. The newer, 'rival', regional institutional constellations with a remit in post-Soviet space like the CIS, the Collective Security Treaty Organisation (CSTO), or the Eurasian Economic Union, as well as broader regional bodies, like the Shanghai Cooperation Organisation (SCO), are non-judgmental and neutral and carry no governance agenda.

[48] The international norm has obvious constitutional implications, even if not expressly requiring constitutional entrenchment. 'This newly emerging "law"—which requires democracy to validate governance—is not merely the law of a particular state that, like the United States under its Constitution, has imposed such a precondition on national governance.' T Franck, 'The Emerging Right to Democratic Governance' (1992) 86 *American Journal of International Law* 46, 47.

In a sense, world constitutionalism has become precisely this hierarchy and evaluative schema: the Central Asian states (inter alia) have passively enabled and inaugurated it by serving as the first graduating class, the first constitutional pupil cohort. This hierarchy was in part internalised by the leaderships, who acknowledged that their constitutions fell short of applicable standards, but pleaded that they were suited to the unripe, callow stage of their societies—they were in effect transitional (a problematic term here, as indicated above and elaborated below). Nazarbaev, for example, has specifically referred to an interim period of several decades of preparation or apprenticeship.[49] This mode, apart from being patently exculpatory and self-serving, presents striking continuities with Soviet developmentalism, only now it is democracy, not communism, that is indefinitely deferred. The use of tropes of immaturity and unreadiness represents a similarly striking concession to culturalist hierarchies of the sort that underlay the original civilising mission of both Bolsheviks and Western colonial powers. They also arguably continue to animate present-day development discourse.[50]

The democratisation paradigm (together with is parent transition paradigm) has been subject to sustained and withering critique.[51] It employs double standards by ignoring the democratic deficiencies of established democracies and forestalls any obligation to query the nature of democracy itself. It focuses excessively on formal rather than substantive criteria, worrying more about what happens at elections than between them. It operates as an ideological filter to prefer some kinds of politics and rights over others, favouring liberalisation and civil and political rights over greater economic redistribution and economic and social rights. It represents a tendentious and simplified view of political evolution the adoption of which has been particularly

[49] 'The real distinction is between a democracy that has evolved over many years and one in the embryonic stage … You had centuries in which to refine concepts of individual liberty. We have had only a few years.' C Robbins, *In Search of Kazakhstan: The Land that Disappeared* (London, Profile Books, 2008) 287 (quoting Nazarbaev).

[50] A Anghie, *Imperialism, Sovereignty and the Making of International Law* (Cambridge, Cambridge University Press, 2007) 179–89. *cf* Gathii and Ngugi (n 41).

[51] S Marks, *The Riddle of All Constitutions* (Cambridge, Cambridge University Press, 2000) 50–75.

unfortunate for Central Asian constitutionalism, since it has played into the hands of authoritarian rulers. By substituting a preoccupation with provisions and language for the substance of the constitutional order, it has allowed them to engage in lawyerly argument about compliance rather than to yield control or power.

But perhaps the problem in facile democratisation and formalist constitutionalism lies at another level: in overburdening Central Asian constitutionalism, rather than letting it off too lightly. Perhaps democratisation entertains unreasonably high rather than demeaningly low expectations. Perhaps the problem lies in overburdening or overvalorising constitutionalism as such. One of the virtues of 'transitional constitutionalism' is that it tames the native hyperbole of constitutionalism, the grandiose meta-political tone. As 'transitional', constitutions can make do with some degree of vagueness to afford time for fundamental constitutional questions to be clarified. Leaving important points constitutionally unspecified allows the interested parties to get on with the political negotiations and avoid premature finality cloaked in elevated language.[52]

As happened, far from embracing plasticity the Central Asian constitutional texts exhibited a singular formal rigidity that stunted the prospects for incremental constitutional development. Unsurprisingly they all came to have preferential recourse to serial and frequent amendment rather than jurisprudential elaboration and interpretation. Still, serial amendments might somewhat counterfactually be regarded as themselves betokening a rolling constitutional design process, addressing arising issues or correcting arising problems. In this light, Central Asian constitutionalism might arguably be viewed as a serviceable idiom for interim political management and getting by, rather than inflated as either a proxy for democratisation (the view from outside Central Asia) or for nation-building (the view from inside). The concept of a *constitutional idiom* could cover both tinkering at the margins whether to placate international opinion or to legitimise or consolidate elite control, and also broader contestation about the political system between clashing interests, as in Kyrgyzstan.

[52] Teitel (n 27).

From the standpoint of developed constitutionalism, this might all look pretty unsavoury and unedifying, a cheapening of the coin of the realm. On the other hand, it might be considered a salutary reminder of the alloy in constitutional coinage generally. The succeeding chapters explore these two contrasting political uses of the constitutional idiom itself, for political control and for political contestation. Chapter four examines the way in which Central Asian presidents have sought to regulate constitutional reform closely, while chapter five confronts the Kyrgyz exception, whereby constitutional politics have escaped such regulation and driven reform.

CONCLUSION

The Central Asian states and constitutional systems took shape at a very distinctive historical conjuncture—hence this natal chart. They had to negotiate not just the path dependence imposed by the Soviet constitutional tradition, but the exigencies of unsought and initially fragile sovereignty, the emerging norms of good governance, rule of law and democratisation discourse, the uncertain call of culture, and the pressing requirements of economic stabilisation and neo-liberal global integration. But if Central Asian constitutionalism faced abundant internal and external constraints, it was also blessed with internal and external resources. The chapters following will examine comparatively how the major constitutional institutions and fields of regulation took shape and how the balance of constraints and resources played out for each of the five systems.

FURTHER READING

1990 Document of the Copenhagen meeting of the conference on the human dimension of the CSCE (CSCE Copenhagen Document), www.osce.org/odihr/elections/14304?download=true (accessed 11 September 2014).

J Anderson, 'Constitutional Development in Central Asia' (1997) 16(3) *Central Asian Survey* 301.

T Carothers, 'The Rule of Law Revival' (1998) 77 *Foreign Affairs* 95.

FJM Feldbrugge, *Russian Law: The End of the Soviet System and the Role of Law* (Dordrecht, Nijhoff, 1993).

P Goldman, G Lapidus and V Zaslavsky, *From Union to Commonwealth: Nationalism and Separatism in the Soviet Republic* (Cambridge, Cambridge University Press, 1992).

VP Kazimirchuk, MM Slavin and BN Toropin (eds), *The Socialist Law-based State: Problems and Discussions* (Moscow, IGiP AN SSSR Press, 1989) [Казимирчук ВП, Славин ММ,Топорнин БН (Отв ред), *Социалистическое правовое государство Проблемы и суждения*, Изд-во ИГиП АН СССР].

S Marks, *The Riddle of All Constitutions* (Cambridge, Cambridge University Press, 2000).

S Newton, 'Transplantation and Transition: Legality and Legitimacy in the Kazakhstani Legislative Process' in M Kurkchiyan and D Galligan (eds), *Law and Informal Practices: The Post-communist Experience* (Oxford, Oxford University Press, 2003).

R Teitel, Post-communist Constitutionalism: A Transitional Perspective" (1994) 26 *Columbia Human Rights Law Review* 167.

P Goldman, G Lapidus and V Zaslavsky, *From Union to Commonwealth: Nationalism and Separatism in the Soviet Republic* (Cambridge, Cambridge University Press, 1992).

4

Super-Presidents and Superpowers

Imbalance of Power – Presidential Particulars: Presidency and President – Presidential Power: Government and Its Subordinate Agencies; Local Administration – Presidential Power: Parliament – Presidential Power: Judicial Structures – Presidential Power: Elections/Referenda – Presidential Power: Administration/*Apparat* and Directly Subordinate Agencies – Presidential Power: National Security – Presidential Power: Lawmaking – Immunity and Impeachment – Doing Justice to Super-presidentialism

IMBALANCE OF POWER

IN THE TWILIGHT of the Soviet Union, a major thrust of Gorbachev's political reform was to make political decision-making for the first time genuinely participatory and consultative. Through the establishment of the Congress of People's Deputies,[1] he sought to redeem parliamentarianism as a mode of substantive political deliberation and determination, rather than a theatre of formal ratification of decisions taken elsewhere. He understood himself as restoring fidelity to the participatory ideals of the revolution embodied in the formal structures of Soviet representative government (discussed in chapter two). Although a Soviet presidency was created to enhance his own legitimacy and to ground his power in a supreme office of state, the USSR remained (formally) a parliamentary state to the end.

[1] J Henderson, *Constitution of the Russian Federation* (Oxford, Hart Publishing, 2011) 48–50.

Even while perestroika lasted, the Union-level push to reset the balance between representative and executive organs of state was never really effective at the level of the peripheral republics. In the Central Asian successor states the new constitutions served to channel and control rather than to continue and intensify the centrifugal force of perestroika reform. Each new Central Asian constitution brought in a presidential system, with a separate mandate for the office of president, and a government appointed by and accountable to it rather than to parliament.

Across Central Asia, presidential power from the moment of independence was in the ascendant, although in Tajikistan only after an interval of chaos and disintegration. Everywhere but Kyrgyzstan it has since only grown more concentrated and unchallengeable. Only Kazakhstan and Kyrgyzstan have exhibited any inter-branch struggle or real contestation of presidential aggrandisement—ephemerally for the former, and definitively for the latter. Uzbekistan and Turkmenistan embraced super-presidentialism[2] from the outset. The other states moved toward it incrementally but inexorably, Kazakhstan in a sudden lurch with its second constitution and Tajikistan and Kyrgyzstan over the course of serial amendments (Kyrgyzstan of course after 15 years dramatically reversed course and repudiated super-presidentialism). As a general rule, the presidency's gain was the parliament's loss: the constitutional fortunes of both branches of government have been intertwined for each of the five states, as this chapter and the next will make plain.

The constitutional question of the roles, relations and balance of power between executive and legislature for the Central Asian states has been overdetermined by a set of mutually aligned political tensions: a geographic tension between national authority and regional power, an institutional tension between concentrated and dispersed state authority (separation of powers), and a historical tension between Soviet and post- (or non-) Soviet cultures of rule. The first two tensions are found in all constitutional systems but the last is a peculiar feature of former party states. In the constitutional chartering of Central Asian presidencies and parliaments, as a rule of thumb

[2] JT Ishiyama and R Kennedy, 'Superpresidentialism and Political Party Development in Russia, Ukraine, Armenia and Kyrgyzstan' (2001) 53 *Europe-Asia Studies* 1177.

the emerging strong presidencies and weak parliaments represented continuity with Soviet patterns of authority. Indeed, as elaborated below, while the Central Asian presidencies appeared to assume many of the organising and controlling functions of the CPSU, Central Asian parliaments like the pre-breakup Soviet Congress of People's Deputies carried the risk of becoming sites of opposition and the contestation of centralised power. That risk was countered by the consolidation of super-presidentialism.

The hyper-centralised nature of the Soviet political system had been replicated at the Republican level, such that Republican political authorities (the Party first secretaries) enjoyed comprehensive control over political affairs in their respective fiefdoms, subject only to instructions from Moscow. Much like former imperial colonies in overseas empires, the newly independent Central Asian ex-SSRs thus carried over comprehensively centralised administrative systems and a 'sovereign bureaucracy'.[3] As discussed in the previous chapter, the overriding challenge of effective sovereignty did not dispose the leaderships at independence to relax their inherited tight control. Moreover, unlike their colleagues in other peripheral Soviet republics like Georgia, they had not faced homegrown nationalist movements agitating for independence and vitiating that control. The perceived fragility of sovereignty at independence in their view effectively made the legislative branch the new state's exposed flank. Legislatures were a source of uncertainty and political unknowns. Deputies were outsiders to politics, unlike the civil servants and bureaucrats staffing the other branches. Judiciaries, by contrast, by virtue of their histories as pliable and reliable servants of the centre carried no real institutional liability and posed commensurately little risk.

The constitutional basis for Central Asian super-presidentialism is not simply a matter of formally conferred powers and prerogatives. Super-presidential systems exhibit a kind of informal colonisation by the executive of the powers and prerogatives reserved to other components of the state, by controlling personnel (cadres determine everything, as Stalin remarked), directly through appointments and indirectly

[3] G Derluguian, 'The Sovereign Bureaucracy in Russia's Modernizations' in P Dutkiewicz and DV Trenin (eds), *Russia: The Challenges of Transformation (Possible Futures)* (New York: New York University Press, 2011) 73–86. The term was originally Trotsky's.

through the manipulation of elections, and by influencing or determining notionally autonomous decision-making processes (including those of adjudication, as in 'telephone justice').[4] In Central Asian super-presidentialism, the presidents not only enjoy sweeping constitutional authority (including direct legislative authority in the form of decrees), but overwhelming penumbral power as well, consolidated and effectively institutionalised by decades-long incumbency in all cases save Kyrgyzstan and Turkmenistan. Presidents Karimov and Nazarbaev have both been at the helm for 25 years, President Rahmon for 20.

In that very longevity of tenure lies the fundamental contradiction at the heart of super-presidentialist constitutionalism. The premise of the Central Asian systems is the unchangeability of elites:

> The reality of politico-economic institutional organization in Central Asia is utterly opposed to … [the Western concept of necessary, regular, lawful elite change], based as it is on the contrary principle of elite unchangeability. Many modern legal instruments are therefore considered not only unnecessary, but even dangerous, especially when they are genuinely effective. In this sense, mechanisms for the rule of law and the unchangeability of politico-economic elites are mutually exclusive notions, whose contradictory character (absolutely realized by the Central Asian ruling class) has proven to be a major obstacle to the effective implementation of Western-oriented legal reforms in the region.[5]

Constitutionalism entails a framework for the orderly succession of elites. The powerful come and the powerful go, but the offices and the powers endure. But in the 'stans, the powerful stay, and constitutional offices and powers serve them—indeed were conceived in the first place to serve them and their claim on rule, and not only the offices but to a degree the very states themselves. In the Soviet constitutional system after Stalin, while the collective or oligarchic leadership of the Politburo also wore (party) offices like costumes of prescriptive authority, they had some defensible sense of the separation of office and office-holder. In post-Soviet Central Asia, by contrast, the reigning

[4] Ishiyama and Kennedy (n 2).

[5] L Golovko, 'The Space for Legal Reform in Central Asia: Between Political Limits and Theoretical Deformations' in *2010 Yearbook of the Organisation for Security and Co-operation in Europe (OSCE)* (Baden-Baden, Nomos Verlagsgesellschaft, 2011) 106–07.

elites would not appear to contemplate ever ceasing to reign *in propria persona*. Apart from Kyrgyzstan, where super-presidentialism itself was fatally wounded in the course of the succession of two presidents, the only other instance of succession in Central Asia, in Turkmenistan, was effectively dynastic (although the heir was designated not familial). However improbably, the institutionalised megalomania of the predecessor has been gradually supplanted by the institutionalised megalomania of the successor, as Berdymukhamedov effortlessly 'slipped on' the eminently serviceable and suitable Turkmen constitutional system, which has been only modestly retailored in the aftermath.[6] But the personalisation of rule in Turkmenistan is only an extreme example of a general Central Asian phenomenon.

And yet the fate of super-presidentialism and of super-presidentialist constitutionalism is far from assured. Yes, the constitutional deck was thus from the outset stacked in favour of the executive, and no amount of cleverness or ingenuity of constitutional design would likely have been adequate for reshuffling it in the interests of a more balanced distribution of power. Controlling, corralling or simply colonising parliamentary space quickly became the standard ploy of the nascent Central Asian executive as a means of neutralising or forestalling challenge to central authority. Nonetheless, these processes of executive domination, though observed generally, have not simply unfolded inexorably and to plan, much less uniformly across the region. Even constitutional politics as severely cabined as the Central Asian sort reveal an irreducible quotient of contingency and surprise: it's still politics, after all. Deputies acquire their own power bases and can always assert their prerogative and defy instructions, even if there is no aisle to cross. As the Soviets discovered with federalism and nationalities, constitutional forms, offices and office-holders possess a kind of vital force of their own, and cannot simply be indefinitely and thoroughly instrumentalised or manipulated without eventual repercussions: constitutional form always threatens sooner or later to acquire substance and escape control in a kind of constitutional blowback against the regime.

[6] S Peyrouse, *Turkmenistan: Power, Politics and Petro-Authoritarianism* (Armonk NY, ME Sharpe, 2012); A Bohr, *Turkmenistan under Berdimuhamedow* (London, Chatham House, 2016).

PRESIDENTIAL PARTICULARS: PRESIDENCY AND PRESIDENT

The functions, powers and privileges of the presidency are elaborated comprehensively in the relevant sections of each constitution. The basic qualifications for office and term length and limits are broadly similar across the five.[7] The two outliers—the Kyrgyz Constitution with a strict one-term limit and straightforward qualifications and the Turkmen Constitution without any term limit and elaborate qualifications—are fair indicators of the respective constitutional cultures and the scope of presidentialism in each; the other three are ranged between. The office of President is one of splendid isolation in all five states: there is no Vice-President, although the first (1993) Kazakh Constitution had provided for a Vice-President and the 1995 Constitution expressly permitted the incumbent to serve out his term but did not re-establish the office.[8]

First it is necessary to address the general place in the constitutional scheme of the office of President: its functions, powers and privileges, together with the procedures for removal from office. Interestingly, whereas Tajikistan, Uzbekistan and Kyrgyzstan are content to leave the regulation of presidential functions and mechanics (including assumption of and departure from office) to the constitutional text itself, Turkmenistan and Kazakhstan have each enacted a separate Law on the President (in the latter case a Constitutional Law which 'in conformity with the Constitution defines the legal position of the President of the Republic of Kazakhstan').[9] Beyond supplementary legislation directly regulating the president as such, there is additional legislation relating to the president or presidency of obvious constitutional import,

[7] Taj 65 (citizen at least 35 years of age, fluent in state language, 15 years continuous residence, 7-year term, 2 consecutive term limit); Kaz 41(2), 42(5) (citizen from birth at least 40 years of age, fluent in state language, 15 years continuous residence, 5-year term, 2 consecutive term limit); Uzb 90 (citizen at least 35 years of age, fluent in state language, 10 years' continuous residence, 7-year term, 2 consecutive term limit); Kyr 62, 61 (citizen between 35 and 70, fluent in state language, 15 years total residence, 6-year term, 1-term limit); Tkm 51 (citizen between 35 and 70 born in Turkmenistan, fluent in state language, 15 previous years consecutive residence working in state organs, social organisations, enterprises, institutions, organisations, 5-year term, no term limit).

[8] Kaz 1993 81, Kaz 94.

[9] Kaz Con Law 26.12.1995.

in particular facilitatory laws supplying 'guarantees',[10] that is, legal wherewithal, for the effective discharge of presidential functions, laws regulating the presidential administration or *apparat* (the presidency in the broader sense), and laws relating specifically to the individual incumbent ('First President').[11]

The Kazakh Law on the President is a compelling demonstration of the characteristic Kazakh formalist approach to constitutionalism, reflected in elaborate specification and discussed in chapter six. Indeed the Kazakh law provides an unexampled legal template for super-presidentialism as a regional constitutional phenomenon in general by so comprehensively parsing and treating all of the dimensions of presidential power in one statute. In the other states either they are implied and/or scattered across multiple enactments. Thus Chapter II 'Powers of the President' first sets forth diplomatic powers and those respecting and national defence and state security.[12] It goes on to enumerate serially presidential powers in relation to Parliament, Government, Constitutional Council, courts and judges, organs of the Procuracy, Central Elections Commission, National Bank, Accounting Committee for Control over Execution of the State Budget, *Akims* (provincial governors), state organs directly subordinate and accountable to the President, and Republican referenda.[13] Finally it elaborates 'other powers of the President', relating inter alia to strategic plans and budgets, award of state honours, mercy, citizenship, asylum, national currency, formation of administration, the National Security Council (NSC), Higher Judicial Council, and Assembly of Peoples and premature termination of *maslikhat* powers.[14] Chapter III elaborates the president's law-making enactments, decrees (*ukazi*, указы) and dispositions (*rasporiahzenia*, распоряжения) and the procedures for their issuance. In Kazakhstan as well, crimes relating only to the president are defined in the Criminal Code. The constitutional status of 'Leader of the Nation' has been conferred on the incumbent president and carries superlative immunities and privileges beyond those in the Constitutional Law on the President—for example, exemption from term limits, lifetime rights

10 Kaz Law 18.06.2003.

11 Kaz Con Law 20.07.2000.

12 Kaz Const, Law 26.12.1995 7, 8 respectively.

13 ibid. 8–18.

14 ibid. 19.

to head the Assembly of Peoples and to sit on the Constitutional Council and the National Security Council.[15] The remit of the enumerated constitutional powers of the other four states may usefully be appreciated by comparison to the magisterial sweep of powers in the Kazakh Law of the President.

PRESIDENTIAL POWER: GOVERNMENT AND ITS SUBORDINATE AGENCIES; LOCAL ADMINISTRATION

Unlike balanced semi-presidential systems (France, for example),[16] where government shares its electoral mandate with the legislature, separate to the president's, in super-presidential systems incorporating a prime minister as well ('semi-super-presidential', perhaps) the legislature's mandate remains separate, but government effectively shares its with the president. That is so because the prime minister and some or all ministers are appointed by and serve at the pleasure of the president. In all constitutions save the Kyrgyz (and only since 2010), the government—the prime minister (except for Turkmenistan, which lacks one) and the cabinet of ministers, together with associated government bodies—is a creature of the president. Although all five constitutions vest parliament with some powers vis-a-vis government, they are entirely trivial and residual in comparison to the president's powers vis-a-vis government. Only in the Kyrgyz case is the proportion largely reversed and the presidential powers are residual. It is not that parliament in the other Central Asian republics does not function as an institution autonomous from government (it emphatically does) or that deputies do not monitor and meddle (they habitually do), but that both parliament and government are ultimately subject to the same instructing authority.

Presidential powers respecting government elaborated in the five constitutions are of three broad types: those of formation, organisation or structure; those of appointment; and those of control over the acts of government. The Turkmen, Kazakh, Uzbek and Tajik constitutions all confer the presidential power, in some cases qualified, to

[15] Kaz Con Law 20.06.2000 1.

[16] S Boyron, *The Constitution of France: A Contextual Analysis* (Oxford, Hart Publishing, 2013) 63–78.

form—meaning to establish, abolish, amalgamate, split or otherwise modify—the component bodies of government (ministries, committees, agencies).[17] The Kyrgyz Constitution confers no such power at all. All five constitutions provide for the presidential power to appoint the most senior government officials, selectively or across the board.[18] Whereas the other constitutions divide posts subject to exclusive presidential powers of appointment/dismissal from posts subject to shared powers, the Kyrgyz Constitution cleanly divides the (very few) posts subject to exclusive presidential powers from the remainder subject to no presidential powers whatsoever. The four super-presidential constitutions also authorise the president to suspend or annul acts of government, either generally or on specified grounds.[19]

Cabinet reshuffling (or the 'carousel', as it is known in Russian) is a constant in Central Asian political life, and would not be notable but for two features distinguishing it from the reshuffling permitted by, and common in, most constitutional systems. First, the office of the prime minister is itself subject to rotation, since in three of five Central Asian states the president is effective though not nominal head of government and can dismiss the prime minister. The Turkmen

[17] Taj 69 (3) (unqualified: 'forms and abolishes ministries and state committees); Tkm 75(6) (qualified: Cabinet itself 'forms in the event of necessity committees, main directorates, and other agencies attached to the Cabinet'); Uzb 91(8) (qualified only insofar as decrees structuring government are presented to Parliament for confirmation: 'forms and abolishes ministries, state committees, and other organs of state governance'); Kaz 44(3) (qualified: upon the presentation of the Prime Minister 'determines the structure of Government').

[18] Taj 69(4) (sweeping: 'appoints and dismisses the Prime Minister and other members of the Government' with submission of the relevant decrees to joint session of parliament); Kyr 63(4.2) (most limited of the five: appoints and dismisses only 'members of Government/leaders of state agencies, dealing with issues of defence and national security, as well as their deputies'); Kaz 44(3) (qualified: submits the candidacy of Prime Minister to the Majlis and appoints with the consent of the Majlis, appoints upon the Prime Minister's nomination the members of Government; appoints directly the Ministers of Foreign Affairs, Defence, Internal Affairs, Justice and dismisses directly all Government members); Uzb 91(10,11) (submits to parliament for confirmation candidacy of the Prime Minister and dismisses the Prime Minister, confirms upon the Prime Minister's nomination the members of the Cabinet and dismisses them); Tkm 72,73; 53(12) (sweeping: is Cabinet Chair and forms the Cabinet but appoints and dismisses Ministers of Defence and Justice with the consent of the Mejlis).

[19] Taj 69(6) (acts of executive organs in the event 'they contradict the Constitution or laws').

President is both since he/she convenes the cabinet, while the Kyrgyz President is neither and lacks any power to dismiss the Prime Minister. The Kazakh, Uzbek and Tajik presidents thus can replace the nominal head of government readily; hence cabinet reshuffles are typically new governments. Second, in virtually every state, former prime ministers, line ministers and or other high officials, have gone into exile or been imprisoned after removal or reshuffle, often in connection with corruption/malfeasance charges.[20] (In Kyrgystan, two presidents have fled, the first to Russia, the second to Belarus.)

Each state has typically adopted a separate statute elaborating inter alia the structure and powers of government, appointment/removal of officials, the types and procedures for the issuance of normative acts, usually appended to which is an identification of the complement of ministries, committees and other state bodies attached directly to the cabinet of ministers but without ministerial designation.[21] Except in Turkmenistan, a separate administration exists for government, essentially an office of the prime minister, often duplicating many of the functions and posts in the presidential administration.

The five Laws on Government are not necessarily reliable guides to government morphology or power hierarchy: in no government are all ministries created equal, as certain offices of state have traditionally been regarded as more influential or fundamental, closer to the heart of sovereign authority (hence eg in the UK the term 'Great Offices of State,' as distinct from lesser or secondary ones). In Central Asia

[20] eg former Kyrgyz Internal Affairs Minister Kulov (S Radnitz, *Weapons of the Wealthy: Predatory Regimes and Elite-led Protests in Central Asia* (Ithaca NY, Cornell University Press, 2012) 66–67), former Kazakh Prime Ministers Kazhgeldin (MB Olcott, *Kazakhstan: Unfulfilled Promise*, Revised Edition (Washington, Carnegie Endowment for Peace, 2010) 119) and Akhmetov ('Former Kazakh PM jailed for 10 years for embezzlement', Reuters 11 December 2015, available at www.uk.reuters.com/article/uk-kazakhstan-akhmetov-sentence-idUKKBN0TU25420151211, accessed 13 February 2016)), former Turkmen Foreign Minister Shikhmuradov (Peyrouse (n 6) 79–80). 'Much of the political opposition in Kazakhstan, as in other Central Asian republics, is made up of politicians who were previous allies of the men in power but have fallen out with them and joined the opposition.' M Haslett, 'Suspicions raised over Kazakh deaths', BBC News, 14 February 2002, available at www.news.bbc.co.uk/1/hi/world/asia-pacific/4712674.stm, accessed 15 November 2015.

[21] Kaz Constitutional Law 18.12.1995 (government), Kyr Constitutional Law 18.06.2012 (government), Taj Law 16.04.2012 (management of state organs), Tkm Law 24.11.1995 (cabinet), Uzb Law 06.05.1993 (cabinet of ministers).

as in Russia and for analogous reasons a clear differentiation seems to have emerged. The Yeltsin-era coinage of *silovyie ministerstva/struktury* (силовые министества/структквы) or power ministries or structures is especially apt here.[22] The role and distinctiveness of the *silovyie struktury* are an emphatically post-Soviet development—the term and the concept could really only have come into currency in a post-Soviet context, however susceptible of wider extension. Power ministries or agencies distinguish themselves not just because their portfolios—security, defence or tax or oil and gas—control especially critical resources, but because a certain authoritarian and autonomous style of management of those resources by their ministries becomes characteristic within the government as a whole. The USSR had its power ministries as well, where ideological, economic, or other resources were concentrated. The status of such ministries is not formal much less constitutional (there are no classes or grades of ministries). Government is not constitutionally tiered in this fashion, but the de facto power hierarchy and relative autonomy of its components is of central significance in the constitutional system. That is why power ministries so readily become states-within-a-state. Much the same might be said of course of their counterparts in mature systems elsewhere.

Presidents also exercise power with respect to local as well as central government. (The structure, functions and place in the constitutional scheme of local government and local/regional administration in the five states are presented in chapter eight below.) Except for Kyrgyzstan, the local representatives of executive authority (governors at provincial and district levels) in the provinces are appointed and accountable to the president.[23] The Kyrgyz Constitution does not directly regulate local administration, referring the matter to subsidiary legislation, which in turn empowers the prime minister, not the president, to appoint governors (*akims*), upon the proposal of the local assemblies (*keneshes*).[24] The other four constitutions grant the president the power to annul or suspend acts of local executive authorities.[25]

[22] Henderson (n 1) 126.

[23] Uzb 93(15) (upon proposal of Prime Minister), Tkm 81, Kaz 87.4 (provincial and equivalent level governors), Taj 69(5) (provincial and equivalent-level chairs, for confirmation by local legislature).

[24] Kyr Law 15.06.2011 10.

[25] Uzb 93(16), Taj 69(6), Kaz 44. In the case of Turkmenistan the power is vested in the Cabinet, of which the President is head. Tkm 75(8).

PRESIDENTIAL POWER: PARLIAMENT

The five constitutions all elaborate the standard presidential powers respecting parliament found in any presidential system: powers arising from the legislative process, to sign and promulgate duly adopted legislation or to veto it[26] (discussed more particularly in the section below on parliamentary legislative process), and to initiate legislation (with the glaring exception of the Kyrgyz Constitution, which excludes a presidential legislative initiative).[27] Presidents by virtue of their general right of legislative initiative also possess the power to initiate the constitutional amendment processes through parliament. More unusually, the Kazakh and Tajik Constitutions permit their presidents directly to submit proposals for constitutional amendment to the electorate in a referendum, bypassing parliament. In Kazakhstan, even parliamentary initiative to amend must be referred first to the President, whose refusal may then be overridden (like a veto).[28] Additional powers include those to nominate the chair of the upper chamber[29] and to terminate the authority of a deputy.[30]

The Kazakh, Turkmen and Uzbek Constitutions confer upon the president the power to dissolve parliament, in the first case either both chambers or the Majilis (but not the Senate) after consultations with both chairs; in the second case if the Mejilis is unable to form parliamentary leadership within a six-month period; and in the third case the entire Olii Majlis (both chambers) in the event of a second refusal to confirm the candidate for Prime Minister.[31] The grounds for a dissolution in the Kazakh Constitution are left unspecified, whereas those in the other two constitutions are narrow (and remote). Only under the Kazakh Constitution does the President also possess the power to terminate prematurely the local assemblies (*maslikhaty*).[32]

[26] Tkm 53(7), Kyr 64(2.1), Uzb 93(17), Taj 69(15) (tersest of the lot: 'signs law').

[27] Kaz 61(1), Uzb 83, Tkm 65, Taj 58, Kyr 79.

[28] Taj 98–99; Kaz 91(1). The other three constitutions all require a parliamentary law (Uzb 127, Tkm 117) or parliamentary referral to the electorate (Kyr 114).

[29] Kaz 58(1), Uzb 86, Taj 69(8) (elected by the chamber upon the President's nomination). There is no such power in respect of either of the unicameral parliaments (Turkmenistan and Kyrgyzstan), or in respect of the lower chamber in the three bicameral parliaments.

[30] Kaz 52(5) (only deputies to the Senate, i.e. not directly elected).

[31] Kaz 63, Tkm 61, Uzb 98.

[32] Kaz 86(5), Kaz Con Law 26.12.1995 19(11).

But the heart of super-presidential power in Central Asia over parliament lies not in the constitutionally specified powers, broad as they might be, but rather in the 'penumbral power' effectively to colonise parliamentary space. Deploying this power, super-presidents exercise strict control over political parties and ultimately over legislative elections, resulting in pliant and biddable deputies and assured steering of the legislative process itself. While this penumbral power is not total, at least outside Turkmenistan, it is often great enough to obviate the need or occasion for the exercise of properly constitutional powers over legislation: vetoes are otiose when bills arrive on the presidential desk in precisely or very nearly the form in which they have been expected. The presidential veto was exercised in Kazakhstan over the 'Leader of the Nation' bill[33] but was then overridden by the Majlis, leaving outsiders to admire the political stagecraft.

PRESIDENTIAL POWER: JUDICIAL STRUCTURES

Presidential power to appoint and remove judges varies across and within the five systems depending on the level of judges and the constitutionally prescribed role of the judicial governance body and/or parliament. In both Kazakhstan and Kyrgyzstan the president nominates supreme court candidates (chair and members) to the Senate and Jogorku Kenesh, respectively, for their election, on the recommendation of the judicial governance body (Higher Judicial Council and Judicial Council, respectively), and appoints lower judges, again as recommended (in Kyrgyzstan by a second body, the Judicial Selection Council).[34] In Uzbekistan and Tajikistan, the president nominates candidates for the Supreme Court and the High Economic Court (chair and members) to the upper chamber (Senate or Majlisi Milli) for its election, and directly appoints (and removes) lower judges, in the latter instance only on the nomination of the judicial governance body (Higher Qualification Commission or Council of Justice).[35] In Turkmenistan, the president appoints the Supreme Court chair on the nomination of the Mejlis and all other judges on the nomination of

[33] Kaz Con Law 20.07.2000.

[34] Kyr 64(3), Kaz 82.

[35] Uzb 93(13–14), Law 02.09.1993 63, Taj 69(8,13).

the Supreme Court chair.[36] (In all cases, however, the procedures for selection and qualification of judicial candidates in the first instance are complex and the subject of subsidiary statutes and regulations, as discussed in chapter six.)

Apart the perennial exception of Turkmenistan, which lacks such a body, much about the judicial appointments process obviously turns on presidential power vis-a-vis the specialised governance/selection organ for the judiciary. In Kazakhstan, Tajikistan and Uzbekistan, that body (Higher Judicial Council, Council of Justice and Higher Qualification Commission, respectively) is a presidential body, the composition of which is determined by the president as well.[37] Only in Kyrgyzstan are both the Judicial Council and the Judicial Selection Council wholly outside executive structures: the Judicial Council is an organ of judicial self-administration and the members of the Selection Council are appointed one-third by the Judicial Council and one-third each by the majority and opposition factions of the Jogorku Kenesh.[38]

PRESIDENTIAL POWER: ELECTIONS/REFERENDA

All constitutions save Uzbekistan's grant presidents powers to call elections and/or referenda.[39] Typically, the president designates parliamentary and local assembly elections[40] (but parliaments designate presidential elections),[41] in the circumstances, at the time, and in the manner constitutionally provided. (In Uzbekistan, the organisation of elections is left to subsidiary legislation, apart from specification of the date. However, the relevant Constitutional Laws on elections do not expressly vest a power to designate elections in either the president or Oliy Majlis, but leave the organisation of general elections to the Electoral Commission in conformity with constitutionally specified terms

[36] Tkm 102, Law 15.08.2009 61(2).

[37] Kaz 82(4), Con Law 25.12.2000 36, Law 17.11.2008 3; Taj 69(12), Law 06.08.2001 95, Statute 14.12.1999 1–2, Uzb Disposition 2.12.2012 Annex 1 29.

[38] Kyr 7, 102.

[39] Kyr 64(1.1, 1.2) (Jogorku Kenesh, local government), Tkm 53(9) (referenda only), Kaz 44(2), Taj 69(14).

[40] Taj 69(14), Kaz 44, Kyr 64(1).

[41] Kyr 74(2), Taj 55(4), Tkm 63(6).

of office and date, and of bye-elections, second round voting, and repeat elections pursuant to norms prescribed by the statute itself.)[42]

Presidential electoral authority is formally most restricted in the Turkmen Constitution, which empowers the Mejlis to set elections for all elective offices (President, Mejlis deputies, local representative assemblies).[43] It is broadest in the Kazakh Constitution, which empowers the President to set regular and before-term parliamentary elections as well as before term presidential elections.[44] More significant than presidential power to call elections is control over the formation and composition of the electoral commissions, the regulatory authorities for elections and influence over their functions. The presidential right to call referenda is significant, particularly but not exclusively in conjunction with the amendment process (notably for the Tajik and Kazakh cases, as noted above), insofar as it amounts to a potential plebiscitary circumvention or supercession of representative government. However, express presidential powers directly to call plebiscites might appear less singular in a context in which electoral processes in general often exhibit a default plebiscitary character (discussed in more detail in chapter five).

PRESIDENTIAL POWER: ADMINISTRATION/*APPARAT* AND DIRECTLY SUBORDINATE AGENCIES

Each constitution provides for the possibility of, though does not typically enumerate or identify, state agencies or 'organs' directly subordinate and accountable to the president, which may or may not be denominated 'pri Presidentie' (при Президенте), that is, under or attached to the president. Sub-constitutional acts establish or regulate these and other agencies.[45] Presidential agencies or organs serving a consultative/advisory function, usually councils, like the Kazakh National Security

[42] Uzb 90, 117, Uzb Const Laws 18.11.1991 (President) 37, 38; 29.08.2003 (Oliy Majlis), 47, 61.

[43] Tkm 63(6).

[44] Kaz 41(3–1).

[45] Kaz Decree 11.03.2008, Annex 2 (list of subordinate organs, including Procuracy, National Bank, corruption and civil service agencies, foreign intelligence, KNB, Republican guard, presidential bodyguard, accounting committee, presidential administration and presidential affairs); Taj Law 16.04.2012 14.

Council or the Kyrgyz Defence Council, may merit constitutional mention.[46] As noted above, in Kazakhstan, Tajikistan and Uzbekistan the judicial administrative body is formed by the president, a power that is constitutionally grounded in the first two.[47] Pre-eminent among the directly subordinate agencies is the presidential *apparat* or administration, which in all five states has either a modest constitutional tethering or none at all, but an immodest constitutional presence and significance.[48] The Kazakh, Tajik and Kyrgyz Constitutions empower the president to 'form', 'create' or 'define the structure of' the *apparat* or administration but provide no further specification, leaving the elaboration of structure and functions to subsidiary acts.[49] Neither the Uzbek nor the Turkmen Constitution mention such a body, leaving its establishment and remit entirely to subsidiary acts.

In each state the presidential administration has grown into a sizeable and comprehensive institution in its own right, with a multitude of offices and departments paralleling the technical or sectoral division of labour in the government proper. In Kazakhstan, for instance, its many subdvisions include a general department, National Security Council (NSC), analytic department, state-legal department, NSC situation centre, internal political department, external politics centre, press service, NSC secretariat, Assembly of Peoples secretariat, chief of administration secretariat, state secretary secretariat, presidential representation in parliament, chancellery, protocol, strategic plans and analysis centre, and departments for state control and organisational-territorial work, civil service, informatisation, law enforcement system and social-economic monitoring.[50] Even in Kyrgyzstan, with by far the slimmest remit of presidential authority in the five states, the presidential administration includes nine departments, as well as assorted secretariats, commissions and councils.[51]

[46] Kaz 44, Kyr 9(1), Taj 69(11).

[47] See n 35.

[48] Compare the hypertrophy of presidential power and administration in the Russian Federation. Henderson (n 1) 117–19.

[49] Kaz 44 (forms administration); Taj 10 ('creates executive *apparat*), Decree 17.01.2104 11.08.2013, Kyr 10(5) ('defines structure of *apparat*, confirms regulation, appoints head'), Uzb 93(8).

[50] www.akorda.kz/ru/executive_office/executive_office_stucture, accessed 14 February 2016.

[51] Kyr Decee 20.12.2010.

The status of the administrative body varies. Turkmen law establishes the *apparat* as a 'state organ,' and vests it with 'facilitation of the activity of the President' and 'unconditional and exhaustive fulfilment of the acts of the President and control over their execution' in the Law on the President.[52] Moreover, inasmuch as the president is simultaneously Head of Government and Head of State, directly convening and chairing the Cabinet of Ministers, the presidential *apparat* functions as an office of the prime minister. Turkmenistan has a unique post of Chief of Staff of the presidential *apparat* and the Cabinet of Ministers. In Tajikistan, the executive *apparat* of the president is established as an organ of state, and is regulated comprehensively by a unique (among the five states) statute[53] that regulates the 'central executive organs of state authority' subordinate and accountable either to the President or to the Government. This constitutional approach is unusual in that it seeks to treat in one instrument the several powers and functions of the presidency (with its *apparat* and its directly subordinate organs) as an institution together with the powers and functions of the government as an institution (with its ministries and committees and directly subordinate and consultative organs). To a degree such an approach appears consonant with a more conventional concept of the executive as one integral branch of government, rather than the super-presidentialist concept of a 'fourth branch'.

PRESIDENTIAL POWER: NATIONAL SECURITY

The Kazakh Law on the President identifies as a distinct subset of presidential powers those concerned with defence and security;[54] all five constitutions alike recognise the president as commander-in-chief (the term, borrowed from the US Constitution, is ubiquitous) of the armed forces[55] and endow the president with the power to declare martial law and/or a state of emergency.[56] The terse and largely formulaic constitutional references to defence and security (invoked also

[52] Tkm Law 21.05.2011 14.

[53] Taj Law 16.04.2012.

[54] Kaz Con Law 26.12.1995 8.

[55] Kaz 44(12), Taj 69(21), Uzb 93(20), Tkm 53(3), Kyr 64(6.8).

[56] Kaz 44(16), Taj 69(24, 22), Uzb 93(19), Tkm 53(14), Kyr 64(9.4, 9.2).

with regard to the curtailment of rights, as discussed in chapter six) give little indication of their service as plinth for the Central Asian national security state, an unsurprising corollary of super-presidential authoritarianism.

The inherited institutional matrix for comprehensive control and surveillance of public life has not only continued as a prominent feature of all five states, but has been reinforced by the emergence of the region after 9/11 as a front-line in global counter-terror policy and strategy. The problem of the security services as states-within-states posed a significant constitutional challenge from the outset, which has never been adequately addressed (and cannot be, where a national security state is simultaneously a super-presidentialist state). The direct constitutional regulation of national security functions and operations in the five states is effectively nil. As has been the case for the rest of the Soviet institutional and governance inheritance, the security institutions all have proved robust and enduring even when shorn of their Cold War ideological justification and torn from their Soviet housing. All five national security agencies, the Uzbek National Security Service, the Turkmen Ministry of National Security, the Kazakh Committee of National Security, the Tajik State Committee of National Security and the Kyrgyz State Committee of National Security, are the direct institutional successors and heirs of the KGB of the respective SSRs. The Tajik Committee and the Turkmen Ministry are not cited in the constitutional text, and the Kazakh and Kyrgyz committees only in connection with appointment of the head, but all are established and regulated by statute.[57] The security agencies command sweeping investigative powers, and they are all detaining authorities as well, as discussed in chapter six, with profound implications for human rights.

Here again constitutional design would seem to be inadequate by omission rather than commission. The Central Asian constitutions did not depart from the norm in initially omitting to regulate at constitutional levels the activities of police, security and intelligence functions (though they may well have departed from the norm in effectively immunising those functions behind an impregnable super-presidentialist wall). However, increasing concern about the liability

[57] Kaz 44, 55 (consent of Senate), 59, Law 06.01.2012, Uzb 93(24), Law 09.12.1992, Taj Law 20.03.2008, Kyr 64(4.2), 74(3.1) (exclusion of Jogorku Kenesh), Law 11.01.1994, Tkm Law 31.03.2012.

of security services to infringe citizens' human rights is one salutary consequence of the post 9/11 'war on terror' and the published and widely criticised excesses of Western states. The requirement that national security operations and personnel abide by human rights obligations has now become part of contemporary human rights discourse as witness the appointment of a UN Special Rapporteur on Human Rights and Counter-Terrorism and the development of standards and guidelines.[58]

The argument for constitutional regulation of the security sector is particularly apposite to the Central Asian states in view of the burdens of the Soviet past they bear. Just as in a former epoch, at the moment of Brezhnev constitutional renewal of 1977, the Soviet authorities found warrant to constitutionalise subordination of the CPSU to socialist legality, so too might the Central Asian successor authorities find warrant at present to constitutionalise subordination of the activities of the security sector to the rule of law and human rights protection. They have taken promising steps but not at the constitutional level, through the adoption in recent years of a 'second generation' of laws incorporating specific guarantees of human rights protection. Thus, for example, the 2012 Kazakhstan National Security Law establishes 'Principles of the Provision of National Security': '1) observance of legality in carrying out the activity of providing national security and 2) priority of the rights and freedoms of the person and citizen.'[59] Similarly, the analogous Turkmen act provides:

> The activity of the organs of national security is based on the principles of legality, equality of the person and the citizen before the law, humanism, respect and the provision of the protection of rights and freedoms of the person and the citizen, centralised management, the use of covert operations and a combination of open and secret methods and means of activity.[60]

However, Central Asian states continue to lack specific mechanisms for the enforcement of human rights protection obligations in the security sector in particular, as for non-executive policing or oversight

[58] Commission on Human Rights Resolution 2005/80, General Assembly Resolution 60/158.

[59] Kaz Law 06.12.2012 3.

[60] Tkm Law 31.03.2012 4.

of intelligence, counter-intelligence, and other national security operations in general. The national security forces continue to serve at the pleasure of the president[61] and their operations are subject to no special legislative or judicial scrutiny or supervision. They have been credibly and repeatedly implicated in torture and arbitrary arrest/detention, use of lethal force in counter-terror operations, intimidation, persecution and compromise of political opponents, as well as targeted assassination—all staples of the Soviet KGB (as also of Western security services).[62] In particular, apart from the evidence of the largely declaratory sub-constitutional principles, oversight as such over domestic counter-intelligence functions has never been an object of constitutional attention. In the super-presidentialist mould, national security is simply taken for granted as an essential and exclusive executive responsibility.

PRESIDENTIAL POWER: LAWMAKING

All five constitutions confer upon the president direct legislative competence to issue normative acts binding across national territory, in order to give effect to enumerated constitutional powers (eg to form directly subordinate agencies).[63] The Kazakh and Turkmen Constitutions permit delegation to the president of competence directly to issue laws (*zakony*, законы), subject to certain conditions; the Kazakh

[61] Even in Kyrgyzstan, where the Government serves at the pleasure of the Jogorku Kenesh not the president, the President retains the capacity to appoint and dismiss both the members of Government and the heads of the organs of state responsible for defence and national security. Kyr 64(4.2).

[62] C Murray, *Murder in Samarkand: A British Ambassador's Controversial Defiance of Tyranny in the War on Terror* (Edinburgh and London, Mainstream Publishing, 2007) at Kindle 2203, 4158; UN Special Rapporteur on Torture Mission to Uzbekistan Report 3 February 2003 (Uzbek SNB torture); Olcott (n 20) ch 8, fn 96; NP Walsh, 'Protest over opposition leader's assassination' *Guardian* 27 February 2006, available at www.theguardian.com/world/2006/feb/27/nickpatonwalsh, accessed 5 November 2015); Haslett (n 17); N Ognianova, 'Kazakhstan's broken promises on human rights,' *Guardian* 22 September 2010, available at www.theguardian.com/commentisfree/libertycentral/2010/sep/22/kazakhstan-osce-values-human-rights, accessed 5 November 2015) (Kazakh KNB corruption, detention, assassination).

[63] Tkm 54, Uzb 94 (*ukazy*, decrees, *postanovlenia*, resolutions or rulings, *rasporiazhenia*, dispositions); Taj 70, Kaz 45, Kyr 65 (*postanovlenia* and *rasporiazhenia*)

delegation is broader.[64] The Kazakh Constitution also gives the President competence to issue decrees having the force of laws for legislative bills determined by the president as requiring urgent consideration, but which Parliament has failed to consider within a one-month period, pending parliamentary adoption. (In the latter instance, Parliament is effectively deprived thereafter of the power to reject legislation or to override a presidential veto, since the urgency provision supersedes the default procedure, making for a kind of constitutional extortion—which has however to date not been exercised.) Given the scope of prescribed presidential authority generally, presidential decrees and other acts have assumed very great significance in all five constitutional systems as sources of law, enhanced moreover by the competence of bodies established by presidential decree themselves to issue in turn binding normative acts within their sphere of competence. Inasmuch as executive lawmaking is a ubiquitous fact of life in all modern constitutional systems, this circumstance is only exceptional to the extent that the predicate authority is exceptionally broad and unconstrained. Arguably the most extended and cumulatively significant use of presidential lawmaking powers in Central Asia was Nazarbaev's during the constitutional interregnum of 1995, particularly since it enabled him to introduce (on dubious constitutional grounds) and submit for referendum a new constitution altogether.[65]

IMMUNITY AND IMPEACHMENT

The force of super-presidentialism is not evident in the scope of authority alone, but as well in the presidential immunity conferred by the constitutions and the grounds for impeachment. All constitutions save the Kyrgyz deem the president inviolable or confer a 'right of inviolability', and the Turkmen, Uzbek and Kazakh further provide that the president's dignity, honour or person is 'protected by law,' and corresponding criminal offences are established in the respective

[64] Kaz 53(4), 61 (upon a two-thirds vote of each parliamentary chamber, for a period not exceeding one year); Tkm 64 (on discrete issues, excluding constitutional amendment, criminal and administrative legislation, and judicial proceedings, and with obligatory subsequent consideration by Mejlis).

[65] Olcott (n 20) 111.

criminal codes.[66] The Kyrgyz Constitution provides that criminal liability may be imposed on the president after removal from office and avoids the term 'inviolable' altogether, reserving it only for the territory of the Republic, property, person, privacy, dwelling and the judge.[67] The constitutions vary provocatively in their treatment of removal of the president from office, both in breadth of grounds and ardour of procedure. The Uzbek Constitution makes no provision for impeachment whatsoever—and indeed only was amended in 2011 to provide a (temporary) succession, in the event of 'impossibility of the fulfilment by the sitting President of his obligations'.[68] The Tajik Constitution makes provision for removal from office only in the event of incapacity owing to illness (on the two-thirds vote of each chamber upon the conclusion of a state medical commission organised by joint session)[69] and for 'deprivation of immunity' for high treason as determined by a two-thirds vote of each chamber following a conclusion of the Constitutional Court.[70] The Turkmen Constitution while similarly providing for removal from office only in the event of illness makes unique provision for a vote of no-confidence in the president 'in the case of the violation by the President of the Constitution and the laws,' determined by a three-quarters Mejlis vote. The effect of such a vote is not specified as such, but presumably on its basis 'the question of the removal of the President is referred to a general referendum.'[71]

The Kazakh constitutional presidential removal provisions mirror the Tajik, but with greater elaboration, providing for 'premature release' from office in the event of incapacity as a result of illness[72] and 'discharge' in the event of a conviction for high treason only.[73] In the latter case the Majilis impeaches by majority vote upon the initiative of no less than one-third of the deputies; the Senate then investigates and

[66] Kaz 46, Kaz Criminal Code 318 (attack on honour and reputation); Tkm 56, Tkm Criminal Code 176 (attempt), Taj 72, Taj Criminal Code 137 (public affront), Uzb 91, Uzb Criminal Code 158 (attempt).

[67] Kyr 67, 8, 12, 29, 30, 94.

[68] Uzb 96.

[69] Taj 71.

[70] Taj 72.

[71] Tkm 57.

[72] Kaz 47(1).

[73] Kaz 47(2).

refers the issue to a joint session of Parliament for final decision (in a multiply hedged and conditioned procedure)

> by a majority of no less than three fourths of the total number of the deputies of each Chamber, in the presence of a Supreme Court conclusion regarding the validity of the accusation and a Constitutional Council conclusion that the established constitutional procedures have been observed. (Kaz 47(2))

Notably, an impeachment proceeding which fails *at any point* entails draconian consequences for its initiators:

> Rejection of the accusation of the President of the Republic of high treason at any stage shall result in premature termination of the powers of the deputies of the Majilis who initiated the consideration of this issue.[74]

Moreover, an additional restriction is imposed to prevent retaliatory impeachment proceedings:

> The issue of discharge of the President of the Republic from office may not be initiated in the period when the President is considering premature termination of the powers of the Parliament of the Republic or the Majilis of the Parliament.[75]

Only Kyrgyzstan has established a broad constitutional basis for removal of a president from office for 'commission of a crime' together with a straightforward procedure. Impeachment is by majority vote of the Jogorku Kenesh on the initiative of one third of the deputies, with confirmation by a finding of the General Procurator of 'indications of a crime'. Conviction is by two-thirds Jogorku Kenesh vote, in the presence of a conclusion of a Special Commission, within a three-month period. The Kyrgyz approach, it will be noted, foregrounds criminal law rather than special presidential immunity (restriction of liability to treason). In general, the presidential removal provisions turn out to be fairly reliable indicators of the underlying constitutional culture in each case: Uzbekistan's presidential absolutism (no removal provision), Turkmenistan's demagogic populism (notional plebiscite), Tajikistan's qualified authoritarianism (restricted legislative authority), Kazakhstan's super-presidentialist proceduralism (elaborate

[74] Kaz 47(2).
[75] Kaz 47(3).

regulation in very restricted compass) and Kyrgyzstan's parliamentary supremacy (broad grounds and legislative control).

DOING JUSTICE TO SUPER-PRESIDENTIALISM

What makes a president a super-president? The lists of presidential powers and prerogatives in the initial set of constitutions were already formidable. The shift from preponderant to overwhelming presidential authority can nonetheless prove incremental and imperceptible. While the constitutional trends toward the consolidation of presidential pre-eminence are everywhere in evidence in Central Asia, it become difficult to fix a point at which the system crosses some Freedom House border post from 'Partly Free' to 'Not Free'. Edgar in *King Lear* cautions—'the worst is not/So long as we can say "This is the worst".' But super-presidentialist features mark the constitutional texts themselves.

The Uzbek, Tajik, Turkmen and Kazakh constitutions all boldly fly their super-presidential colours in the introductory presidential articles:

> The President of the Republic of Uzbekistan is head of state and facilitates the co-ordinated functioning and mutual operation of the bodies of state authority.
>
> The President of the Republic of Tajikistan is Head of State and of the executive authority of Government. The President is the guarantor of the Constitution and the laws, human and citizen rights and freedoms, national independence, unity and territorial integrity, the continuity and longevity of the state, the co-ordinated functioning of state bodies, the observance of the international treaties of Tajikistan.
>
> The President of Turkmenistan is the Head of State and executive authority, highest official of Turkmenistan, stands guarantor of the state independence and neutral status of Turkmenistan, of its territorial integrity, observance of the Constitution, and the fulfilment of international obligations.
>
> The President of the Republic of Kazakhstan is Head of State, its highest official, defining the fundamental directions of internal and external policy of the state and representing Kazakhstan within the country and in international relations.
> The President of the Republic is the symbol and guarantor of the unity of the people and state authority, inviolability of the Constitution, human and citizen rights and freedoms.

> The President of the Republic facilitates the co-ordinated functioning of all branches of state authority and the accountability of all organs of authority before the people.[76]

The formulation in the Kyrgyz Constitution is by contrast demure:

> The President is Head of State.
>
> The President embodies the unity of the people and state authority.[77]

In the wording of the other four constitutions, and most grandiosely in the Kazakh, the president is effectively established as meta-branch of government, elevated above all other state bodies, legislative, judicial and executive, and performing a co-ordinating function among them as impartial arbiter. The echoes of the transcendent status of the Party in the Soviet constitutional order are rather hard to miss here, in context. However, whereas the Party was notionally a collective guarantor, the president is very much an individual guarantor, and in Central Asia perhaps most emblematically across post-Soviet space, a de facto oligarchy would appear to have given way to a de jure monarchy, more securely constitutionally anchored. The much-remarked rituals and ceremonies of Central Asian presidential monarchism are not merely an expression of a homegrown 'sultanistic' (or borrowed US) political culture, but a function of the constitutional status of the office and its sub-constitutional elaboration, as witness the specificity of provisions in the Kazakh and Turkmen Laws on the President and the Kazakh Law on the First President-Leader of the Nation.[78]

Judged severely, Central Asian super-presidentialism can be seen to retard constitutionalism. Yet constitutional amendments do not open closed political space, they can at most reflect and then regulate openings. There may be democratic constitutions, but there are no real democratisation constitutions, that is, constitutions designed to enable and sustain ongoing processes of democratisation. Transitional constitutionalism is a theory of constitutional processes not constitutions. The literature on the opening of authoritarian regimes suggests that complex processes of ongoing bargaining structure, pace and sequence democratic openings, and that constitutional reform typically reflects

76 Uzb 89, Taj 64, Tkm 50, Kaz 40.

77 Kyr 60.

78 Kaz Con Law 26.12.1995, Tkm Law 21.05.2011, Kaz Con Law 20.06.2000.

such processes.[79] With the exception of Kyrgyzstan however, politics have yet to come to the region (in the sense of publicly contested positions, issues and programmes, espoused by differentiated parties and politicians): they are barred at the gates by super-presidentialism, denied the right of citizenship. Super-presidentialism is a constitutional system in its own right—authoritarianism anchored in express and implied constitutional arrangements—which seeks a pre-emptive closure, or severe straitening, of the space for political dynamics in general, and a fortiori the space for metapolitical (ie constitutional) dynamics. That is, super-presidentialism is if anything *counter-transitional*, a system which is structurally fortified against the possibility of transformation or constitutional development, a constitutional mortmain.

But regional perspectives reveal Central Asian super-presidentialism in rather a different light, and caution against one's dismissing it as self-evidently a travesty or abuse of constitutionalism. Central Asian constitutional discourse itself construes a super-presidential system (though avoiding the somewhat pejorative term) as precisely transitional, an envelope for progressive constitutional reform.[80] The presidency appears as effectively a steward or regent for a set of emerging institutions which have not yet attained majority: in its role as regulator of the relations among executive, legislative and judicial branches, the presidency serves as guardian or guarantor of the constitutional order itself. The Legislative Monitoring Institute under the Uzbek presidential *apparat* (transferred thereto from the Olii Majlisi by presidential decree) furnishes a particularly stunning and exemplary instance of the presidency's role meta-constitutional role, insofar as it is tasked with

> systematic analysis of the course of democratic reforms in the sphere state and social construction, the consequent realisation of the constitutional

[79] G O'Donnell and PC Schmitter (eds), *Transitions from Authoritarian Rule, Volume 4; Tentative Conclusions About Uncertain Democracies: Prospects for Democracy* (Baltimore MD, Johns Hopkins University Press, 1986) 37–47.

[80] Constitutional Council of the Republic of Kazakhstan (2010), *The Constitution of Kazakhstan: A Scientific–Practical Commentary* (Almaty, Raritet) available at www.ksrk.gov.kz/data/filedat/default/28-10-10-3-rus.zip, accessed 6 November 2015) [Конституция Республики Казахстан: Научно-практический комментарий.– Алматы: Раритет, 2010] 7–8 ('progressive dynamic of Kazakh statehood' [поступательная динамика казахстанской государственности]).

> principle of the division of powers, the preparation of proposals for strengthening the self-reliance and independence of executive, legislative and judicial branches of power, the balance among them, and the creation of an effective system for checks and balances in the system of state authority and governance.[81]

Though not so avowed by its regional champions, this concept of presidential guarantor rather than a simple continuation of the functional role of the CPSU in the Soviet order becomes a defensible adaption and rearticulation of it in changed circumstances, as precisely transitional. Just as communism was once upon a time understood as on the horizon, and socialism (the party state) as the intermediate managerial stage preparing society for it, so now has democracy become the goal and super-presidentialism the provisional order pending and enabling its attainment. This 'regency' argument, while it might not be inherently unsound, is problematic insofar as it is manifestly self-serving, like Putin's 'managed democracy.' It also reanimates or perpetuates colonialist tropes, as raised in chapter three.

Thus a salient feature of Central Asian super-presidentialism, and an index of the self-avowed transitional status of Central Asian constitutionalism, is the effective constitutionalisation of constitutional reform itself. The systems are distinguished from mature or stabilised counterparts by their quasi-formalised character as *works-in-progress*. All constitutional orders provide for contingent amendment processes, but these provide for *planned or contemplated* reform, consolidation and maturation processes—not exactly a rolling design, but certainly a programmatic one. And the reform-planning function is of course vested in the presidency, which remains for the four super-presidential states the sole impetus and source of constitutional change, the exclusive author and initiator of constitutional amendments. To the extent that these systems are indeed transitional and transformable, any processes of transformation remain closely superintended and controlled from the top, in a calculated and calibrated political decompression.

[81] Uzb Decree 02.04.2005.

FURTHER READING

D Lewis, 'Understanding the Authoritarian State: Neopatrimonialism in Central Asia' (2012) 19 *Brown Journal of World Affairs* 115, 126.

L Golovko, 'The Space for Legal Reform in Central Asia: Between Political Limits and Theoretical Deformations' in *2010 Yearbook of the Organisation for Security and Co-operation in Europe (OSCE)* (Baden-Baden, Nomos Verlagsgesellschaft, 2011) 105, 115.

HE Hale, 'Democracy or Autocracy on the March? The Colored Revolutions as Normal Dynamics of Patronal Presidentialism' (2006) 39 *Communist and Post-Communist Studies* 305.

J Heathershaw, *Post-conflict Tajikistan: The Politics of Peacebuilding and the Emergence of Legitimate Order* (London, Routledge, 2009).

JT Ishiyama and R Kennedy, 'Superpresidentialism and Political Party Development in Russia, Ukraine, Armenia and Kyrgyzstan' (2001) 53 *Europe-Asia Studies* 1177.

MB Olcott, *Kazakhstan: Unfulfilled Promise*, Revised Edition (Washington, Carnegie Endowment for Peace, 2010).

J Šír, '*Halk Maslahaty* in the Context of the Constitutional Evolution of Post-Soviet Turkmenistan' (2005) 6 *Perspectives on European Politics and Society* 321.

5

Talking Shop or Governing Body

Parliament

Parliamentary Basics: Composition, Parliamentarians and Parties – Parliament as Institution: Structure, Leadership, Development – Parliamentary Powers: Lawmaking – Other Parliamentary Powers – The Meta-rules of Representation – Elections and Term of Office – A Tale of Two Parliaments, and Two Constitutions: Tajik and Kyrgyz

THE FIVE PARLIAMENTS—THE bicameral Tajik, Uzbek and Kazakh, and the unicameral Turkmen and Kyrgyz, making eight chambers in total—present a compelling disparity in their constitutional circuitry and operational dynamics, even where broad commonalities are evident. The overriding question remains what share of the actual governing they shoulder. The answer is largely determined by the scope of presidentialism set out in the previous chapter.

The analysis in the present chapter looks first to the fundamentals of the parliamentary systems: the composition of the seats in the eight chambers and the basis for their occupation, the honourable members themselves (qualifications, rights, responsibilities, privileges and liabilities), and the regulation of parties in the general political system and then in the parliamentary scheme. Then it takes up the structure and organisation of parliament as an institution, its leadership and committee structure and the course of its development over more than twenty years in the five cases. Next it takes up parliamentary powers: first and foremost legislative power and the legislative process, then powers of appointment, dismissal, oversight and control over executive and judiciary. Following this general exposition, there are two sections looking at meta-rules, or rules for rules: the first analysing the representative formulas and frameworks themselves (districting, proportional and first-past-the-post, and bi- and unicameralism), then another exploring the regulation of the electoral system generally, respecting both president and parliament. Finally a concluding section examines more closely the vicissitudes of the Tajik Majlisi Olii and the Kyrgyz Jogorku Kenesh, the two most volatile parliamentary cases and, from a comparative standpoint, the most intriguing and instructive as well.

PARLIAMENTARY BASICS: COMPOSITION, PARLIAMENTARIANS AND PARTIES

Composition

The territorial constituency is the exclusive basis for parliamentary representation in the Kazakh and Uzbek lower houses (Majilis and Legislative Chamber), as in the unicameral Turkmenistan Mejlis. Proportional representation (PR) is the basis for roughly one-third of seats in the Tajik lower house (Majlisi Namoyandogan) and the basis for all the seats in the unicameral Kyrgyz Jogorku Kenesh. In a regionally unique provision, nine deputies to the Kazakh Majilis are elected by the Assembly of Peoples, the constitutional inter-ethnic relations body.[1] The principle for representation in the three upper houses is a mix of territorial (larger administrative subdivisions, ie provinces or equivalent) for the bulk of the seats and national (at-large) for a designated remainder. Seats in the Tajik Majlisi Milli, Kazakh Senate and Uzbek Senate are allocated on an analogous basis: indirect election for the territorial seats by local councils according to a set representative formula, and presidential appointment of the at-large seats (sixteen in Uzbekistan, fifteen in Kazakhstan, and one quarter in Tajikistan), in the Kazakh and Uzbek cases on the basis of specified criteria.[2] The Tajik

[1] Kaz 51, 44; the Assembly of Peoples is only referenced in the Constitution respecting the presidential competence to form it. See the discussion in ch 8.

[2] Two seats per province or equivalent in Kazakhstan, yielding 98 seats, with an additional 15 appointments 'taking account of the need to facilitate

Constitution alone leaves the number of deputies for both chambers to subsidiary legislation, as well as the electoral basis (a mixture of single mandate and national lists) for the Majlisi Namoyandagon, the lower house, since the make-up of the Tajik parliament was a particularly contentious issue in the peace negotiations.[3]

Deputies and Senators

The qualifications and terms of office for deputies of the eight chambers are broadly similar but least stringent in the Kyrgyz Constitution.[4] Legislators all enjoy immunity from prosecution or arrest save when revoked by the chamber,[5] but are subject to disciplinary measures and can lose their mandate for unexplained absence from a session, occupation of a post incompatible with service as a deputy, and (in Kazakhstan and Kyrgyzstan only) crossing the aisle—leaving their faction or the party on whose behalf they were elected.[6] Members of all

the representation in the Senate of national cultural and other significant societal interests' (Kaz 51(1)); 6 seats per province or equivalent in Uzbekistan (14 including Karakalpakstan and the city of Tashkent), yielding 104 seats, with an additional 16 seats appointed by the President 'of the most authoritative citizens with great practical experience, and distinct services in the fields of science, art, literature, production, and other spheres of state and social activity' (Uzb 77); and equivalent but constitutionally unspecified representation in Tajikistan for provinces and republican cities and districts, with no constitutional criteria specified for presidential appointments. Taj 49.

[3] The Law on the Majlisi Oli as currently amended provides for 33 indirectly elected deputies of the Majlisi Milli and eight presidential appointees and 63 deputies of the Majlisi Namoyandagon, Taj Con Law 19.04.2000.

[4] Uzb 77 (deputies of the Legislative Chamber and members of the Senate must be citizens of at least 25, with continuous residency of five years prior to election); Tkm 60, 90 (Mejlis deputies must be citizens of at least 25, with continuous residency of ten years, five-year term); Kaz 50(5), 51(4) (deputies must be citizens, with continuous residency of ten years, Majlis deputies must be at least 25, Senate deputies at least 30 with higher education, five-year term for Majlis deputies, six-year term for Senate deputies); Taj 48–49 (Majlisi Namyandogan deputies must be citizens of at least 25 with higher education; Majlisi Milli deputies must be citizens of at least 35, with higher education, five-year term for both); Kyr 70(2) (Jogorku Kenesh deputies must be citizens at least 21 with the right to vote, five-year term).

[5] Kyr 72, Kaz 52(6), 57, Taj 51, Uzb 88, Tkm 67.

[6] Kaz 52(5) (Majilis deputies only), Kyr 73(3.1).

chambers save the Tajik Majlisi Milli are prohibited from occupying other remunerated or official posts while serving (to varying degrees of rigour and specificity);[7] members of the Majlisi Milli are barred only from occupying *more than two representative* posts.[8] Only the Kyrgyz and Tajik constitutions include an express provision that parliamentarians are to vote their conscience.[9]

Organisational Parties

Although Central Asian political parties are not constitutionally regulated, they remain constitutionally fundamental political institutions. Each of the five constitutions does protect the right of political association[10] and all save Kazakhstan the right specifically to form parties, as discussed in more detail in chapter six. The formation, organisation and regulation of political parties in developed multiparty democratic systems have not typically merited comprehensive regulation, nor has the legal status of party organisations generated particular controversy or concern. Concern with party financing has however in recent decades led to the adoption of new party-regulatory statutes.[11] In the Central Asian states political parties have

[7] Taj 50 (other representative organ, official post, business, save scholarly/creative), Kyr 72(2) (state or municipal service, business, company management or supervisory board, except scholarly/creative), Kaz 52(3) (other representative organ, paid work except scholarly/teaching/creative; business; company board), Uzb 88 (other kinds of remunerated work, save scholarly or creative), Tkm 69 (member of cabinet, *hiakim*, *archina*, judge, prosecutor) but not scholarly or creative activity.

[8] Taj 50. They are thus not barred from holding simultaneous executive office or a second representative office; members have frequently been members of local councils (who elect the Majlisi Mjilli) or local executive officials, like the Dushanbe mayor. MB Olcott, *Tajikistan's Difficult Development Path* (Washington, Carnegie Endowment for Peace, 2012) 116.

[9] Kyr 73(1) ('not bound by imperative mandate'), Taj 51 ('right to express his/her opinion, vote according to his/her conviction').

[10] Taj 28, Kyr 4(2), Tkm 30, Uzb 34, Kaz 23(1) (umbrella right to association).

[11] In the UK, only since 2000 has there been a parliamentary Act specifically regulating the formation, registration and financing of political parties, the Political Parties, Elections and Referendums Act 2000 c.41.

been closely and comprehensively regulated by special statute since independence as an integral aspect of super-presidentialism.

Each state has enacted a law on political parties;[12] these laws typically regulate substantive matters such as party aims and purposes as well as procedures. They provide for threshold numbers of members or signatories for formation (Kyrgyz parties require ten, Uzbek parties 20,000, and Kazakh Kyrgyz and Turkmen parties 1,000 signatories),[13] requisite geographic diversity of membership (two-thirds of oblasts and equivalents for Kazakh parties, all oblasts for Uzbek parties, a majority of towns and regions for Tajik parties, no such requirement for Kyrgyz or Turkmen),[14] due registration (requirements and procedures, grounds for rejection and appeal of rejection),[15] rights and duties of parties (access to state media, activities outside working hours),[16] and grounds and procedures for suspension or termination by authorities.[17] Compliance under such meticulous and comprehensive regulation is challenging even for the best organised and most determined parties, particularly in a context of invidious application and political manipulation of the rules by the authorities. Numbers of would-be parties have failed to clear the registration procedures or have

[12] Kaz Law 15.07.2002, Kyr Law 12.06.1999, Uzb Law 26.12.1996, Taj Law 13.11.1998, Tkm Law 10.01.2012.

[13] Kaz Law 15.07.2002 6(1); Taj Law 13.11.1998 3; Tkm Law 10.01.2012 3; Uzb Law 26.12.1996 6; Kyr Law 12.06.1999 5.

[14] ibid.

[15] Kaz Law 15.07.2002 10–11; Taj Law 13.11.1998 7; Tkm Law 10.01.2012 14–17; Uzb Law 26.12.1996 8–9; Kyr Law 12.06.1999 10. Uzb Law 8–9. Requirements typically include submission of charter, opening of bank account and other due formalities of creation of a legal person. See eg Kaz Law 10(7–8). State registration is the heart of the matter: in the Soviet and post-Soviet civilian understanding all legal persons only commence to exist and attain cognisability upon their official registration (these are all 'registration jurisdictions'); eg Kaz Civil Code 42(3): 'A legal entity shall be deemed to be created from the moment of its state registration.'

[16] Kaz Law 15.07.2002 15; Taj Law 13.11.1998 10; Tkm Law 10.01.2012 23; Uzb Law 26.12.1996 12; Kyr Law 12.06.1999 11.

[17] Kaz Law 15.07.2002 13; Taj Law 13.11.1998 20–26; Tkm Law 10.01.2012 35; Uzb Law 26.12.1996 10–11; Kyr Law 12.06.1999 14.

been subsequently de-registered[18] for trivial non-compliance, and even duly registered parties have run afoul of requirements of the election laws, as discussed below. Further, the rights of political parties as such must be evaluated against the general protection regime for the exercise of political rights, notably those of expression and assembly, which, as discussed in chapter six, has not been encouraging in any of the states except Kyrgyzstan.

The treatment of political parties is perhaps best considered as a particular and particularly charged instance of a more general phenomenon in post-Soviet Central Asia, the state regulation of social organisations or 'civil society' through comprehensive registration requirements—effectively a form of state licensing. Freedom of association and the commensurate evacuation of social space by political authority is a chronic sticking point in the transformation of the Soviet constitutional order. From the perspective of central authorities, all social associations are latently, presumptively or potentially political (and hence subject to registration in all five states)[19] whereas parties are manifestly so. Political parties across Central Asia are always separately regulated and subject to special requirements and scrutiny; they may or may not be regarded as a category of social association.[20]

Parliamentary Parties

Pseudo-pluralism and phony parties are the hallmark of the regional constitutional systems: staged or managed contestation among formally distinct parties organised and instructed by the same (supreme) political interests. Indeed if Putin has pioneered 'managed democracy',[21] the Central Asian regimes have essayed 'staged democracy'. Organisational

[18] See eg OSCE/ODIHR 2012, 4, 11 (history of party registration refusal, party and candidate de-registration in Kazakh parliamentary elections); OSCE/ODIHR 2005, 18 (de-registrations of candidates in Kyrgyz parliamentary elections).

[19] Kaz Law 31.05.1996 13, Kyr Law 15.10.1999, Tkm Law 03.05.2014, Uzb Law 15.02.1991, Taj Law 12.05.2007.

[20] In Kyrgyzstan, provisions relating to political parties were expressly removed from the law on associations and placed in a separate statute. Kyr Law 12.06.1999 22.

[21] P Anderson, 'Russia's Managed Democracy' (2007) 29(2) *London Review of Books* 3–12.

parties seem more to be creatures of parliamentary blocs (or rather of the regime acting through parliament) than the other way around, that is, the parties serve the regime by conferring deliberative legitimacy and an appearance of parliamentary plurality. This is a plurality only of diverse client constituencies, who compete with one another for political favour or spoils from the presidential regime but are united in their undeviating support for it.[22]

Nonetheless all constitutional systems expressly accommodate party pluralism in the parliamentary scheme, though not necessarily in the constitution itself. In the Uzbek and Kazakh constitutions, parliamentary parties are recognised as factions for purposes respectively of electing the prime minister, or consulting with the president on his/her appointment,[23] but merit no other constitutional mention. Otherwise, the two constitutions refer only to generic 'deputies'. Neither the Turkmen nor the Tajik Constitution expressly contemplates any role for parliamentary parties as such; the Kyrgyz Constitution by contrast predicates the very functioning of the Jogorku Kenesh on parliamentary parties. However, the parliamentary-regulatory statutes and chamber rules for the Kazakh Majlis, Uzbek Legislative Chamber, and Tajik Majlisi Namoyandogan (but not the Turkmen Mejlis[24] or the Kazakh, Uzbek and Tajik upper chambers) provide a general basis for deputies to unite in either party factions or non-party (thematic or functional) groups; Kazakh senators are however permitted to unite in groups only (not on the basis of party affiliation).[25]

Whereas in the other cases, the organisation of parliamentary factions appears to be at the choice of the deputies, the Kyrgyz Constitution requires deputies to join parliamentary factions, inasmuch as they are elected on the basis of party lists. Jogorku Kenesh deputies who leave their faction lose their power. Kazakh deputies who leave or are expelled from the party in whose name they were elected

[22] B Dave, 'Kazakhstan's 2004 Parliamentary Elections: Managing Loyalty and Support for the Regime' (2005) 52(1) *Problems of Post-Communism* 3, 7.

[23] Uzb 98, Kaz 44(3).

[24] Uniquely, the Turkmen Mejlis Law makes no mention of either parties or factions. Tkm Law 09.01.2009.

[25] Taj Con Law 19.04.2000 52–53, Uzb Law 29.08.2003 9, Kaz Con Law 16.10.1995 34, Rules 08.02.1996 (Senate) 14.

lose their mandate.[26] Loss of party affiliation and its consequences do not seem to be contemplated for the Uzbek Legislative Chamber, the Tajik Majlisi Namoyandogan or the Turkmen Mejlis, a circumstance suggesting that party affiliation and party discipline are not in the end deemed essential for parliamentary processes (the role of factions in parliamentary structure and processes is discussed below). The Kyrgyz Constitution alone defines and provides for a parliamentary opposition (and moreover vests express powers and rights in it);[27] Uzbek legislation in the wake of the 2008 reforms however now also employs the term 'opposition' (and confers on the opposition express rights), but its practical as opposed to formal significance remains prospective only.[28] In the Kazakh, Tajik and Turkmen parliamentary systems, both the term and the underlying concept are lacking.

PARLIAMENT AS INSTITUTION: STRUCTURE, LEADERSHIP, DEVELOPMENT

In their brief life, the Central Asian parliaments have undergone significantly greater institutional development and sophistication as legislative bodies than their predecessor Republican Supreme Soviets did over many decades. Professionalisation of the legislator; elaboration of a committee system; socialisation to parliamentary usages and the rules of order; familiarisation with budgets, government records and documents; monitoring of the activities and responsibilities of officials; use of constituent surgeries and devotion to constituent relations generally; and development of legislative review and drafting

[26] Kyr 73(3.1), Kaz 52(5).

[27] Kyr 70 ('the faction or factions not entering into the composition of the parliamentary majority and having announced their opposition to it'); Kyr 74 (3.4, 3.5), 95(7) (elects one third of Electoral Commission, Accounts Chamber and Judicial Selection Council); 76(1) (representative chosen as chair of Budgetary Committee and Legal Order Committee); 75(1) (election to Deputy Toraga (Speaker) posts facilitated).

[28] Uzb 12.12.2002 Constitutional Law 25, Law 29.08.2003 (Legislative Chamber) 9 ('faction having announced itself the opposition', enjoys rights to present alternative versions of bills and minority reports to committees, present its own views on issues set for plenary discussion, and guaranteed participation in reconciliation commissions in the event of Senate rejection of a bill).

expertise are all general trends to be observed in parliaments across the region, although to significantly varying degrees.[29] Institutional development cannot simply be read off the regulatory framework, but it remains essential to understand the relations between the two.

The regional parliaments with the exception of the Jogorku Kenesh are the subject of dedicated constitutional laws, for the Uzbek Legislative Chamber and the Senate individually, and for the Kazakh Parliament, the Tajik Majlisi Olii, and the (single-chamber) Turkmen Mejlis. All eight chambers have also adopted internal Rules.[30] The need for separate parliamentary-regulatory statutes in the first place strikes the comparative constitutionalist as odd. The only quasi-parliamentary system in Central Asia lacks one: the Jogorku Kenesh is not regulated by any law save the constitution and its own Rules. The regulatory statutes typically repeat the constitutional provisions and supply further elaboration regarding the legislative process, the rights, privileges, liabilities and immunities of members, the structure of the chamber, and the regulation of parliamentary offices. Although these statutes are of course themselves laws adopted by the respective parliaments, they have not necessarily been authored or introduced by parliamentarians (unlike the Rules, which are at least presumptively drafted and adopted by them without any executive involvement, and so a species of parliamentary auto-regulation). They carry a constitutional charge even in the one instance (Turkmenistan) where they do not carry the title of constitutional law, and so seem in the nature of a framework externally provided for, rather than internally designed by, the lawmakers.[31]

Parliamentary leadership is constitutionally regulated for all eight chambers, variably but analogously, and then elaborated in the parliamentary-regulatory statutes. Typically, the chair of the chamber (eg Speaker of the Uzbek Legislative Chamber and Toraga of the Jogorku Kenesh), elected from among deputies, calls sessions to order and presides, prepares the legislative agenda, and co-ordinates the

[29] See eg Olcott (n 8) (lack of professionalism of Tajik Majlisi Oli).

[30] Tkm Resolution 09.01.2009, Uzb Law 29.08.2003 (Legislative Chamber), Law 29.08.2003 (Senate), Kaz Rules 08.02.1996 (Majlis), Rules 08.02.1996 (Senate), Taj Rules 10.11.2000 (Majlisi Milli), Rules 07.11.2001 (Majlisi Namoyandagon).

[31] The Kazakh Law on Parliament, Kaz Con Law 18.12.1995, was passed into law under presidential interim lawmaking authority prior to the convocation of the first parliament under the 1995 Constitution (indeed, two months prior to the first elections to that body).

committee work, and enforces discipline, among other responsibilities.[32] All the systems except Turkmenistan incorporate conciliar leadership for each chamber in a body of senior officials (typically, chair and deputy chairs of the chamber and chairs of the committees), charged with setting the legislative agenda, organising committee composition and work, administering disciplinary proceedings, and other global functions; the Jogorku Kenesh Coordinating Council alone also includes coalition heads and faction leaders.[33] The Kyrgyz Constitution in singular fashion provides that the deputy speakers are to be chosen in a manner and quantity 'facilitating their election' from among the opposition; the Uzbek Legislative Chamber Rules guarantee each faction a deputy Speaker post.[34] The parliamentary-regulatory statute and/or chamber rules for the Kazakh Majlis, Uzbek Legislative Chamber and Tajik Majlisi Namoyamdogan, but not the Turkmen Mejlis, provide for representation of parliamentary factions in leadership posts and/or procedures (eg questions or minority analyses).[35]

Each constitution provides for the formation of parliamentary legislative committees; the Kazakh Constitution uniquely limits their number to seven for each chamber.[36] The committee system is now well developed in all states. The parliamentary-regulatory statutes and/or the individual chamber rules elaborate the details of committee formation, typically vested with the speaker or chair of the chamber, and function in the legislative process (committees generally first review

[32] Taj 53, Kaz 58(3), Tkm 70, Law on Mejlis 17, Uz 85, 86, Kyr 75(1, 2).

[33] Uzb Con Law 12.12.2002 (Senate) 16 (Kengash), Uzb Con Law 12.12.2002 (Legislative Chamber) (Kengash); Kaz Con Law 16.10.1995 10 (Majilis Bureau, Senate Bureau); Taj Con Law 19.04.2000 27, 44 (Council of Majlisi Milli, Council of Majlisi Namoyandogan); Kyr Law 25.11.2011 24 (Coordinating Council)

[34] Kry 75 (1), Uzb Law 29.08.2003 4.

[35] Kaz Con Law 16.10.1995 10(2), Regulations (Majlis) 08.02.1996 161; Uzb Con Law 12.12.2002 (Legislative Chamber) 25, Taj Rules 07.11.2001 5, 63(1), 83, 106(4).

[36] Kaz 60(1), Uzb 87, Tkm 62, Taj 53, Kyr 76(1). There are at the time of writing 8 Legislative Chamber committees, 6 Uzbek Senate committees, 9 Majlisi Namoyandogan committees, 5 Majilisi Milli committees, 7 Kazakh Majilis committees, 6 Kazakh Senate Committees, 14 Jogorku Kenesh committees and 8 Mejlis committees. Detailed information on the current committee structure is available on the respective parliamentary websites (for the Turkmen Mejlis on the general government website, see www.turkmenistan.gov.tm/?id=5647, accessed 5 November 2015).

legislation and then report it out to the chamber). The Jogorku Kenesh Rules alone provide for PR of parliamentary factions on committees,[37] and moreover the Kyrgyz Constitution directly requires that the Chairs of the Budgetary and Legal System Committees be appointed from the parliamentary opposition, a genial innovation, thus ensuring pluralism of committee leadership as well as membership.[38] Of the other four cases, only the Uzbek parliamentary-regulatory statute provides that committee leaders and members be elected 'with account' of their party allegiance.[39]

The varying accommodation of parliamentary pluralism in the rules framework for the legislative bodies in the five states reveals a largely formalist approach. The Kyrgyz case stands out strikingly in its meticulous and comprehensive treatment: pluralism in parliamentary structure and functions is regulated at the level of the Constitution and factions are treated passim in virtually every provision of the Jogorku Kenesh rules. Indeed the Kyrgyz parliamentary system does not accommodate pluralism, it is premised on it—as indeed any parliamentary system worth the name ought to be. By contrast, in the Tajik, Uzbek and Kazakh systems, parliamentary pluralism is regulated discretely rather than integrally. The failure to ensure factional or minority representation on committees (as opposed to leadership posts and structures) is especially telling; of the three, only the Uzbek system even addresses the issue.

PARLIAMENTARY POWERS: LAWMAKING

As noted above,[40] in each state a sub-constitutional law on normative acts regulates the hierarchy of legislation generally. Normative legal acts are duly adopted and published legal documents which establish, abolish or modify a legal norm binding on its addressees. Normative legal acts may originate legislatively, with parliament or local representative bodies, or sub-legislatively, with officials or state organs (bodies) specifically authorised by legislation to promulgate them (ie analogous to

[37] Kyr Law 25.11.2011 25(3).
[38] Kyr 76.
[39] Uzb Con Law 12.12.2002 17.
[40] See ch 1.

regulatory acts in a common law context). They are of specific enumerated types: indeed, all five Central Asian legal systems have embraced the menagerie of legal acts[41] developed over first Russian and then Soviet bureaucratic practice, which can be daunting for English speakers since there are no precise equivalents to capture the nuances and degrees. Normative legal acts specifically exclude acts, determinations or decisions of bodies and officials of an individual character. Parliaments generally enjoy the unique competence to adopt laws and constitutional laws (*zakony* and *konstitustionnyie zakony*).

The constitutions vary revealingly in the breadth of legislative initiative they confer. The Kazakh Constitution is the most restrictive; the Uzbek broadest, including all three apex courts (only the Turkmen Constitution also vests initiative in the Judiciary) and the Procuracy, but excluding the Senate. The Kyrgyz Constitution is unique in excluding the President from the legislative prerogative and extending it to the general electorate (10,000 voters).[42] The parliamentary right of initiative is restricted in Tajikistan in respect of budgetary and tax bills and amnesty bills (vested in the Government and President alone, respectively); in Kazakhstan bills contemplating a decrease in state revenues or increase in expenditures are subject to Government pre-approval for parliamentary introduction.[43]

The legislative process across the three bicameral systems is broadly similar, but the two unicameral cases differ (unsurprisingly perhaps, since one is the chief governing organ in a parliamentary democracy, and the other a servile tool in a super-presidential autocracy). The Tajik, Uzbek and Kazakh constitutions all provide for consecutive consideration of proposed legislation first by lower, then upper,

[41] See eg Kaz Law 24.03.1998 3, Kyr Law 20.07.2009 4, Uzb Law 14.12.2000 5, Taj Law 08.12.2003 6, Tkm Law 07.12.2005 3.

[42] Kaz 61(1) (president, deputies of parliament, government), Tkm 65 (president, Cabinet of Ministers, deputies of the Mejilis, Supreme Court), Uzb 83 (president, legislature of Karakalpakstan, deputies of the Legislative Chamber, Cabinet of Ministers, Constitutional Court, Supreme Court, Higher Arbitration Court, General Procuracy); Taj 58 (members of the Majlisi Namoyandogan, deputies of the Majlisi Milli, president, government, Majlis of Gorno-Badakshan); Kyr 79 (10,000 voters, deputies of the Jogorku Kenesh and government).

[43] Taj 59, Kaz 61(6) (a 'positive conclusion of the Government must accompany any such bill, save when introduced by the President').

chamber.[44] Ordinary laws require a simple majority of votes in either chamber; constitutional laws (in Kazakhstan and Tajikistan) a two-thirds supermajority (and Kazakh Senate amendments to constitutional laws require a two-third Majlis majority to be sustained); in Tajikistan, uniquely, the lower chamber has the exclusive power to adopt budgetary and amnesty legislation.[45] In the event of rejection by the upper chamber, the Uzbek and Tajik constitutions both provide for a lower chamber override by two-thirds supermajority, in which case the bill is deemed adopted;[46] the Kazakh Constitution in the same event instead provides for a second consideration and vote by the Senate.[47] The Uzbek and Kazakh constitutions, in the absence of an override, or in the event of a partial rejection by the upper chamber, respectively, provide for reconciliation of the differences between the chambers;[48] the Tajik Constitution makes no express provision for reconciliation. All three constitutions provide that a presidential veto can be overridden by a two-thirds supermajority of both houses for ordinary laws, and a three-quarters majority in Kazakhstan and Tajikistan for constitutional laws.[49] The Kazakh Constitution provides uniquely that a bill for which a presidential veto has been sustained (at least one chamber has failed to reach the two-thirds threshold) is deemed not adopted *or adopted in the version proposed by the President.*[50]

Of the two unicameral systems, the Turkmen Constitution strikingly omits any treatment of legislative procedure; leaving the matter to subsidiary legislation, save in respect of the presidential veto, for

[44] Taj 59, 69 Kaz 54(1).

[45] Taj 60, 61, Kaz 61(5, 5.1). The Uzbek Constitution does not differentially regulate procedure for adoption of constitutional laws, save in requiring a three-quarters quorum in each chamber for their consideration. Uzb 81.

[46] Uzb 84, Taj 60, Kaz 61 (5) (only in the event it is returned by the Senate to Majlis with modifications; if rejected in toto by the Senate, a bill may be reaffirmed by a two-thirds Majlis supermajority and referred for a second Senate cons (Kaz 61(6)).

[47] Kaz 61(6) (a bill referred for repeat Senate consideration cannot then be re-introduced in the same session). Thus, the will of a rejecting Kazakh Senate, unlike even the will of a rejecting Kazakh president, stands regardless, for the duration of the session, at least.

[48] Uzb 84, Kaz 61(5).

[49] Kaz 54(2), Taj 62, Uzb 84.

[50] Kaz 54(2).

override of which a two-thirds supermajority is required.[51] Thus, the only constitutional regulation of Turkmen legislative procedure is to be found in the section relating to presidential powers. The Kyrgyz Constitution requires three readings of a legislative bill (the only constitutional provision in the region regarding this detail of the lawmaking process, and underscoring the extent to which Kyrgyz is a legislative republic), passage by a simple majority of deputies voting but no less than 30 of the 125 deputies. Constitutional laws require passage by a two-thirds majority of all 125 deputies.[52] A presidential veto of either a constitutional or an ordinary law may be overridden by a two-thirds supermajority of all 125 deputies. Uniquely, the Kyrgyz Constitution provides that in the event of the president's failure to sign a law following parliamentary override of a presidential veto, the *Toraga* (Speaker) signs it.

OTHER PARLIAMENTARY POWERS

Appointments/Removals

The constitutions generally afford parliaments (or particular chambers in bicameral systems) broad powers respecting the appointment and dismissal of the prime minister (all save Turkmenistan) and heads of state organs and apex courts (all five, and in the case of Kazakhstan members of apex courts; in the unique case of Tajikistan, lower-ranking judges as well), and ministers (Tajikistan, Kyrgyzstan, Turkmenistan). The powers of appointment and dismissal vary in their force and formulation (with or without presidential proposal, choice, confirmation, consent, consideration of the issue, approval of presidential decree), as in the chamber or chambers empowered (exclusive upper, exclusive lower, joint). The breadth of parliamentary authority in the Kyrgyz Constitution is sweeping; the powers of appointment and dismissal of the Jogorku Kenesh eclipse those of all other Central Asian parliaments and exceed those of the Kyrgyz President.

The Tajik Constitution empowers the two parliamentary chambers in joint session to approve the President's decrees of appointment or

[51] Tkm 53(7).
[52] Kyr 80 (3,4).

dismissal respecting not just the Prime Minister, but the members of Government as well.[53] The Tajik Majlisi Milli has the exclusive power to elect and recall upon presidential proposal the entire complement of judges of all courts (discussed in the next chapter below);[54] whereas the lower chamber, the Majlisi Namoyandogan, has the power to approve presidential decrees of the appointment of Central Bank chair and vice-chairs.[55] In Turkmenistan, the only pure presidential system in the region (without a prime minister), Mejlis powers respecting the Cabinet of Ministers are slender in the extreme. The Mejlis has the power to 'consider upon presentation by the President the issue of the appointment [NB the qualified formulation, unique among the five constitutions: not 'consider the appointment' or 'confirm the appointment'] to or removal from office of the Supreme Court Chair, General Procurator, Minister of Internal Affairs and Minister of Justice'.[56]

In Uzbekistan, the Senate has exclusive powers of election (upon presidential proposal), appointment and dismissal (upon presidential proposal), or confirmation of presidential decrees of appointment of dismissal, for a range of heads of state bodies.[57] The joint Olii Majlis possesses the power to review and confirm the candidacy of the Prime Minister, to confirm presidential decrees on the formation and disbanding of ministries, state committees and other state organs.[58] In Kazakhstan each chamber enjoys the power to appoint two members of the Constitutional Court, the Central Electoral Commission and the Accounts Committee.[59] Uniquely across the four super-presidential systems, the Kazakh Constitution establishes a procedure

[53] Taj 55.
[54] ibid. 56.
[55] ibid. 57(10).
[56] Tkm 63(7).
[57] Election: President of Constitutional Court, Supreme Court, Higher Economic Court (Uzb 80(2, 3, 4)); appointment/dismissal Head of State Environmental Protection Committee, diplomatic representatives, Chair of Central Bank (Uzb 80(5, 8, 9)); General Procurator, Chair of Accounts Chamber, Chair of National Security Service (Uzb 80(6, 7)).
[58] Uzb 78(13).
[59] Kaz 57.

for either chamber to request presidential dismissal of any member of Government for failure to uphold the laws.[60]

Pursuant to the great regional anomaly of the Kyrgyz Constitution, the majority faction of the Jogorku Kenesh, alone or in coalition, possesses the competence to choose within a 15-day period the candidate for Prime Minister (not from within its ranks, however, as deputies, unlike Westminster MPs, are forbidden simultaneously to hold any other post).[61] The candidate Prime Minister prepares the programme, structure and composition of Government for submission to the Jogorku Kenesh for confirmation and determination, all within the allotted period.[62] The President must issue a decree of appointment of the Prime Minister within three days (a purely secretarial function); otherwise she or he is deemed appointed.[63] Of the other four constitutions, only the Uzbek vests in the majority party of the Legislative Chamber the power to propose the candidacy for Prime Minister to the President.[64] The Kazakh Constitution, by contrast, grants the factions of the Majlis only a consultative role in selection of the Prime Minister by the President.[65]

Other Powers Vis-a-vis Government and President

Beyond their powers of appointment/removal of senior state officials, the parliaments, either jointly or as separate chambers, constitutionally

[60] At the initiative of one third of the deputies, the chamber summons a member of Government to report on questions of his/her performance, and by majority vote refers the issue of dismissal to the President. In the event the President declines to act, the chamber may make a second reference by majority vote within six months, obliging the President to dismiss. Kaz 57(6).

[61] Kyr 72(2).

[62] Kyr 84(1). In the event of the failure of the Jogorku Kenesh to comply with these requirements, the President asks another faction (on no specified basis) to form a majority coalition, choose a Prime Minister, and confirm and determine Government programme, structure and composition within a further 15-day period. Following a second failure to comply, the President asks a second faction; following a third failure, factions are free to form a coalition at their initiative. If a Government cannot be formed in the prescribed fashion, the President calls early parliamentary elections, as noted in ch 4 above. Kyr 84(2, 3, 4, 6).

[63] Also as noted in ch 4, the president retains the competence to appoint the members of Government with defence and security portfolios.

[64] Uzb 98.

[65] Kaz 44.

command additional ultimate control measures, notably including impeachment of the president (discussed above) and no-confidence in the government or ministers. The Uzbek, Kazakh and (necessarily) Kyrgyz constitutions authorise a parliamentary vote of no confidence (for the first 'in the Prime Minister', for the other two 'in the Government');[66] the Tajik and Turkmen do not.[67] The Kazakh Constitution also interestingly equates the failure by Parliament in joint session to confirm the Government's Report on the Execution of the Budget to a no-confidence vote (as well as authorising a no-confidence vote at Government call in the event of parliamentary rejection of government-introduced legislation).[68] Parliaments also exercise operational or supervisory responsibilities with respect to government programmes and the budget.[69] Individual deputies, even Turkmen Mejlis deputies, possess the constitutionally grounded rights to put questions to state organs or officials.[70]

All constitutions save the Turkmen contemplate a parliamentary role in the formation, appointment or oversight of the electoral commission (see the section immediately below). Pursuant to the Kyrgyz Constitution, the Jogorku Kenesh exercises control over the Ombudsman; Uzbek, Tajik and Kazakh subsidiary legislation contemplate some more limited parliamentary role respecting the ombudsmen or human rights plenipotentiary (the point is moot in Turkmenistan which lacks a human rights office).[71] The constitutions all grant parliaments (one or both chambers) authority for ratification or denunciation of international treaties.[72]

[66] Kaz 56(2) (majority vote of Majlis only upon initiative of at least one fifth number of deputies); Uzb 98 (two-thirds vote of both chambers upon initiative of one third vote of the Legislative Chamber in the event of 'persistent contradictions between Prime Minister and Legislative Chamber'; Kyr 85(3, 4) (majority vote on initiative of one third; no grounds specified).

[67] The Turkmen Constitution as noted above does contain a no-confidence proceeding respecting the President, effectively an impeachment. Tkm 57.

[68] Kaz 53, 61(7).

[69] The Mejlis has powers also (expressed with characteristic curious qualification) to 'review the issue of the approval of the programme of activity of the Cabinet of Ministers' as of 'the issue of the confirmation of the state budget' Tkm 63(2, 3).

[70] Tkm 66, Law 09.01.2009 37.

[71] Kyr 74.4(6, 7), 74.6(2), 108.

[72] Kaz 54.1 (jointly), Taj 57.5 (Majlisi Namoyandogan), Kyr 74.2(3), Tkm 63.9, Uzb 78.20 (jointly).

THE META-RULES OF REPRESENTATION

In any form of representative government, the meta-rules governing representation exercise profound effects on the outcome of the secondary rules governing representative decision-making. So the framework—bicameralism as against unicameralism, PR as against first-past-the-post territorial constituencies, boundaries for electoral districts, indirect versus direct election versus appointment—is a fateful matter. In Central Asia, these issues, and the multiple configurations of representative architecture they yield, have generally been matters for mandarins and not public debate or deliberation much less struggle and passion, save in the anomalous Tajik and Kyrgyz cases (which are treated in some detail in the final section of this chapter). For a constitutional analyst, the Central Asian comparative parliamentary laboratory is particularly fascinating and instructive at this meta-rule or representational framework level.

Districting

Electoral districting, usually an object of political contestation in developed electoral democracies (think of 'safe seats' in the UK characterised by observed consistencies between party affiliation and demographics), appears to be largely mechanical across Central Asia, following from inherited and unaltered Soviet administrative boundaries (see the discussion on local government in chapter eight). Save for Kyrgyzstan, which lacks them, territorial electoral districts are constitutionally or sub-constitutionally required to reflect rough parity of numbers of voters, though with account of territorial-administrative boundaries.[73] In some instances, however, the results have produced districts of very unequal size;[74] indeed it was a constitutional challenge to districting that was the ultimate trigger for the demise of the first post-Soviet Kazakh Republic.[75] The fixing of district boundaries for parliamentary elections (lower or single house) is vested in all four systems with the electoral

[73] Kaz Con Law 28.09.1995 21.2, Uzb Law 28.12.1993 7, Tkm 60.

[74] See eg Olcott (n 8) 10 (very populous Tajik district boundaries drawn in area not loyal to president).

[75] See ch 1.

commissions, by subsidiary legislation.[76] This power alone would make the electoral commissions of critical constitutional importance, even did they not command sweeping other powers.[77] The determinations of the electoral commissions are not subject to parliamentary approval (the electoral commissions are discussed in the section immediately below). The specified criteria for determination of Turkmen Mejlis, Kazakh Majilis, Tajik Majlisi Naomyandogan and Uzbek Legislative Chamber district boundaries are strictly numerical, that is, non-political, to ensure parity of representation, but the course of democratic politics elsewhere suggests that numbers inevitably become politicised, albeit perhaps not avowedly or formally. The Central Asian pattern of stunted or constrained party development might mean that the issue of presidential party 'safe seats' is some time away from emerging, and that districting will remain below the political waterline.

Proportional Representation versus First-Past-the-Post Territorial Constituencies

Only the Kyrgyz and Tajik constitutions adopt PR, in the former case across the board in the single chamber; in the latter case for a fair portion (one third) of the seats in the Majlisi Namoyandogan. In both cases the threshold for parliamentary seats for contesting parties is 5 per cent. PR is one proven constitutional device for ensuring a potential for national representation of parties without either territorial concentration or widespread depth of support, that could therefore not readily return candidates on the basis of single-mandate constituencies. The trade-off obviously is in the loss of 'local knowledge', close constituent-representative connections and communications, and a

[76] Kaz Elections Law 22 (Central and territorial commissions); Taj Law 10.12.1999 12.2; Uzb Law 28.12.1993 7 (Central Electoral Commission on proposal of provincial authorities); Tkm Electoral Code 04.03.2013 26.9 (Electoral Commission)

[77] In the UK, parliamentary constituencies are determined by Parliament on the basis of periodic reports of Boundary Commissions for England, Wales, Scotland and Northern Ireland, prepared after a lengthy public hearings process. In federal states, districts can be determined by legislatures of the component states (eg Congressional districts in the US) or by the national parliament (eg federal divisions in Australia, on the basis of Commission reports).

conveyor belt for concerns and claims straight from the voting periphery to the deliberative centre. There are formidable arguments for and against PR and alternatives (first-past-the-post, weighted voting, etc), but ideally those arguments should be raised and entertained in public fora: the representative formula itself, the constitutional meta-rules, should be a matter for public debate and contest. They should themselves be politicised and foregrounded rather than remaining ostensibly technical or background matters.

In both Central Asian cases, PR was brought in as a decidedly political objective only after an extended initial phase—almost a decade in Tajikistan, half a decade in Kyrgyzstan—of first-past-the-post single mandate constituencies, which were established as universal regional norm for all first generation constitutions. (In Kyrgyzstan, as discussed in the final section below, single mandate districts were brought back in again after another five years, and then eliminated definitively in favour of PR four years after that.) Whatever might be said on behalf of the objective merits or putative greater fairness of PR, the rapid consolidation of super-presidentialism could be conjectured to have settled the matter decisively, as first-past-the-post was clearly a superior political control device. The passage of anti-regime interests through the representational filter into parliament was less likely if that filter were territorially fine, not nationally coarse. In both Tajikistan and Kyrgyzstan PR became a rallying cry of the opposition as a constitutional device for undercutting super-presidential domination of parliament. In Tajikistan, it had the further political valence of enabling the fortunes of expressly Islamic parties. But first-past-the-post versus PR is not simply a binary choice: they are not mutually exclusive approaches, and the post-conflict Tajik Constitution incorporates them both. Indeed, in Tajikistan, the proportion of single to national Majlisi Namoyandogan seats was specifically contested between the UTO and the Government in negotiations, and remained unsettled until the eve of elections.[78]

Unicameralism versus Bicameralism

The predecessor SSRs all vested supreme legislative (as well as executive power) in a single-chamber parliament, the Supreme Soviet (unlike the

[78] OSCR/ODIHR 28.11.1999, 5.

Union Supreme Soviet, which was bicameral), with representatives elected on the basis of territorial electoral districts.[79] Bicameralism was tolerated in the Soviet scheme only as a pillar of Stalin's resolution of the national question and the creation of the Union: it was apposite exclusively to the federal level in a multinational scheme and hence unnecessary in the SSRs.[80] Otherwise, in the socialist understanding the very concept of an upper house betokened constitutionalised elitism and class domination. All of the independent states save Kyrgyzstan carried the unicameral scheme intact over into their initial post-Soviet constitutional arrangements. All of these but Turkmenistan have since added a second chamber (Kazakhstan in 1995, Tajikistan in 2000 and Uzbekistan in 2002), while reliably anomalous Kyrgyzstan has shifted in the opposite direction, inaugurating a bicameral parliament five years after the 1993 Constitution and then reverting to unicameral five years after that (2003). The regional experimentation with single versus plural chambers is intriguing and demonstrates that the question of single or dual chambers does not have a simple valence or political rationality.

The exclusion of party affiliation from the Kazakh and Uzbek Senates and the Tajik Majlisi Milli, ostensibly in order to ensure that deliberations are trans-partisan and statesman-like, as befits a senior body, sounds somewhat anachronistic and anomalous in context. If the lower houses in the three instances were in fact robustly partisan, there would be greater warrant in banning partisan politics at the senior chamber threshold. As matters stand, whatever the ostensible degree of partisanship in the lower houses (outside of Tajikistan and Kyrgyzstan, perhaps best described as token), the upper house members are to a man or woman (informal) presidential partisans, loyal to the incumbent. In the context of super-presidentialism the constitutional exclusion of partisanship from the Majlisi Milli and Kazakh and Uzbek Senates does not make them non-partisan or apolitical, it makes them reliably political and partisan in the only sense that matters: regime stalwarts. In Kazakhstan, the Senate has become a convocation of the politically eminent and trustworthy. Its chair was between 2011 and 2013 perhaps the country's best-respected jurist, the former and now once again Supreme Court chair (and former General Procurator as well).[81]

[79] eg Kaz SSR 1978 90.

[80] Venice Commission 11.12.2002.

[81] See Kazakh Supreme Court website, www.blog.sud.kz/en.

ELECTIONS AND TERM OF OFFICE

Even the cursory review of the series of Central Asian presidential elections in the first chapter reveals the striking fact that in no state has the initially established constitutional framework proved enduring, resembling more a collapsible wooden yurt-frame than structural steel. On one pretext or another, in every single one of the 'stans, terms have been extended (Kazakhstan 1995, Uzbekistan 2002, Turkmenistan 1994 and again 1999—the second time for life), and/or the clock has been reset for an incumbent with a new constitution (Uzbekistan 2002, Kazakhstan 1999), and/or terms limit have been extended (Kazakhstan 2000 yet again, Tajikistan 2003). The constitutional regulation of parliamentary elections has similarly although less brazenly undergone revision in all cases where a legislative chamber has been added (Kazakhstan 1995, Uzbekistan 2002, Tajikistan 1999) or subtracted (Kyrgyzstan 2003), the number of deputies augmented or diminished (Kyrgyzstan 1998), or changes to the basis of constituencies introduced (PR in Tajikistan 1999).

Rules and Referees

All five states have adopted comprehensive electoral legislation and all five constitutions have established a special regulatory body to administer and enforce it, the central electoral commissions.[82] The commissions delimit electoral districts, register voters and candidates, determine eligibility, monitor campaigning and financing, prepare and conduct polling, count and report results, issue regulations and directives, and entertain complaints at all stages. In each state, the commission has emerged as an immensely significant and powerful constitutional actor, effectively gatekeeper for the system as a whole: on its probity, independence and

[82] The constitutions provide for appointment of its chair and/or membership by parliament and/or president (the Turkmen Constitution alone creates an entirely presidential body with no parliamentary involvement whatsoever save to confirm its chair) Kyr 107, 74.4 (Jogorku Kenesh, nomination 1/3 president, 1/3 parliamentary majority, 1/3 opposition), Tkm 53.8 (president), Taj 57.1 (Majlisi Namoyandogan), Uzb 78.14 (Olii Majilis jointly), Kaz 44.7, 52.6, 57.1 (president and each chamber of parliament).

competence rides the legitimacy of all elected officials. As with other state organs, rules regulating the appointment and accountability of leadership and membership are critical, as are those ensuring adequate and fair representation of contending political forces in decision-making at all levels from headquarters to polling place.

All of the election laws have been the object of sustained and critical international engagement, in the context of monitoring of both parliamentary and presidential (though as a rule not local) elections by international bodies, most prominently the OSCE. Some laws contemplate a role for international monitors, with a view towards compliance with international standards (or placation of international actors). Candidacy rights have proved a recurrent sticking point in election law evaluation: onerous qualification requirements and correlative ease of disqualification, unequal access to public resources and systemic biases in favour of incumbents or ruling party candidates. The Tajik Majlis Oli election law, amended expressly pursuant to the 1997 peace accord (described in the section below) and subsequently amended again in 2003, was a particular focus of concern in the circumstances, and presents exemplary issues.[83]

Enforcement and Results

As noted in chapter three, in an age of programmatic democratisation, elections have assumed special prominence in 'transition states', for better or worse, as general proxy for democratic consolidation. Much may be said on the point against low-intensity democracy and the low standards thereby imposed, but Central Asian elections have as a general matter fallen short even at this 'technical' level. Litigation over candidate eligibility or selection, campaigning and electoral mechanics has been a recurrent feature of parliamentary and presidential elections, as the OSCE reports make plain. Even in sophisticated Kazakhstan,

83 Taj Law 10.12.1999, OSCE/ODIHR 26.07.2006, 4 (no criteria specified for CEC appointment, on presidential proposal), 7 (barriers to nomination), Assessment 17.09.2003, 5–6 (registration and de-registration). Similar issues have been identified in the other cases, eg Uzbekistan, OSCE/ODIHR 21.02.2005 Assessment (discriminatory registration requirements, neutrality of and appointments to electoral commission).

where challenge to presidential diktat has even been attempted, the courtroom rather than the ballot box has proved the principal arena of contestation.

As an example of the regional trends, in Kazakhstan, at every election there have been a flurry of complaints and legal proceedings, although most have been of a minor nature.[84] There have been numbers of adverse administrative rulings, citizen challenges and a smaller number of judicial appeals. In respect of minor violations and infractions, the system seems to function well enough; of greater concern are the infrequent but fateful disqualifications, de-registrations and the like, which undermine the democratic process. Opposition candidates standing for parliamentary and presidential elections routinely have been disqualified, often on the ground of dubious, trivial or politically motivated criminal convictions.[85] Authorities' clever manipulation of choice rather than crude manipulation of results is preferred, a perverse testament to their sophisticated appreciation of electoral legitimisation in the constitutional scheme (in distinction to the farcical process in Turkmenistan).

Elections do matter. In Kyrgyzstan, the reinstatement of single mandate constituencies by the 2003 amendments (see the final section below) fomented the Tulip Revolution: the results obtained at the first elections under the new system were so widely perceived as illegitimate that they sparked disturbances which eventuated in the ouster of the president. Of the 75 seats, ten were the subject of ongoing review or invalidation by the Central Election Commission (CEC) two months after the elections.[86] Popular resentment was running sufficiently high that the acting President called for new parliamentary as well as presidential elections, though only the former were held. Ironically, it was the illegitimate 2005 Jogorku Kenesh that led the parliamentary charge in the ultimately successful drive for a new Constitution.

Do elections and election laws really merit the hype, though? Election-law reform, elections-monitoring and elections-fetishism generally in unconsolidated democracies might compound the problem.

[84] See eg OSCE/ODHIR 15.12.2004, 16–17, 19–20.

[85] Olcott (n 8) 11; OSCE/ODIHR 15.12.2004, 11 (two opposition candidates not permitted to participate on the basis of presumptively politically motivated convictions).

[86] OSCE/ODIHR 20.05.2005.

The 'juridification' or 'lawyering' of the electoral process might produce the paradoxical result of more not less opportunity for interference with the process of democratic will-formation. Obviously, removal of discretionary authority and the elimination of potential for using substantive criteria of any sort for the qualification of either voters or candidates are desirable. But even the most assiduous and comprehensive reform of this nature will still leave any regulated process open to the manipulation of its formal elements for political gain. That is the ineradicable problem of all formal regulation of any sort, and its significance is mitigated only by background, extra-legal factors, such as the political culture. No amount of reforming and refining will prevent clever lawyers from finding purchase for their talons in the smoothest and most polished regulatory surfaces, in the Central Asian states as elsewhere. That's what lawyers are trained to do, particularly when they stand in the formidable tradition of Soviet legal formalism and of *diktat* in impeccable legal dress.

But here as elsewhere the critical issues are not ones of 'political technology' and foreground (or even background) rule-manipulation but of politics itself, not of contests but contestation, not of the exercise of choice but the nature and terms of choice. Soviet elections were always regarded as a sham, but as plebiscites or referenda they were really just a particularly exaggerated instance of a widespread phenomenon: the presentation of a single issue or a single candidate to an electorate, asked only to approve or reject. Plebiscites suffer from multiple democratic defects in the eyes of political theorists, since they do not offer the possibility of true contestation or alternatives: it is always yea or nay to a proposition the terms of which have been set elsewhere or to a candidate selected beforehand. This plebiscitary tradition has been continued across post-Soviet Central Asia, and is a feature of all systems except Kyrgyzstan. It commences with the constitutions themselves, all presented to citizens as *faits accomplis* after purely notional consultative processes.[87] (One might imagine as a thought experiment a plural constitutional election where alternative provisions, or even alternative drafts, were put to the vote instead of an agreed text, as elaborated in the last section below on Kyrgyzstan.) As chronicled in

[87] eg in the Tajik referendum of 2003, and the Kyrgyz referenda of 1996 and 1998, the ballots required a simple yes or no response to an elaborate list of highly technical and complex changes, which would have been sufficiently challenging

outline in chapter one, the five constitutions have undergone iterative amendment and in two cases wholesale replacement. Each set of amendments, has, like the original charter itself, been the subject of a plebiscite in the form of a referendum.

As the constitutional texts and amendments themselves have been plebiscites, so for the most part have the elections conducted under them. The invidious application of qualification and disqualification rules (in the context of much else, from campaign restrictions to voter list compilation) reduces the names on the slate and narrows the field of political choice. The inherited plebiscitary tradition of Soviet elections rather burdens the issue of elections in general. The answer to an incorrigibly plebiscitary system is not necessarily to try to reform the election process (or processes: candidacy, campaigning, polling, counting) itself, to move towards free and fair elections. Of course that is a good thing, but free and fair plebiscites are not much of an improvement over rigged and fraudulent ones. The opening up of the political process and the rise of democratic contestation is itself a process which will take place, when and if it ever does, within the political culture and not necessarily or even preferably in the run-up to and conduct of elections.

A TALE OF TWO PARLIAMENTS, AND TWO CONSTITUTIONS: TAJIK AND KYRGYZ

The course of constitutional development in Kazakhstan (after 1995), Uzbekistan and Turkmenistan has been entirely a function of presidential will. In Tajikistan and Kyrgyzstan, however, constitutional arrangements are the outcome of a struggle, of two very different kinds and with two very different outcomes. Not only is each constitution and its tumultuous narrative instructive in its own right, but the juxtaposition of the two affords particular critical insights about the fate of constitutionalism in Central Asia and generally. What follows is not a chronicle but an analysis of especially salient features.

for someone with a higher legal education to parse, let alone ordinary Tajik and Kyrgyz citizens. In the Tajik case, the multitude and meticulousness of the changes is something of a testament to the status of constitutional formalism. Kyr Laws 16.02.1996, 21.10.1998; Taj 22.06.2003 Amendments.

Post-Conflict Constitutionalism: Tajikistan

The history of Tajik politics since 1999[88] offers yet another depressing demonstration of the regional pattern of the colonisation of parliamentary space by executive authority but the circumstances are singular. The Tajik parliamentary system is unique not only as the product of a negotiated resolution of an armed conflict but as the product of an *internationally mediated* resolution, 'international peace-building'. Indeed the very constitutional idiom of the resolution and the resulting prominence of the constitutional reforms may be attributed in significant part to the role of the international community and to the liberal conceits of constitutionalism animating it.[89] The belligerent sides might not have gone to war over the structure of the state as such but they were eventually persuaded to end the war in part by redesigning it (or at least tweaking it).[90] However, far from redeeming the good name of liberal constitutionalism, the long-term conceptual and political involvement of international expertise and prestige in the Tajik normative framework for governance may sooner have revealed it as hollow. However 'reformed' (and as the discussion below suggests, the term is at least problematic), the Majlisi Namoyandogan and the Majlisi Milli, together with the all the other constitutional contrivances of Tajik government, remain artefactual and remote from the lives of the citizenry, ruses and pageants of power to which people resign themselves and adapt, much as they did with their Soviet-era equivalents.

[88] J Heathershaw, *Post-conflict Tajikistan: The Politics of Peacebuilding and the Emergence of Legitimate Order* (London, Routledge, 2009) 87–116; Olcott (n 8) 11–16.

[89] The Tajik peace agreement in 1997 came at the height and in the full hubris of international peace-building as a signature enterprise of post-Cold War multilateralism. See Heathershaw (n 88) for a critique of the 'performance' aspect of peace-building and democratisation in Tajikistan, the script of democratisation which international actors enact and stage by proclaiming progress rather than objectively assessing actual political dynamics.

[90] The Tajik agreement gave the National Reconciliation Commission and the president the following functions and powers 1) referendum for amendments and additions to the existing Constitution; 2) new law on elections to Parliament and the local representative bodies; 3) establishment of a Central Elections Commission; and 4) reform of the Government (UTO representatives in ministries, departments, local authorities, judicial bodies and law enforcement agencies). General Agreement 27.06.1997.

The Tajik civil war, by a wide margin the most violent and destructive of the conflicts in the wake of the Soviet collapse, was particularly complex, with a welter of factions representing rival bureaucratic power centres, ethnic labour migrants from peripheral areas, reform elements, Islamists, youth gangs, party militias and opportunistic warlords, as well as decisively intervening Russian and Uzbek forces. After a complete disintegration of state authority, the conflict coalesced around the Russian-backed reconstituted government under Rakhmon (then Rakhmonov) and the United Tajik Opposition under Said Nuri, an unlikely coalition of Islamists and reformers. Rakhmon and Nuri would go on to negotiate the 1997 peace agreement between them, under the auspices of a UN-sponsored process, with participation from the other four Central Asian states as well as Russia, Afghanistan, Iran, Pakistan, the OSCE and the Organisation of the Islamic Conference.[91] The Tajik constitutional system, to be reformed in the interests of accommodating pluralism, had initially been cobbled together in the throes of the conflict itself by one of the belligerent parties (the Constitution was adopted in 1994 and the first presidential elections held that year), and so could hardly claim general credibility. It was never a particularly promising prospect for redemption.

The post-1999 Tajik political system, with the amended Constitution itself a post-conflict document, subordinated constitutional reform to the realpolitik of conflict resolution. The result can be judged leniently: whatever its super-presidentialist shortcomings, it has rendered a renewal of hostilities remote. It can also be judged harshly: the missed opportunity effectively to secure pluralism, constitutionalism or democracy meant a hollow peace. The devil is in the details, though: the 1999 amendments adopted in the referendum pursuant to the accord were succeeded in 2003 by a further set of amendments which arguably contravened at least the spirit of that accord. The first amendments enhanced and transformed parliamentarianism by creating the Majlisi Milli and establishing election by party lists for 34 per cent of the Majlisi Namoyandogan seats but affected presidentialism more ambiguously, extending the presidential term to seven years

[91] ER Hay, 'Methodology of the Inter-Tajik Negotiation Process' in K Abdullaev and C Barnes (eds), *Politics of Compromise: The Tajikistan Peace Process* (London, Conciliation Resources, 2001) 39.

but imposing a one-term limit. The further amendments four years later clearly strengthened and entrenched presidentialism, doubling the term limit and resetting the clock, thus granting the incumbent the possibility to serve a further fourteen years at the expiry of the then-current term in 2006. As noted earlier, at the same time as a bid for greater presidential self-aggrandisement, the referendum displayed some considerable concern for the text.

The 1999 amendments may be viewed as militating in divergent ways. The creation of an upper chamber favoured regional interests, while the allotment of a portion of seats in the lower chamber to national party lists favoured cross-regional interests and more faithfully reflected national political pluralism, particularly in conjunction with the legalisation of confessional parties (the only such constitutional provision in the entire region). However, in the first parliamentary elections under the new dispensation (and the new election law, which had been an integral part of the deal and was discussed above), the opposition which had fought the conflict and negotiated the agreement took only two seats. While it might be urged that the amendments were not bold enough (eg as might have been an all-PR Majlisi Namoyandagon), the Majlisi Oli election results then and in the years since soberly remind us that no amount of constitutional engineering, however inspired or internationally endorsed, is sufficient to achieve the desired accommodation of pluralism.[92] As was argued above in the case of election laws generally, any set of formal rules of choice (whether for the post-conflict Tajik elections or the 2000 US presidential elections) is subject to manipulation and instrumentalisation, crude or clever, and can be evaluated only for the degree of its susceptibility.

As significant as what the 1999 constitutional amendments did to seal the peace deal is what they omitted to do, since the other major agreed provision—the power-sharing arrangements, by which 30 per cent of central government positions were to be awarded to the UTO—was in effect a side-deal, memorialised but never constitutionalised.[93] The failure of the constitutional text itself as amended to pluralise the

[92] See Heathershaw (n 88) 94–103 for a sobering analysis of the 2005 elections as 'authorised by the elite'.

[93] 18.05.1997 Protocol on political issues, annexed to General Agreement 27.06.1997 3 (percentage not specified).

appointments procedures for state institutions or government posts (in the manner of, eg, the 2010 Kyrgyz Constitution) is damnable; changes in posts without changes in rules, division of the spoils in the absence of mechanisms of and structural constraints on decision-making, is nothing but a one-off.[94] In any event, the 30 per cent distribution formula was never fully carried through, and attrition in the years following resulted in the current occupation of all public offices by the President's men and women.[95] Indeed the opposition as such appears to have vanished from the Tajik parliamentary and bureaucratic scene altogether. It only existed while outside the constitutional system, on the wrong side of the law; once it was enfranchised and legalised it effectively melted away (or was co-opted by and incorporated into the presidential patronage system),[96] an occurrence which says as much about the capacity of the constitutional system to sustain effective pluralism and diversity as it does about the staying power or political will of politicians.[97]

Roundheads Triumphant: Kyrgyzstan

The Kyrgyz constitutional fortunes of presidency and parliament described a regionally familiar and not especially edifying course for its first decade and a half. A succession of amendments in 1996, 1998 and 2003 had the effect of augmenting presidential at the expense of parliamentary authority, as well as of fundamentally altering the parliamentary structure and electoral basis. But in the years since, those fortunes have dramatically departed from type, culminating in a triumph of the roundheads. The 2010 Kyrgyz Constitution, unlike any of its sibling regional constitutions, is the outcome of serious, informed

[94] See R Zoir and S Newton, 'Constitutional and Legislative Reform' in K Abdullaev and C Barnes (eds), *Politics of Compromise: The Tajikistan Peace Process* (London, Conciliation Resources, 2001).

[95] Heathershaw (n 88); Olcott (n 8) fn 90.

[96] As discussed in ch 7 below, the patronage or neo-patrimonial system has good claim to being deemed the operative constitutional system, the real 'material constitution'.

[97] The Islamic Revival Party secured two seats (national list) out of 63 in the 2010 elections, but lost those in the 2015 elections. OSCE/ODIHR 05.02.2014, 6, 33, OSCE/ODIHR 15.05.2015.

political bargaining over fundamental matters of constitutional design, by political factions with distinct interests and corresponding constitutional positions. It is exceptional not just by regional but also by world standards, and recalls the South African constitutional negotiations.[98] Such noisy, foreground contestation in a constituent process might appear unseemly but it illustrates in an exemplary fashion the manner in which the ostensibly extraordinary politics of constitutional moments is permeated with ordinary politics, and combines low political calculation with lofty regard for posterity.

Over the same course of amendments, the make-up of the Jogorku Kenesh itself has undergone dizzying serial alteration—think of a mad geneticist inducing mutations and reverse mutations to the constitutional DNA to see what would happen to the political system. The original 1993 Constitution established a unicameral Jogorku Kenesh of 105 deputies representing single territorial constituencies. The 1998 amendments created an upper house of 70 representatives indirectly elected by region and a lower house of 35 representatives directly elected on the basis of a single national district. The amendments two years later reversed the proportions, reducing the seats in the upper house to 45 and raising those in the lower house to 60. In 2003, a further set of amendments restored a unicameral Jogorku Kenesh of 70 seats, once again elected on the basis of single-member constituencies. In 2007, that number was raised to 90, only this time in another volte face territorial districts once again ceded place to nationwide party lists. Thus, the Kyrgyz parliament has see-sawed between unicameralism and bicameralism, within bicameralism between ratios of seats in the two chambers, and between PR and single member constituencies for the lower or single chamber. The very volatility of the formulae for the Jogorku Kenesh seats is testament to the political salience of representation in an endemically decentralised polity, much less susceptible to central management than the similarly regionalised case of Tajikistan.[99] However, the ongoing tussles over parliamentary seats and chambers in the years leading up to the 'Second Kyrgyz Republic' of 2010 must

[98] H Klug, *The Constitution of South Africa: A Contextual Analysis* (Oxford, Hart Publishing, 2010) 29–32.

[99] S Radnitz, *Weapons of the Wealthy: Predatory Regimes and Elite-led Protests in Central Asia* (Ithaca NY, Cornell University Press, 2012).

be assessed against the background pattern of inexorable presidential encroachment: a rearrangement of orchestral forces under the direction of a Toscanini determining and conducting the score.

Nonetheless, unlike any other Central Asian state, any other post-Soviet state, any other post-socialist state, and indeed any other state in this heyday of World Constitutionalism, Kyrgyzstan had become habituated or socialised to ongoing constitutional experimentation of a fairly fundamental sort—a kind of constitutional Maoist 'permanent revolution'. An enthusiast for the dynamic constitutionalism of Kyrgyzstan in the context of regional stasis and stagnation should resist the temptation to put it all down to 'democratisation'. Kyrgyz constitutional ferment, while it might carry democratic implications or create conditions favourable to subsequent democratic development, reflects the play of elite interests—politics emphatically, but democratic politics only dubiously. From a constitutional lawyer's standpoint, however, whatever the motivations and the dynamics bringing about the new constitutional order, what counts is the further development and consolidation (or not) of that order. What fascinates is that it was *constitutional* politics, rather than the usual sort, that got activated in Kyrgyzstan, even if largely for partisan and parochial reasons. Kyrgyz constitutionalism is very much the most absorbing and intriguing in the region precisely because it has been politicised, cathected by the energies and interests of politicians (not necessarily or especially 'democratic' politicians, whatever such might be).

'Subversive clientelism' has been proposed as the mechanism for the 2005 'Tulip Revolution': the mobilisation by emergent regional elites of cultivated networks of poor clients against an authoritarian centre, clients dependent on them for substitute social service provision in the absence of reliable state support.[100] In such circumstances democratic rhetoric and popular participation do not necessarily equate to 'bottom-up' democratic politics. The constitutional activation so striking a feature of the recent Kyrgyz scene might well be a concomitant or corollary of 'subversive clientelism'. The same regional elites mobilising their clients against the regime appear through their parliamentary factions to have been seeking to remould the political system nearer to the heart's desire, that is, from presidential to parliamentary form.

[100] ibid. 20.

Elite-manipulated street-level regime change in 2005 and 2010 could be viewed in this light as a condition precedent to system redesign (making future 'regime change' less significant a strategy). Once the balance of power was shifted to the Kyrgyz roundheads (as it appears to have been in the 2010 quasi-parliamentary republic) and 'the Crown' was brought to heel, the sense of their struggle necessarily changed.

In 2006, for the first time, multiple alternative drafts of fundamental constitutional provisions governing the balance of powers between executive and legislative, comprehensively elaborated, were in circulation and under general discussion (at least by the interested factions, if not by the wider public).[101] This circumstance is unprecedented not only in Central Asian constitutionalism, but is a rarity anywhere—the author is not aware of a comparable process across the entire transition zone. This simultaneous breadth of choice was a freak of Kyrgyz politics but raises some fascinating counterfactuals. What if this sort of thing were the norm in world constitutionalism—what if alternative conceptions of the organisation of government, at the level of the fundamental nature of the system (parliamentarianism as against presidentialism) as well as at the level of particular constitutional parameters (terms of office, appointment powers, etc) were a matter of simultaneous choice and comparison? What if constitutions or constitutional provisions were like candidates, that is, competing and contrasting? What if the constituent process itself were made contestatory and competitive, rather than consultative and consensual? What if alternative constitutions (constitutional provisions) stood against *each other* and fought for votes? What if the constituent process itself were fully and openly politicised, if not democratised?

The Kyrgyz constituent processes also benefitted from international involvement, but in a starkly different manner to the Tajik case: not in the form of prescriptive straight-jacketing (the democracy/liberal institutions agenda and stock script of international peace-building), but of open-ended consultation and consideration of genuine alternatives. The Kyrgyz *Toraga* applied to the Venice Commission in June 2005 in the wake of the Tulip Revolution to request assistance in constitutional reform. The Commission, deepening its constitutional engagement with Kyrgyzstan underway since 2002, provided sus-

[101] Venice Commission 28.09.2006.

tained and meticulous expertise throughout the tumult of 2005–06 and again in the context of the drafting of the 2010 Constitution.[102] More important in the reform process than international expertise, however sound, was the rough-and-tumble of political negotiations and manoeuvres, the constitutional academy of the streets. The Kyrgyz lawmakers themselves all underwent accelerated on-the-job constitutional law training, of a sort that most constitutional lawyers themselves never have the benefit of, as the author can attest, having interviewed opposition deputies of the Jogorku Kenesh in the spring of 2007. Here the alternative formulations carried immediate practical implications and were vigorously (indeed clamorously) debated.

FURTHER READING

K Abdullaev and C Barnes, *Politics of Compromise: The Tajikistan Peace Process* (London, Conciliation Resources, 2002).

M Bader, 'The Legacy of Empire: A Genealogy of Post-Soviet Election Laws' (2012) 37 *Review of Central and East European Law* 449.

J Heathershaw, *Post-conflict Tajikistan: The Politics of Peacebuilding and the Emergence of Legitimate Order* (London, Routledge, 2009).

S Khakimovr, 'Constitutionalism in Tajikistan: Toward Democracy or Greater Authoritarianism?' (2013) 14 *Central Asia and the Caucasus Journal of Social and Political Studies* 122.

S Radnitz, *Weapons of the Wealthy: Predatory Regimes and Elite-led Protests in Central Asia* (Ithaca NY, Cornell University Press, 2012).

A Stepan and C Skach, 'Constitutional Frameworks and Democratic Consolidation: Parliamentarianism Versus Presidentialism' (1993) 46(4) *World Politics* 1.

[102] Venice Commission 24.10.2005, 28.09.2006, 17.12.2007, 04.06.2010. The Venice Commission has rendered isolated opinions for Uzbek (1), Kazakh (2) and Tajik (2) legislation as well, but the depth and breadth of its relationship with Kyrgyzstan (multiple opinions over more than a decade on fundamental constitutional reform inter alia) is unique.

6

Honour in the Breach

Rights, Courts and Justice

Constitutional Role and Functions of the Central Asian Judiciaries – Constitutional Evolution of the Central Asian Judiciaries – Governance: Judicial Personnel Management and Court Administration – Structure and Functions: The Five Court Systems – Constitutional Basis of the Central Asian Justice System: Internal Affairs, Justice and the Procuracy – Rights and Remedies – Judicial Protection – International Protection – Supplementary Protection: Procuracy and Human Rights Institutions

IN CONTEMPORARY CONSTITUTIONAL discourse, a great deal appears to ride on the role of the judiciary in the regulation of the constitutional system itself—'world constitutionalism' is really a matter of the spread of constitutional adjudication.[1] For the societies of the Bloc, this phenomenon acquired particular force and significance. Constitutional courts emerged as the pivotal or hinge institution in the post-communist moment and judicial review became the defining process of transitional constitutionalism, in places like Poland

[1] B Ackerman, 'The Rise of World Constitutionalism' (1997) 83 *Virginia Law Review* 771.

and Hungary.[2] Constitutional courts played an indispensable role in the consolidation of post-communist constitutional systems, umpiring the fractious relations between legislative and executive branches and enforcing rights and rules. In the Russian Federation itself, which faced vertical as well as horizontal separation of powers issues in the context of its inherited complex ethno-territorial federalism, the Constitutional Court also flexed its institutional muscle and asserted its designated authority.[3]

By contrast, although formally embracing judicial supremacy and enshrining judicial review in the new constitutions (with the exception of Turkmenistan), the Central Asian states were not prepared to cede any real ground to a neutral enforcement institution. Rather than progressively resolved through constitutional jurisprudence, Central Asian legislative–executive tensions were pre-empted by the super-presidentialist turn—immediately in Uzbekistan and Turkmenistan, within a brief period in Kazakhstan, after the war in Tajikistan, but only provisionally and incompletely in Kyrgyzstan. Even in Kyrgyzstan, where inter-branch struggles became chronic and constitutional separation-of-powers and rights protection issues have remained live and in play, constitutional adjudication has proved a marginal factor. That is not to deny that a constitutional jurisprudence of considerable sophistication or ingenuity has in some instances (notably Kazakhstan and Kyrgyzstan) arisen, but rather to gauge soberly its relation to the structure of constitutional authority.

In the Soviet period, courts figured not at all in the maintenance and maturation of the constitutional scheme, save in the endgame. They played no 'process-policing' role; they had no powers of constitutional review of legislation; they did not guard against executive over-reaching; and they did not enforce or protect citizen rights as such. They were as weak and acquiescent (subject to political instruction) as

[2] R Teitel, 'Post-Communist Constitutionalism: A Transitional Perspective' (1994) 26 *Columbia Human Rights Law Review* 167 ('Instead of new constitutional texts, the dominant constitutional phenomenon in the post-communist transitions … is the emergence of constitutional courts.')

[3] J Henderson, *Constitution of the Russian Federation* (Oxford, Hart Publishing, 2011) 206–14; R Sharlet, 'Transitional Constitutionalism: Politics and Law in the Second Russian Republic' (1995–96) 14 *Wisconsin International Law Journal* 495; see generally A Trochev, *Judging Russia: Constitutional Court in Russian Politics, 1990–2006* (Cambridge, Cambridge University Press, 2008).

any other 'organ of state power', perhaps even weaker because farther removed from decision-making structures. The generally supine and subordinate place of the Soviet judiciary and its complete removal from constitutional (indeed governmental) affairs were fateful for the successor Central Asian judiciaries. These judiciaries would have required a near-miraculous (and accelerated) institutional transformation as well as a nurturing political climate in order to stand any chance of assuming their newly prescribed constitutional stature.

The congenital weakness of the Central Asian judiciary was burdened by new complications: the sudden severance of access to the material, technical and professional support and development resources concentrated at the Union level, super-presidentialist control mania and corruption, for starters. The court systems were not only unlikely to achieve substantive supremacy at the apex of the constitutional systems, they were largely incapacitated from fulfilling their basic constitutional role to protect citizen rights and administer justice. The constitutional courts and councils might have been innovations, but the ordinary courts (including the supreme courts) and the rank-and-file judges were just the rebaptised courts and judges of the SSRs, making for significant continuity not merely in judicial culture and practice, but in institutional structure and governance—as well as personnel. In consequence, the now-sovereign Central Asian states, despite placing impressive catalogues of rights at the head of their independence constitutions, rapidly acquired a reputation as laggard in their enforcement of those rights, as in their compliance with the concomitant international obligations they had assumed as well.[4] Indeed, they seemed to out-Herod the late Soviet Herod.

This chapter accordingly tracks both the constitutional and wider enforcement vicissitudes of the Central Asian judiciaries. It takes up the issues of constitutional review, structure and governance of the judiciary and of the justice system more broadly, including particularly the role of the Procuracy and the Justice and Interior Ministries. It also examines the human rights protection framework for each of the five states and its effectiveness and evaluates the significance of international monitoring and assistance.

[4] All five acceded to the International Covenants, though not immediately (Kyrgyzstan 1994, Uzbekistan 1995, Turkmenistan 1997, Tajikistan 1999, Kazakhstan 2006), as well as the other principal human rights instruments. See discussion below.

CONSTITUTIONAL ROLE AND FUNCTIONS OF THE CENTRAL ASIAN JUDICIARIES

Determination of the constitutionality of a legal norm was an innovation of late perestroika[5] which had previously been unknown to the Soviet constitutional order but was carried on by most of the successor states. The Uzbek, Tajik, Kazakh and Kyrgyz constitutions have all created constitutional tribunals: either a dedicated council (Kazakhstan), a dedicated apex court (Uzbekistan, Tajikistan) or a dedicated chamber of an apex court (Kyrgyzstan). The Turkmen Constitution omits to provide a dedicated constitutional organ or indeed any mechanism for judicial review of legislation or the challenge of the constitutionality of a legal act even on the grounds of its infringement of fundamental rights. The four Central Asian review bodies are variably authorised not only to determine the constitutionality of challenged laws and other normative acts (judicial review in the strict sense), but also to review elections, resolve disputes over constitutional authority, clarify meaning of constitutional provisions, and strike down laws and other acts infringing citizen rights. In all four constitutions the review is abstract, that is, relating to a norm, not a case (the issue of the constitutionality of the norm may arise in a pending case, but the review by the constitutional tribunal is strictly confined to the norm).

The remit of and standing to apply to the constitutional review bodies vary in subtle but significant ways. All bodies have abstract review over the constitutionality of legislation:[6] the Kazakh Council only over laws (*zakony*) between parliamentary adoption and presidential signature, as well as over parliamentary resolutions[7] (but not regulations, ordinances, decrees of other competent central state or local government organs); the Uzbek and Tajik Courts and the Kyrgyz Chamber over all normative acts (including laws already in force) at

[5] Henderson (n 3) 201–03.

[6] 'Conformity with the constitution' for Uzbek and Tajik Courts and the Kazakh Council; 'declaration of unconstitutionality' for the Kyrgyz Chamber.

[7] Competence respecting parliamentary resolutions established pursuant to the wake of the 2007 amendments. Constitutional Council of the Republic of Kazakhstan (2010), *The Constitution of Kazakhstan: A Scientific–Practical Commentary* (Almaty, Raritet) available at www.ksrk.gov.kz/data/filedat/default/28-10-10-3-rus.zip, accessed 6 November 2015) [Конституция Республики Казахстан: Научно-практический комментарий.– Алматы: Раритет, 2010] 312.

all levels (enumerated and specifically including presidential acts for the first two); the Tajik Court can review all apex court acts as well, a review power not possessed by the other three constitutional review bodies, thus becoming a 'meta-supreme' judicial instance for matters of constitutionality.[8] All review bodies also determine the constitutional conformity of international treaties before entry-into-force or (for the Uzbek Court) of 'international treaty obligations,' and all bodies review proposed constitutional amendments.

The Kazakh Council and the Tajik Court have final judicial review over elections and referenda;[9] the Kazakh Council and the Uzbek Court have the power to issue authoritative interpretations of constitutional norms. The Tajik Court alone has the express power to resolve disputes between and among central and local organs over competence, independently of the determination of constitutionality of normative legal acts (an important umpiring role not accorded the other review bodies).[10] The Uzbek Court alone has federalist review over the conformity of the Karakalpak Constitution and laws with the umbrella Uzbek Constitution.[11] Finally and critically, the Kazakh Council, the Tajik Court and the Kyrgyz Chamber all have a separate and distinct constitutional rights jurisdiction, apart from their general review powers, which permits them to review any legal normative act infringing constitutionally guaranteed rights and freedoms (the only way in which the Kazakh Council can review a law already entered into force, but only on the reference of a court not the application of an individual claimant). Standing is broadest in Kyrgyzstan and Tajikistan; both constitutional panels entertain petitions from any natural or legal person alleging the infringement of a right by a legal act (such standing is itself constitutional in the Kyrgyz case, but sub-constitutional in the Tajik).[12]

For all review bodies, a wide range of state actors has standing (by designation or inclusion) to make application depending on its subject matter: the president, prime minister and/or government, leaders of the parliamentary chambers and/or parliament and chambers, groups

[8] Taj 89(1).

[9] Kaz 72(1), Taj Con Law 03.11.1995 14(d).

[10] Taj 89(2), Taj Con Law 03.11.1995 14(e).

[11] Uzb 109(2).

[12] Kaz 78, Taj Con Law 03.11.1995 14 (pursuant to Taj Law 20.03.08), Kyr 97(7).

of deputies, apex court or all courts (Kyrgyz Chamber and Kazakh Council); other central and/or local officials and/or bodies; the General Procurator; (Tajik and Uzbek Courts, Kyrgyz Chamber) and the Ombudsman (Tajik Court for rights cases and Kyrgyz Chamber generally).[13]

In none of the jurisdictions is incidental review contemplated of the 'cases or controversies' sort. That is, a dispute may not be appealed to the constitutional review bodies on the grounds that it raises constitutional issues; the review bodies exercise no appellate or supreme jurisdiction. In this respect, they all are specialised constitutional tribunals (like the French *Conseil Constitutionnel* or the German *Bundesverfassungsgericht*) rather than apex courts deciding constitutional questions inter alia (like the US Supreme Court). Neither are the four constitutional review bodies courts of human rights as such, although their jurisdiction clearly encompasses rights insofar as they are alleged to be infringed by legislation which would thereby contradict the constitution (for the Tajik, Kazakh, and Kyrgyz review bodies expressly). A recurring issue is the boundary between supreme court and judicial review jurisdiction. Although, as discussed below, three of the four Central Asian judicial review bodies do have specialised rights jurisdiction, it is over normative legal acts (legislation)[14] and not individual official actions or decisions.

The jurisprudential record of the Uzbek and Tajik Courts, the Kazakh Council and the Kyrgyz Chamber is something of a mirror of the constitutional soul for the respective states. As an umbrella point, no review body appears to have taken a decision directly adverse to the central authorities (apart from individual rights cases). The Uzbek Court, which has no constitutional rights jurisdiction as such, has rendered a total of 22 decisions in about as many years, and thus can appear largely ornamental. The Kyrgyz Chamber (successor to the Court under the pre-2010 Constitution, which had a similar remit) and the Tajik Court have both entertained a significant number of individual rights applications, as well as ruling on the constitutionality of a range of normative acts and elections.

[13] Kyr Con Law 13.06.2011 20, Taj Con 03.11.1995 37, Uzb Law 30.08.1995 19, Kaz Con Law 29.12.1995 20.

[14] See discussion in ch 2 and Henderson (n 3) 5–6.

The stand-out exception is Kazakhstan's Constitutional Council, which has consistently produced cogently and comprehensively argued decisions, and has amassed an impressive cumulative record of meticulous constitutional deliberation. It has treated routine constitutional issues (such as limits and time periods) as well as protected substantive rights (like freedom of expression in the context of a new Law on Media) and ruled on separation of power issues (like Majlis authority for self-dissolution or extension by referendum of Presidential term).[15] Just as 'telephone justice' was after Stalin exceptional rather than routine for the simple reason that political prosecutions ('anti-Soviet activity') accounted for a marginal percentage of criminal cases, so has a serious constitutional tribunal like the Kazakh Council managed 'impartially' to address sundry issues that do not implicate the presidential balance of power. In other cases, like the 2011 extension-of-term referendum (a bravura piece of constitutional theatre, see chapter one above), it has employed sophisticated but results-orientated constitutionalist reasoning to preserve appearances and leave the formal balance of power undisturbed, exhibiting a stark disparity between the force of constitutional reasoning and its consequences: the mountains have laboured and brought forth a mouse. Of course, even in resolving quotidian issues, judges of the Constitutional Council may be subject to all sorts of ideological and political biases stemming from their socialisation in an authoritarian and super-presidentialist milieu.

Nonetheless, the place of the Constitution in Kazakh legal and political culture is now supreme and secure, and prodigious talent and expertise have been developed and deployed in the process. Constitutionalism has been thoroughly nativised, as witness the evident quality of the Constitutional Council's decisions and of constitutional scholarship,[16] demonstrating the formidable conceptual capacities

[15] Kaz Constitutional Council Rulings 21.04.2004 (Media Law unconstitutionally infringes right to freedom of expression); 13.04.2012 (period of years or months runs from constitutionally triggering event and expires on the corresponding month and date of the last year, or corresponding date of the last month, of specified period); 18.06.2007 (Majlis self-dissolution unconstitutional); 20.01.2011 (amendment authorising referendum to extend presidential term unconstitutional).

[16] The comprehensive article-by-article Commentary published under the aegis of the Council, with contributions from leading constitutionalists, judges and statesmen, is *sans pareil* across the region. Kaz Constitutional Commentary (n 7).

of both inherited Soviet legalism and the constitutional minds of Kazakhstan. Constitutionalism has itself developed into the justificatory ideology of super-presidentialism (at least in Kazakhstan) and its dialectical nimbleness has proved the equal of Marxism-Leninism. The result is a constitutional *caudillismo* which is as much the one as the other.

Much Western constitutional scholarship has been pre-occupied with the so-called 'counter-majoritarian conundrum':[17] the capacity of an elite apex panel (constitutional or supreme court) in the course of judicial review to annul democratically enacted legislation. How can an allegedly democratic system tolerate such a manifestly anti-democratic ('counter-majoritarian') device and moreover grant it such a pivotal role? This perennial chestnut has not figured as an issue in Kazakh (or wider Central Asian) constitutional jurisprudence or the analysis of it. The role of an elite Council in a democratic system does not register as paradoxical or provocative in a context in which that institution is not discernibly more elite than any other governing institution and no further removed from the possibility of majoritarian constraint. The procuracy, or for that matter the parliament, is just as exposed to critique on counter-majoritarian grounds.

CONSTITUTIONAL EVOLUTION OF THE CENTRAL ASIAN JUDICIARIES

For all Central Asian states, the relationship between the constitutional redefinition and reconfiguration of the place of the judiciary in the post-Soviet order, on the one hand, and the institutional transformation of the judiciary itself, on the other, has been exceedingly fraught and complex. Whereas constitutional dynamics have centred on the governance of the judiciary and the elusive goal of effective separation from the executive (discussed next below), institutional dynamics have involved much more besides. The inherited institutional disabilities of the Central Asian judiciaries have proved especially challenging to overcome, if not intractable, particularly amidst diminished support

[17] N Sultany, 'The State of Progressive Constitutional Theory: The Paradox of Constitutional Democracy and the Project of Political Justification' (2012) 47 *Harvard Civil Rights–Civil Liberties* 371, 373–75.

and resources, declining skills and competence, rapidly spreading corruption and executive domination. Although every country undertook a programme of judicial reform early on, often with donor assistance or at donor instigation, the Central Asian judiciaries have gained a singular reputation in post-Soviet space for incompetence, venality and corruption, as both judicial decisions and judgeships themselves became effectively commodified, available for sale.[18] The institutional dependence of the judiciary on the executive endured as justice ministries continued (for the first decade) to exercise significant administrative and budgetary control over the court systems. 'Telephone justice' or political instruction in judicial decision-making not only remained but was now exacerbated by corruption and bribery (which had not featured in the Soviet judiciary).[19] These matters are discussed at greater length in the next chapter.

All the five states inherited a dual judicial system: a system of ordinary courts for civil, criminal and administrative matters,[20] and state and agency *arbitrazh*, a special system of economic tribunals for the resolution of disputes between state enterprises (notwithstanding the name, the proceedings were adjudicative, although the procedure was somewhat less rigid and formal than in the ordinary courts).[21] A threshold issue for the new constitutional systems was how to re-organise this dual system for a market economy. The initial configuration in four constitutions, which has endured to the present in Uzbekistan and Tajikistan,[22] preserved the inherited institutional distinctiveness of

[18] See discussion of judicial corruption in ch 7 below.

[19] eg International Crisis Group, 'Kyrgyzstan: The Challenge of Judicial Reform, Asia Report No 150, 10 April 2008', available at www.crisisgroup.org/~/media/Files/asia/central-asia/kyrgyzstan/150_kyrgyzstan__the_challenge_of_judicial_reform.ashx, accessed 6 November 2015, 8–9 ('In many ways, the judge has become just another political "resource" in a corrupt state system').

[20] Administrative liability was a separate category of liability (essentially for minor infractions of public obligations, analogous to misdemeanours) in Soviet law, subject of a dedicated Code of Administrative Violations for each SSR, and was carried over into the legal systems of all five states. Kaz Code 30.01.2001, Kyr Code 04.08.1998, Taj Code 31.12.2008, Uzb Code 22.09.1994 (Administrative Liability), Tkm Code 17.12.1984 (the Turkmen SSR Code still in effect as amended).

[21] H Berman, *Justice in the U.S.S.R.: An Interpretation of Soviet Law* (Cambridge MA, Harvard University Press, 1963) 124–29; OS Ioffe and PB Maggs, *The Soviet Economic System: A Legal Analysis* (Boulder, CO, Westview Press, 1987) 54; Henderson (n 3) 7.

[22] Taj 84, Uzb 107.

the arbitrazh system by establishing in its place a separate economic court system alongside the regular court system (and the constitutional court). The economic courts, with the Higher Economic Court at its head, enjoy jurisdiction over disputes between businesses (legal persons) relating to commercial transactions and other matters. That configuration has since been modified in Kazakhstan and Kyrgyzstan by the merger of the economic system into the regular system after serial constitutional amendment and legislation, thus eliminating the separate economic apex court. In Turkmenistan only the Supreme Court received constitutional status; the Soviet state arbitrazh system had been abolished but a single 'arbitrazh court' (its decisions reviewable by the Supreme Court) was eventually established by subsequent law.[23] These matters will be taken up in the next chapter, where the fate and function of the economic or commercial court system are examined in detail.

The constitutions vary in the depth of treatment accorded the court system, but the judicial sections or chapters are generally brief (8–11 Articles); the Turkmen is most laconic in providing no elaboration of court structure and function, naming only the Supreme Court.[24] The Kyrgyz, Uzbek and Tajik sections afford some regulatory detail respecting the constitutional tribunal alone;[25] the Kazakh section does not treat the Constitutional Council, which merits its own chapter (and is formally not a court), but does treat the Procuracy (like the Russian Constitution).[26] The Kyrgyz Constitution provides at some length for judicial selection, appointment and removal; the Tajik and Kazakh in condensed fashion; the Uzbek and Turkmen leave the matter to subsidiary legislation.[27] All five constitutions resoundingly proclaim the full and equal status of the judiciary and the special dignity of judges.[28] All constitutions forbid the creation of 'extraordinary courts';[29] Kazakhstan's also forbids 'special and extraordinary courts

[23] Tkm Law 14.02.2000. All other courts, including the arbitrazh courts and provincial and district courts, are formed or disbanded on presidential authority alone. Tkm Law 15.08.2009 15(2).

[24] Tkm 99–109.

[25] Kyr 93–103, Uzb 106–16, Taj 84–92.

[26] Kaz 75–83.

[27] Kyr 95, Kaz 82, Taj 86.

[28] Kaz 77, Uzb 112, Tkm 101, Kyr 94, Taj 97, 91.

[29] Taj 85, Uzb 107, Tkm 100, Kyr 94(3), Kaz 75(4).

under any name' and Turkmenistan's 'other structures, vested with the powers of a court.' Such language appears framed against the Soviet tradition of para- or quasi-judicial bodies in executive ministries (the NKVD tribunals, eg) passing criminal sentences, but could also arguably restrict the creation of conventional administrative tribunals (eg for immigration).[30]

The question of the role, dignity and authority of the judiciary loomed large in early Central Asian constitutionalism. In the initial enthusiasm of independence, the historically subaltern status of judges (at Soviet trials, judges were as a rule deferential to party or administrative authority, represented by procurators)[31] was repudiated. Central Asia politicians, judges themselves and public opinion generally, called for an independent and institutionally strong judiciary. Judicial independence was resoundingly declared in all five constitutions (for the judiciary as branch in the Tajik and Uzbek cases as well as for judges),[32] buttressed by newly adopted laws on the status of judges, with the intention of duly elevating the judicial profession and the societal place of adjudication: the very use of the term 'status' is revealing.[33] The call for judicial reform was echoed by international donors, who saw the emergence of a strong, effective and independent judiciary as a sine qua non of successful transition, both to democratic, constitutional governance and a market economy. But the reconstitution of the Central Asian judiciary appeared largely declaratory. The first generation constitutions did not facilitate much less secure judicial independence. They did not embrace novel procedures (respecting appointments or discipline) or governance arrangements (in the direction of self-administration or independent administrative bodies). Though subsequent amendment in the cases of all constitutional systems has made redoubtable progress in both respects, as discussed below, judicial independence remains a very live issue everywhere in the region.

[30] The Kyrgyz Constitution expressly permits the creation by law of 'specialised courts'. Kyr 93(3).

[31] G Ginsburgs, 'The Political Undercurrents of the Legal Dialogue' (1967–68) 15 *UCLA Law Review* 1226, 1226–27 (in context of 'established practice of ad hoc administrative guidance of judicial affairs … procuracy [used] as an intrusive watch-dog over the routine functioning of the judicial branch for tactical policy purposes'); Berman (n 21) 270–71 ('outside pressure' on judges).

[32] Kaz 77, Kyr 94, Taj 84, 87, Uzb 106, 108, Tkm 101.

[33] Tkm Law 29.05.1991 (invalid), Kaz Decree 20.12.1995 (invalid), Kaz Con Law 25.12.2000, Kyr Con Laws 25.12.2000 (invalid), 09.07.2008.

GOVERNANCE: JUDICIAL PERSONNEL MANAGEMENT AND COURT ADMINISTRATION

The Soviet judiciary had not been self-administering. Rather, the Ministry of Justice (Union Ministry at the centre, and Republican ministries for the SSRs) managed court affairs, both respecting 'organisational matters' and 'material-technical' support. Organisational issues encompassed such matters as case-processing, workload, scheduling and general effectiveness (ministerial court departments would conduct periodic evaluations or *spravki* of all courts). Material-technical issues included everything from the management of support personnel (clerks to drivers) and the upkeep of courthouses to the payment of judges' salaries and the preparation of court budgets. This arrangement, not uncommon in civilian jurisdictions but increasingly regarded as outmoded and insufficiently conducive to judicial independence, was preserved (initially) in all five states. Judges of SSR provincial courts had been elected by the provincial soviets; judges of the Supreme Court by the Republican Supreme Soviet (judges of district courts were elected directly by voters);[34] but the Ministry of Justice played the central role in the selection and preparation of candidates and the training and management of the judicial corpus.

Kazakhstan, Kyrgyzstan and Tajikistan have all, albeit not initially, established constitutional bodies, and Uzbekistan and Turkmenistan sub-constitutional bodies, regulating recruitment, promotion, and removal of judicial personnel. They have all as well relieved the Ministry of Justice of some or all court organisational, financial and material support functions, transferring these to the management organ (Tajikistan and Uzbekistan)[35] or a separate administrative unit in the judiciary itself (Kazakhstan, Kyrgyzstan, Turkmenistan).[36] Only in Uzbekistan does the Ministry of Justice continue to exercise any residual direct court control functions.[37]

[34] Constitution Kaz SSR 152.

[35] Taj Con Law 06.08.2001 96–98 (Council of Justice); Uzb Law 02.09.1993 11 (Higher Qualifications Commission, charged with organisational but not material-technical support, which remains with the Ministry of Justice).

[36] Kaz Con Law 25.12.2000 56, Decree 03.11.2010 (Court facilitation department of the Supreme Court), Kyr Law 18.07.2003 (Court department of the Supreme Court), Tkm Law 15.08.2009 88 (Directorate for organisation of court operations of the Supreme Court).

[37] Uzb Law 02.09.1993 11, Statute 23.08.2011 8.6.

Of the judicial managerial bodies, the Kazakh Higher Judicial Council was first established as a consulting body in 2001, but was only constitutionalised and re-organised in 2007. It discharges the gamut of judicial personnel advisory and supervisory responsibilities: recruitment and selection through competitive examination (qualification) of judicial candidates, selection on the basis of competitive examination of candidates for vacant lower courts posts, review and recommendation of candidates for higher court posts, review of removal from office of judges at all levels, on disciplinary and other grounds (court reorganisation, health, etc), review of complement of judicial posts for lower courts, all for disposition by the relevant authority (president or Supreme Court).[38] The Kyrgyz Judicial Selection Council, a constitutional body, performs analogous functions;[39] as do the Tajik Council of Justice, established as a constitutional body pursuant to the 1999 amendments and subsidiary legislation, the Uzbek Judicial Qualifications Commission, a sub-constitutional body (both also discharging court administrative functions as noted above), and the several Turkmen Qualification Panels of Judges, also sub-constitutional (one for each provincial and equivalent court and the Supreme Court, regulating selection, appointment, promotion, removal and discipline).[40] Uzbek, Kazakh and Tajik judicial managerial organs are executive, with the membership appointed by the president; the Turkmen Qualification Panels are judicial only; and the Kyrgyz Judicial Selection Council is judicial-parliamentary, appointed one third by the judiciary itself and one third each by the parliamentary majority and opposition and consisting of 'judges and representatives of civil society', in an unparalleled constitutional arrangement.[41]

Only in the Kyrgyz Constitution does the phrase 'judicial self-governance' figure, and indeed the Kyrgyz judiciary is fully self-governing, through a unique system of constitutional bodies: the Congress of Judges, consisting of the entire judicial corpus, the Council of Judges, elected by the Congress, and the meeting of judges, consisting of the entire judicial staff at each court.[42] The Congress 'determines the

[38] Kaz Law 17.11.2008 2(1).

[39] Kyr 64(3), 95(4, 5, 7).

[40] Tkm Law 15.08.2009 68.

[41] Kyr 95(7)

[42] Kyr 102, Law 20.03.2008 4(2), 6, 8, 10–11.

fundamental policy lines of the judicial branch' and addresses state organs on behalf of the judiciary, functioning as in effect a constitutional trade union; the Council forms and implements the budget for the entire court system, imposes disciplinary liability, recommends removal of judges to the President, and organises training and continuing education for judges (inter alia).[43] Its sweeping budgetary authority alone, constitutionally established,[44] would make the Council a unique organ. Thus the Kyrgyz scheme alone is not *institutional* self-governance, with decision-making vested in an apex court or similar designated authority, but *professional* self-governance, with decision-making vested in the judges themselves, through prescribed democratic procedures. In other words, the Kyrgyz Constitution constitutionally establishes the judiciary on the model of a parliament (a democratically self-governing structure) rather than an executive (a hierarchically governed structure).

The constitutional and subsidiary framework for governance of the judiciary thus presents a strikingly varied landscape across the five states. Kyrgyzstan assumes its customary position as outlier: a thoroughly and imaginatively reconceived scheme of judicial self-governance, self-administration, and shared (with citizens) management, liberated from any executive involvement whatsoever. Kazakhstan follows after with significant residual (indirect) executive control over regulation of judicial personnel, but court administration solidly in the hands of the judiciary, and then in sequence Tajikistan and Uzbekistan, buffering to a limited degree judicial personnel regulation, and lacking direct judicial administration of courts. In the absence of a specialised management organ, Turkmenistan vests a surprising degree of authority directly in the judiciary itself, both respecting the regulation of judges (the Qualifications Panels) and court administration (the Directorate under the Supreme Court). Given the suffocating weight of presidential authority generally in Turkmenistan, the impressive formal independence of the judiciary is not necessarily cause for celebration.

One should resist the obvious temptation of awarding Kyrgyzstan the laurels here, for the race for judicial independence has not obviously been already won.[45] The constitutional governance framework,

[43] Kyr Law 20.03.2008 7, 9.

[44] Kyr 98(2).

[45] In 2013, 37 per cent of citizen complaints to the Akytkachy (Ombudsmen) concerned the courts. Ombudsmen's Report 25.07.2014, table 4. The Ombudsmen

however genially conceived, can only facilitate independence, not secure or guarantee it. As discussed in the next chapter, corruption of public officials is endemic throughout the region, and no degree of insistence on either the inviolability or sacred charge of judges is sufficient to differentiate them from other civil servants when it comes to susceptibility to influence or instruction or the temptations of office. Judicial independence is multiply conditioned. Even where the institution itself is adequately insulated from executive or other outside pressure (an empirical evaluation, rather than a regulatory one), its culture remains as resolutely hierarchical as that of its Soviet predecessor. Although 'in individual cases judges are not accountable',[46] judges are under strong professional pressure not to offend or run afoul of superiors, and so are exposed to the possibility of subtle or direct *judicial* instruction from above. Moreover, the disciplinary system can operate to penalise judges for reversals on appeal if they are deemed 'illegal decisions' (incorrect decisions), a potentially elastic term.[47]

STRUCTURE AND FUNCTIONS: THE FIVE COURT SYSTEMS

The territorial, jurisdictional and hierarchical structure of the courts of the Central Asian SSRs was passed on intact to their successor independent states, and is still discernible in broad outline notwithstanding the serial reorganisation that at least four of the five systems have since undergone. Two opposing tendencies in restructuring may be observed across the region, but they do not serve merely to distinguish alternative reform strategies among the states, but as well successive or even simultaneous policies within them: consolidation and specialisation of

comments, 'The majority of citizens requesting a representative of the Akytkachy (Ombudsmen) at a hearing were motivated by distrust of the judicial system. Citizens in their applications cite violations of their rights to a fair and public hearing of their case in court and request the presence of the Akytkachy (Ombudsmen) at court hearings as an observer.'

46 Kaz 77(2).

47 See eg Kaz Con Law 25.12.2000 39(1): 'A judge may be brought to disciplinary liability 1) for violation of the law in adjudicating a case …; 39(3) The reversal or modification of a judicial act does not in and of itself carry liability for a judge, if in the course of its issuance gross violations of the law have not been allowed, as indicated in the decision of the higher-standing judicial instance.' *cf* Taj Con Law 06.08.2001 119(a) ('gross violation of the law in the trial of a case').

courts. Consolidation is represented by the merger of the economic (*arbitrazh*) courts in Kazakhstan and Kyrgyzstan, and by the merger of the Constitutional Court in the latter (now the Constitutional Chamber of the Supreme Court). Specialisation is represented by the recreation of the Arbitrazh Court in Turkmenistan, by the inauguration of juvenile justice courts in Kazakhstan,[48] and by the reconstitution of the inherited military justice system.[49] Obviously there are multiple ways to rationalise a judicial system, and the inter-country differences reflect different approaches.[50] One halting trend in the region has been the revival or neo-institutionalisation of traditional folk modes of dispute resolution, such as the *bi* courts in Kazakhstan (subject of intermittent discussion but still on the drawing board) and the *aksakal* courts in Kyrgyzstan (constitutionally established as community, ie non-governmental, institutions but of waning significance).[51] These efforts are discussed in chapter eight on the constitutional significance and role of culture.

The Soviet era provincial boundary lines have for the most part been preserved (see the discussion on local government in chapter eight), as have the district lines, for purposes both of local administration and court structure. In some instances lines of territorial jurisdiction have changed in conjunction with corresponding administrative changes, but as a rule administrative and judicial boundaries are overlapping. District courts are generally the lowest-tier courts, and are courts of first instance for ordinary criminal and civil matters, as specified by the provisions of the corresponding procedure codes respecting jurisdiction.[52] In Kazakhstan, Uzbekistan and Kyrgyzstan,

[48] Kaz Decree 23.08.2007.

[49] eg, Taj Con Law 06.08.2001 61–74; Uzb 02.09.1993 39–42; Kyr Law 20.03.2008 25(2).

[50] The universal reliance on some form of specialisation for commercial disputes across the republics is analysed in ch 7 following.

[51] Kyr 59, Law 06.07.2002, see A Ranjbar, 'The Declining Use of Aksakal Courts in Kyrgyzstan,' Eurasia Foundation report, available at equalbeforethelaw.org/sites/default/files/library/The_Declining_Use_of_Aksakal_Courts_in_Kyrgyzstan.pdf, accessed 4 November 2015). The constitutional regulation of *aksakal* courts was more elaborate in earlier versions of the constitution, Kyr 1998 85 (agreed jurisdiction over property and family disputes specified). See discussion in ch 8.

[52] eg Kaz Criminal Procedure Code 13.12.1997 290, Civil Procedure Code13.12.1997 27.

inter-district courts have been established as courts of first instance for designated categories of action.[53] Provincial or oblast courts are intermediate tier, and exercise appellate jurisdiction over decisions of district judges as well as original jurisdiction for more serious crimes and disputes.[54] Oblast appellate jurisdiction is generally of two kinds: de novo review or appellate review in the strict sense (of the facts and the application of the law) of decisions before they have entered into force, and cassational review (of the application of the law only) of decisions that have entered into force.[55] Additionally, oblast-level courts may exercise supervisory review over lower court decisions that have entered into force, broader review on the basis of legality, and review on the basis of circumstances newly come to light as well.[56]

The higher level courts are typically divided into chambers or panels, for criminal, civil, administrative and (in those systems which have merged the former *arbitrazh* courts) economic matters. Supreme courts have supervisory jurisdiction and can exercise other forms of review as well, including cassational and appellate; they can also sit as a first instance court for designated matters.[57] As befits an apex court, the supreme courts exercise multiple other leadership functions as well: generalisation of practice, issuance of authoritative guidelines, discipline, nomination of judicial candidates and court administration (in Kazakhstan and Kyrgyzstan). The supreme courts have their own complex internal organisation, in the context of their varying role in

[53] Kaz Con Law 25.12.2000 3(2.2), Decrees 16.01.2001 (economic courts), 23.08.2007, Criminal Procedure Code 13.12.1997 290–91 (juvenile courts), Criminal Procedure Code 13.12.1997 290–92 (criminal courts), 290–93 (military courts); Uzb Law 02.09.1993 37 (civil matters); Kyr Law 20.03.2008 25(1.1), Criminal Procedure Code 30.06.1999 240(5) (jury trials in specified criminal matters).

[54] eg Kaz Civil Procedure Code 13.12.1997 28, Criminal Procedure Code 13.12.1997 291.

[55] Kaz Con Law 25.12.2000 11, Kyr Law 20.03.2008 30(7).

[56] Taj Con Law 06.08.2001 78, 81, Tkm Law 15.08.2009 24(1) (cassational, supervisory, new circumstances), Uzb Law 02.09.1993 30 (appellate, cassational, supervisory).

[57] Supervision and first instance only: Kazakhstan (Kaz Con Law 25.12.2000 18(3), 22, Civil Procedure Code 13.12.1997 29, Criminal Procedure Code 13.12.1997 292); supervision, new circumstances: Kyrgyzstan (Kyr Law 20.03.2008 14(2.1); first instance, cassation, supervision, new circumstances: Tajikistan (Taj Con Law 06.08.2001 44), Turkmenistan (Tkm 15.08.2009 24(1)); first instance, supervision: Uzbekistan (Uzb Law 02.09.1993 13).

administration of the judiciary as a whole. All of these functions have been carried over from the predecessor SSR supreme courts, as have the types of appellate jurisdiction for all second-instance courts. Apart from the marginal tweaking noted above (amalgamation, specialisation, redistribution of appellate burden, modification of supreme court final instance jurisdiction), there is nothing novel about the basic set-up or machinery of adjudication across the Central Asian republics. It is manifestly derivative of the antecedent Soviet scheme, however much modified to comply with contemporary standards and (formally) to incorporate adversarial process and judicial supremacy (as might equally be asserted of the structure and functions of the Russian judiciary).[58]

One notable feature of the Soviet system was the ideological and practical prominence of lay justice. Judges sat with two people's assessors, who with no higher legal education nonetheless had equal votes in the decision on cases,[59] but were as a rule deferential to their sole professional colleague. The institution of the assessors has been preserved (with some modification) in Tajikistan, Turkmenistan and Uzbekistan pursuant to sub-constitutional legislation.[60] Jurors have been introduced only in Kazakhstan and are pending introduction in Kyrgyzstan six years after the enabling legislation. The Kyrgyz Constitution alone incorporates a right to a jury trial (for contemplated cases) among fundamental rights.[61] Both the respective criminal procedure codes have been comprehensively amended to provide for all dimensions of juror participation: selection and vetting, presentation of evidence and general trial issues, rights to put questions after examination, summation, jury instructions, jury deliberations.[62] The Kazakh and Kyrgyz jurisdictional provisions are restrictive,[63] granting defendants a right to

58 Henderson (n 3) 214–27.

59 USSR Constitution 1977 154; Berman (n 21) 34, 63.

60 Taj Con Law 06.08.2001 16, Tkm Law 15.08.2009 50, Uzb Law 02.09.1993 62.

61 Kaz 75, Law 16.02.2006, Kyr 26(6), Law 15.07.2009, Venice Commission Opinion 16.12.2008.

62 Kaz Criminal Procedure Code 13.12.1997 542–77, Kyr Criminal Procedure Code 30.06.1999 331(1–34).

63 Kaz Criminal Procedure Code 13.12.1997 543 (with a further restriction exempting from jury trial specified capital crimes such as treason, attempt on the life of the president and terrorism); Kyr Criminal Procedure Code 30.06.1999 240(5).

petition for jury trials only when charged with crimes subject to capital or life sentence (Kazakhstan) or specified crimes of violence including murder and rape with aggravating factors (Kyrgyzstan).

Kazakh experience demonstrates that jurors can be and have been successfully accommodated, but the question remains: what is their ultimate role and relevance to criminal justice? The rigorously prescribed procedures in both Kazakh and Kyrgyz legislation clearly afford a far firmer and more carefully conceived foundation for lay justice than the assessors in the other three states. In Kazakhstan, there have been instances of jury acquittals even in politically charged cases, but jurors remain subject to the same general political climate as judges.[64] However, the introduction of jury trials is on a far lesser scale than in the Russian Federation, raising questions of 'tokenism' or placation of international opinion in the context of significant enthusiasm for jury trials (particularly on the part of common lawyers). For successful institutionalisation, juries demand significant and sustained efforts from all justice system actors. It is ultimately incumbent on the justice system professionals to accommodate the lay element; the only labours burdening the jurors should be hearing and trying the evidence as instructed. Jurors only have to be 'educated' to the technical aspects of the justice system when they are sworn, whereas the system has to undergo a fairly profound re-education to accommodate jurors in the first place. Jurors are not expected to know anything about trials before they are summoned to one, whereas trial professionals (judges, advocates, procurators) need to know everything about juries and how they work.

CONSTITUTIONAL BASIS OF THE CENTRAL ASIAN JUSTICE SYSTEM: INTERNAL AFFAIRS, JUSTICE AND THE PROCURACY

The constitutional development of the five states' judiciaries, and particularly their relations with the executive, cannot well be appreciated

64 See eg Kaz Sentence 28.08.2012 (human rights advocate accused of extortion partially acquitted, conditionally sentenced only and freed after trial). The verdict was subsequently overturned on appeal and in a second jury trial the defendant was convicted and sentenced to 12 years in a hard labour colony. Kaz Sentence 07.12.2012.

without an understanding of the parallel constitutional development of the other institutional components of the justice system. The criminal justice system has been the object of particular attention on the part of donors and observers, with a focus on the rights of the accused and those in custody (judicial guarantees). This section focuses particularly on three bodies: the Ministries of Justice and Internal Affairs, and the Procuracy. (Other institutional actors play an equally significant role in criminal justice, most notably perhaps the presidential administration—the president's legal office can be the pivotal decision-maker in matters of criminal justice policy.) Typically, only the Procuracy receives any constitutional mention, and then of utmost brevity, and the formal chartering of the principal executive organs of the justice system is the work of subsidiary legislation. The criminal procedure codes authoritatively map out the role and functions, rights and duties, of the various institutional actors in the criminal justice system in the serial phases of preliminary, pre-trial, trial and post-trial, and enjoy supremacy over specific legislation regulating the Procuracy, ministries and other actors.

Internal Affairs

As noted in chapter four in the context of national security, the ministries of internal affairs loom large in the constitutional framework of all five states. As holds true for Central Asian parliamentary, judicial and executive institutions in general, policing institutions were carried over from their SSR predecessors. This congenital acquisition presented its particular challenges. While the prominence of policing, public order and investigative functions was hardly unique to the Soviet system, as discussed in chapter two, the power, prerogatives and institutional forms of the Soviet police were sufficiently exaggerated vis-a-vis the common run of states as to justify the appellation 'police state'. All five states might thus be considered to have been confronted with the urgent need at independence to tame or domesticate the police constitutionally. They have addressed this task with varying degrees of determination, good faith and success.

The inherited Soviet-era internal affairs apparatus, much like the UK Home Office before the 2007 reforms (which saw prisons, probation and criminal justice transferred to the newly created Justice Ministry), had a very broad remit, including police and security forces, investigative services and the penitentiary system. One direction of constitutional reform across the region has been the reduction in size of the internal affairs empire and the hiving off of functions like the penitentiary system (in Kyrgyzstan and Tajikistan). The delineation of functions and responsibilities of internal affairs ministries has been left to subsidiary legislation. Each jurisdiction typically has a set of regulations for its Ministry of Internal Affairs and/or a law on the organs of internal affairs, elaborating structure, functions and responsibilities and procedures, as well as supplemental and subsidiary regulations. Kyrgyzstan has created a unique Civilian Observer Council under the Internal Affairs Ministry, exercising advisory functions.[65] Unlike eg the Independent Police Complaints Commission for England and Wales, the Kyrgyz Observer Council is a ministerial body.

Police

Internal affairs ministries all have under their jurisdiction the criminal police (as well as the traffic police and the administrative police). Additionally, internal affairs ministries also have their own armed force, the interior troops, intended for large scale public-order operations, as well as counter-narcotics agencies and 'spetsnaz' or special forces (something like Special Branch in UK policing).[66] All five states carry over the two principal Soviet detention facilities or 'isolators': the *IVS* (ИВС, Temporary Detention Isolator, Изолятор Временного Содержания), the police lock-up, where suspects may be detained for no more than 72 hours (generally), and the *SIZO* (СИЗО, Investigative Isolator, Следственный Изолятор), the prison or pre-trial investigative detention facility.[67] These facilities have typically remained within the jurisdiction of internal affairs,[68] but the *SIZO* have been transferred to the Government in Kyrgyzstan and to the Ministry of Justice in

[65] Kyr Rules 12.05.2011 (Civil society observers' board, Ministry of Internal Affairs). This is one of several such observers' boards, enabled by the Statute 29.09.2010.

[66] Kaz Internal Affairs Statute (Regulations) 22.06.2005 1 (Committee of internal troops, Committee against narco-business and drugs trafficking).

[67] eg Kaz Criminal Procedure Code 5-2, 5-3; Tkm Criminal Procedure Code 18.04.2009 173.

[68] eg Tkm Law 07.07.2001 7, Kaz Law 21.12199 5-2, 5-3.

Tajikistan, along with the rest of the criminal enforcement system.[69] Other detaining authorities, such as the National Security agency, narcotics agency and the military, can also maintain 'isolators'.[70] Beyond detention, a range of other pre-trial restrictive or compulsory measures with constitutional implications is provided, for example, house arrest, bail or travel ban.[71]

Investigation

Internal Affairs typically maintains the primary or default investigative service in the criminal justice system, but a range of other ministries and agencies (organs) in the five states typically is authorised to conduct investigations or inquests as well (and thus to detain suspects) and maintain their own investigative services, employing investigators (*sledovateli*, следователи) or examiners (*doznavateli*, дознаватели). In Kyrgyzstan, for example, the Procuracy, National Security agency, customs, financial police, penal service and counter-narcotics agency are investigative agencies.[72] A broad range of investigative techniques and procedures is contemplated and their use is regulated in the main by the criminal procedure codes.[73] The investigator exercises formidable, quasi-judicial authority in his or her own right (somewhat as a French *juge d'instruction* would do), including that to initiate a criminal case, as discussed below in the section on judicial guarantees and fair trial rights. Investigative services are at the same time detaining authorities, and can maintain detention facilities (*SIZO*).

Prisons and Penal Sanctions

The Central Asian penitentiary system is in direct genealogical descent from the Soviet system including prisons and Gulag, the Soviet Main Administration of Camps and Places of Incarceration (as are all post-Soviet systems). The Gulag loomed much larger in the public

[69] Kyr Law 31.10.2002 7, 8, Taj Law 23.05.1998 15(5).

[70] eg Kyr Law 31.10.2002 7.

[71] eg Kaz Criminal Procedure Code 04.07.2014 136–65.

[72] Kyr Criminal Procedure Code 30.06.1999 5. Additional agencies are also authorised to carry out searches. Kyr Law 16.10.1998 16. *cf* Kaz Criminal Procedure Code 04.07.2014 7(23), 61.

[73] eg Kaz Criminal Procedure Code 04.07.2014 179–305.

imagination (and the lives of the citizenry) than prison systems elsewhere. It permeated society to such an extent that one can speak of the USSR as a carceral state as much as a police state, characterised by the vast numbers of the politically repressed, as well as the 'thieves-in-law' (*vory-v-zakone*), the all-powerful organised criminal network anchored in the camps and prisons.[74] The Gulag was a correctional empire within the Soviet empire, and the Kazakh, Kyrgyz, Tajik, Uzbek and Turkmen systems retain the quality of an imperial fortress (indeed, Kazakhstan had been the site of one of the most extensive series of Gulag complexes).[75]

In Kazakhstan, Uzbekistan and Turkmenistan, the penitentiary system is administered by a subdivision or agency of the Ministry of Internal Affairs, in Kyrgyzstan an agency directly subordinate to Government, and in Tajikistan an agency of the Ministry of Justice.[76] The administration of penal sentences, including custodial sentences, is regulated in all five states by a quasi-constitutional code, the criminal enforcement code.[77] Though the penitentiary system merits no particular constitutional treatment as such, save in connection with the rights against torture and ill-treatment and the rights of those in custody (in the section below dedicated to which its generally dire state across the 'stans will be analysed at greater length), it is a defining and integral dimension of the constitutional order. In Kyrgyzstan, Kazakhstan and Tajikistan the prisons agency has been transferred between the Ministries of Internal Affairs and Justice—twice for the first two—without perceptible alteration in culture of governance and conditions of incarceration, a testament to its institutional solidity and stubbornness: it

[74] International Crisis Group (ICG), 'Kyrgyzstan's Prison Nightmare', Asia Report No 118, 16 August 2006, 3.

[75] A Applebaum, *Gulag: A History of the Soviet Camps* (London, Penguin, 2004) 102, 258, 374.

[76] Kaz Committee of the criminal-enforcement system, 22.06.2005 Statute 1; Kyr State service for the enforcement of penalties (ГСИН, GSIN), Statute 18.12.2009 1; Taj State administration for the enforcement of penalties (GUIN, ГУИН), Ministry of Justice Statute 01.04.2008 5, 6(5), appendix 3; Uzb State administration for the enforcement of penalties (GUIN, ГУИН), Tkm Department of the enforcement of penalties, Law 21.05.2011 10.

[77] Kaz Criminal Enforcement Code 13.12.1997, Kyr Criminal Enforcement Code 11.11.1999, Taj Criminal Penalty Enforcement Code 06.08.2001, Tkm Criminal Enforcement Code 25.03.2011.

has proved a very hard nut to crack indeed.[78] The shift of penitentiary system governance from the police to the justice sector endorsed by the international community has proved largely cosmetic.

Ministry of Justice

Soviet Ministries of Justice at Union and Republican levels had as their core responsibility and raison d'etre the administration of the court system;[79] additionally they regulated the bar (*advokatura*) and *notariat*, oversaw higher legal education and organised legislative research and codification. Thus for the most part they performed service and support functions and did not play a major role in justice system policy or affairs. All the new Central Asian Ministries of Justice carried their institutional structures over intact from their SSR predecessors—departments, directorates, staffing levels and job descriptions, etc—but their organisation charts underwent significant subsequent modification. They acquired a widened set of responsibilities, becoming in effect the line ministries for legal reform and legislative planning and drafting, adding a policy role respecting the justice system to their court-related functions.

Long before the new parliaments had built up any degree of legislative expertise (or the presidential administrations and apparatuses, for that matter), and while the legal staffs of other government ministries, agencies and committees were modest, the Ministries of Justice became the default repositories of state legal expertise simply because they commanded the only significant staff of lawyers. Ministries of Justice took the labouring oar in drafting work generally, organising drafting working groups and co-ordinating the work of lawyers elsewhere in the government. Ministries of Justice have typically been intimately involved in the drafting of constitutions and constitutional amendments. Even when not involved in drafting or coordination work per se, the Justice Ministries typically performed legislative expertise (technical review of legislative drafts) on bills prepared elsewhere, whether in the president's office or other line ministries or agencies. These critical functions were not expressly provided for in the constitutions or

78 See eg ICG 2006 (n 74) (state of Kyrgyz prison system).

79 USSR Ministry of Justice (MoJ) Statute 21.03.1972 2.

even referenced, and generally were established pursuant to subsidiary regulation.

Beyond the expansion of their remit in legislative matters, they gained new prominence as repositories of legal information (electronic databases of legislation and court rulings) and as central registries for normative acts, pledges (security), legal persons (in the context of rapidly proliferating businesses and social organisations as well as political parties) and civil acts (births, deaths, marriages, etc). The Kyrgyz, Kazakh and Tajik Justice Ministries lost their court-administrative functions (as noted above), but retained essential justice system functions such as control over judicial expertise and judicial enforcement (court bailiffs), the notariat and the defence bar. Those three ministries also assumed additional justice-centred functions transferred from other ministries, notably the penitentiary system from internal affairs; in the case of Kazakhstan only to be restored to the jurisdiction of the latter after ten years, and in the case of Kyrgyzstan to be transferred after seven years to a new central government service.[80] Other ministerial functions may include receipt of citizen complaints/applications, provision of legal aid, legal public awareness/propaganda, continuing legal education, legal consulting, compliance with international obligations and provision of international legal assistance.

The assumption by Ministries of Justice of augmented responsibilities for the criminal justice system has at times placed them at odds with Procuracies. The drafting of substantive and procedural criminal legislation has been a bone of contention between them, as their divergent ideas and concepts regarding legal reform tend to reflect agency interests (eg issuance of arrest warrants and direction of investigation). In the recent revision of the Kazakh Criminal Procedure Code, for example, the Procuracy gained the upper hand and took the lead role in drafting.

Procuracy

The Procuracy was the cornerstone of the imperial Romanov—and then the imperial Bolshevik—criminal justice system from its founding

[80] Kaz MoJ Statute 28.10.2004 16; Kyr MoJ Statute 18.12.2009 6 (includes legal aid); Taj MoJ Statute 01.04.2008 6(1–9) (includes criminal enforcement/penitentiary system); Uzb MoJ Statute of 23.08.2011; Tkm MoJ Statute 06.08.2008.

as the *oko gosudarstva*, the eye of the state, by Peter the Great in 1722. It remains the defining institution of the justice system across the independent republics of Central Asia, as other post-Soviet jurisdictions. Anomalous in the breadth of its authority, an imperial anachronism in a post-imperial age, it confronted all post-Soviet states at birth with a constitutional reform challenge. All five Central Asian states retained the institution in its inherited form, as a self-contained system independent of any other state organ, and with its full complement of both supervisory and justice process powers. The language in the very first line of the respective provision in each of the five constitutions carries over word-for-word the defining formulation of the function of the Soviet Procuracy in Union and Republican constitutions: 'supervision of exact and uniform enforcement of the laws.'[81]

As noted above,[82] apart from their government-wide watchdog-cum-ombudsman's role ('general supervision'), Soviet procurators played a multitude of (conflicting) roles within the justice system, participatory and supervisory. They and not judges issued arrest warrants; they directed investigation, as well as presenting the case for prosecution at trial; they made effectively judicial assessments of evidence and guilt (the promiscuous admixture of adjudicative with investigative and prosecutorial functions remains a problematic feature of post-Soviet criminal procedure in Central Asia).[83] Over and above their direct participation in proceedings, they had supervisory responsibility for ensuring the 'legality' (conformity with procedural and substantive norms) of the justice process itself and the corresponding power to protest any judicial act.

The constitutions both regulate the office of the General Procurator and the institution of the Procuracy itself.[84] All five constitutions provide that the General Procurator is appointed by the president with consent of the upper house (in Tajikistan, Uzbekistan and Kazakhstan) or the unicameral legislature (Turkmenistan and Kyrgyzstan).[85]

[81] Kaz 83, Kyr 104(10), Taj 93, Uzb 118, Tkm 110, USSR 1977 164.

[82] See ch 2.

[83] L Golovko, 'The Space for Legal Reform in Central Asia: Between Political Limits and Theoretical Deformations' in *2010 Yearbook of the Organisation for Security and Co-operation in Europe (OSCE)* (Baden-Baden, Nomos Verlagsgesellschaft, 2011) 114–15.

[84] Kaz 83, Kyr 2010 104, Uzb 118–20, Taj 93–97, Tkm 110–14.

[85] Kyr 64(4), Kaz 44, Taj 69(9), Uzb 93, Tkm 53(12).

In Tajikistan, uniquely, the Constitution expressly subordinates the General Procurator jointly to the Majlis Milli as well as the president, in accord with the 1999 amendments.[86] Additional constitutional provision in Kazakhstan is made for the General Procurator to attend open or closed parliamentary sessions[87] and to present the case for rescinding a deputy's inviolability to the relevant chamber.[88] In Kyrgyzstan, uniquely, the General Procurator's finding of 'the presence in the President's actions of the marks of a crime' is necessary to support conviction by the Jogorku Kenesh[89] in impeachment proceedings (discussed in chapter four).

The five constitutions vary significantly in their depth of regulation of the institution itself: in the Kazakh and Kyrgyz Constitutions the Procuracy is treated in one article;[90] in the Uzbek, Turkmen and Tajik constitutions under a separate chapter or section consisting of four or five articles.[91] The Kyrgyz and Kazakh provisions elaborate procuratorial functions (the former exhaustively); the other three leave the elaboration to dedicated Laws on the Procuracy.[92] The Kyrgyz Constitution, where reform of the Soviet institutional profile and powers of the Procuracy has gone furthest, trims the list of procuratorial functions to a lean six (by contrast the Uzbek Law on the Procuracy enumerates fifteen, the Tajik Law twelve). Save in Turkmenistan, the Procuracy has been shorn of the authority to issue arrest warrants, and the scope of its authority to conduct (as opposed to supervise) investigations has been reduced.[93]

In all Soviet-derived criminal justice systems, equality of arms between defence and prosecution has presented a distinct challenge, notwithstanding the fact that criminal procedure (in Central Asia as in Russia and other former Soviet Republics) has been formally converted

[86] Taj 94.

[87] Kaz 59(6).

[88] Kaz 57.

[89] Kyr 67(2).

[90] Kaz 83 (Section VII, Court and Justice), Kyr 107 (Chapter VII Other State Organs); *cf* Constitution of the Russian Federation 129, Henderson (n 3) 199.

[91] Uzb 118–21 (Chapter XXIV), Tkm 110–14 (Section VII), Taj 93–97 (Section VIII).

[92] Taj Con Law 25.07.2005, Uzb Law 09.12.1992, Tkm Law 15.08.2009 3.

[93] Kaz Law 21.12.2005 4, Kyr Law 17.07.2009 3 (investigation only of officials), Taj Con Law 25.07.2005 5, Uzb Criminal Procedure Code 22.09.1994 35, Tkm Law 15.08.2009 3.

from inquisitorial to adversarial (constitutionally in the Kyrgyz, Tajik and Turkmen cases).[94] All five constitutions provide for legal assistance to citizens, but the institutional disadvantage of the defence bar carried over from Soviet times has remained a live issue. A unique and allied carryover from the Soviet justice system is the inequality between Procuracy and judiciary, running in favour of the former. For the Soviet judiciary itself and not just the bar was also at an institutional disadvantage with respect to the Procuracy. Procurators were typically better educated, more informed and more authoritative than judges before whom they appeared. Although the Procuracy has been variably relieved of some of its arms and shorn of some its armour over the course of reforms, it retains in each of the five criminal justice systems its warrior brawn and bearing (Central Asian procurators carry on the Russian/Soviet tradition of quasi-military uniforms and insignia of ranks): still the most formidable institution in criminal proceedings and in the justice sector generally. As discussed in the section on rights below, justice reform efforts in Central Asia have left intact the central Soviet institutions and their roles and relations (and hence the institutional culture), notwithstanding the new rules. Those Soviet roles and relations amount to 'complex deformations' of the justice system, not amenable to straightforward legislative amelioration and invisible to legal system actors because taken for the norm.[95]

RIGHTS AND REMEDIES

An old Soviet *anekdot* (joke) had an elderly patron sitting forlornly in a sparsely furnished restaurant waiting to be served, perusing the mimeographed menu. When the frumpy, surly waitress finally ambles over, and the diner asks her hopefully in succession for borshch, shchi (cabbage soup) and solyanka, he is told curtly each time, 'Nyet, citizen. Not available.' Finally, he looks at her plaintively, 'Tell me, dearie, is this a menu or a constitution?' When it comes to the enforcement of rights in contemporary Central Asia, alas, the difference is still hard to detect.

[94] Kaz Criminal Procedure Code 04.07.2014 23, Kyr 99 (3), Criminal Procedure Code 30.06.1999 18, Taj 88, Criminal Procedure Code 03.12.2009 20, Uzb Criminal Procedure Code 22.09.1994 25, Tkm 107, Criminal Procedure Code 18.04.2009 22.

[95] Golovko (n 83) 111.

Of all former Soviet states, the 'stans bear a stigma as singularly derelict in their observance of human rights obligations. Turkmenistan and Uzbekistan are both widely regarded as among the very most repressive regimes of the hour. For example, Freedom House has consistently accorded both its worst possible score of 7 for civil liberties and political rights, placing them at the extremity of the 'not free' category, which includes Kazakhstan and Tajikistan as well with more modest scores. Only Kyrgyzstan, with scores of 5, is rated as 'partially free', and only just.[96] Still, the Central Asian republics are repressive in a complex way that is distinctly post-Soviet: generally heavy-handed and ruthless with perceived opponents, but still anxious about norm-compliance.

The following sections treat text and context for selected principal categories of civil and political rights as formulated in the five constitutions (a comparative survey of selected economic and social rights is deferred until chapter seven) and then take up the available remedies, including judicial, international and supplementary. Although courts have been generally regarded as the principal organ for the protection of rights, however, other bodies, including procuracies in their traditional supervisory function as well as dedicated new agencies such as ombudsmen and human rights bodies, have played significant enforcement roles in Central Asia.

At a formal, textual level, the catalogues of rights elaborated in the five constitutions are, save as remarked more particularly below, generally unimpeachable and conform to the international human rights standards to which the states have acceded. Only the Kyrgyz and Tajik constitutions make fundamental rights absolute, that is, non-derogable even in extremis.[97] The Kazakh and Turkmen constitutions provide for derogation in states of emergency, but do not qualify the

[96] Freedom House, Freedom in the World Country Ratings 1972–2013, available at www.freedomhouse.org/sites/default/files/Country%20Ratings%20and%20Status%2C%201973-2014%20%28FINAL%29.xls, accessed 11 November 2015. However problematic the methodological insufficiencies and ideological biases (see D Giannone, 'Political and Ideological Aspects in the Measurement of Democracy: The Freedom House Case' (2010) 17(1) *Democratization* 68) and redolent of 'low intensity democracy' (S Marks, 'Guarding the Gates With Two Faces: International Law and Political Reconstruction' (1998–99) 6 *Indiana Journal of Global Legal Studies* 457, 464–66), the Freedom House ranking would appear to tally in a rough way with the results of the present comparative constitutional analysis.

[97] Kyr 20(4.1–10, 5.1–10), Taj 47.

derogation; the Uzbek Constitution omits reference to derogation altogether. Inasmuch as all states have ratified the ICCPR, they remain bound by the non-derogability provisions of Article 6, but the failure of three of them to make commensurate constitutional provision for non-derogability remains concerning.

Rights of Life and Liberty, and Against Torture and Ill-Treatment; Prisoners' Rights

The formulations of the basic rights to life and integrity of person might be imagined as uniform and uniformly unobjectionable across the five constitutions, but they are not. The Turkmen and Kyrgyz constitutions impose a flat ban on the death penalty; the Tajik Constitution reserves it for 'especially grave crimes', the Kazakh Constitution exclusively for 'terrorist crimes with loss of life and especially grave crimes committed in wartime' but provides a 'right of clemency.'[98] The Kazakh exception is difficult to justify, particularly in view of the elasticity and liability to invidious application of the term terrorism, discussed below. The right to life provision in the Uzbek Constitution omits any reference to the death penalty (which has been abolished by subsidiary decree)[99] and employs an odd usage, which is somewhat unsettling in light of Uzbekistan's regional reputation for reliance on lethal state violence: 'The right to life is the inalienable right of each person. Any attempt on life is regarded as the gravest crime.'[100]

The constitutions all duly prohibit torture and ill-treatment.[101] However, torture and ill-treatment were endemic to Soviet police and prison culture (far from uniquely) and they have proved stubbornly

[98] Kaz 15(2), Kyr 21, Taj 18, Tkm 22.

[99] Uzb Decree 01.08.2005.

[100] Uzb 24. See C Murray, *Murder in Samarkand: A British Ambassador's Controversial Defiance of Tyranny in the War on Terror* (Edinburgh and London, Mainstream Publishing, 2007) (circumambient menace of Uzbek state violence, both in and out of custody). See also Human Rights Watch, 'Bullets Were Falling Like Rain: The Andijan Massacre, May 13, 2005', available at www.hrw.org/sites/default/files/reports/uzbekistan0605.pdf, accessed 6 November 2015, 'Until the very end, politically motivated imprisonment in Uzbekistan' www.hrw.org/sites/default/files/reports/uzbekistan0914_ForUpload.pdf, accessed 4 November 2015.

[101] Uzb 26, Kaz 17, Kyr 22, Taj 18, Tkm 23.

ineradicable in the 'stans, all of which have gained notoriety for the brutality and lawlessness of law enforcement. Forced or induced confessions and fabricated evidence are still common for suspects, and ill-treatment and poor conditions for convicts:

> In all five Central Asian states there is overwhelming evidence of pervasive torture and other ill-treatment of detainees by both regular police and security services. Over the past two decades thousands of people across the region have alleged that they have been arbitrarily detained and tortured or ill-treated in custody in order to extract a forced confession or money from relatives.[102]

Only the Kyrgyz Constitution specifically provides for humane treatment of prisoners,[103] though the Soviet culture of ill-treatment of prisoners from which the five states emerged might have been thought to supply ample reason for all to have constitutionalised the rights of those deprived of liberty. All states are parties to the Convention against Torture but only Kazakhstan and Kyrgyzstan have signed the Optional Protocol, which requires states parties to establish National Preventive Mechanisms as well as to permit visits to place of detention by members of the Subcommittee on the Prevention of Torture. Kazakh legislation has now transferred oversight of prisoners' rights protection from the Ministry of Justice to civil society observatory commissions at the provincial level.[104]

The International Committee of the Red Cross has a headquarters agreement authorising prison inspection visits and interviews with detained persons with Kyrgyzstan and Kazakhstan; elsewhere the prisons are largely inaccessible by outsiders (and for that matter local human rights advocates).[105] As noted earlier, the penitentiary system across the region remains largely unreconstructed, with endemic

[102] Amnesty International, Return to Torture Extradition, Forcible Returns and Removals to Central Asia, EUR 04/001/2013 (2013), available at www.amnesty.org/download/Documents/12000/eur040012013en.pdf, accessed 4 November 2015, 11.

[103] Kyr 22(2).

[104] Kaz Criminal Enforcement Code 13.12.1997 1, 3.1, 21.1–21.11, Law 02.07.2013, Rules 26.09.2013 (3 sets); Kyr Criminal Enforcement Code 11.11.1999 21.1–11.

[105] ICRC news release 25.02.2011, available at www.icrc.org/eng/resources/documents/news-release/2011/kazakhstan-news-2011-02-25.htm, accessed 4 November 2015.

ill-treatment, harsh conditions and exposure to infectious disease. In Turkmenistan, which has been the object of particularly grave concern on the part of human rights organisations, it constitutes a black hole, with no published or authoritative information identifying facilities and numbers of inmates, let alone opportunities for visits and inspection. The wife of the convicted former Turkmen Foreign Minister Shikhmuradov has had no communications with nor information about him for over a decade.[106]

Rights of Social and Political Association and Activity

In the catalogue of rights, political rights and rights of association and assembly[107] have proved the most difficult to assert effectively, the most 'honoured in the breach', across the region. Unlike other basic rights, where the difficulties arise in the enforcement and application, the problems regarding rights of assembly and association in the five constitutions are discernible in the formulation, where the differences are revealing. The Tajik and Turkmen provisions regarding assembly, for example, are terse but (relatively) unqualified ('right to participate in gatherings meetings, demonstrations, peaceful marches as established by law'; 'freedom of gatherings, meetings, and demonstrations in the manner established by law'); the Uzbek and Kazakh provisions expressly qualified ('authorities may stop or forbid the holding of such measures [meetings] only on justified concern for security'; 'use of this right may limited by law in the interests of state security'). The Kyrgyz provision by pointed contrast is elaborate, not merely unqualified but amplified to include a right to facilitation by the authorities of the assembly with or without notice and a right against organisers' liability for failure to notify.[108]

[106] Amnesty International, Turkmenistan: The authorities should reveal the whereabouts of the disappeared, Public Statement, AI Index: EUR 61/007/2012 (2012), available at www.amnesty.org/download/Documents/24000/eur610072012en.pdf, accessed 4 November 2015. ('The whereabouts of dozens of people convicted in unfair trials in 2002 and 2003 for the alleged assassination attempt on then President Niyazov remained unknown.')

[107] The constitutional regulation of political parties and religious organisations is discussed in more detail in chs 5 and 8, respectively.

[108] Kaz 32, Kyr 34, Taj 29, Uzb 33, Tkm 29.

The right to associate freely is guaranteed in all constitutions, but is more or less elaborately hedged against associations seeking the 'violent overthrow' of the established order. All constitutions forbid the formation of associations or parties on a religious basis, save the Tajik, which permits religious parties on the basis of the 1999 amendments pursuant to the peace accord.[109] The Kazakh Constitution draws a firm line between civil society and the state, establishing 'that illegal interference of the state in the affairs of social organisations is not permitted, and of social organisations in the affairs of the state, or the imposition on social organisations of the functions of state organs.'[110] Such a starkly dichotomous conception, notwithstanding its ostensible evenhandedness (you keep off the state's patch, the state keeps off yours), is curious, not to say anachronistic, and redolent of the Soviet assertion of state prerogatives and obsessive policing of the bounds of state authority. It fails to understand that civil society is emphatically political through and through.

Perhaps the chief impediments to free association lie not so much in the particular constitutional restrictions on the purposes for which they may be formed (which are at least arguably reasonable for the defence of the constitutional order itself) as in the state registration requirements. In a carryover from Soviet practice when the state had effectively colonised civil society through comprehensive regulation and control (indeed direction) of associational life, Central Asian social associations (CSOs, NGOs, charities, clubs, etc) continue to be subject to official registration.[111] Indeed, the Uzbek Constitution itself defines social associations qua registered, in a comprehensive enumeration of types that is concerning in its very specificity.[112] Technically, social associations acquire legal capacity as legal persons only upon registration (and hence are not strictly illegal without it), but only Kyrgyz legislation specifically permits social associations to be created without the formation of a legal person or registration.[113] Registration imposes significant administrative burdens (initially and on an ongoing basis in the form of reporting and accounting obligations) in an excessively bureaucratic

[109] Kyr 4(3), Kaz 5(4), Uzb 57, Tkm 30, Taj 28 (authorising 'among others democratic, religious and atheistic parties', a carefully hedged formulation).

[110] Kaz 5(2).

[111] Kaz Law 31.05.1996 13, Tkm Law 21.10.2003 15, Taj Law 12.05.2007 6, 21.

[112] Uzb 56.

[113] Kyr Law 15.10.99 6.

context and exposes social associations to state scrutiny and control. Foreign and foreign-funded associations are typically permitted (outside of religious organisations and political parties) but may be subject to additional requirements. In the wake of the massive efforts by bilateral and multilateral donors across Central Asia, particularly in the initial years after independence, to assist the growth of 'civil society,' many civil society organisations (CSOs) have essentially been artefacts of donor programming and foreign funding. They have been regarded as politically suspect and potentially oppositional, and are frequently elite-dominated where they have not themselves been co-opted by state authorities.[114]

Rights of Expression and Conscience; Rights of Dissemination and Communication

The rights to expression and dissemination are variably formulated.[115] The Turkmen formulation is stunningly feeble, without mention of the press or mass media as such, and indeed without any reference to dissemination: 'the right to freedom of conviction and its free expression, and also to receive information, if it does not constitute a state or other protected secret'. The other constitutions all provide explicitly for freedom of the press and dissemination of information as freedom of expression, with signature differences: the Uzbek provision merely noting that 'mass media shall be free and act in conformity with the law'; the Kyrgyz provision uniquely omits reference to state secrets (a further Kyrgyz provision is dedicated to freedom of information, including access to state information and specifically to information about oneself);[116] the Kazakh, Uzbek and Tajik provisions all include an express ban on censorship.

Notwithstanding the constitutional guarantees, Central Asian publishers, broadcasters and internet providers have been subject to restrictive regulation, which is sometimes very onerous. Censorship appears in the guise of self-censorship and obedience to understood

[114] SN Cummings, *Understanding Central Asia: Politics and Contested Transformations* (Abingdon and New York, Routledge, 2012) 82.

[115] Uzb 29, 67, Taj 30, Kyr 31(2), Kaz 20, Tkm 28.

[116] Kyr 33.

(and sometimes express) instructions from authorities. Laws on media serve as the principal regulatory device (supplemented by laws on broadcasting, publishing and access to public information) and while typically providing for the range of necessary subjects of regulation, such as journalistic investigation, diversity of opinion, rights and obligations of editors and publishers, and right of refutation, are problematic insofar as they impose licensing and registration requirements on all forms of media with the exception of the internet.[117] Codes regulating liability (administrative, criminal and civil) can obviously also significantly condition and constrain press freedom, with respect for example to libel or failure to observe licensing requirements.[118]

The resulting state of the fourth estate varies dramatically across the 'stans. Broadcast media everywhere are likely to be directly or ultimately in firm state control but print media display greater independence (in ownership and expression). Particularly in Kazakhstan and Kyrgyzstan, the reading, listening, viewing and surfing public is very sophisticated and discriminating (as well as able for the most part to access unhindered outside sources of news and information, including reporting of domestic affairs in the foreign media). However, whereas the lines of permissible views and content in Kazakhstan are fairly tightly policed, Kyrgyzstan's press like its politics has always been rather anarchic and freewheeling, and media freedom there exceeds the regional average by a very wide margin. Elsewhere, in a regionally recurring pattern, independent media companies have been forced to close or have been driven out of business, foreign media have been denied licences or had

[117] See eg Article 19 analysis of Tajik Media Law, available at www.article19.org/data/files/medialibrary/37717/Tajik_Media-Law_Final-.pdf, accessed 4 November 2015); Memorandum on the Law of the Republic of Uzbekistan on Mass Media, available at www.article19.org/data/files/pdfs/analysis/uzbekistan-mass-media-law-06-2004.pdf, accessed 4 November 2015); Memorandum on Kazakhstan's Law on Mass Media August 2006, available at www.article19.org/data/files/pdfs/analysis/kazakhstan-media-la.pdf; Memorandum on Kyrgyz Mass Media Law and the Law on Journalists' Activities 15 September 2005, available at www.article19.org/pdfs/analysis/kyrgyzstan-media.pdf, accessed 4 November 2015.

[118] eg Article 19, Comment on the provisions concerning the right to freedom of expression in the Draft Code of Administrative Offences of Kazakhstan, May 2010, available at www.article19.org/resources.php/resource/1537/en/kazakhstan:-comment-on-the-provisions-concerning-the-right-to-freedom-of-expression-in-the-draft-code-of-administrative-offences, accessed 4 November 2015.

them revoked, and independent journalists harassed, intimidated or prosecuted. The case of Turkmenistan is simplest: notwithstanding the first-ever Media Law adopted in 2012, which resoundingly proclaims unhindered freedom of the press, of dissemination and receipt of information, of the establishment, ownership, operation and use of mass media, all media are state-controlled, full stop.[119] However even in the relatively benign cases, repressive measures remain endemic and reflexive:

> In Central Asia, draft laws and new legislation in Kazakhstan and Kyrgyzstan are aimed at further restricting the rights of people to free expression and stifling the media. In Kazakhstan and Tajikistan, politically motivated prosecutions and law suits are being used to silence dissent.[120]

The five constitutions endorse freedom of conscience and confession. However, as ever the devil is in the details, and this particular devil resides in the dedicated laws on religion, of which each state boasts one, analysed in chapter eight. The very need for a statute regulating religious activity strikes a constitutionalist as odd, inasmuch as in most jurisdictions it is only really the charitable status of religious associations that comes in for any sort of scrutiny and regulation, and the constitutional guarantees place very severe limits on regulating much of anything else. In Central Asia, much as was the case for social associations or political parties, religious activity is a source of anxiety and a provocation to vigilance on the part of authorities. Both as a matter of conscience and confessional particularity, religious activity provides an incomparably righteous ground for challenge, contestation or condemnation of Caesar, and Caesar's forms of rule.

Rights in Criminal Proceedings (Judicial Guarantees)

The constitutions all provide fair trial rights (against self-incrimination, arbitrary arrest/detention, double jeopardy, retroactivity, to due

[119] Tkm Law 22.12.2012 1, 2; Reporters without Borders 2014 Index. The Media Law is called 'a complete fiction' and Turkmenistan is ranked 177 out of 181 states.

[120] Article 19 Statement, 02 May 2014, 'Central Asian governments must stop violating freedom of expression', available at www.article19.org/resources.php/resource/37537/en/central-asian-governments-must-stop-violating-freedom-of-expression#sthash.Ux3TjEti.dpuf, accessed 4 November 2015.

process, criminal defence, presumption of innocence, appeal) but vary in the detail of elaboration. The Kyrgyz provisions are singularly comprehensive, in distinction to the Turkmen bare bones (but then the language of the Turkmen Constitution is generally economical). Habeas corpus rights are constitutionally guaranteed unequivocally only in Kazakhstan and Kyrgyzstan; the other three constitutions adopt weaker formulations.[121] While all five constitutions provide the right to counsel for the accused,[122] only the Tajik, Kazakh and Kyrgyz constitutions include unequivocal guarantees in the text to a defence lawyer 'from the moment of custody'.

Criminal procedure in Central Asia is the bell jar of the tensions and contradictions of constitutional or limited government: nowhere is the disparity between the power of the state and the vulnerability of the individual more starkly in evidence than in the circumstances of custody, investigation and trial. Judicial guarantees, constitutional constraints on policing, detaining, investigating, prosecuting and adjudicating authorities, are as easy to enumerate as they are difficult to actualise and enforce. The criminal procedure codes are of greater constitutional moment for rights protection in the justice system itself that the constitutionally enumerated guarantees.

The Soviet state perfected criminal proceedings and procedure as preferred tool of political control and repression: if for Vyshinsky, confession was the 'queen of evidence', prosecution in general was the queen of enforcement. All five states have carried over the gestalt of Soviet criminal procedure, its stages and sequence, actions and actors, fundamental concepts and categories: a Soviet lawyer plucked by TARDIS from 1950s Moscow and deposited in an investigation or trial in contemporary Dushanbe or Almaty would have no difficulty getting orientated. The roles of the procurator may have been curtailed (diminished direct investigative authority, no issuance of arrest warrant) and of the *advokat* expanded (rights of participation at all stages), but the basic procedures and roles would all be very familiar (inquest, preliminary investigation, enquirers and investigators, etc).

All the states have introduced non-negligible reforms, such as jury trials (Kazakhstan and prospectively Kyrgyzstan), adversarial justice,

[121] Kaz 16, Kyr 24(4), Uzb 25, Taj 19.

[122] Kaz 16(3), Kyr 24, Taj 19, Uzb 116, Tkm 108 (right to counsel at all stages of proceedings).

right to counsel, judicial warrants), but those reforms show divergent degrees of penetration. They can often seem more like modifications and patches to a venerable software programme, the equivalent of a late-generation Microsoft Windows version with DOS running unperturbed underneath the glossy new features. The prestige factor attaching to the adoption of internationally validated and *de rigeur* justice process components is a significant driver of reforms. It reflects the reigning international legal ideology operating in domains as widely removed as criminal justice (foregrounding human rights) and trade law ('economic constitutionalism'—immunising entrepreneurial and trade rights against any political challenge):

> There is an additional key factor that contributes to the promotion of legal reforms and the expansion of the political space for positive legal evolution in Central Asian countries. The governments and political elites of the region absolutely need to enhance their prestige, image, and legitimacy before the international community, especially when one takes into account the recent independence of these states and their lack of institutional traditions. For instance, the desire for international prestige explains, at least in part, most of the positive legal reforms enacted in Kazakhstan during and immediately prior to the country's OSCE presidency, in particular the laws on domestic violence and gender equality adopted with the support of the OSCE's Office for Democratic Institutions and Human Rights (ODIHR) in December 2009.[123]

Indeed, many of the heralded reforms to criminal procedure across contemporary Central Asia, such as habeas corpus, signify as largely cosmetic add-ons which leave the functioning of the justice process undisturbed but convey a misleading impression of convergence on accepted criminal practice.[124] Thus the requirement of judicial intervention in the event of detention of a suspect after either 48 or 72 hours in all states except Turkmenistan (requirement only of the

[123] Golovko (n 83) 109.

[124] Human Rights Watch, 'No One Left to Witness: Torture, the Failure of Habeas Corpus, and the Silencing of Lawyers in Uzbekistan' (2011), available at www.hrw.org/sites/default/files/reports/uzbekistan1211webwcover.pdf, accessed 4 November 2015 (reporting, inter alia, practice of 'habeas without corpus', obtaining judicial warrant for a detention prospectively and using it to deny judicial access to the detainee once detained).

decision of a procurator) does not ipso facto secure the generally accepted benefits of habeas corpus.[125]

Beyond departures from due process standards, the venerable Soviet device of the invidious use of criminal process to punish or forestall political opposition remains a major human rights concern and focus of critique for the republics. The Ashgabat show trial of 2003 against the alleged perpetrators of the November 2002 attack on Niyazov is perhaps the most egregious contemporary Central Asian example but more routine cases abound in every jurisdiction.[126] The habitual invocation of constitutional guarantees too readily equates to reform as sloganeering, rather than structural transformation: 'habeas corpus' is one such slogan. Rights, or their due protection, are outcomes of systemic changes, not quick-fix amendments: they cannot simply be legislated as such into being, which is why the translation of constitutional catalogues into a rights protection framework is a prodigious, long-term labour. For this reason, the actual mechanism elaborated in the criminal procedure code, and not the label—for example, 'habeas corpus'—or the constitutional provision, demands evaluation and analysis.

Other Issues Arising from Rights Formulation

When presented with this selection of rights catalogues, differential rights ordering and organisation within them, and finally of alternative particular rights formulations, the observer may be inclined to put the question: what difference does any of this make at the end of the day? The enumerated differences might mean a great deal or very little, but in the absence of developed rights jurisprudence and a progressive elaboration and exegesis of the texts, who can say? Of course one might easily read into observed differences all sorts of telling political

[125] Kaz Criminal Procedure Code 04.07.2014 14(2) (72 hours), Kyr Criminal Procedure Code 30.06.1999 39(2) (48 hours), Uzb Criminal Procedure Code 22.09.1994 226 (72 hours), Taj Criminal Procedure Code 03.12.2009 92(3), 95(3), 96(2) (72 hours), Tkm Criminal Procedure Code 18.04.2009 144(2) (48 hours).

[126] See E Decaux, 'OSCE Rapporteur's Report on Turkmenistan' 12 March 2003, available at www.osce.org/odihr/18372, accessed 9 February 2016, for the Turkmenistan case. For other exemplary or notable instances, see Human Rights Watch 2011 (Uzbekistan), HRC Communications 09.11.2010, 24.05.2014 (Kazakhstan, Zhovtis and Kuramshin cases).

and cultural nuances, but at great peril. The significance of the right ultimately turns on the adequacy of the remedy: the skeletal text only takes on flesh when courts enforce rights by applying the provisions to concrete complaints of infringement and in so doing interpreting them.

Nonetheless, the observed differences in the formulations do seem to tally with the human rights culture and capabilities of the respective constitutional systems. Thus, for example, in addition to the points noted earlier (comprehensiveness of judicial guarantees, express non-derogability, etc) the Kyrgyz Constitution makes international human rights norms immediately justiciable, as well a priority over other international treaties.[127] All constitutions make some reference to duties, principally those of citizens,[128] as well as rights, but rights and duties are not specifically correlative. The Turkmen Constitution in singular fashion appears to condition rights protection on the fulfilment of duties in a quasi-contractual formulation (almost an exchange of performance obligations): 'the effectuation of rights and freedoms is inseparable from the performance by person and citizen of his obligations before society and the state.'[129]

Not expressly formulated in any of the constitutions are rights of newly identified marginalised and vulnerable populations. To the traditional categories of minorities (the constitutional protection of whom is discussed in chapter eight), elderly, poor, women, children and prisoners, have in recent years (as a result of human rights mobilisation) been added: the disabled, mental patients, lesbian/gay/bisexual/transgender persons (LGBT), people with aids (PWAs), sex workers and injecting drugs users (IDUs), among others. Many of these groups have been the object of discrimination and persecution in Central Asia, and have formed interest groups or associations to lobby for adequate legal protection or recognition, with some success (particularly in Kyrgyzstan, where representatives of marginalised groups regularly come to parliamentary surgeries to convey concerns or comment on draft bills).

Finally, although terrorism is expressly referenced only in the Kazakh Constitution (as noted above, in a rights context, and negatively), it

[127] Kyr 6(3).

[128] Uzb 47–52, Kyr 55–56, Kaz 34–38, Taj 42–45, Tkm 40–42. Duties of parents to children, and of grown working children to non-working parents also figure (Kaz 27), as do those of respect for elders and care for relatives and sick (Kyr 37).

[129] Tkm 40.

casts a very long shadow over constitutional rights protection in all five cases. Issues of ill-treatment and torture have gained particular prominence in light of the counter-terrorism drive of the last decade, which has had a particularly unfortunate impact on the Central Asian states. Counter-terror has served all five states as a pretext for suppression generally of political opposition and officially unsanctioned or unregulated Islamic association and activity. As noted in chapter four, new Kazakh and Turkmen security sector legislation has begun to address the internationally recognised nexus between human rights and counter-terror measures, but only in declaratory fashion. The Shanghai Cooperation Organisation, to which all states save neutral Turkmenistan belong, along with Russia, China and Iran, has adopted a draconian regional counter-terror convention.[130] In the context of the Soviet-era institutional roles and dynamics, the war on terror, the region's perceived strategic vulnerabilities, and the states' fears of Islamist challenges to authority, the security services have come to play a critical and overwhelmingly negative role in respect of rights (much as the KGB once did).[131]

JUDICIAL PROTECTION

The remedies available for infringement of constitutional rights by normative legal acts were discussed above in the section on constitutional tribunals. For individual acts of a non-normative nature, for example, administrative decisions, by state bodies or officials, four constitutions expressly grant citizens a remedy against infringements of right,[132] although the formulations vary intriguingly. Uzbekistan provides 'a right to appeal in court the illegal action of state organs, officials, and

[130] 2001 Shanghai Convention, see analysis Amnesty International (n 102) 15–16.

[131] Murray (n 100) 17–27 (detailed account of reality behind a terrorism trial): Amnesty International (n 102) 11 (noting 'the practices of torture and other ill-treatment that are often used in relation to people suspected of ordinary crimes, and routinely used in relation to political opponents and individuals suspected of involvement in extremism and terrorism-related activities or in banned religious groups').

[132] Kyr 39 (made non-derogable by 20(5.7)), Taj 32 (oddly as the second paragraph in the article on the right of ownership), Uzb 44, Tkm 44.

social associations.' Turkmenistan, Kyrgyzstan and Tajikistan provide for compensation for harm caused by unlawful actions: Turkmenistan provides only a 'right to demand compensation for material and moral damage in judicial proceedings'; Kyrgyzstan a 'right to compensation for harm'; and Tajikistan that 'material and moral damage shall be compensated in accordance with the law.' On the other hand, whereas in the Kyrgyz provision the infringing actions are those of 'organs of state authority, of local government and officials in the performance of their duties', in the analogous Tajik provision they are those of 'state organs, social organisations, political parties, and individuals' and in the Turkmen provision those of 'state organs, other organisations, their personnel, and also private persons.' It is clear that only the Kyrgyz provision is drafted clearly and in a rule-of-law spirit to protect citizens against the state alone. In the other cases the constitutional waters are muddied and state violation of individual right is effectively conflated with a general civil liability attaching to sundry non-state actors as well.

INTERNATIONAL PROTECTION

The Central Asian republics have been well-integrated into the UN Human Rights system from the outset; they were all born into the human rights age, just as the system took on its mature, definitive form. All five have ratified the principal human rights instruments, save that Tajikistan, Uzbekistan and Turkmenistan have not signed the Optional Protocol to the Convention against Torture and Kazakhstan and Tajikistan have not signed the Second Optional Protocol to the Civil and Political Rights Covenant (by which states parties undertake to abolish the death penalty).[133] Unlike the Russian Federation, no Central Asian state is a member of the Council of Europe or has acceded to the

[133] International Covenant on Civil and Political Rights (ICCPR), Protocols 1 and 2: Kaz 24.01.2006, 30.06.2009, not acceded; Kyr 07.10.1994, 07.10.1994, 06.12.2010; Taj 04.01.1999, 04.01.1999, not acceded; Uzb 28.09.1995, 28.09.1995, 23.12.2008; Tkm 01.05.1997, 01.05.1997, 11.01.2000; International Covenant on Economic Social and Cultural Rights (ICESCR): Kaz 24.01.2006, Kyr 07.10.1994, Taj 04.01.1999, Uzb 28.09.1995, Tkm 01.0.1997; Convention against Torture (CAT) and Protocol: Kaz 26.08.1998; 22.10.2008, Kyr 05.09.1997, 29.12.2008, Taj 11.01.1995, not acceded; Uzb 28.09.1995, not acceded; Tkm 25.06.1999, not acceded.

European Convention of Human Rights, thereby making itself subject to the jurisdiction of the European Court of Human Rights.[134] They are not therefore subject to sustained, detailed and cumulative international scrutiny, through adjudication of individual cases by an eminent tribunal, of the human rights consequences of their normative framework and state practice. Nor therefore do they enjoy the benefit of the attendant pressure and notoriety as a driver of reform to improve their compliance with international obligations.

All five states have however acceded to the First Optional Protocol of the ICCPR, allowing the Human Rights Committee to entertain individual communications alleging violations of rights. While not as effective a protection mechanism as the jurisdiction of an international court issuing binding decisions, the Committee's consideration and opinion afford the principal international quasi-judicial forum for evaluating the constitutional commitments of the five states respecting human rights.[135] All states participate in the Universal Periodic Review mechanism, and have made regular reports and responses in connection with it.[136] The Kazakh Constitution establishes the supremacy over domestic legislation of all international treaties, whereas the Kyrgyz Constitution provides that human rights 'are self-executing and have priority over norms of other international treaties', thus not in need of enabling enactment (like the Human Rights Act in the UK). The Kyrgyz Constitution further alone incorporates an express right to apply to international human rights organs.[137]

[134] They are not geographically eligible (saving arguably Kazakhstan which, like Turkey, straddles continents and has a European toehold). Kyrgyzstan has however since 1992 been a member of the COE's Venice Commission, which renders advisory constitutional opinions on legislation (but cannot hear or adjudicate cases), and Kazakhstan joined in 2012; the opinions of the Venice Commission have been noted in this analysis where relevant.

[135] The HRC's jurisprudence regarding communications under protocol 1 encompasses all five states: Kazakhstan (3 communications considered but acceded only 2009), Kyrgyzstan (12), Tajikistan (22), Uzbekistan (34), Turkmenistan (3).

[136] All five states have participated in the both first and second UPR cycles. See www.ohchr.org/EN/HRBodies/UPR/Documents/uprlist.pdf and www.ohchr.org/Documents/HRBodies/UPR/UPR-FullCycleCalendar_2nd.pdf, accessed 11 November 2015.

[137] Kaz 4(3), Kyr 6(2), 41.

SUPPLEMENTARY PROTECTION: PROCURACY AND HUMAN RIGHTS INSTITUTIONS

The rights protection system and its deficiencies have been the subject of sustained international concern, criticism and engagement. The sphere of right extends well beyond judicial guarantees in criminal matters and well beyond the remit of courts and adjudication. Rights of assembly, expression and organisation have been prominent as well. As noted in chapter two, Soviet law did make allowance for rights enforcement but through the Procuracy not the courts. Whatever may be urged against its role in human rights infringement, the five Central Asian Procuracies continue to play a significant role in human rights protection, perhaps more significant than the courts or the special mechanisms (ombudsmen and other national human rights mechanisms).[138]

In post-Soviet Central Asia as elsewhere in post-Soviet space, special rights-monitoring bodies have been established to play a critical para-judicial role in rights enforcement. Kyrgyzstan, Uzbekistan, Kazakhstan and Tajikistan all have established an Ombudsman or Human Rights Plenipotentiary, though only in the first case as a constitutional organ effecting 'parliamentary control over human rights'.[139] Turkmenistan has established a National Institute for Democracy and Human Rights, as well as a Commission for the Review of Complaints of Abuse by Law Enforcement, both under direct presidential auspices. The former was not vested with human right protection jurisdiction or the capacity to receive complaints, but created rather to serve an applied research function. The Commission, by contrast, was established expressly for the purpose of receiving complaints.[140]

The Paris Principles promulgated under UN auspices require that national human rights institutions have the capacity to present regular and occasional reports and make policy and legislative proposals to responsible authorities, to facilitate ratification of and compliance with international human rights obligations and participate in preparation of periodic reports, to publicise and promote for general awareness and educational purposes. They also require that such institutions enjoy free

138 As it does in the Russian Federation, Henderson (n 3) 240.

139 Kaz 19.11.2002 Decree, Statutes 10.12.2002, Kyr 108, Law 31.06.2002, Taj Law 20.03.2008, Uzb Law 24.04.1997.

140 Tkm Decrees 23.10.1996, 19.02.2007.

and timely access to persons, documents and information, free communication with press and public and consultation with other public bodies and NGOs. The composition must be reflective of societal pluralism, and include NGOs and academics, and must be appointed or elected with a specific mandate. Institutions with jurisdictional competence should inform complainants of their rights and remedies, seek amicable resolution, hear or transmit complaints and make recommendations.[141] The Central Asian human rights bodies vary in their conformity to the requirements of the Paris Standards and their capacity to discharge their functions independently and authoritatively, as well as in their remit and authority generally, as noted above. The Kyrgyz *Akyitkachy* (Ombudsman) has proved the most active and effective and the Uzbek Plenipotentiary the least.

Their role recapitulates in certain respects the supervisory role of the Procuracy, including action at the instigation of citizen complaints. However, as relatively new, comparatively modestly staffed and funded bodies, they cannot command anything remotely touching the institutional force and authority of the venerable Procuracy as they prepare to take on other powerful state actors (including possibly the Procuracy itself). As Stalin once reportedly remarked of the Vatican's wartime significance, 'How many divisions has the Pope?' As elsewhere in constitutional affairs, institutional weight or clout must be secured over time in the course of the play of events and personalities and is not susceptible of being ordained ab initio, even with the necessary political will. If long-established but weak institutions like courts must engage in an extended struggle for due constitutional stature and authority, brand new institutions like the Ombudsman have a yet tougher row to hoe, particularly insofar as they are called upon to challenge the authority and correctness of formidable vested bureaucratic interests, the power agencies or ministries. They are as a rule armed with slingshots against the constitutional Goliaths. The international community may well laud the creation of new rights champions on paper, but it is not well-positioned to appreciate the developmental rigours that inevitably await them before they attain their institutional age of majority.

[141] UN Human Rights Commission Resolution 1992/54, 1992 and General Assembly Resolution 48/134, 1993.

FURTHER READING

L Golovko, 'The Space for Legal Reform in Central Asia: Between Political Limits and Theoretical Deformations' in 2010 *Yearbook of the Organisation for Security and Co-operation in Europe (OSCE)* 105, 115 (Baden-Baden, Nomos Verlagsgesellschaft, 2011).

Human Rights Watch, 'Uzbekistan: Nowhere to Turn: Torture and Ill-treatment in Uzbekistan' (2009) hwww.hrw.org/sites/default/files/reports/uzbekistan1107webwcover.pdf.

Human Rights Watch, 'No One Left to Witness: Torture, the Failure of Habeas Corpus, and the Silencing of Lawyers in Uzbekistan' (2011) www.hrw.org/sites/default/files/reports/uzbekistan1211webwcover.pdf.

International Crisis Group, 'Kyrgyzstan: The Challenge of Judicial Reform, Asia Report No 150, 10 April 2008' (2008).

UN 03.02.2003 Report of the Special Rapporteur on the Question of Torture, Theo van Boven, Addendum: Mission to Uzbekistan, Submitted in Accordance with Commission Resolution 2002/38, E/CN.4/2003/68/Add.2.

7

Plan to Clan

Transitions, Economic and Social

Constitutional Regulation of the Economy: Basic Rules – Constitutional Regulation of the Economy: Basic Institutions – Economic Constitutionalism: Foreign Investment and International Integration – The 'Material Constitution': Crony Capitalism, Corruption, Crime – Social Provision and Protections (Pensions, Unemployment, Poverty, Gender)

THE ECONOMIC DIMENSIONS of constitutions are rarely singled out for special treatment, and indeed economic constitutional provisions as such are generally terse and formulaic, particularly in these days of universal markets. But the Central Asian states derive from a constitutional order which defined itself economically and socially before anything else, and which prominently constitutionalised its fundamental economic and social institutions (socialist ownership and the plan, sweeping social protection and provision). As a consequence economic and social regulation necessarily comes to assume particular significance for the Central Asian constitutions, even if by implication or omission rather than by express treatment. Such economic and social provisions have proved surprisingly stable, given the emergent or market-transitional circumstances in which the constitutions were drafted.

This chapter does not confine itself to the constitutional regulation of the market and the social system or the constitutional elaboration of social and economic rights. It adopts an unconventionally broad approach meriting an explanatory justification. For one, the Central Asian states had to establish the legal foundations of market systems to begin with, thereby undertaking a 'constituent process' for the economy itself. For another, as discussed in chapter three, beyond their Soviet derivation, the Central Asian systems have been profoundly marked by their emergence into a globalised world defined by neoliberal norms and institutions. The 'economic constitutionalism' of, for example, the World Trade Organization (WTO) and foreign investment rules has arguably constrained their freedom of legislative manoeuvre and conditioned their constitutional architecture. Finally, the divergence between constitutional and legal norms on the one hand and the actual practices of economic governance (administrative and judicial actions and decisions) on the other is so profound a feature of the Central Asian states as to merit sustained constitutional examination.

In the sections below, the analysis takes up first the establishment of the basic property and contract rule of the game, the 'economic constitution', in the civil codes and related legislation. Then it considers three constitutional bodies charged directly with economic regulatory authority: the central bank, the accounts chamber (committee) and the economic courts. Following is a discussion of the harmonisation of the constitutional framework of the Central Asian states with the demands of global integration and international economic norms. The penultimate section looks critically at the rise of crony or clan capitalism, corruption and crime across all five states, and examines the continuing paradox of punctilious constitutional formalism in the context of the endemic violation of basic constitutional norms across the Central Asian states. At the end is a consideration of the social constitution—the social support and protection system for work and health.

CONSTITUTIONAL REGULATION OF THE ECONOMY: BASIC RULES

The economic and social provisions of the five constitutions were framed in such anodyne and plastic terms, save as noted below, that they would have been serviceable for a broad set of market configurations—and perhaps that was the point. They were not economically transitional in any linear sense or to any definite end, but were instrumental, intended to afford the greatest breadth of maneuvering room to elites keeping options open. However, it was the civil code in each of the five states that indisputably served as the economic constitution, the basic legal framework for the new economic system. The states all embraced speedy codification rather than an expressly provisional or transitional regime of economic regulation. They might have deferred codification, relying instead for a more extended period on interim economic institutions—and a 'transitional economic constitution'—in the context of the progressive, gradual relaxation of state control, cession of economic decision-making and transfer of economic assets (means of production) from state to non-state actors. Instead, the five states moved expeditiously towards a market economy though at significantly varying rates, with the 'K' states in the lead. As a result, though they effectively constitutionalised a new property regime by codifying it, they did not constitutionalise (entrench or protect) the process by which that regime was created—privatisation. Typically they relied on a (constitutionally unregulated) state property committee to manage the disposition of the portfolio of state holdings (major state enterprises, typically) and serve as the central regulator of the privatisation process, as discussed in the section on crony capitalism below.

The parliaments except the Turkmen Mejlis adopted their respective civil codes[1] on the basis of the CIS Model Civil Code of 1994–96[2] (as has the Duma of the Russian Federation).[3] There are some notable differences in arrangement, organisation and formulation. The Turkmen Code, apart from being the only one to bear the name of the then-president,[4] was independently elaborated on the basis of the German Civil Code, the Bürgerliches Gesetzbuch (BGB), and differs in numerous respects from the other four. These latter are all sister instruments, having been produced as so many (for the most part trivial or modest) variations on a theme. They all carry on the robust Russian civilist tradition and thus bequeath to the Central Asian states a common stock of

[1] Kazakhstan adopted its Civil Code, Parts I & II in 1994; Tajikistan 1999; Kyrgystan 1995, 1998; Uzbekistan 1996; Turkmenistan 1998.

[2] MS Korableva, 'A Comparative Study of the Protection of Civil Rights: The Civil Codes of CIS Countries' (2002–03) 28 *Review of Central and East European Law* 167.

[3] J Henderson, *Constitution of the Russian Federation* (Oxford, Hart Publishing, 2011) 86–87.

[4] 17.07.1998 Turkmenistan Civil Code of Saparmurat Turkmenbashi No 294-I.

legal concepts, definitions and terms. Indeed the story of post-Soviet codification represents but another serial chapter in the history of Soviet codification. Much as the Union-wide Principles of Civil Law[5] were conceived to serve as template on the basis of which the respective SSRs were free (within severe constraints) to introduce locally appropriate nuances, so did the CIS Model Code function for the post-Soviet jurisdictions which adapted it. The Kazakh, Kyrgyz, Uzbek and Tajik civil codes are indeed striking in their consistency and conformity with one another, exhibiting in most respects less variation than among state or provincial jurisdictions in most federal states (Canada, US, Australia).[6] One might even say that the Central Asian republics share with the Russian Federation almost an identical civil–legal morphology (such fairly strict parallelism does not carry over into other fields, notably criminal law, which lacked a post-Soviet model codification process and thus exhibits greater diversity of arrangement, language and provisions). Despite this commonality of economic architectural plan, the economies of the Central Asian states have all come to look quite different one to another, as to that of the Russian Federation. This divergence raises the issue of the relevance of the basic economic rule framework to the outcomes.

All five states carried over the emerging mixed ownership provision of the penultimate Soviet moment. The first generation constitutions all provided for a diversity of forms of ownership, meaning private as well as state.[7] Whether expressly (as in the case of Uzbekistan) or by implication, they all provided for an emerging economic system (since it was emergent from the antecedent regime more definitively than it was leading to a definite successor regime). The very need to distinguish private and state ownership and provide constitutional guarantees against expropriation of objects in private ownership serves as an index of an interim property regime. All constitutions save the Turkmen reserved to exclusive state ownership all natural resources, including notably land.[8] Kyrgyzstan expressly prohibited the sale and purchase of

[5] USSR Law 08.12.1961.

[6] PB Maggs, 'The Civil Codes of Central Eurasia—A Comparison,' Paper presented at the Central Eurasian Studies Society Fourth Annual Conference, Cambridge, Mass., 2003, available at www.law.illinois.edu/p-maggs/codes.htm, accessed 4 November 2015.

[7] 1993 Kaz 45, 1993 Kyr 4, Uzb 53, Taj 12, Tkm 9.

[8] Kaz 1993 46, Kyr 1993 3, Uzb 55, Taj 13.

land. Turkmenistan was anomalous in both permitting sale of land and in omitting to include an article establishing state ownership in natural resources. Restrictions or prohibitions in land transactions were relaxed in all cases by subsequent legislation and amendment.

Some constitutions recognise a broad express right to personal ownership and market participation.[9] The Turkmen Constitution does not include particular property or market rights in the catalogue of individual rights; rather the right to ownership, including expressly the 'ownership of means of production, land, other material and intellectual objects of value', is incorporated in the general article on ownership, and while the state 'shall encourage and support the market and facilitate the growth of small and medium enterprises', it does not guarantee any entrepreneurial right as such.[10] The Tajik Constitution treats ownership in an economic context (guarantee of 'the freedom of economic and entrepreneurial activity, equal right, and legal protection of all forms of ownership, among them private') as well as additionally in a rights context, albeit interestingly in a negative formulation ('no one has the right to remove or limit a citizen's right of ownership').[11]

CONSTITUTIONAL REGULATION OF THE ECONOMY: BASIC INSTITUTIONS

National or Central Bank and Accounts Organ

The constitutional texts themselves make very slender direct provision for economic policy-making and regulation. Only two purely 'economic' institutions carry constitutional status: the national or central bank[12] and the Accounts Chamber or Committee.[13] Central banks of course carry primary responsibility for anchoring and regulating a country's

[9] Kaz 26, Taj 32.

[10] Tkm 7, 8.

[11] Taj 12, 32.

[12] Taj 57(10), 69(7), Kaz 44, 55, 57, Uzb 124, 80 (9, 12), Kyr 64(5.1), 74(4.3), 105. Only the Kyrgyz and Uzbek constitutions establish the role and functions of the central bank; the Turkmen Constitution omits mention of it altogether.

[13] Kyr 107, Kaz 53, 57, Uzb 78(17), 93(12); omitted in the Tajik and Turkmen constitutions.

banking system, as for determining and implementing monetary policy. Typically central banks are constitutionally insulated from political pressure and are not answerable in their day-to-day conduct of monetary and banking affairs to the executive.[14] The head of a central bank cannot usually be recalled or removed by the president who has appointed her or him, and her or his term of office may not coincide with that of the elected executive. In none of the Central Asian constitutions may such safeguards be found; the leadership of central banks is not regulated differentially relative to that of other executive organs. The chief bankers in the Central Asian republics are as much creatures of the executive as the procurators general or the chairs of the central elections commissions. The Accounts Chamber in each jurisdiction is an oversight, control and audit body at the highest level for implementation of the state budget (expenditures and disbursements of all manner of state funds).[15]

Courts and Markets: Judicialism

Of course, in all five states government or cabinet plays the lead role (as supervised by the corresponding offices in the presidential apparat or administration) in state fiscal and economic policy: Ministries of Finance, Economy and Planning, Agriculture, Industry, Mining, etc, together with subsidiary economic regulatory organs, like the property committee. Indeed, it would be hard to come up with government functions which have no economic relevance whatsoever. Due consideration of their place in the constitutional scheme for the economy is however beyond the scope or pretensions of this analysis, which rather takes up an institution which traditionally does not figure in discussions of the 'economic constitution': the judiciary.

As introduced in the preceding chapter, each state inherited an SSR *arbitrazh* system, which was re-established as an economic court under the new constitutions, apart from Turkmenistan which relied on supplementary legislation after an interval. The precise jurisdictional remit of these courts varied, but in general, like their predecessor *abritrazh* tribunals, they were authorised to adjudicate disputes between legal

[14] Bank of England Act 1998, s 1(2), US Federal Reserve Act § 10.

[15] See eg Kaz Accounts Committee Statute 05.08.2002 1(7), 2.

entities but not disputes one party to which was a natural person.[16] The advantage of continuing the old system in new guise was the development and maintenance of a special body of judicial expertise and experts for cases entailing particular complexities—a sophisticated tribunal for sophisticated disputes. Unlike the old *arbitrazh* system, where the proceedings were less formal and the evidentiary requirements less strict than in civil cases (in this respect the Soviet system more resembled commercial arbitration), those of the new economic courts have been tightened up.

The last chapter took note of the salience of 'judicialism' in the transition paradigm and of the expectations placed on the Central Asian judiciaries by the international community (and the resources and support channelled to them for the purpose). The role of the judiciary in ensuring the success of the 'project of markets' was if anything accorded more attention and concern (and a great deal more funding) than its role in the correlative 'project of democracy'.[17] Constitutionalists and human rights groups may have insisted that Central Asian courts police separation of powers and enforce rights, but the World Bank and a host of like-minded donors insisted yet more stridently that courts referee the emerging market and enforce property and contract—and zealously supplied abundant technical assistance and financing. A powerful new rationale for these projects had been authoritatively articulated by then-General Counsel of the World Bank Ibrahim Shihata on the formalist, neo-Weberian grounds that capitalist growth was premised on a market-enabling legal framework of rules and institutions, and that courts were indispensable as enforcers.[18]

If the civil code and related commercial legislation supply the basic rules for economic actors, so ran the arguments, then the umpire is the court system. Transition means a shift from vertical to horizontal

[16] Kaz Decree 16.01.2001, Taj Economic Procedure Code 05.01.2008, Tkm Law 14.02.2000, *Arbitrazh* Procedure Code 19.12.2000.

[17] DM Trubek 'The 'rule of law' in development assistance: past, present, and future' in DM Trubek and A Santos (eds), *The New Law and Economic Development: A Critical Appraisal* (Cambridge, Cambridge University Press, 2006).

[18] DM Trubek, 'Max Weber on the Role of Law in the Rise of Capitalism' (1972) *Wisconsin Law Review* 720; Trubek (n 17); I Shihata, 'Governance and the Role of Law in Economic Development' in A Seidman, RB Seidman and T Walde (eds), *Making Development Work: Legislative Reform for Institutional Transformation and Good Governance* (Amsterdam, Kluwer Law International, 1999) xviii–xxi.

modes of co-ordination, from one supreme economic decision-maker to a myriad of individual decision-makers. In that case the default role of state authorities in economic maintenance should shift commensurately from determining choice to refereeing the choices of others, from executive to judicial. To the Central Asian judiciary (both the economic courts and the regular courts insofar as they were resolving disputes over property and contract) was thus imputed a critical *constituent* role securing the nascent market economy. No constitutional provision in the region charged the courts expressly with this function, but the nature of the transition process itself demanded it: courts were imagined to be the definitive market-transitional institution discharging a composite function of consolidating and legitimising newly introduced market rules and stabilising actors' expectations.

The ordinary and specialised economic courts in the five states all have come routinely and comprehensively to apply the rules of the market to civil and commercial disputes. They have accumulated a substantial body of economic jurisprudence through the decisions and interpretive guidelines of the apex courts or panels. But if Central Asian courts have served a constituent or pedagogic function in the transition to the market, it has been rather by unedifying example than precept. The regional prevalence (if not ubiquity) of judicial bribery and corruption (see discussion below) suggests Central Asian judges have themselves been integrated into the market system as much as they preside over or enforce it, and that judicial decisions (and offices) are regulated by commerce rather than regulate it. Judges have risen to the challenges of commercial disputes, not to consolidate the market, but for the reason Willie Sutton gave the FBI when asked why he robbed banks: that's where the money is.[19]

[19] eg in a dispute worth in excess of $150 million involving the takeover of a mobile telephone company by interests associated with then-President Bakiev's son, the Kyrgyz Supreme Court rendered a decision in favour of the latter which defied logic and strongly suggested corruption. Decision of the Supreme Court of the Kyrgyz Republic 15.12.2005, Case No 07-000287/05ED. See characterisation of that decision in Judgment of the Privy Council JCPC 2009/0065, JCPC 2009/0065 *Altimo Holdings and Investment Limited and Others (Appellants) v Kyrgyz Mobil Tel Limited and Others (Respondents)*, para 40. For an analogous case of judicial expropriation see *Sistem Muhendislik Sanayi Ve Ticaret AS v Kyrgyz Republic*, ICSID Case No. ARB(AF)/06/1, Award of 30 September 2009.

ECONOMIC CONSTITUTIONALISM: FOREIGN INVESTMENT AND INTERNATIONAL INTEGRATION

The Central Asian constitutional systems all came of age just as the wave of globalisation was cresting. The five states were not just newly enfranchised subjects of the international community and international law, they were new entrants to the global field of economic play, new international market actors. As such, they found themselves confronted with pressing issues of positioning, strategy and national development policy. Conversion to a market economy required not just thinking like a state in organising the domestic framework for commerce (constituting the market, laying down the ground rules and fashioning the essential institutions), but thinking like a state in a competitive global economic context. That context was itself in the process of becoming ever more comprehensively regulated by the emerging field of international economic law, and the Central Asian Five discovered that they were expected to assume international obligations governing (and constraining) their choice and use of economic rules and institutions. The WTO, for instance, came into being and immediately asserted its global significance when the states were three years and some old.

All such issues were particularly accentuated because three of the five states—Kazakhstan, Turkmenistan and Uzbekistan—possessed very substantial hydrocarbon reserves and mineral deposits, and were therefore poised immediately to become very significant global economic players. In a world obsessed with the quest for natural resources, Central Asia was one vast greenfield suddenly and unexpectedly opened for economic exploitation and investment. Resource endowments, the material riches of the states at emergence, have exercised profound shaping effects on their constitutional systems generally, even though not formally reflected in constitutional language. In these globalising circumstances, the constitutional systems themselves came under scrutiny on the basis of the degree of their perceived openness to the world at large, their 'economic hospitality'. The Soviet economic order had been singularly closed and controlled, permitting the very most marginal penetration by the capitalist outside and then only very late in the day.

All five constitutional systems contemplate the insertion of their economies into global systems of exchange, production and distribution; they make provision for trade and investment and the foreign agents of trade and investment. However, only the Kyrgyz Constitution itself makes specific reference to rights of foreigners. All five civil codes provide that foreign persons be governed by the same rules, or may acquire the same rights and obligations, as citizens.[20] In each state's civil domain, foreign individuals or entities are thus generally free to acquire, possess and dispose of property; to establish, modify or terminate multiple forms of civil relations or conduct transactions with citizens and local legal entities; to form or participate in the formation of local legal entities, and to establish branch or representative offices, subject to the requirements and restrictions (eg licensing restrictions for sensitive sectors) of applicable legislation. Soviet-era restrictions or blanket prohibitions on the participation of non-citizens in domestic economic transactions or activity or their use of domestic civil forms, rights and rules are not in evidence: the Central Asian economies are all at least in the formal sense fully open and in conformity with the prevailing neo-liberal norms.

Each of the states has regulated foreign investment from the inception, supplementing the general rules of the civil code with a special set applicable to foreign direct investors establishing a physical presence in the jurisdiction, usually contained in a law on investment or foreign investment (special laws on foreign investment have been phased out in Kazakhstan and Tajikistan).[21] The states have also negotiated bilateral investment treaties with significant foreign partners. Additionally, each major investment project itself is usually the object of a special contractual regime, effectively a 'project constitution' that can modify the application of default background legislation (tax, labour, social, banking, civil and commercial laws and regulations). Pipeline and resource extraction projects can involve particularly complex regimes involving multiple actors, sovereign and private. Examples of complex individual project regimes include the Kumtor gold mining operation in Kyrgyzstan,[22] the Tajik aluminium company[23] and the North

[20] Kaz Civil Code 01.07.1999 3(7), Kyr Civil Code 08.05.1996 1(3), Taj Civil Code 30.06.1999 1(2), Uzb Civil Code 21.12.1995 2(3), Tkm Civil Code 17.07.1998 2(3).

[21] Kaz Law 08.01.2003 (general including foreign), Kyr Law 27.03.2003, Taj Law 12.05.2007 (general including foreign), Uzb Law 30.04.1998, Tkm Law 03.03.2008.

[22] See discussion of ownership structure in *Sistem Muhendislik Insaat Sanayi Ve Ticaret Anonim Sirketi v Kyrgyz Republic* (n 19).

[23] MB Olcott, *Tajikistan's Difficult Development Path* (Washington, Carnegie Endowment for Peace, 2012).

Caspian Operating Company offshore, a consortium of Kazakhstan's KazMunaiGas, Royal Dutch Shell, Exxon Mobil, Agip, TOTAL and others.[24]

The types of provisions in all three instruments (investment laws, bilateral investment treaties and project agreements) are similar, offering special protections, guarantees and privileges (national treatment, repatriation of profits, tax and other privileges, visas, legislative moratoria, dispute resolution), though of progressively narrower application: to all investors, to those of the treaty partner, and to those involved in a particular projects.[25] The very narrowest rules can have the greatest economic consequences in view of the scope and significance of the projects. The very need for the special incentives of investment laws reflects the competition for capital and the Central Asian republics' interest in attracting investment and capturing its benefits balanced against their interest in controlling its effects. All three types of instruments are outside the formal constitutional framework but may be said to supplement it, particularly since the provisions of international agreements are typically accorded constitutional superiority over domestic legislative provisions.[26] For instance, standard international arbitration clauses in such instruments have the effect of removing investment disputes from the constitutionally grounded national judicial systems and the resulting decisions from national jurisprudence.[27]

Kyrgyzstan and Tajikistan have now both acceded to the WTO (long years apart, in 1998 and 2013, respectively); Uzbekistan and Kazakhstan have been negotiating their accession; and Turkmenistan finally established a commission in 2013 to begin the process.[28] Accession requires a comprehensive schedule of commitments to bring national legislation into conformity with WTO requirements. Unlike constitutional commitments under the OSCE Copenhagen Document, or indeed unlike international treaty obligations under the human rights instruments, the trade undertakings place the Central Asian states under a

[24] See North Caspian Sea Production Sharing Agreement (NCSPSA).

[25] See eg UK–Kazakhstan bilateral investment treaties, Agreement 23.11.1995. Kazakhstan has 48 such treaties. www.investmentpolicyhub.unctad.org/IIA/CountryBits/107, accessed 9 November 2015.

[26] Kaz 4(3), Taj 10, Tkm 6, Kyr 6.

[27] W Scheuermann, 'Economic Globalization and the Rule of Law' (2001) 8(4) *Constellations* 1, 6–8.

[28] www.turkmenistan.ru/en/articles/17033.html, accessed 9 November 2015.

stringent enforcement and monitoring regime. (The states have also assumed economic—and other—obligations in joining regional intergovernmental organisations such as the Eurasian Economic Union and the Shanghai Cooperation Organisation,[29] which become part of their wider constitutional landscape). One of the standing ironies of the age of globalisation is that whereas allegations of torture or political repression may be discussed and condemned in the Torture or Human Rights Committees, industrial subsidies or tariffs violating WTO obligations can authorise direct retaliatory measures by other members. The 'economic constitutionalism' of multilateral trade agreements or investment agreements requiring parties effectively to entrench legislative provisions[30] is subject to greater enforcement than 'human rights constitutionalism'.

THE 'MATERIAL CONSTITUTION': CRONY CAPITALISM, CORRUPTION, CRIME

The 'stans impinge on the world's imagination not through their imposing new halls of parliament or state-of-the-art constitutional tribunal hearing chambers, but as south-of-the-(Russian)border stage sets for the machinations of ruthless rulers, venal ministers and governors, and billionaire bankers and businessmen—oligarchies with local colour and intrigue. Granted the popular image is shaped by sensationalist (and orientalist) coverage, uninformed by any sense of legal or constitutional structure; it still to a degree corresponds to the reality. Central Asian societies are characterised by stark inequality and conspicuous concentration of wealth, pervasive official self-dealing and abuse of office, and entrenched organised crime networks of trafficking (drugs, weapons and humans). And yet the constitutionalist trappings explored over the preceding three chapters are in fact a critical part of the scene and not just decoration.

[29] T Dadabaev, 'Shanghai Cooperation Organization (SCO) Regional Identity Formation from the Perspective of the Central Asia States' (2014) 23(85) *Journal of Contemporary China* 102.

[30] D Schneiderman, 'Investment Rules and the Rule of Law' (2001) 8(4) *Constellations* 522, 523.

Informal mechanisms of decision-making and exercise of authority are nothing new in Central Asia. They were characteristic of Soviet governance generally, at the centre and on the peripheries. But the nature, function and types of these mechanisms have been transformed in contemporary Central Asia, along with the constitutional context. The actual wiring of power in the Central Asian republics does not correspond to the constitutional circuit diagram (any more than the actual wiring of Soviet power ever did). But the formal constitution and the 'informal constitution' for each of the five remain reciprocally conditioning and accommodating. Accordingly, this section takes up the constitutional implications of three allied, economically defining phenomena of progressive degrees of departure from the formal constitutional rules framework: 'crony capitalism,' the disordered (really a distinctive locally ordered) form[31] in which 'the market' has come to Central Asia, corruption and crime.

Crony Capitalism

In the Land of the Soviets, the political elites controlled all productive economic assets and made all economic decisions. But they had no proprietary interests as such (at least not until late in the day when the system began to deteriorate). For the *nomenklatura*, the pursuit of power, not profit, was the motivation; and control, not ownership, was the default legal relation to capital. All of that changed dramatically once the political and economic systems came crashing abruptly down together, leaving the Central Asian elites (as those in the other peripheral SSRs) with a historically matchless windfall: disposition as they determined of whatever quotient of Soviet state assets happened to be located on their territory (with certain exceptions, like nuclear facilities or the Baikonur space centre in Kazakhstan). Long before the constitutional drafting processes were commissioned, the processes of privatisation and conversion of title to the inherited capital stock of the USSR had been set fatefully in motion.

[31] J Gray, *False Dawn: The Delusions of Global Capitalism* (London, Granta, 1998), identifies the various 'disordered' forms of capitalism which have flourished in the age of globalisation.

As in Russia and elsewhere, privatisation in Central Asia rapidly assumed first place among the economic imperatives of transition, even before 'marketisation', that is, the furnishing of market rules and institutions, pre-eminently a property regime.[32] The privatisation processes unfolded in divergent ways both within and among the five republics, involving a mix of methods: small-scale, mass, auction and case-by-case.[33] But notwithstanding such divergence, the constitutional systems were alike in omitting to regulate privatisation in a comprehensive or controlled fashion—a deafening silence in the circumstances. While the constitutional place and function of a general property regime for an emergent or transitional market economy were self-evident, the constitutionalisation of the process of creating such a regime in the first place was not. Thus the Central Asian constitutions (no more than any other post-Soviet constitutions) were emphatically not transitional in this literal sense: they did not specify transitional mechanisms of privatisation, leaving such to subsidiary legislation.[34]

One might well query why separation of powers, the balance of public authority among constituent government branches, is properly matter for constitutional regulation but not 'separation of wealth', that is, the balance of economic power among the state and emergent social actors. The failure to regulate 'separation of wealth' constitutionally is symptomatic not just of deficiencies of the Central Asian systems but equally of contemporary world constitutionalist discourse. A property regime replacing near-total concentration of societal wealth in state hands necessarily pivots around the disposition and distribution of that wealth. It is bound to involve the highest possible stakes for society and

[32] J Stiglitz, 'Whither Reform? Ten Years of the Transition. Annual Bank Conference on Development Economics', World Bank, Washington, DC, 28–30 April 1999.

[33] Eskender Trushin and Eshref Trushin, 'Problems of Market Transition' in B Rumer (ed), *Central Asia and the New Global Economy* (Armonk, NY, M E Sharpe, 2000) 112–14. See AE Peck, 'Foreign Investment in Kazakhstan's Minerals Industries' (1999) 40(7) *Post-Soviet Geography and Economics* 471 for case studies of privatisation in the Kazakhstan minerals sector and MB Olcott, *Kazakhstan: Unfulfilled Promise*, Revised Edition (Washington, Carnegie Endowment for Peace, 2010) 136–44 for a general account of Kazakh privatisation and its modalities.

[34] An unusual late example is Tkm Law 18.12.2013. Most laws on privatisation came and went in the initial decade after independence, eg Kaz Decree 23.12.1995 (since annulled).

therefore to be vulnerable to all sorts of manipulation. Some degree of constitutional safeguarding of the national patrimony as it is in the process of disaggregation seemed called-for. But it apparently was never contemplated, either by international experts or regional constitutionalists and drafters. Indeed, certain zeal is to be observed on the part of constitutionalists for the swiftest eradication of any traces of the privileged place of state ownership. Some endorsed the express and emphatic constitutional protection of private property and contract in the post-socialist context—never before necessary because in most prior cases the property regime had long predated the constitution. But such an endorsement mislocated the chief peril for 'transition states' in residual state encroachment rather than elite usurpation.[35]

The subsequent development, elaboration and entrenchment of regionally characteristic patterns of clan, dynastic or familial aggrandisement and neo-patrimonialism[36] are attributable (in part) to this absence of constitutional controls over the rate, scope and process of deconcentration of state wealth. The result has been a rapid reconcentration. Central Asian elites retained public power but *augmented* now by proprietary power. Kazakhstan is exemplary:

> Nazarbayev and his various relatives have been working hard to ensure that their family group will be by far the most powerful of all families, holding controlling interests in every major sector of the country's economy.[37]

It is misleading to think of this scenario in terms of the undiminished might of the state or the continued domination of the long-monopolistic public over the nascent private sector. Rather, *those in control* of state assets at independence—who were in control of the constituent processes as well—devised a system premised on a promiscuous mix of political and economic power, whereby positions of public constitutional authority brought privileged claims to private assets (or privileged disposition of them). If the Soviet system had

[35] CR Sunstein, 'On Property and Constitutionalism' (1992–93) 14 *Cardozo Law Review* 907.

[36] See ch 2 and A Ilkhamov, 'Neopatrimonialism, Interest Groups and Patronage Networks: The Impasses of the Governance System in Uzbekistan' (2007) 26 *Central Asian Survey* 65.

[37] MB Olcott, *Kazakhstan: Unfulfilled Promise*, Revised Edition (Washington, Carnegie Endowment for Peace, 2010) 188.

colonised the forms of private right (companies, title, contract) for public authority, the new Central Asian systems colonised the forms of public authority for private right. The consequence was an entirely sui generis form of the market, a privatised Soviet system similar to Russia's '*sistema*',[38] which happily dispensed with state ownership, command and administration (as with ideology) but retained a significant degree of elite privilege and control.[39]

> In such a system selected economic elites receive preferential treatment and privileges, making support from the state rather than market forces a crucial factor for maintaining and accruing wealth.[40]

The rise of crony or clan capitalism has not been a simple consequence of the original division of the Soviet spoils (indeed many of the inherited capital assets were wasting or rapidly depreciating, thanks to the ramshackle state of Soviet industrial plant). Over the years since, an extraordinary amount of new wealth has been created, in multiple forms, across the region, pre-eminently though not exclusively from natural resource exploitation[41] (as well the rise of diversified services, communications, food, transport, etc sectors)—and a new generation of wealth-creators has concomitantly arisen. Examples of this regionally distinct breed of tycoon-politicians include former Kazakh diplomat, security chief and media mogul Rakhat Aliyev, who recently died in an Austrian prison awaiting trial on murder charges, and former Kazakh energy minister and billionaire banker Mukhtar Ablyazov, sought by the Russian Federation on fraud charges and by Kazakhstan on embezzlement charges (and the High Court of England and Wales for contempt), who is currently awaiting extradition from France. Both owe their political and economic fortunes and misfortunes to their ties to Nazarbaev (Aliyev was his ex son-in-law), of whom they ran afoul.

[38] A Ledeneva, 'Cronies, Economic Crime and Capitalism in Putin's *Sistema*' (2012) 88(1) *International Affairs* 1, 149.

[39] See Gray (n 31) 133–67 for an argument of the derivation of post-Soviet patterns of the acquisition, distribution and exercise of economic power from Soviet antecedents.

[40] G Sharafutdinova, *Political Consequences of Crony Capitalism Inside Russia* (Notre Dame, IN, University of Notre Dame Press, 2011) 3.

[41] See generally P Jones Luong, *Institutional Change and Political Continuity in Post-Soviet Central Asia: Power, Perceptions, and Pacts* (Cambridge, Cambridge University Press, 2002).

Aliyev and Ablyazov have been at the centre of extended and elaborate civil and criminal legal proceedings in the UK, Austria, France, Ukraine and Russia.[42] An undeniable dimension of the connection here has been affective or clan-related. Clan and local or familial ties, though disavowed and discouraged, never disappeared during the administration of the planned economy, and have again become salient in the brave new post-Soviet economy of banking, construction, resource extraction, and services. But it is the patron–client ties which have emerged from that economy itself, rather than traditional ties as such, which define Central Asian crony capitalism.[43]

The new corporate and entrepreneurial networks which make up the Central Asian business sector owe their existence and prominence to an enabling and conditioning legal and constitutional environment. The ascendant economic elites have availed themselves of the legal forms provided by the civil code—closed and open joint stock companies, limited liability partnerships, etc. Indeed, the very elasticity and adaptability of such forms—virtues praised by champions of private law as bulwark of markets and democracy[44]—have made possible a bewildering interpenetration of public and private interests through ownership and transactional structures as elaborate as can be found in any multinational enterprise.[45] It has also permitted the Central Asian state itself to continue to play a dominating role as a private market actor, not only through the Soviet state enterprise form, which survives

[42] 'Arrest warrant for Kazakh billionaire accused of one of world's biggest frauds,' *Guardian* 16 February 2012, available at www.theguardian.com/business/2012/feb/16/arrest-warrant-kazakh-billionaire-mukhtar-ablyazov, accessed 6 November 2015.

[43] Olcott (n 37) 184–89 (qualified political/economic salience of clans Kazakhstan); Ilkhamov (n 36) 68–72 (distinction between clan and patronage networks in Uzbekistan); S Radnitz, *Weapons of the Wealthy: Predatory Regimes and Elite-led Protests in Central Asia* (Ithaca NY, Cornell University Press, 2012) 77–102 (community clientilism more significant in Kyrgyzstan than clan ties).

[44] Sunstein (n 35).

[45] See eg the Tajik Aluminium company, MB Olcott, *Tajikistan's Difficult Development Path* (Washington, Carnegie Endowment for Peace, 2012) 182–216. See also discussion of variety of ownership structures in the natural resource industry, P Jones Luong and E Weinthal, *Oil Is Not a Curse (Cambridge Studies in Comparative Politics)* (Cambridge, Cambridge University Press, 2011) 11–31 (Turkmenistan and Uzbekistan retaining Soviet-era state ownership with control, with Kazakhstan opting for significant foreign private ownership).

in all five jurisdictions, but through wholly- and majority-state-owned joint-stock companies.[46]

> [T]he Soviet-educated drafters of the new post-Soviet civil codes, particularly in Central Asia, chose to embrace the horizontal relations theory of state participation in civil-law relations and to rely on it as a pillar of the free-market economy… [and so] the state became a normal participant in the domain of private law. Should one be surprised that the state, officially allowed to enter the market as a 'subject of private law', rapidly forced out other actors and started dominating economic life in all the countries of Central Asia?[47]

Corruption

The massive conflict of interest which underlay the elites' drafting of the constitutional rules by which they themselves would play and occupy privileged roles led ultimately past crony or clan capitalism to corruption. The Central Asian Five have acquired a singular and singularly deserved reputation for corruption and self-dealing on the part of state officialdom. Turkmenistan and Uzbekistan are ranked among the ten most corrupt states (169 and 166 out of 177 contenders) in Transparency International's 2014 Corruption Perceptions index, a ranking they have consistently held. Tajikistan at 152, Kyrgyzstan at 136 and Kazakhstan at 126 rank somewhat better.[48] The phenomenon cuts across all levels: custodians and operatives of the state alike, senior ministers and low-level functionaries, have been implicated. It needs to be approached with caution and critical scrutiny, however, particularly in light of the hegemony of international anti-corruption discourse exemplified by Transparency International itself. For 'corruption' is susceptible to overbroad, careless and invidious application, and its

[46] eg Turkmenneft, Turkmengaz, Uzbekneftegaz, Jones Luong and Weinthal (n 45) 77–78.

[47] L Golovko, 'The Space for Legal Reform in Central Asia: Between Political Limits and Theoretical Deformations' in *2010 Yearbook of the Organisation for Security and Co-operation in Europe (OSCE)* (Baden-Baden, Nomos Verlagsgesellschaft, 2011) 113.

[48] Transparency International, 2014 Corruption Perceptions Index, available at www.transparency.org/cpi2014/results, accessed 6 November 2015.

presumptive relationship to economic or political development (or rule of law) is not self-evident. '[T]he anti-corruption campaign transforms the politically or ideologically contestable into the technically necessary and the morally imperative.'[49] Venality, conversion, abuse of office, nepotism, bribery, rent-seeking, lobbying, favouritism, etc are distinct phenomena across societies in respect of their economic, social and cultural nature as well as in respect of their legal status. Lumping them together under a problematic moralistic umbrella term reflects an institutionally and culturally narrow model of governance and law. Moreover, 'corruption' connotes dysfunctionality and illegitimacy, whereas informal governance mechanisms may be both functional and legitimate.

However problematic the term, it nonetheless appears to capture a fundamental and nearly universally acknowledged condition of the contemporary Central Asian polities and economies. The general question of corruption, like cronyism, is compounded across the region by issues of political and cultural context and continuity. Numerous observers have contended that contemporary Central Asian corruption represents a reversion to regional cultural type, that ties traditionally structuring collective life in these societies have hydraulically found new modes of expression and outlets.[50] The instrumentalisation for personal ends of normative structures of authority, channels of transaction and forms of organisation, was part and parcel of life in Soviet Central Asia, as witness phenomena like the Rashidov cotton scandals and the indigenisation or cultural infiltration of the collective farm and local party apparatus.[51]

[49] D Kennedy, "The International Anti-corruption Campaign" (1999) 14 *Connecticut Journal of Int'l Law* 455, 462.

[50] See R Urinboyev and M Svensson, 'Living Law, Legal Pluralism, and Corruption in Post-Soviet Uzbekistan' (2013) 45(3) *Journal of Legal Pluralism and Unofficial Law* 372 for a summary of scholarly views. '[T]he boundaries between "public office" and "private sphere" are not clear-cut and even the meaning of the word 'abuse' varies according to local legal and cultural standards.' ibid. 373.

[51] See ch 2; D Kandiyoti, *Agrarian Reform, Gender and Land Rights in Uzbekistan*, UNRISD 2002, available at www.unrisd.org/80256B3C005BCCF9/(httpAuxPages)/C2919AC1CD7B5379C1256CCA00369D07/$file/kandiyoti(sml).pdf, accessed 5 February 2016; and I Lipovsky, 'The Central Asian Cotton Epic' (1995) 14(4) *Central Asian Survey* 529, 537–38; D Hiro, *Inside Central Asia: A Political and Cultural History of Uzbekistan, Turkmenistan, Kazakhstan, Kyrgyzstan, Tajikistan, Turkey, and Iran* (London, Duckworth Overlook, 2013), Kindle 2515 (Rashidov scandal).

The question remains: just what might corruption have to do with the five constitutional systems? Obviously, the definition of corruption depends on the mapping of legality and the disjunction in a given society between published constitutional and other binding legal norms, on the one hand, and the background norms actually governing behaviour, on the other. But 'corruption' is also a function of the very cultural and societal significance of such a disjunction in the first place. The lines between legal and illegal as between licit and illicit official comportment are drawn very differently in different places. Just as there does not exist one ordained form of market economy, neither does there exist one concept of an honest or pure economy as distinct from dishonest or corrupted economies. The cumulative evidence suggests that the constitutional systems of the Central Asia permit or tolerate, even if they do not formally legitimise, a very substantial degree of lax application of the published rules, or of differential application of those rules to office-holders and ordinary citizens. This might be construed as rather a feature of the background constitutional culture—the attitude or value-disposition to legal constraints on official powers and actions—than of the system as such, but regardless the view taken here is that 'corruption'—or more broadly, informal governance—is of vital importance in understanding Central Asian constitutionalism.

The principal constitutional issue here is effective constraint, the 'problem of instrumentalism' posed by the Soviet constitutional order.[52] Although each of the constitutions makes abundantly clear the sacrality of the constitutional order and imposes duties on all citizens to uphold and support it, what appears lacking or deficient is the Weberian ideal of the quasi-clerical calling of public service and the severe discipline imposed on public servants. A double standard for officials and ordinary mortals would appear to be as defining a feature of the Central Asian constitutional systems as of the Soviet system whence they derive: one set of rules for the *nomenklatura* (and its modern heirs and assigns), another for the citizenry. Ironically, the articulated rules for the former are more stringent, while the applicable rules are more lax: public servants bear a higher normative burden of probity, but one from which they are more likely to be relieved.

Now, a constitutional system might not be imagined to be required to regulate positively against corruption: ground rules of prohibition

[52] See ch 2.

would seem to suffice, and, say, a constitutional article against corruption would seem altogether odd and out-of-place. But in systems such as these, given their history and vulnerabilities, some degree of the constitutionalisation of 'virtue in office' might not have been inapposite. The constitutional systems of the Central Asian states made no reference to their fateful emergence from the Soviet constitutional womb, in this as in other respects. The initial division of the inherited wealth, or the spoils of the Soviet collapse, was an extraordinary and irresistible opportunity for private gain at public expense, as suggested above. Privatisation was itself a process of a historically unique initial distribution, an unprecedented dealing of the deck of property at the commencement of a high-stakes game of poker. In a sense, an original sin of corruption tainted the very birth of the constitutional systems, which they masked or legimitised. But the conversion of use rights to ownership rights at the inception has since been vastly compounded by exploitation of the rents made available through the new states—rents which were not available in the Soviet period (apart from the vodka bottle for queue-jumping at the local clinic) because of the tightly policed nature of the system and its illiquidity.

The picture of political power built up on the basis of constitutional authorisation (see the analysis of super-presidentialism in chapter four) has to be supplemented by an appreciation for the economic power (really a form of political power) deriving from a command over 'rents from the state'.

> In these regimes, power lies not so much in formal control over institutions of the state, such as government ministries or the military, as it does in the ability to provide (or block) access to business opportunities or posts in government that allow officials to benefit from corruption. The leadership distributes these moneymaking opportunities in exchange for a cut of the financial proceeds and maximum political loyalty. Anybody thinking of turning against the regime risks losing business, property, and access to power; they may even face legal charges and imprisonment. Legal cases are easy to concoct against erstwhile insiders: everybody involved in these informal politico–business networks is likely to have at one time broken the law.[53]

There are two kinds of power at issue here. One is the express power which is ultimately anchored in constitutional provisions, and which

[53] D Lewis, 'Understanding the Authoritarian State: Neopatrimonialism in Central Asia' (2012) 19 *Brown Journal of World Affairs* 115.

is the subject of conventional constitutional analysis, for example, the executive power of appointment. The other kind of power is a derivative of the first, and represents the value which can be extracted from either the exercise of that constitutional power or forbearance from its exercise—what an economist would term an 'economic rent' arising from the scarcity of this constitutional resource (the 'spoils of office'). If President Rahmon has the constitutional power to appoint a Tajik judge, he simultaneously possesses a derivative *para-constitutional* power to obtain a benefit (monetary, eg a kickback, or political, eg pliancy, or both), and the appointed judge now has the constitutional power(s) to adjudicate disputes and issue binding decisions, as well as to make subordinate appointments (eg of staff) or to assign cases on a docket to other judges (if she is a court chair), and to do (or not do) other things as well, all of which in turn command rents. Neo-patrimonialist 'corruption' is not a travesty of the constitutional system, it *is* the constitutional system (or the way it operates).

Now the use of public office for private gain or other forms of influence-peddling are blatantly unconstitutional in that they violate clear norms articulated in the constitution itself, both general norms for everyone and special norms for public officials. But they are in a different sense part and parcel of the de facto constitutional system, and their very illegality or unconstitutionality is what ties them in. In the passage quoted above, the illegality of 'corruption' is precisely what makes it politically functional. The co-existence of punctilious constitutional formalism and endemic rule-breaking is perplexing. But a neo-patrimonial system is premised precisely on that co-existence: there would be no 'corruption,' nor would corruption be functional, as it incontrovertibly is in a neo-patrimonial system, unless there were a formalised, constitutionally grounded rule-structure as foil. If departure from the rules is itself regulated neo-patrimonially, then patently the rules have to be in place and always at least presumptively enforceable.

The formal constitutional order imposes strict standards of probity and rules of comportment on public officials,[54] including, beyond the constitutional provisions themselves and supplementary civil service legislation and regulations, specific, targeted anti-corruption measures. But the patrimonial system which is at least in this sense 'meta-constitutional' *licenses* the relaxation of the standards and waiver or

[54] Taj Code of ethics15.09.2010, Kaz Law 23.07.1999.

variance of the rules in particular circumstances, to particular degrees, and in respect of particular persons. The constitutional rules of prohibition are paradoxically enabling rules as well. The result is a kind of constitutional spoils system, where the office is expressly regulated but the spoils tacitly: Tammany Hall plus sovereignty—and sovereignty's cloak of constitutionalism. Indeed institutionalised public corruption in Central Asia appears considerably less puzzling if it is approached as municipal corruption scaled up. What makes it outlandish is the elevated idiom of constitutionalism that in a perverse way enhances and enlarges the field of neo-patrimonial play, rather than serving as eyewash. The parallels to Soviet constitutionalism have perhaps been insufficiently remarked (although the currency there was control not lucre).

The constitutional anti-corruption system not only consists of positive rules of public probity on the part of officials, but express negative rules of prohibition. Laws against corruption have been adopted and anti-corruption commissions established as the scale of the problem has gained notoriety and international pressure has been applied.[55] Criminal codes have been amplified to incorporate a range of economic crimes, from embezzlement to money-laundering.[56] But the negative rules are as susceptible of invidious and selective enforcement as the positive rules are of relaxation and waiver. The periodic ferocity of anti-corruption rhetoric and action and the ostentatious punishment of selected offenders[57] are a carry-over from the late Soviet era, when the post-Brezhnev leadership mounted anti-corruption drives to counter the black market (Central Asia was a particular target in the 1982 Andropov campaign).[58] The contemporary Central Asian elites

[55] eg Kaz Law 02.07.1998, Taj Law 25.07.2005, Kyr Law 08.08.2012.

[56] Kaz Crim Code 16.07.1997 190–226, Kyr Crim Code 01.10.1997 178–220, Taj Crim Code 21.05.1998 258–97, Uzb Crim Code 22.09.1994 175–85, Tkm Crim Code 12.07.1997 238–66. The Uzbek code notably and uniquely includes in the chapter (XII) 'Crimes against the fundamentals of the economy' such actions as 'transactions against the interests of the Republic' (175) and 'concealment of foreign currency' (178, an old Soviet chestnut, *cf* RSFSR Criminal Code 88), while placing money-laundering (243) in the chapter (XVII) 'Crimes against public safety.'

[57] A recent example is the sentencing of former Kazakh Prime Minister Akhmetov to ten years in prison on corruption charges. See ch 4 (n 20).

[58] G Ubiria, *Soviet Nation-Building in Central Asia: The Making of the Kazakh and Uzbek Nations* (London, Routledge, 2015) 237.

have recourse to these same measures; they conveniently invoke and 'activate' a constitutional principle (that is internationally endorsed) to suit the needs of the hour and the purposes of power. In the same manner, as discussed in chapter five, they have invoked and activated the international norms of counter-terror to undercut political opposition and grass-roots mobilisation. Of course, they can run afoul of foreign anti-corruption legislation, over the application of which they have no direct influence.[59]

Crime

Not simply liable to corruption on the part of their official custodians, the 'stans also became variably susceptible to penetration by organised crime. If clan capitalism and corruption have become woven into the economic and political fabric of Central Asian life, and are accommodated by the formal constitutional order, so too is organised criminal activity. In part this represents the general continuation of the Soviet system's accommodation of the 'black market' and of its homegrown organised criminal network, the 'thieves-in-law'. In part it is a function of Central Asia's particular 'geocriminal positioning'. Turkmenistan, Uzbekistan and Tajikistan all border Afghanistan, source of much of the opium for the international drugs trade even before it became exceptionally volatilised by war, revolution and the counter-terror crusade after 9/11. Once liberated from Soviet control, Central Asia was destined to become a drugs-trafficking corridor.

The thieves-in-law are the direct heirs of the Soviet organised criminal structures headquartered in the prison camps and colonies, and like the Sicilian Mafia are governed by rituals and an elaborate code, almost a 'criminal constitution'.[60] They are active across all former Soviet

[59] Kazakhstan eg settled a US Foreign Corrupt Practices claim and agreed to the establishment of a World Bank-administered social fund ('BOTA Fund') to distribute allegedly stolen assets held in a Swiss bank account. Memorandum of Understanding among the Governments of the United States of America, the Swiss Confederation, and the Republic of Kazakhstan 1 December 2006, www.state.gov/documents/organization/108887.pdf, accessed 13 February 2016.

[60] F Varese, *The Russian Mafia: Private Protection in a New Market Economy* (Oxford, Oxford University Press, 2001) 145–66; International Crisis Group (ICG), 'Kyrgyzstan's Prison Nightmare', Asia Report No 118, 16 August 2006, 3 ('Guards

republics and preserve their ties, constituting an invisible, surviving 'black USSR'. They do not merely engage in criminal activity, they also carry on commerce—they are market actors, and important ones—and they can govern, or at least participate in the governing, both at local and at national levels. Kyrgyzstan furnishes a particularly notorious example. During the Bakiev era, channels of political influence and instruction allegedly ran from the prison colonies to the highest levels of government.[61] Kyrgyzstan is not a narco-state, but it certainly has many of the attributes of one, as does Tajikistan, both serving as vital trafficking corridors to Russia and Europe. In an even more obvious sense than for more mundane form of corruption, organised criminal activity is 'extra-constitutional'. But also like corruption, it is integral to the constitutional system: criminal elements penetrate the state; they do not simply defy its writ on the outside.

SOCIAL PROVISION AND PROTECTIONS (PENSIONS, UNEMPLOYMENT, POVERTY, GENDER)

If the civil codes and allied basic market legislation may be viewed as equating to a constitution for the economy and hence meriting inclusion in a study of the Central Asian constitutional systems, what of social welfare/protection legislation? In the triumphalism attendant on the collapse of socialism amidst the ascendancy of neo-liberalism, while rights *of* the market (so-called entrepreneurial or commercial rights, rights of participation) assumed arguably constitutional proportions, rights *against* the market fared less felicitously. Economic and social rights as such, qua formulated, seemed to pass through the great filter of the Soviet collapse and to retain their constitutional prominence undiminished in the new Central Asian states. But what they in fact signified for citizens was subtly, progressively and profoundly transformed. Unlike civil and political rights, social and economic rights had not simply been items on the Soviet constitutional menu; they were staples of the Soviet social system's kitchens.

no longer control the prisons, which are run by criminals, who enforce a strict and sometimes violent caste system … At the centre of the system until mid-2005, one inmate, Aziz Batukayev, controlled a criminal empire within the prison walls.').

[61] ICG (n 60).

The same logic of constitutional regulation by constitutional omission described above carries over to the social system as well. The Soviet schemes for social insurance (income support against disability, sickness, old age, loss of breadwinner) and social services (health and hospitalisation, maternity and child care, sport and recreation, etc) were integral to the USSR constitutional order, and elaborated in the Constitution itself.[62] But by comparison the laconic treatment of social benefits and services in the post-Soviet Central Asian constitutions, in the context of a unilateral revision of the social contract and a shift away from broad universal to narrow, means-tested or otherwise qualified benefits, operates to exclude rather than include by implication.

As they do for civil and political rights, all five constitutions enshrine social and economic rights, but this time in a fairly uniform and misleading manner. All provide for social security (formulations vary between 'a right to' and 'are guaranteed') support in old age, in the event of illness or disability and for survivors.[63] The constitutions are alike in providing a right to free medical care, albeit only on legislatively prescribed terms[64]—a pale shadow of the Soviet single-payer, single-provider Semashko health system, the most comprehensive ever attempted and the inspiration and model for the NHS in the UK.[65] The availability, quality and comprehensiveness of state-provided health care vary dramatically across the five states, but marketisation of health care has proceeded to such an extent that very few patients receive gratis services.[66] The Kazakh and Kyrgyz constitutions guarantee the inviolability of the dwelling (a property-centric formulation)[67] but the other three (the Tajik, Uzbek and Turkmen constitutions) provide an express right to housing. The Turkmen Constitution uniquely guarantees universal state support in the acquisition or construction of a

[62] USSR 1977 41–42.

[63] Kaz 28, Kyr 53(1–2), Taj 39, Uzb 39, Tkm 36.

[64] Taj 38, Uzb 41, Tkm 35, Kaz 29, Kyr 47(3).

[65] F Stevens, 'The Convergence and Divergence of Modern Health Care Systems' in William C Cockerham (ed), *The Blackwell Companion to Medical Sociology* (Oxford, Blackwell, 2008) 465.

[66] M Borowitz and R Atun, 'The Unfinished Journey from Semashko to Bismarck: Health Reform in Central Asia from 1991 to 2006' (2006) 25(4) *Central Asian Survey* 419.

[67] Kyr 46(4), Kaz 25(2).

dwelling.[68] Beyond universal economic rights granted to all citizens, special economic rights are in a few instances recognised for vulnerable or qualifying individuals, for example, a right to housing support for low income or other statutorily qualifying categories in the Kyrgyz and Kazakh constitutions.

All Central Asian republics have by now made a decisive shift away from the Soviet defined benefit pension scheme to a defined contribution scheme, a shift of seismic proportion with regard to the constitutional social model. Now individual workers are required to contribute to their own pension accounts (as are employers) at a statutory rate, and the cumulative funds are invested in a beneficiary-designated fund against retirement. Workers have the right to supplement their obligatory contribution with voluntary contributions on the basis of an individual agreement. Kazakhstan brought in the first such pension plan in 1997 on the Chilean model (Chile was well-known for its pioneering adoption of an individual accounts-based pension scheme in 1981),[69] while Uzbekistan and Turkmenistan, the last stalwarts of the inherited Soviet scheme, shifted to the new pension model in 2009 and 2012 respectively.[70] Defined contribution schemes exemplify the 'risk society': they seek to transfer from public paternalistic authority to self-responsible citizens the burden of managing life risks and planning for the future. The Kazakh scheme initially enabled workers to elect a default state-managed option or else shop their individual account among competing private funds in quest of the best returns, like any canny investor. However, in 2013, Kazakh legislation brought the private funds (for the obligatory pension) under a publicly managed unified fund, effectively nationalising them and reversing its neoliberal course (which had won accolades from international financial institutions).[71]

Though the subsidiary social legislation clearly marks the advent of this underlying revolution in the social and providential role of the

[68] Taj 36, Uzb 27, Tkm 24, Kaz 25, Kyr 30.

[69] S Newton, 'Transplantation and Transition: Legality and Legitimacy in the Kazakhstani Legislative Process' in M Kurkchiyan and D Galligan (eds), *Law and Informal Practices: The Post-communist Experience* (Oxford, Oxford University Press, 2003) 151–70.

[70] Uzb Law 03.09.1993, Tkm Social Protection Code 19.10.2012, Tkm Law 31.03.2012.

[71] Kaz Law 21.06.2013.

state, the constitutions do not clearly signal it. The rights formulations, even when hedged and qualified, betoken as much continuity as rupture with the Soviet tradition of broad social protection programmes and multiple discrete forms of support, the cradle-to-grave largess of the social state. Only the Kyrgyz Constitution in an altogether unique provision (dating from the 1993 original version and hence antedating the change in the basis of pensions) expressly eschews a paternalistic social model: 'State social [activity] should not assume the form of state guardianship limiting the economic freedom, agency, and opportunity of the citizen.'[72] The revision of the social contract undergirding Soviet socialism can be argued to have commenced with Gorbachev. But it never seems to have become properly constitutionalised, as witness the many lingering equivocations to be found in the treatment of entrepreneurial and ownership rights identified above, which are perhaps matched here in the catalogues of social and economic rights.

The shift away from redistributionist policies (like pay-as-you-go defined benefit pensions) towards qualified universal entitlements (free medical care within strict limits) and residual safety-net redistribution for the vulnerable is detectable in the constitutional texts 'between the lines', even if it is not articulated. The constitutions reveal a divided social soul, most starkly in the case of the Kyrgyz Constitution and its admonition against state guardianship and inclusion of the right to freedom of work in the same article as the right to property (marking the shift from a social to proprietary model of labour). Virtually all European post-war constitutions expressly adopted a constitutional 'social model'.[73] But the Central Asian constitutions, poised between socialism and neo-liberalism, struggle to articulate a coherent one. Of the lot, the Turkmen and Uzbek retain the greatest formulaic fidelity to the Soviet comprehensive social entitlements. Turkmenistan boasts the region's only codification of all social legislation, the Turkmen Social Protection Code, which provides for maternity, child care, veteran and invalid benefits (inter alia), in addition to pensions.[74] The robustness of the constitutional social guarantees notwithstanding, the reality across

[72] Kyr 53(4).

[73] eg Italian Constitution 32, 38 (free medical care to indigent, comprehensive state income support).

[74] Tkm Social Protection Code 19.10.2012.

the region is often grim; the general level of social support and services, from the adequacy of pensions to the quality and availability of medical care, plummeted with independence and has never recovered.[75]

Perhaps the most telltale shift in the constitutional basis of the social system in the 'stans is the position of labour. The Central Asian constitutions establish a right to work, rest and leisure, but the formulations differ: the Kazakh and Kyrgyz constitutions use the formulation 'right to the freedom of work', the others 'right to work'; none supplies the all-important Soviet gloss 'that is, right to guaranteed employment'.[76] The labour codes clearly all descend from the respective SSR labour codes (similar organisation, similar terms, similar provisions),[77] yet another example of broad conceptual continuities with Soviet regulation underlying the constitutional systems though not evident in the constitutional texts themselves (as in the case of criminal procedure discussed in the previous chapter).

All five preserve the guaranteed monthly minimum wage; all preserve the 'labour booklet', the core document of Soviet labour discipline and control, a cumulative performance record that moved with the worker from employer to employer; all except Uzbekistan preserve the establishment of work norms agreed by management and labour, with account of published model norms.[78] Of course the fundamental shift has occurred insofar as the state enterprise is no longer the default or even a significant employer, but that shift has not fundamentally altered the wording of the provisions. For the Uzbek and Turkmen labour codes, even the absence of a right to strike has been continued (although strikes are not prohibited). The Kazakh, Kyrgyz and Tajik codes all include the right to strike prominently, as indeed do the Kazakh and Kyrgyz constitutions directly, the latter unconditionally.[79]

[75] See International Crisis Group (ICG), 'Central Asia: Decay and Decline,' Asia Report No 201, 3 February 2011 (deterioration of social infrastructure and disappearance of social services a region-wide phenomenon).

[76] Tkm 33, 34, Kyr 42, 43, Taj 35, 37, Uzb 37, 38, Kaz 24.

[77] See eg Kaz SSR Labour Code 1971.

[78] Taj Labour Code 15.05.1997 102, 56, Kyr Labour Code 04.08.2004 154, 65, 179, Kaz Labour Code 15.05.2007 122, 35, Tkm Labour Code 18.04.2009 79, 42,105, Uzb Labour Code 12.12.1995 155, 81.

[79] Kaz 24, Labour Code 15.05.2007 298, Kyr 3, Labour Code 04.08.2004 436, Taj Labour Code15.05.1997 211.

The provisions for collective agreement (as indeed all the other provisions regarding labour agency through representative organs) might be supposed in contemporary conditions at last to have become enforceable. But where state interests are at stake, independent trade unionism faces similar constraints in Central Asia to independent social associations or political parties; in Turkmenistan, for example, trade unions continue to be organised in inherited Soviet fashion with a single national federation at the top of a hierarchy of sectoral branches and workplace locals (the enabling statutory provision disguising the unitary reality, as in the case of political parties).[80] An extreme episode was the December 2011 Zhanozen police shooting of 14 striking workers in western Kazakhstan, which is sadly emblematic of the practical significance of labour legislation even in a (notionally, by regional standards) enlightened jurisdiction with a history of post-Soviet independent trade unionism. Long-standing union grievances at three oil companies (all with significant Kazakh state involvement) had brought mass dismissals and led to the strikes, in the context of court rulings of illegality and administrative and criminal actions against the organisers.[81]

In spite of the resource and resulting building boom evident in most capitals, Central Asian societies remain pervasively rural, with a preponderant portion of the population residing and pursuing a livelihood in the countryside, many in one way or another off the land. Poverty, masked in the Soviet dispensation through Moscow's capacity to organise inter-regional, inter-sectoral and inter-occupational transfers and subsidies at will (essentially channelling development assistance to its internal third world), has become chronic and severe, particularly in Tajikistan, Uzbekistan and Kyrgyzstan. The regulation of agricultural land, labour, production and credit therefore figure prominently in the social and economic landscape. The hollowness of constitutional property guarantees, on the one hand, and constitutional social guarantees, on the other, is ironically united in the exceptionally precarious status of Uzbek cotton workers. Years after the early-independence land tenure reforms, they find themselves working on the same (re-organised)

[80] Tkm Law 04.11.2013 11 ('trade unions may unite in national centres, unions, councils and other associations').

[81] International Crisis Group (ICG), 'Kazakhstan: Waiting for Change' Asia Report No 20, 30 September 2013, 13–14. Needless to add, in the aftermath, union leaders, and not the police, were prosecuted and convicted.

collective farms for the same bosses, but on considerably poorer terms (reduced, delayed, in-kind wages; reduced hours), lacking enforceable rights in the agricultural concern, the land, or their labour. Similar patterns crop up in Tajikistan, where 15 years after independence most *dekhan* farms represented re-organised collective farms and farmers enjoyed little security.[82]

Finally but critically, the treatment of gender in the Central Asian constitutions appears lamentably diminished. The USSR had constitutionalised gender equality in a comprehensive and categorical manner, together with the affirmative action to achieve it, in the context of the incorporation of women in the workforce and the provision of generous support for reproductive labour (maternity leave, crèches, ante- and post-natal services and support):

> Exercise of these rights is ensured by according women equal access with men to education and vocational and professional training, equal opportunities in employment, remuneration, and promotion, and in social and political, and cultural activity, and by special labour and health protection measures for women; by providing conditions enabling mothers to work; by legal protection, and material and moral support for mothers and children, including paid leaves and other benefits for expectant mothers and mothers, and gradual reduction of working time for mothers with small children.[83]

All five Central Asian constitutions confine themselves by stark contrast to a one-line, terse declaration of the equal rights of men and women, or in the case of the Kazakh Constitution, simply to the inclusion of 'gender' in a serial enumeration of prohibited grounds of discrimination (along with descent, race, language, religion and social position) in the general equality article.[84] In view of the abiding patriarchal characteristics of Central Asian societies, the relegation of gender equality to little more than an obligatory formality in all five constitutions is to be regretted—particularly given that the international normative framework for gender equality has undergone its greatest

[82] Kandiyoti (n 51), D Kandiyoti, 'The Cry for Land: Agrarian Reform, Gender and Land Rights in Uzbekistan' (2003) 3 *Journal of Agrarian Change* 225; O Porteous, 'Land Reform in Tajikistan: From the Capital to the Cotton Fields' Action Against Hunger, 2003, available at www.ecnr.berkeley.edu/vfs/PPs/Porteous-ObiC/web/landreform.pdf, accessed 3 November 2011, 3–7.

[83] USSR 1977 35.

[84] Kyr 16(4), Taj 33, Uzb 46, Tkm 20, Kaz 14.

elaboration and deepening across the brief span of the emergence of independent Central Asia, as reflected for example in the CEDAW framework, UNWomen, gender-analysis, gender-mainstreaming, etc. No longer adequately supported for reproductive work, and forced in tightened economic circumstances to shoulder a larger portion of the burden of productive work, in a pattern common across the transition zone, Central Asian women confront the further challenges of a family culture now no longer checked by centrally imposed gender-egalitarian policies (from Moscow).[85]

FURTHER READING

G Gleason, *Markets and Politics in Central Asia* (Economies in Transition to the Market) (London, Routledge, 2013).

SM Hersh, 'The Price of Oil' *The New Yorker*, 9 July 2001, 48–65.

A Ilkhamov, 'Neopatrimonialism, Interest Groups and Patronage Networks: The Impasses of the Governance System in Uzbekistan' (2007) 26 *Central Asian Survey* 65.

D Kandiyoti, 'The Cry for Land: Agrarian Reform, Gender and Land Rights in Uzbekistan' (2003) 3 *Journal of Agrarian Change* 225.

D Kennedy, "The International Anti-corruption Campaign" (1999) 14 *Connecticut Journal of Int'l Law* 455, 462.

A Khasanbaev and WD Pfau, 'The Funded Pension Scheme in Uzbekistan: An Analysis' (2009) 31 *Sophia International Review* 75.

D Lewis, 'Understanding the Authoritarian State: Neopatrimonialism in Central Asia' (2012) 19 *Brown Journal of World Affairs* 115.

P Jones Luong and E Weinthal, *Oil Is Not a Curse* (Cambridge Studies in Comparative Politics) (Cambridge, Cambridge University Press, 2010).

PB Maggs (2003) 'The Civil Codes of Central Eurasia—A Comparison'. Paper presented at the Central Eurasian Studies Society Fourth Annual Conference, Cambridge, Mass., www.law.illinois.edu/p-maggs/codes.htm, accessed 4 November 2015.

[85] See K Rittich, *Recharacterizing Restructuring: Law, Distribution and Gender in Market Reform* (Amsterdam, Kluwer Law International, 2002) (differential gender impact of market transition); Kandiyoti (n 51); Kandiyoti (2003) (n 82).

S Newton, 'Transplantation and Transition: Legality and Legitimacy in the Kazakhstani Legislative Process' in M Kurkchiyan and D Galligan (eds), *Law and Informal Practices: The Post-communist Experience* (Oxford, Oxford University Press, 2003).

O Porteous, 'Land Reform in Tajikistan: From the Capital to the Cotton Fields,' Action Against Hunger, 2003 www.cnr.berkeley.edu/vfs/PPs/Porteous-ObiC/web/landreform.pdf, accessed 3 November 2011.

K Rittich, *Recharacterizing Restructuring: Law, Distribution and Gender in Market Reform* (Amsterdam, Kluwer Law International, 2002).

8

Central Asia Constitutions and Central Asian Difference

The Regulation of Pluralism

Identity: Who, the People? – Citizenship and Ethnicity ('Nationality') – Federalism, Devolution – Language – Culture – Religion – Local and Regional Government

IDENTITY: WHO, THE PEOPLE?

IN THE WAKE of the sudden socialist collapse three fundamental matters, which for most political systems are resolved sequentially over decades if not centuries, had to be addressed simultaneously: the question of collective identity in the first place (the constitutional subject); the question of the appropriate constitutional framework of rules, procedures, rights and governing institutions; and then the question of the ongoing distribution of political power and economic resources in accordance with that framework. The tasks of defining the nature of the decision-making authority, agreeing the modes of decision-making, and then undertaking the decision-making processes themselves all had to be confronted urgently at the same time.[1]

The greatly condensed time horizon for the first question was especially anomalous. Constitutional identity is usually formed only through

[1] C Offe, *Varieties of Transition: The East European and East German Experience* (Boston, Polity, 1996) 32–33.

collective historical experience, well before constituent assemblies ever assemble. But the overnight disintegration of the Bloc, and then the Union which was its organiser and master, forced the issue. Across all the vast extent of the 'transition zone', from the Danube to the Sea of Japan, the threshold question of the constitutional subject and constitutional identity was probably no more fraught than for the five contrived 'ethnostans' of Central Asia.

At first glance, the national community for the Central Asian states might seem to be settled matter. Each new state bore an ethnic nation in its name, and so Kazakhstan was self-evidently the state of the Kazakh nation, Tajikistan of the Tajik nation, etc. But the nation-state is a contested and dubious construct even in seemingly clear-cut cases. For the 'artefactual' nations of Central Asia created by Soviet federalism it was particularly so. The shift from 'nationality-autonomies' to 'nation-states' in formal terms was deceptively straightforward, both in international and constitutional law. In international law, it involved an elevation of existing status, the achievement of internationally recognised sovereignty for a pre-existing subnational political jurisdiction. In constitutional law, it required a re-characterisation and modest re-organisation of inherited political institutions. The international promotion and national rebranding however masked the latent tensions and contradictions of the Soviet national scheme which the Central Asian states had inherited. All five carried the indelible marks of the Soviet juridification of culture and ethnicity as the basis of political community and organisation.

The Central Asian constitutions all proclaimed the identity of the political or constituent community in an ostensibly inclusive manner. Each, echoing Philadelphia 1787, commenced with a ringing preamble, 'We, the people of …', although Uzbekistan's omits the first person plural. The expression employed in all five constitutions was 'the people of [Kazakhstan, Uzbekistan, Tajikistan, Turkmenistan, the Kyrgyz Republic]', which is not co-terminous with the expression 'the [Kazakh, Uzbek, Tajik, Turkmen, Kyrgyz] people'. The constitutions invoked stock constitutional formulas of the age of mature self-determination to meet the requirements of a civic rather than a primordial nation; they were all avowedly 'colour-blind', forbidding discrimination and guaranteeing all citizens equal protection. But they failed simultaneously to incorporate counter-majoritarian or minority-protecting constitutional mechanisms which would safeguard the multinational character of the national communities at independence. Each of the five is to varying degrees significantly less ethnically plural after two decades of independence.

The Soviet constitutions (Union and sub-Union) reflected a complex multinational project, requiring of citizens and authorities alike concerted energies over the *long durée*. The Constitution of the Russian Federation preserves important aspects of this project, both institutional and aspirational, although the justificatory ideology has changed.[2] But the constitutions of the Central Asian states have supplanted a multinational with a national project and a correlative multinationalist ideology with a nationalist one. In part this circumstance is itself a Soviet legacy: in contrast to the fractal ethnic geometry of the Soviet heartland, the RSFSR, the ethnic geometry of the Central Asian periphery was designed to be simple: the republics were constituted in the first place as ethnic homelands, in which would reside the titular nation as well as non-titular communities or individuals. They were diverse to begin with because of the complex demographics of Turkestan from which they were carved—the Ferghana valley particularly had historically been an ethnic and cultural mosaic. They became secondarily more diverse with the incentivised in-migration ('settlement') of large numbers of ethnic Russians and the compulsory exile (particularly to Kazakhstan and Kyrgyzstan) of 'enemy' and 'problem' nations (Poles, Koreans, Germans, etc).

The five constitutions all moved away from the avowedly and structurally multinational character of Soviet constitutionalism, both in their institutions and in their rhetoric. They all failed to provide specifically multinational institutions of governance at the centre like the USSR Soviet of the Nationalities or the Russian Federation Council (with the marginal exception of the Kazakh People's Assembly) or ethno-territorial jurisdictions in the regions (with the exceptions of Karakalpakstan in Uzbekistan and Gorno-Badakhsan in Tajikistan, discussed below). Conspicuously absent as well is a multinational constitutional ideology structuring the conception of rights and responsibilities. Whereas the Soviet-era constitutions imposed positive duties to further the multi-

[2] The preamble to the Russian Constitution opens, 'We the multinational people of the Russian Federation …' Russian Federation Constitution 3, J Henderson, *Constitution of the Russian Federation* (Oxford, Hart Publishing, 2011) 85.

national project,[3] the constitutions of the independent states impose positive rights to (or state 'facilitation' of) ethno-cultural expression as well as to non-discrimination and prohibit discriminatory propaganda.[4] The constitutional protection of cultural/ethnic pluralism is nowhere particularly robust.

Cutting against regional type is the unique constitutional institution of the Assembly of the Peoples of Kazakhstan, established expressly for the purpose of

> the facilitation of interethnic agreement in the Republic of Kazakhstan respecting the process of formation of the Kazakh civic identity and the competitiveness of the nation on the basis of Kazakhstani patriotism, civic and spiritual-cultural commonalty of the people of Kazakhstan and the consolidatory role of the Kazakh people[5]

The careful balance struck here between Kazakh (ethnicity) and Kazakhstani (nation) in this formulation is indicative of the Kazakh 'primus inter pares' approach to the constitutional relations of the titular and constituent peoples.

The Assembly functions as a presidential advisory and policy body in the sphere of inter-ethnic relations, with a remit including central and local government, business and civil society. As a result, it is of peripheral constitutional significance—it is an advisory or consultative organ, and an ethnic 'electoral college', not a governing body. Apart from developing legislative and policy proposals, conducting seminars and public awareness measures, supporting ethno-cultural associations, and promoting the state and other languages (and the use of Kazakh among the Kazakh diaspora abroad), its chief role is to elect nine Majlis deputies. It also supervises the work of subsidiary assemblies at oblast and equivalent levels. Its membership and that of the oblast bodies is

[3] Kaz SSR 62—obligation to 'national dignity' strengthen friendship of nations and nationalities of the multinational Soviet state'.

[4] Kaz 19 (right to native culture and language), Uzb 4 (state 'facilitates a respectful attitude toward languages, customs, and traditions'), Kyr 37 (state support for customs and traditions 'not infringing human rights and freedoms), Taj 2 and Tkm 14 (weakest of all; use of native language only).

[5] Kaz Law 20.10.2008 3. The body was in fact initially established during the 1995 interregnum as a parliament-substitute in an effort to legitimise Nazarbaev's rule-by-presidential-edict. MB Olcott, *Kazakhstan: Unfulfilled Promise*, Revised Edition (Washington, Carnegie Endowment for Peace, 2010) 11.

nominated from among 'representatives of ethno-cultural and other social associations, representatives of state organs and other persons with account of their authority in society.'[6] The loosely formulated scope of capacity or action and basis of membership suggests that the People's Assembly mechanism is designed along loose consociational, consultative, non-Western lines, precisely to avoid a rigidly juridified structure, based on hard representational criteria and quotas.

CITIZENSHIP AND ETHNICITY ('NATIONALITY')

The five constitutional orders all formally embraced a civic rather than ethnic or primordial concept of nation. However, in each case, over the two and half decades since independence, and for the most part in the very first years, the underlying character of the constitutional order has become ethnically hegemonic—in some cases subtly, in others overtly. The titular elites at independence were in a position to secure substantive ethnic domination after the intervening decades of largely formal ethnic domination—domination over two principal categories: residual ethnic Russians and resident ethnic minorities (both native, eg Tajiks in Uzbekistan, and settled, eg Germans, Poles and Koreans in Kazakhstan). The elites all inherited ethnically plural, multinational polities, but in which (save for Kazakhstan) the titular ethnicity constituted a majority of the population. They owed their positions and prominence in the first place to the perennial Soviet policy of *korenizatsia* or indigenisation,[7] promoting titular candidates for leadership positions in political bureaucracies (as of course in republican cultural institutions themselves, academies of science, universities, etc). While Soviet *korenizatsia* as a policy of Moscow had always been tempered by a co-ordinate principle of 'ethnic balance' (meaning effective central/Russian control—if

[6] Kaz Law 20.10.2008 15(1). Neither the number of members at national or oblast levels, nor the composition of the bodies as between the identified candidate pools is further specified.

[7] T Martin, *The Affirmative Action Empire: Nations and Nationalism in the Soviet Union, 1923–1939* (London and Ithaca NY, Cornell University Press, 2001) (early Soviet *korenizatsia*); B Dave, *Kazakhstan—Ethnicity, Language and Power* (Abingdon and New York, Routledge, 2008) 76–77 (late-Soviet *korenizatsia* and ethnic preference).

First Secretaries were Uzbek, Tajik, etc, then Second Secretaries were usually Russian), post-Soviet *korenizatsia* as a policy of the new national elites faced no restraints and was free to become a matter of wholesale ethnic replacement.

Fatefully, while the independent Central Asian republics rejected the formally multinational components of the Soviet constitutional order, they carried over the predicate juridified concept of nationality intact, without expressly constitutionalising it. The juridical status of nationalities was not a matter for direct constitutional regulation in the USSR either, but was rather the object of subsidiary legislation (in conformity with which nationality was officially registered in the internal Soviet passport and other civil documentation).[8] Similarly, in post-Soviet Central Asia, nationality (ethnicity) has continued to be recognised and defined juridically in statutes and regulations so reflexively and consistently that it can justifiably be deemed an integral part of the constitutional order. The Kazakh and Kyrgyz constitutions emphatically repudiate the Soviet practice of compulsory indication of ethnicity.[9] The sub-constitutional regulation of ethnicity in Kazakhstan is representative of the region. A child's ethnicity is determined by that of the child's parents; in case of divergent ethnicity, the child may elect the ethnicity of either parent upon the issuance of an identity document or passport (but ethnicity is indicated in the document itself only upon the holder's election).[10]

Citizenship is governed by subsidiary legislation. Each state has adopted a comprehensive law on citizenship. The inclusion of a right (or the absence of bar) to carry dual (or multiple) citizenship varies: citizenship of another state is not recognised but not prohibited in Turkmenistan, Kyrgyzstan and Uzbekistan, whereas in Tajikistan and Kazakhstan dual citizenship is forbidden.[11] Dual citizenship is of

[8] R Brubaker, 'Nationhood and the National Question in the Soviet Union and Post-Soviet Eurasia: An Institutionalist Account' (1994) 23(1) *Theory and Society* 47, 53.

[9] Kaz 29(2) (right to indicate or not indicate ethnicity), Kyr 20(4.9) (bar on compulsory indication of ethnicity non-derogable).

[10] Kaz 19(1), Family Code 26.12.2011 65, 26.08.13 Rules 3.4.

[11] Kaz Law 20.12.1991 21(5) (acquisition of citizenship of another state entails loss of Kazakh citizenship), Kyr Law 21.05.2007 5 (save where otherwise provided by treaty), Taj Law 04.11.1995 4, Uzb Law 02.07.1992 10, Tkm Law 22.06.2013 5 (categorically).

particular significance to ethnic Russians whose interest in remaining in Central Asia is (partially) a function of the retention of their freedom both to travel and, if necessary or desirable, to immigrate to the Russian Federation. Kyrgyzstan and Kazakhstan alone among the five recognise a 'right of return' on an ethnic basis: ethnic Kyrgyz[12] are entitled to a waiver of residency and otherwise applicable additional requirements; '*oralmany*' (foreign ethnic Kazakhs) are entitled to citizenship on the basis of a simplified procedure but subject to residency requirements.[13]

The five states have all undergone a significant degree of ethnic de-diversification, most dramatically in those states which had significant populations of Russians (Kazakhstan notably) or exiled/'enemy' nations (again Kazakhstan, also Kyrgyzstan). These 'post-colonial' cultural dynamics are obviously complex and would be a challenge to the most sophisticated constitutional system to accommodate or regulate. But a 'non-ethnic' Uzbekistan or Tajikistan in the circumstances was always a rather more improbable prospect than, say, a non-racial South Africa,[14] owing to the post-Soviet possibilities for repatriation to now external 'homelands'. The 'unmixing of peoples'[15] is a widespread phenomenon after the Soviet collapse: the emigration or 'repatriation' of Russians to Russia and of ethnic minorities to kin-states inside or outside post-Soviet space. Although not regulated as such in the constitutional systems (any more than it was regulated in the Soviet system), the status of ethnic Russians is necessarily a feature of them (as everywhere in the post-Soviet periphery) and has been a contentious matter. As Anglo-Indians or Anglo-East Africans of a former day, Russians found themselves in an uncomfortable or disadvantageous situation post-independence: bearers of a colonialist nationality at an anti-colonialist conjuncture, formerly privileged power-holders now cut off from the circuitry of power.

Non-Russian exiled minority populations, in Kyrgyzstan and Kazakhstan primarily, have also emigrated in large numbers, particularly

[12] Kyr Law 21.05.2007 14(2).

[13] Kaz Law 20.12.1991 16(1).

[14] Constitution of the Republic of South Africa 1996, Art 1(b).

[15] R Brubaker, 'Aftermaths of Empire and the Unmixing of Peoples: Historical and Comparative Perspectives' (1995) 18(2) *Ethnic and Racial Studies* 189.

where they have been encouraged by repatriation schemes of kin-states (Germany, Greece, Poland).[16] Insofar as they afford insufficient minority protections or guarantees (or otherwise simply fail affirmatively to forestall or vitiate ethnic hegemony), the Central Asian constitutional systems can arguably be regarded as among the 'push' factors contributing to emigration. They would seem to be outweighed by the pull factors, such as more promising economic fortunes (the attractiveness of the Greek or German schemes may owe less to the prospect of ethnic homecoming and more to the lure of a First World ticket).

Ethnic Russians have fared variously under the five constitutional systems, notwithstanding the fact that the constitutional protections they enjoy are essentially uniform across the region. Unlike, say, the Baltics, the Central Asian states have not mounted invidious legislative efforts to disenfranchise Russians or condition their citizenship on onerous new requirements (mastery of the official language).[17] However, whereas Russians in Kazakhstan (and to a lesser extent in Kyrgyzstan and Uzbekistan) have continued to play an economic if not a political role in post-Soviet independent national life, albeit in reduced numbers, they have for the most part abandoned Tajikistan and Turkmenistan. In part this pattern has been a function of demographics: the major capital cities in the region were all mostly Russophone. Bishkek and Almaty had been Russian garrison towns and Tashkent a major centre of Soviet-promoted Russian resettlement, whereas Northern Kazakhstan had historically (from the time of Catherine) had a preponderant Russian settler population, which over time secured increasing land rights at the expense of the nomadic population thanks to tsarist legislation.[18] But the hospitality, in operational rather than written terms, of the new constitutional orders to non-titulars and especially to Russians has undoubtedly played a part.

[16] See eg K Iglicka, 'Are they Fellow Countrymen or Not? The Migration of Ethnic Poles from Kazakhstan to Poland' (1998) 32(4) *International Migration Review* 995, 1007.

[17] WR Brubaker, 'Citizenship Struggles in Soviet Successor States' (1992) 26(2) *International Migration Review* 269, 279–84 (restrictive citizenship laws in Estonia and Latvia).

[18] MB Olcott, *The Kazakhs* (Stanford CA, Hoover Institution Press, 1995) 86–89.

FEDERALISM, DEVOLUTION

Of separate concern is the constitutional fate of non-titular nationalities, native to the territory of the states, both those for whom territorial autonomy had been provided (Karkalpaks and Pamiris) and those deprived of it (Uzbek Tajiks). The Republic of Karakalpakstan in Uzbekistan and the Gorno-Badakhshan Autonomous Oblast or Province (GBAO) in Tajikistan are the only autonomous jurisdictional units (autonomies) in the region. Under the Uzbek and Tajik constitutions, respectively,[19] each of Karakalpakstan and the GBAO is a self-governing entity with legislative capacity within its defined sphere, as well as its own complement of executive and judicial institutions (in the case of GBAO elaborated more particularly in subsidiary federal legislation, in that of Karakalpakstan in its own constitution). Karakalpakstan and Gorno-Badakhshan differ in their (inherited) status as autonomies: Karakalpakstan, having been an Autonomous Soviet Socialist Republic within the Uzbek SSR, now enjoys the constitutional status of sovereign Republic within the Republic of Uzbekistan[20] (a Soviet ASSR, like an SSR, did have its own constitution; it was also granted the authority to 'deal independently with matters within its jurisdiction').[21] GBAO had been an 'Autonomous Region', and as such regulated by a Law (rather than a constitution), drafted by its own soviet (legislature) but adopted by the soviet of its parent SSR, to which it was subordinate. It was now an Autonomous Province of Tajikistan co-ordinate with the other provinces.[22] Neither the Uzbek nor Tajik constitutions define

[19] Taj 81–83, Uzb 70–75. The treatment in the Uzbek Constitution is more extensive, as befits the status of Karakalpakstan as a sovereign Republic.

[20] 'The sovereign Republic of Karakalpakstan enters into the composition of the Republic of Uzbekistan. The sovereignty of the Republic of Karakalpakstan is guarded by the Republic of Uzbekistan.' Uzbek Constitution Art 70. 'The Republic of Karakalpakstan has its own Constitution. The Constitution of the Republic of Karakalpaktan cannot contradict the Constitution of the Republic of Uzbekistan.' Art 71.

[21] USSR 1977 82. An SSR, defined as 'sovereign' (Art 76) had a greater degree of autonomy, manifest in its authority over the 'activity of enterprises, institutions, and organisations subordinate to the Union' (Art 77), ie an SSR controlled central government entities on its territory whereas an ASSR did not.

[22] 'Gorno-Badakhshan Autonomous Province is a constituent and inseparable part of the Republic of Tajikistan.' Taj 81.

themselves as federal; indeed the Tajik state is declared 'unitary',[23] whereas the integrity of Uzbek state is not defined at all.

Both Gorno-Badakhsan and Karakalpakstan enjoy the right of national legislative initiative pursuant to the Tajik and Uzbek constitutions.[24] But unlike the Russian Constitution,[25] neither the Uzbek nor the Tajik constitutions elaborate lists of exclusive and shared powers or vest residual powers vis-a-vis the autonomous entities. Hence from a strict constitutionalist analysis, not even the Uzbek arrangements would qualify as federalist, although the Karakalpak Constitution kits out the Republic with a full complement of governance institutions. Indeed, while the Law on Gorno-Badakhsan specifies the 'economic fundamentals of the activity of the GBAO', the 'financial fundamentals' and the 'social and cultural fundamentals',[26] only with respect to the last does it elaborate 'powers' (*polnomichia*, полномочия) in education, culture and public health.

However, in distinction to simple devolution, some marginal constitutional special provision is made for participation of the autonomies in central government. Under both the Tajik and Uzbek constitutions, one of the deputy chairs of the senior chamber (Majilisi Milli and the Senate) must be chosen from among the GBAO deputies and Karakalpakstan representatives, respectively,[27] and one member of each of the Constitutional Courts must be a representative of Gorno-Badakhshan and Karakalpakstan, respectively.[28] Additionally, in Uzbekistan only, the Head of Government of Karakalpakstan is an ex officio member of the Cabinet of Ministers and the Procurator of the Republic of Karakalpakstan is appointed by the highest organ of government of Karakalpakstan (with consent of the General Procurator).[29] Karakalpakstan also has its own judicial system, with a supreme court and an economic court,[30] whereas the Gorno-Badakhshan court is on the level of a

23 Taj 1.

24 Taj 58, Uzb 83.

25 Russian Federation Constitution 71–73; Henderson (n 2) 4.

26 Law on GBAO, Chapter 2, 6–10, Chapter 3, 11–15, Chapter 4, 16–18, respectively.

27 Taj 53, Uzb 86.

28 Taj 89, Uzb 108.

29 Uzb 98, 119.

30 Uzb 107.

provincial (oblast) court.[31] In all other respects (basis for parliamentary representation, appointment of judges, eg) GBAO and Karakalpakstan are treated as equivalent to the other (non-autonomous) provinces.

In terms of their formal relation to the constitutional governance arrangements of the polity in general, Gorno-Badakhshan could perhaps best be analysed as a devolved jurisdiction with limited specified powers of self-government, like Scotland or Wales; whereas Karakalpakstan appears closer to a subordinate but sovereign component of a federal state, recalling in its status a Subject of the Russian Federation.[32] Notably, 'mutual relations' between the greater Uzbek and lesser Karkalpak Republics are to be regulated by 'treaties and agreements' concluded between them,[33] though there is no 'treaty of federation,' such as the autonomies of the RSFSR concluded with Moscow in 1992 to establish the Russian Federation or other bilateral treaties between Subjects of the Russian Federation and the Federation itself.[34]

The degree of substantive as distinct from formal autonomy enjoyed by GBAO and Karakalpakstan in Tajikistan and Uzbekistan is as pointed an issue now as it was for them in the predecessor SSRs (or as indeed it was for those SSRs themselves within the Union). The situation in the two autonomies is rather different, however: whereas Karakalpaks are a minority even in Karakalpakstan, which is in any case subject to perhaps the most centralised and authoritarian state in the region, the Pamiris of the GBAO occupy a remote corner of perhaps the most regionalised (albeit progressively presidentialist) state, and also as Ismailis enjoy the significant presence and support of a powerful and influential international patron in the Aga Khan Foundation. It is difficult for one not to view them as sham autonomies in the Soviet way, ironically bearing the same yoke from which their parent entities were themselves liberated with the Soviet collapse.

Beyond Karakalpakstan, and furnishing an instructive contrast with it, one further special problem of accommodation of native ethnic diversity confronted independent Uzbekistan. Tajik-speakers

[31] Taj 84.

[32] Henderson (n 2) 3–4, 94–101.

[33] Uzb 75. It is endowed with the right to secede on the basis of a referendum, Uzb 74, as well (doubtlessly as significant as the analogous right of the SSRs to secede from the Union).

[34] Henderson (n 2) 97–100.

in Uzbekistan were of sufficient demographic significance at independence (something like 10 per cent of the population, considerably in excess of Karakalpaks) that Uzbekistan could well have been regarded as binational. Owing to the vicissitudes of Stalin-era 'national delimitation', the urban-dwelling Persian-speakers ('Tajiks') of historical Transoxiana found themselves incorporated in an Uzbek republic, outside the borders of what eventually became the Tajik SSR (initially Tajikistan had been an ASSR within the Uzbek SSR, like the Kyrgyz ASSR within the Kazakh SSR). The Tajik 'irridenta' of Samarkand and Bokhara (and other towns) in Uzbekistan during the life of the USSR were catered to by Soviet nationalities policies (education, media, cultural institutions, preference policies) generally even though not benefitting directly from a homeland (no other Soviet ethnic population of comparable size and concentration was stranded outside its 'proper' autonomy in this way). However, in the late Soviet period, assimilationist Republican policies confronted them with a choice of either tactically adopting Uzbek nationality (most were bilingual in any case) or decamping for Tajikistan. Uzbekistan at independence thus inherited a 'Tajik problem' and witnessed the entrenchment and intensification of those policies.[35]

Uzbekistan's facially colour-blind constitution[36] was never likely to afford the large Tajik minority full participation in national life and group autonomy in the context of the modern Uzbek history of majoritarian politics and resurgent exclusivist nationalism. Whereas the Karakalpaks have at least continued to merit a form of self-determination, however qualified and attenuated, in the new dispensation, the Tajiks are more exposed than they were throughout the Soviet period. A similar fate befell other non-titulars in peripheral SSRs after independence, for example, Abkhaz in Georgia, who were subject to discrimination and persecution now that they were completely exposed to the policies of the parochial (titular) capital, no longer buffered by cosmopolitan

[35] See R Foltz, 'The Tajiks of Uzbekistan' (1996) 15(2) *Central Asian Survey* 213.

[36] N Gotanda, 'A Critique of "Our Constitution is color-blind"' (1991) 44 *Stanford Law Review* 1 (US Constitution's freedom from positive discrimination on racial grounds does not make it colour-blind in view of necessity for redress of present effects of past discrimination).

Moscow.[37] Indeed, the existence of Tajikistan as an independent state of Tajiks rather worsens the plight of their co-ethnics next door, who now constitute a stubbornly 'foreign' element in the heart of the Uzbek polity, notwithstanding that they are emphatically autochthonous and indeed themselves represent the historic Persian heart of the region. Uzbek Tajiks confront a fate like the Ottoman Greeks or Egyptian Copts: the constitutional logic of majoritarian self-determination has effectively rendered them aliens in their own land, *natio non grata*, in their case without any formal-constitutional protection.

One leftover problem bequeathed by Stalin to the region is a prism refracting at once all the many constitutional shades of space and identity: the arbitrarily ethno-territorialised Ferghana Valley, Central Asia's great fruit and vegetable garden and home to one quarter of the total population. The Ferghana is parcelled among Tajikistan, Uzbekistan and Kyrgyzstan in a crazy mosaic which leaves each with significant non-titular local minorities, heightened inter-ethnic tensions, competition for common resources and artificial barriers to commerce and movement.[38] The Kyrgyz share of the valley has been the site of the worst ethnic riots in post-Soviet space, in two terrible episodes 20 years apart, just before the denouement of *Sovietskaia vlast'*, in 1990, and again two decades on in the year of the second rout of the president, 2010.[39]

The social and legal position of the local minorities (particularly Kyrgyz Uzbeks, Uzbek Kyrgyz, Tajik Uzbeks) has deteriorated, in respect of access to resources and human security generally (especially in an atmosphere of counter-terrorist witch-hunting). The baroque borders, splitting villages and creating extra-territorial islands, remain unsettled in a number of areas. During Soviet times, the administrative

[37] See L Broers, 'Containing the nation, Building the State: Coping with Nationalism, Minorities and Conflict In Post-soviet Georgia', PhD. dissertation, SOAS, 2004.

[38] The 'crisis-ridden Ferghana' is also a discursive construct. See M Reeves, 'Locating Danger: Konfliktologiia and the Search for Fixity in the Ferghana Valley Borderlands' (2005) 24(1) *Central Asian Survey* 67, 67–69.

[39] Y Ro'i, 'Central Asian Riots and Disturbances, 1989–1990: Causes and Context' (1991) 10(3) *Central Asian Survey* 21, 23–33; International Crisis Group (ICG), 'The Pogroms in Kyrgyzstan,' Asia Report No 193, 23 August 2010, available at www.crisisgroup.org/~/media/Files/asia/central-asia/kyrgyzstan/193%20The%20Pogroms%20in%20Kyrgyzstan, accessed 11 November 2015.

borders were the object of both negotiation and re-delineation (eg sorting out collective farm jurisdiction) in an ongoing process. With the acquisition of statehood and the deployment of its symbolic and legal apparatus, the logic of national identity has been imposed simultaneously with the logic of national territory, disturbing and deforming local patterns of life.

> Contemporary cartographic and political complexity … arises … from the conjunction of multiple logics—with 'national' border overlaid upon kinship networks, trade routes, grazing patterns, pilgrimage circuits, canal systems and memories of historical landholdings that follow entirely different spatial patterns and social logics.[40]

Just as the Ferghana is a demographic microcosm of the region, so is it a constitutional microcosm, as the policies and the legal arrangements within and across the borders exhibit not just the constitutional personalities of the states (Uzbekistan as sheriff and bully), but the force of constitutionalism itself, of distinct uniform national orders in the first place, here juxtaposed, superimposed, and counterposed.

LANGUAGE

Not surprisingly, language policy and regulation has become a recurrent focus of nationalist tension in independent Central Asia, and the place of language in the constitution has been contentious. All five constitutions make the national language the state language; Russian is accorded special status in the constitutions of Kazakhstan, Kyrgyzstan and Tajikistan and not mentioned in those of the other two states. Uzbekistan and Turkmenistan have gone the farthest in de-Russifying governance and employing Uzbek and Turkmen respectively as the default language for official purposes.[41] All five states however continue to rely on Russian in many contexts.

[40] M Reeves, 'Materialising State Space: 'Creeping Migration' and Territorial Integrity in Southern Kyrgyzstan' (2009) 61 *Europe-Asia Studies* 1277, 1287.

[41] In Turkmenistan provision is made for foreign languages of instruction in (foreign state-organised or sponsored) international schools but not for Russian (Law on language 5(4)); in Uzbekistan Russian has been progressively demoted in state functions and relegated to marginal use. 'Language policy and ethnic relations in Uzbekistan' in G Smith, V Law, A Wilson, A Bohr and E Allworth, *Nation-building*

Language policy is a fair proxy or indicator for the strength and significance of nationalist ideology. Privileging of the national language as medium of instruction, communication (print, broadcast and electronic media) and official state business is legally anchored in all states, as is accommodating other languages (to varying degrees). Laws on language do the general regulation; laws on education, media, etc include relevant linguistic provisions.[42] Restricting the use of other languages of otherwise discriminating against their speakers is legally prohibited in all states. However, particularly but not exclusively where the ideology of the nation-building project has been ethnic (as in Turkmenistan and Uzbekistan) the problem lies not in facially discriminatory regulation but either in invidious application of norms or discriminatory effects of decisions ostensibly on other grounds—or simply in the social consequences for individuals of the duly protected exercise of language rights. Just as in the Soviet context education in a non-Russian school could impair later career choices,[43] so too in contemporary Central Asia can education in non-state language schools. Non-speakers of the state language (and minority language-speakers eg Tajik-speakers in Uzbekistan) as well as Russian-speakers have been increasingly marginalized.[44] Thus, for example, Uzbek schools have been closed in Kyrgyzstan and Tajik schools in Uzbekistan. In Samarkand (the largest Tajik-speaking centre in Uzbekistan), 'the number of schools with instruction in Tajik has been reduced to one mixed Tajik-Uzbek language primary school.'[45]

in the Post-Soviet Borderlands: The Politics of National Identities (Cambridge and New York, Cambridge University Press, 1998) 109–202 (progressive entrenchment of Uzbek at expense of Russian in language legislation).

[42] eg Kaz Law 27.07.2007 9 (instruction in other languages facilitated where possible), Taj Law 22.07.2013 7 (guaranteed choice of language of instruction, state facilitation where possible), Tkm Law 15.08.2009 5 (Turkmen basic language of instruction, state assistance in native language study), Uzb Law 21.10.1989 throughout (state language for all official/business purposes but provision made for use of other languages as well for documents, citizens' application in circumstances where speakers a majority or residing compactly).

[43] JM Landau and B Kellner-Heinkele, *Politics of Language in the Ex-Soviet Muslim States: Azerbaijan, Uzbekistan, Kazakhstan, Kyrgyzstan, Turkmenistan, Tajikistan* (London, Hurst, 2001) 55–58.

[44] Smith, Law, Wilson, Bohr and Allworth (n 41).

[45] M Sadykov, 'Uzbekistan: Tajik Language Under Pressure in Ancient Samarkand' Eurasianet, 5 November 2013, available at www.eurasianet.org/node/67724, accessed 11 November 2015.

The status of the Russian language assumes a somewhat ironic dimension with respect to law and legislation itself. Inasmuch as all five constitutional and legal orders are to the same extent direct heirs of the Russian legal tradition and have carried over the root stock of Russian concepts, terms and rules intact, the installation of the vernacular as official state legal language has presented a challenge. Legislation in all five states is published in the state language and in Russian on official sites. However, Russian continues to be the drafting and conceptual language of the law in most capitals (and in some provinces), and the official controlling version of a law in the national language is often back-translated from the Russian. Indeed, many of the standard legal terms in the vernacular are transliterations from the Russian in any case. The constitutional systems in future may diverge from their Russian/ Soviet origins, but for the foreseeable future they will all in some fundamentally recognisable sense continue to 'speak Russian', and thus be in a kind of constitutional conversation with one another and with the other post-Soviet Russophone traditions, even when they purport to speak in the native tongue.

CULTURE

Soviet nationalities policy was instrumental in forging for each nationality a canonical cultural heritage: a (materialist-inflected) history, a literature (national epic and lyric poetry), a musical tradition (instruments, repertoire of folk and authorial compositions), a dance and dramatic tradition (troupes, productions, performances), as well as vernacular media (newspapers and magazines, television and radio) and new (socialist realist) national literature. This was not purely the 'invention of tradition', but it was certainly the official identification and certification of tradition. These inherited cultural templates continue to inform and legitimise the constitutional systems of the new Central Asia even though they are not referenced (save perhaps in the preambles) much less prescribed or regulated.

Certainly independence has stimulated and encouraged renewed exploration and revision/redefinition of the contours of traditional national culture. Universities, research institutes and performing and fine arts organisations (arts academy, opera and ballet, philharmonia, traditional dance ensemble, etc) often directly descend from SSR predecessors and, although re-organised, carry on (in part) Soviet ethnographic approaches and conceptual frameworks.[46] Even while cultural production and research have been mobilised in a consciously revisionist mode, against the received Soviet interpretation (eg in new 'anti-Soviet' historiography highlighting the oppressive or colonialist nature of Soviet rule and with it policies like collectivisation, sedentarisation and the systematic repressions of the 1930s),[47] the appropriation of culture for political purposes and the style of official cultural rhetoric and cultural endorsement remain recognisably derivative of Soviet practices. The materials have been altered to suit the purposes of the new leaderships, but the moulds remain familiar. Thus, to cite an extreme example, Niyazov's Turkmenbashi cult, his use of images, slogans and new purpose-produced scripture, all in the context of an imposed 'totalitarian' organisation of collective existence and indeed of individual subjectivities, was classically Stalinist. It could not imaginably have been so comprehensively conceived and meticulously executed by anyone but an heir to that political system.

Thus, while the constitutions all endorse universalist liberalism and expressly proscribe divisive, exclusivist nationalism, they have accommodated and legitimised a continuation of the Soviet cultural project (an official, state-endorsed version of national history, identity and cultural production), but liberated from the (very significant) constraints of multinational socialism. The Soviets managed to keep the nationalist genie inside the bottle while tooling, decorating and polishing the nationality lamps and installing them in the grand cultural exposition in which all Soviet citizens lived and which was embodied in the VDNKh.[48] The post-Soviet Central Asian authorities have raided the display, making off with their respective lamps and remov-

[46] For the persistence of Soviet categories in post-Soviet Central Asian academic discourse see L Yountchi, 'The Politics of Scholarship and the Scholarship of Politics: Imperial, Soviet, and Post-Soviet Scholars Studying Tajikistan' and Z-A Auezova, 'Kyrgyz—Muslim—Central Asian? Recent Approaches to the Study of Kygrgyz Culture in Kyrgyzstan', both in M Kemper and S Conermann (eds), *The Heritage of Soviet Oriental Studies* (Abingdon, Routledge, 2011), 217–40 and 241–62, respectively.

[47] Notably in Kazakhstan; see H Yilmaz, 'History Writing as Agitation and Propaganda: The Kazakh History Book of 1943' (2102) 31(4) *Central Asian Survey* 409.

[48] See ch 2, 67.

ing the stoppers. Karimov has made '*uzbekchilik*', Uzbekness, a core component of his ideology,[49] and elevated Tamerlane to national hero—notwithstanding the historical inconvenience that Uzbeks and Timurids were enemies; the nomadic Shaybanids led by Uzbek Khan drove the Timurids out of the region to India where they became Moghuls.[50] Niyazov during his lifetime fashioned an elaborate confessional creed out of Turkmen identity and tradition.[51] The Uzbek and Turkmen policies recall nineteenth-century nationalist projects but with twenty-first century techniques of propagation. While neither is to be found in the constitutional text, they are integral to the constitutional order.

Of course, in a globalised world with instantaneous circuits of cross-cultural communication, the new Central Asian nation-building and culture-defining projects face a lot of competition and cannot be so assuredly prosecuted or uncritically received. Looking forward though, and bearing in mind the concept of an evolving constitutional identity,[52] it proves difficult for one to say in just what something like Karimov's *uzbekchilik* is likely ultimately to issue, particularly as memories of Soviet times fade and a generation more drawn to global popular than official national culture grows ascendant. The liberal letter of the constitutional systems is in tension with the parochial spirit informing them, particularly as culture has been instrumentalised in a fairly transparent way in the interests of a narrow political class.

RELIGION

The ringing proclamation of freedom of conscience and profession of belief in the constitutions is belied by an unusually close and comprehensive statutory and regulatory regime for religion in every state, encompassing organisations, places of worship, practices, activities,

[49] Dave (n 7) 20 fn 3.

[50] For Karimov's ideological project see AF March, 'The Use and Abuse of History: "National Ideology" as Transcendental Object in Islam Karimov's "Ideology of National Independence"' (2002) 21 (4) *Central Asian Survey* 371 (invention of history serves Uzbek state not Uzbek nation).

[51] S Turkmenbashy (Niyazov), *Rukhnama: Reflections on the Spiritual Values of the Turkmen* (Ashgabat, 2005).

[52] G Jacobsohn, 'Constitutional Identity' (2006) 68 *The Review of Politics* 361.

education and materials. All five states had early on adopted dedicated statutes regulating religion, religious organisation, or religious activity. The coming-to-prominence on the wider global stage (and in the immediate regional vicinity) of Islamist organisations and agendas with concrete political objectives coincided with the first decade of Central Asian constitutionalism and exercised a quasi-formative influence on its accommodation of Islam. The threat posed or perceived to the legitimacy and stability of the new regimes by Islamist movements reinforced the inherited Soviet regulatory approach to religious forms and organisations, that is, to confine them to officially sanctioned, state-patrolled and controlled expression.

Religion had been the object of especially comprehensive and assiduous state regulation throughout the Soviet period. In the Central Asian republics, Islam was the focus of particular and sustained attention, although Orthodoxy was also prominent, particularly in Kazakhstan and in Russophone cities. The default Soviet approach for Muslims was the creation of ostensibly self-regulatory confessional authorities, the Spiritual Directorates of Muslims, which have survived into the independent republics as state bodies. As a rule, indigenous or historically present religious traditions, meaning for Central Asia Islam, Judaism and Orthodox Christianity, occupy a privileged status, whereas newly introduced religions (eg Baptism or Mormonism, ie missionary sects, particularly those of North American, evangelical provenance) have been disfavoured.

Generally, each law on religion sets out categories of recognised religious association, from religious communities or congregations, to national religious administrations or directorates, and specifies the requirements and procedures for state registration (the Tajik law micro-regulates Islamic organisations, eg specifying the population requirements for establishment of Friday and weekday mosques).[53] In all five cases, religious associations are subject to mandatory state registration, which may be refused or revoked; no religious association may operate legally on the national territory unless registered.[54] Religious education

[53] Taj Law 26.03.2009 11.

[54] Kaz Law 11.10.2011 L3(11), 15, Taj Law 26.03.2009 13, Uzb Law 14.06.1991 11, Tkm Law 21.10.2003 11, Kyr Law 31.12.2008 10.

and publication/dissemination of religious materials may be subject to further licensing requirements. A state religious affairs agency, variously denominated and structured, is also established to administer the regulatory regime and supervise compliance. Also common to the five religious affairs regimes is the rather Orwellian practice of 'state confessional expertise',[55] a process of scrutiny of teachings, materials, practices and rituals to ensure these are all bona fide—conforming to acceptable religious norms as well as the law of the land. Missionary activity is subject to special regulation in Kazakhstan and Kyrgyzstan (licensing requirements) and is banned outright in Uzbekistan.[56] A distinctive zone of religious regulation is the intersection of religion and financial activity, exemplified by Islamic banking, which has undergone some significant development in Kazakhstan.[57]

LOCAL AND REGIONAL GOVERNMENT

Each of the constitutions under study here also organises national space for purposes of governing. The ethno-territorial Soviet scheme achieved only partial coverage insofar as large areas (the bulk of the territory in fact) of the RSFSR remained outside it—they were not ethnicised for purposes of notional self-determination or self-administration. They were simply *oblasti,* provinces, the basic intermediate administrative–territorial subdivision of a Soviet republic. The same principle of non-ethnicised territorial administrative subdivision also effectively applied within the non-Russian SSRs: the territory in them not further allocated to sub-Republican autonomies like Karakalpakstan and GBAO was divided into provinces, districts, town, villages and rural population centres.

[55] Kaz Law 11.10.2011 6, Taj Law 26.03.2009 17, Uzb Law 14.06.1991 19, Regulations 21.04.2004 7 (foreign-published religious materials only), Tkm Law 21.10.2003 7, 20, Kyr Law 31.12.2008 10(3), 11(4), (8) (foreign missions), 12(4) missionaries, 22 (religious literature).

[56] Kaz Law 11.10.2011 8, Kyr Law 31.12.2008 12, Uzb Law 14.06.1991 5.

[57] GN Khaki and B Ah Malik, 'Islamic Banking and Finance in Post-Soviet Central Asia with Special Reference to Kazakhstan' (2013) 1(1) *Journal of Islamic Banking and Finance* 11; PB Maggs, 'Islamic Banking in Kazakhstan Law' (2011) 36 *Review of Central and East European Law* 1.

Each state constitutionally provides for and differentiates between *local state administration* and *local self-government*. The usage varies: in Turkmenistan, Uzbekistan and Tajikistan 'local state administration' includes officials and agencies of central executive authority assigned to the larger administrative territorial divisions (usually province, city and district), as well as corresponding elected representative bodies (councils or assemblies), and 'self-government' refers only to communes or gatherings at the very lowest levels and their corresponding administrative staff. Only in Kyrgyzstan and Kazakhstan does 'local self-government' embrace all sub-national representative assemblies.[58] Only in Kyrgyzstan does local mean local, the 2010 Constitution having abolished provincial level administration (but not provinces) and devolving both executive and representative functions to district levels.

The procedures for appointment of the governors/local chief executives vary (usually appointed by the president at higher levels), as does their accountability. Again, the precise delineation of authority varies, but there is a generally consistent distribution of labour between representative and executive functions. The local representative bodies have ordinance-making (local acts) and revenue-raising power; the local chief executive typically signs and implements ordinances and oversees the activities of the local branches and offices of central ministries and agencies as well as a general executive staff.[59] The delineation between

[58] Tkm 77–83 (local administration consisting of *halk maslahata* and *akim*), 84–88 (local self-government consisting of *gengeshes* at town, village, rural levels), Uzb 99–105 (local administration consisting of *hokim* and *kengashes*; local self-government of citizen gatherings at town, village, neighbourhood or mahalla levels), Kaz 85–89 (local administration headed by *akim*; local self-government in form of elected *maslikhat* at provincial, district, village levels and population directly at lowest levels), Kyr 110–13 (local state administration only incidentally referred to and not constitutionally elaborated; local self-government in form of local *kenesh* and mayor or head of village *okomot*), Taj 77–78 (local administration in form of presidential representative (chair) and *majlis* at provincial, city and district levels; local self-government at village level in form of *jamoat*).

[59] Kaz Law 23.01.2001 (akims govern in conjunction with corresponding representative maslikhats in parallel arrangement from provincial/city levels down to town, rural, village), Uzb Law 02.09.1993 9 (citizen gatherings of villages, settlements and mahallas (neighbourhoods), often generically referred to simply as mahallas), Tkm Law 01.10.2011 (halk maslahats at provincial or town, village levels, a remnant of the once-mighty Halk Maslahat system described in ch 1 above), Kyr Law 14.06.2011 administration (akims appointed by prime minister on nomination

functions is less distinct for the very most local authorities, which have commensurately limited jurisdiction. The nomenclature is confusing owing to the use in the five states' legislation of similar-sounding Persian or Turkic terms for the various bodies and officials, not always with the same legal field of reference.

The functionality of the local administrative and local self-government arrangements is uneven: where central institutions continue to exhibit significant deficits in governance capacity (eg accounting/auditing systems, training and command of procedures, efficiency and integrity), local institutions are even more compromised. Even in more advanced or developed jurisdictions (eg Kazakhstan), the quality of local institutions can vary significantly with province and locality. Provincial presidentially appointed governors and mayors (*akims, hokims, hiakims*) often command considerable regional authority in their own right (as local power brokers) and dominate local representative councils (particularly in highly regionalised polities like Kyrgyzstan, Kazakhstan and Tajikistan), replicating the democratic deficit (or sham) at the centre. Even in Kyrgyzstan, where the framework supports a fair degree of autonomy of local authorities, the oversight role of central state authority is extensively detailed. At the most local levels, where the village and rural communes or gatherings decide issues of purely local significance, there might ironically be greater latitude for democratic processes than at district, provincial or national levels. On the other hand, in Uzbekistan and Turkmenistan, local government functions as political surveillance and control mechanism for central authorities—yet another instance of vintage Soviet institutions decanted into new constitutional bottles. The Uzbek mahallas have manifested about as much authentic citizen capacity for unconstrained deliberative self-governance as did Los Comités de Defensa de la Revolución in Cuba or the networks of Stasi informers in the GDR.[60]

of corresponding representative keneshes), Law 15.06.2011 (keneshes as representative authority and mayors/akims as executive authority, local organs of self government subject to state authority as specified per Art 10).

60 Human Rights Watch, 'Uzbekistan, From House to House: Abuses by Mahalla Committees' (2003), available at www.hrw.org/sites/default/files/reports/uzbekistan0903full.pdf (accessed 4 February 2016).

Finally, one of the five states has experimented with devolved adjudication at the level of local self-government. As noted above in chapter six, the 2010 Kyrgyz Constitution authorises *aksakal* (greybeard or elder) courts, which had been established by presidential decree in 1995 and then further institutionalised pursuant to sub-constitutional legislation.[61] The *akasakal* courts represent a modern take on a folk dispute resolution practice, reinvented with state warrant, something like *gacaca* jurisdictions in Rwanda[62] (but without high state purpose as in the latter). They are not formal judicial bodies; their members, who do not need legal training to qualify, stand for election from the community and serve on a voluntary basis, to resolve village disputes.[63] Their popularity (save among scholars of alternative or customary dispute resolution) has waned, chiefly because their authority does not extend to the pressing problems which most frequently prompt locals to seek redress, like land or civil registration, for example, nor in any case to enforcement (for which the *aksakal* courts must apply to local courts, to which parties can similarly appeal).[64] It is noteworthy that this essay in devolved justice has been attempted in the one jurisdiction which is comparatively free of central instruction and pressure—and certainly of the Soviet-style co-optation of ostensibly autonomous local institutions still characteristic of Turkmenistan or Uzbekistan. Its failure to thrive suggests that the practical and institutional design aspects (eg limited authority) matter more to citizens than its intimacy or authenticity: in contemporary Central Asia, access to and facilitation of the state machinery might count for more than humanistic or culturally resonant alternatives.

[61] Kyr 59, Decree 25.01.1995, Law 06.07.2002.

[62] P Clark, *The Gacaca Courts, Post-Genocide Justice and Reconciliation in Rwanda: Justice Without Lawyers* (Cambridge, Cambridge University Press, 2010).

[63] Kyr Law 06.07.2002; J Beyer, 'Revitalisation, Invention and Continued Existence of the Kyrgyz Aksakal Courts: Listening to Pluralistic Accounts of History' (2006) 53–54 *Journal of Legal Pluralism* 141.

[64] Finland, Ministry of Foreign Affairs, 'The Declining Use of Aksakal Courts in Kyrgyzstan' Eurasia Foundation, 2012.

FURTHER READING

WR Brubaker, 'Nationhood and the National Question in the Soviet Union and Post-Soviet Eurasia: An Institutionalist Account' (1994) 23(1) *Theory and Society* 47, 78.

——, 'Aftermaths of Empire and the Unmixing of Peoples: Historical and Comparative Perspectives' (1995) 18 (2) *Ethnic and Racial Studies* 189.

B Dave, *Kazakhstan—Ethnicity, Language and Power* (Abingdon and New York, Routledge, 2008).

A Farrant, 'Mission Impossible: The Politico-geographic Engineering of Soviet Central Asia's Republican Boundaries' (2006) 25 *Central Asian Survey* 61.

JM Landau and B Kellner-Heinkele, *Language Politics in Contemporary Central Asia: National and Ethnic Identity and the Soviet Legacy* (London, IB Tauris, 2012).

N Megoran, 'Rethinking the Study of International Boundaries: A Biography of the Kyrgyzstan–Uzbekistan Boundary' (2012) 102 *Annals of the Association of American Geographers* 464.

A Rashid, *The Resurgence of Central Asia: Islam or Nationalism?* (London, Zed, 1995).

Y Ro'i, *Islam in the Soviet Union: From the Second World War to Perestroika* (London, C. Hurst, 2000).

G Smith, V Law, A Wilson, A Bohr and E Allworth (eds), *Nation-building in the Post-Soviet Borderlands: The Politics of National Identities* (Cambridge and New York, Cambridge University Press, 1998).

Tables of Authorities

TABLE OF CASES

UK Privy Council

JCPC 2009/0065, JCPC 2009/0065 *Altimo Holdings and Investment Limited and Others (Appellants) v Kyrgyz Mobil Tel Limited and Others (Respondents)*

International Centre for the Settlement of Investment Disputes (ICSID)

Sistem Muhendislik Sanayi Ve Ticaret A.S. v. Kyrgyz Republic, ICSID Case No. ARB(AF)/06/1, Award of 30 September 2009

Ontario, Canada

Judgment of the Superior Court of the Province of Ontario, 15.04.2014, *Sistem Muhendislik Insaat Sanayi Ve Ticaret Anonim Sirketi v. Kyrgyz Republic, 2014 ONSC 2407*

Kazakhstan

06.03.1995 Ruling of the Constitutional Court of the of the Republic of Kazakhstan in the matter of the verification of the constitutionality of the 17.12.1993 resolution of the Central Elections Commission of the Republic of Kazakhstan 'on the formation of electoral districts for elections of deputies of the Supreme Soviet of the Republic of Kazakhstan' in the part relating to the formation of the Abylai Khan electoral district no. 12 of the city of Almaty, Kazakhstanskaia Pravda, 08.03.1995. [Постановление Конституционного Суда Республики Казахстан от 6 марта 1995 «По делу «О проверке конституционности постановления Центральной избирательной комиссии Республики Казахстан от 17 декабря 1993 «Об образовании избирательных округов по выборам депутатов Верховного Совета Республики Казахстан» в части обр азования Абылайхановского избирательного округа № 12 города Алматы, *Казахстанская Правда* 8 Марта 1995]

21.04.2004 Ruling of the the Constitutional Council of the Republic of Kazakhstan on the conformity of the Law of the Republic of Kazakhstan on mass media of information with the the Constitution of the Republic of Kazakhstan [Постановление Конституционного Совета Республики

Казахстан от 21 апреля 2004 № 4 «О проверке Закона Республики Казахстан «О средствах массовой информации» на соответствие Констит уции Республики Казахстан » »]

18.06.2007 Normative Ruling no. 7 of the Constitutional Council of the Republic of Kazakhstan on official interpretation of the norm of the Constitution of the Republic of Kazakhstan in connection with the adoption of the 21.05.2007 Law of the Republic of Kazakhstan no. 254-III bringing in amendments and additions to the Constitution of the Republic of Kazakhstan [Нормативное постановление Конституционного Совета Республики Казахстан от 18 июня 2007 года № 7 «Об официальном толковании норм Конституции Республики Казахстан в связи с принятием Закона Республики Казахстан от 21 мая 2007 года № 254-III «О внесении изменений и дополнений в Конституцию Республики Казахстан» »]

31.01.2011 Normative Ruling no. 2 of the Constitutional Council of the Republic of Kazakhstan on the verification of the Law of the Republic of Kazakhstan bringing in amendments and changes to the Constitution of the Republic of Kazakhstan for its conformity with the Constitution of the Republic of Kazakhstan [Нормативное постановление Конституционного Совета Республики Казахстан от 31 января 2011 № 2 «О проверке Закона Республики Казахстан «О внесении изменения и дополнения в Конституцию Республики Казахстан» на соответствие Конституции Республики Казахстан»]

13.04.2012 Normative Ruling no. 2 of the Constitutional Council of the Republic of Kazakhstan on official interpretation of the norms of the Constitution of the Republic of Kazakhstan on the issue of the expiry of constitutional periods [Нормативное постановление Конституционного Совета от 13.04.2012 года № 2 «Об официальном толковании норм Конституции Республики Казахстан по вопросу исчисления конституционных сроков»]

28.08.2012 Sentence of the specialised inter-district court for criminal cases with juror participation of Zhambyl *oblast'* no. 1-64/2012 [Приговор Специализированного межрайонного суда по уголовным делам с участием присяжных заседателей Жамбылской области от 28 августа 2012 года № 1-64/2012]

07.12.2012 Sentence of the specialised inter-district court for criminal cases with juror participation of Zhambyl oblast' [Приговор Специализированного межрайонного суда по уголовным делам Жамбылской области с участием присяжных заседателей от 7 декабря 2012 года]

Kyrgyzstan

15.12.2005 Decision of the Supreme Court of Kyrgystan, Case No 07-000287/05ED

Submissions to the Human Rights Committee for consideration under the First Optional Protocol to the International Covenant on Civil and Political Rights

24.05.2014, Communication to the Human Rights Committee In the case of Vadim Kuramshin against the Republic of Kazakhstan

09.11.2010, Communication to the Human Rights Committee In the case of Yevgeniy Zhovtis against the Republic of Kazakhstan

TREATIES AND INTERNATIONAL DOCUMENTS/REPORTS

Commonwealth of Independent States (CIS)

21.12.1991 Accord (Belavezha Accords) on the creation of a Commonwealth of Independent States, Protocol to the Accord on the creation of a Commonwealth of Independent States [Соглашение от 21.12.1991 о создании Содружества Независимых Государств (1991); Протокол к Соглашению о создании Содружества Независимых Государств]

Bilateral treaties

23.11.1995 Agreement between the Government of the United Kingdom of Great Britain and Northern Ireland and the Government of the RepUblic of Kazakhstan for the Promotion and Protection of Investments, London, 23 November 1995, Treaty Series No. 30 (1996)

Tajik Peace Process

27.06.1997 General Agreement on the Establishment of Peace and National Accord in Tajikistan, signed in Moscow on 27 June 1997, UN Doc. No. A/52/219

Organisation for Cooperation and Security in Europe (OSCE)

1990 Document of the Copenhagen meeting of the conference on the human dimension of the CSCE (CSCE Copenhagen Document) http://www.osce.org/odihr/elections/14304?download=true (accessed 11 September 2014)

Delegations of Armenia, Belarus, Kazakhstan, Kyrgyzstan, Russia, Tajikistan, Uzbekistan and of the Kyrgyz Republic to the OSCE, Appeal of the CIS Member States to the OSCE Partners, Astana, 15 September 2004, SEC.DEL/225/04, 16 September 2004 (2004 Astana Appeal)

2005 OSCE Human Dimension Commitments: Thematic Compilation, Second edition 2005 http://www.osce.org/odihr/elections/16363?download=true (accessed 11 September 2014)

OSCE/ODIHR Election Mission Reports (final save as indicated) and Election Law Assessments:

Kazakhstan

05.02.1999 Republic of Kazakhstan Presidential Election 10 January 1999

20.10.2000 Republic of Kazakhstan Parliamentary Elections 10 and 24 October 1999

15.12.2004 Republic of Kazakhstan Parliamentary Elections 19 September and 3 October 2004

21.02.2006 Republic of Kazakhstan Presidential Election 4 December 2005

30.10.2007 Republic of Kazakhstan Parliamentary Elections 18 August 2007

16.06.2011 Republic of Kazakhstan Early Presidential Election 3 April 2011

03.04.2012 Republic of Kazakhstan Early Parliamentary Elections 15 January 2012

Kyrgyzstan

16.01.2001 Kyrgyz Republic Presidential Elections 29 October 2000

20.05.2005 Kyrgyz Republic Parliamentary Elections 27 February and 13 March 2005

07.11.2005 Kyrgyz Republic Presidential Election 10 July 2005

24.04.2008 Kyrgyz Republic Pre-Term Parliamentary Elections 16 December 2007

02.10.2009 Kyrgyz Republic Presidential Election 23 July 2009

27.07.2010 Kyrgyz Republic Constitutional Referendum 27 June 2010

10.04.2000 Kyrgyz Republic Parliamentary Elections 20 February and 12 March 2000

20.12.2010 Kyrgyz Republic Parliamentary Elections 10 October 2010
10.01.2012 Kyrgyz Republic Presidential Election 30 October 2011

Tajikistan

28.11.1999 Observations and recommendations draft law on elections to the Majlisi Oli of the Republic of Tajikistan

17.05.2000 Republic of Tajikistan Elections to the Parliament 27 February 2000

17.09.2003 Republic of Tajikistan OSCE/ODIHR Assessment of draft amendments to the law on elections to the Majilisi Oli

31.05.2005 Republic of Tajikistan Parliamentary Elections 27 February and 13 March 2005

26.07.2006 Assessment of the Law on election of the President, Republic Of Tajikistan

18.04.2007 Republic of Tajikistan Presidential Election 6 November 2006

06.07.2010 Republic of Tajikistan Parliamentary Elections 28 February 2010

05.02.2014 Republic of Tajikistan Presidential Election 6 November 2013

Uzbekistan

28.04.2000 Limited Election Assessment Mission, Republic of Uzbekistan election of deputies to the Oliy Majlis (Parliament) 5 & 19 December 1999

21.02.2005 Assessment of the Law on elections of the Oliy Majlis, Republic of Uzbekistan

07.03.2005 Limited Election Observation Mission Report, Republic of Uzbekistan Parliamentary Elections 26 December 2004

23.04.2008 Limited Election Observation Mission, Republic of Uzbekistan Presidential Election 23 December 2007

07.04.2010 Republic of Uzbekistan Parliamentary Elections 27 December 2009

Turkmenistan

11.11.1999 Turkmenistan Parliamentary Elections 12 December 1999 Needs Assessment Mission

11.02.2007 Turkmenistan Presidential Elections 8 January 2007 Needs Assessment Mission

20.10.2008 Turkmenistan Early Parliamentary Elections 14 December 2008 Needs Assessment Mission

17.02.2012 Turkmenistan Presidential Elections 3 January 2012 Needs Assessment Mission

23.07.2012 Turkmenistan Assessment of the Electoral Legislation

Shanghai Cooperation Organisation

2001 Shanghai Convention on Combating Terrorism, Separatism and Extremism

United Nations

1993 Principles relating to the Status of National Institutions, adopted by General Assembly resolution 48/134 of 20 December 1993 (The Paris Principles)

1985 Basic Principles on the Independence of the Judiciary Adopted by the Seventh United Nations Congress on the Prevention of Crime and the Treatment of Offenders held at Milan from 26 August to 6 September 1985 and endorsed by General Assembly resolutions 40/32 of 29 November 1985 and 40/146 of 13 December 1985

12.12.1995 General Assembly Resolution 50/80 'Maintenance of international security,' A/RES/50/80

03.02.2003 Report of the Special Rapporteur on the question of torture, Theo van Boven, Addendum: mission to Uzbekistan, submitted in accordance with Commission resolution 2002/38, E/CN.4/2003/68/Add.2

21.05.2005 Commission on Human Rights Resolution 2005/80, 'Protection of human rights and fundamental freedoms while countering terrorism chap. XVII, E/CN.4/2005/L.10/Add.17

16.12.2005 General Assembly Resolution 60/158, 'Protection of human rights and fundamental freedoms while countering terrorism,' A/RES/60/158

Council of Europe, European Commission for Democracy through Law (Venice Commission)

11.12.2002 Comments, Draft amendments to the Constitution of the Kyrgyz Republic, comments by Ms Hanna Suchocka (Member, Poland), no. 229/2002

16.12.2008 Opinion on the constitutional law on court juries of Kyrgyzstan no. 480/2008

24.10.2005 Opinion on Constitutional Reform in the Kyrgyz Republic no. 42/2005

28.09.2006 Preliminary comments on three drafts for a revised Constitution of the Kyrgyz Republic 383/2006

05.06.2007 Opinion on the possible reform of the Ombudsman institution in Kazakhstan, no. 425 / 2007

17.12.2007 Opinion on the constitutional situation in the Kyrgyz Republic no. 457/2007

04.06.2010 Opinion on the draft Constitution of the Kyrgyz Republic (version published on 21 May 2010), no. 582/2010

17.06.2011 Joint opinion on the Constitutional Law on the judicial system and status of judges of Kazakhstan, no. 629 / 2011; ODIHR Opinion no. JUD–KAZ/186/2011

17.12.2012 Joint opinion on draft amendments and addenda to the Law 'on elections to the Oliy Majlis of the Republic Of Uzbekistan' and 'on elections to the regional, district and city councils (kengesh) of people's deputies of Uzbekistan', no. 693/2012

10.12.2013 Opinion on the draft Code on judicial ethics of the Republic of Tajikistan No. 739/2013

16.06.2014 Opinion on the draft Constitutional Law on the Constitutional Court of Tajikistan, no. 765/2014

European Commission

22.07.1996, 'The Tacis Programme Annual Report 1995', Brussels, 22.07.1996 Com (96) 345 final, https://core.ac.uk/display/5091226/tab/similar-list) (accessed 29 September 2016)

TABLE OF LEGISLATION

OTHER NATIONAL LEGISLATION

USSR

30.07.1937 Operational Order, NKVD USSR no. 00447 on the operation for the repression of former kulaks, criminals and other anti-Soviet elements [Оперативный приказ Народного комиссара внутренних дел СССР № 00447 от 30.07.1937 «Об операции по репрессированию бывших кулаков, уголовников и других антисоветских элементов»]

1959 Dictionaries of nationalities and languages for responses to questions 7 and 8 of the census form (on nationality and mother tongue), Central statistical administration under the USSR Council of Ministers, All-Union 1959 Census administration, Moscow: State statistical publishers 1959 [Словари национальностей и языков для шифровки ответов на 7 и 8 вопросы п ереписного листа (о национальности и родном языке), Центральное Статистическое Управление при Совете Министров СССР, Управление по проведению Всесоюзной переписи населения 1959, Государственное Статистическое Издательство Москва 1959]

27.10.1960 Law, RSFSR on the confirmation of the Criminal Code of the RSFSR [Закон РСФСР от 27.10.1960 «Об утверждении Уголовного кодекса РСФСР»]

08.12.1961 Law, USSR confirming the Principles of civil legislation of the USSR (together with the Principles of legislation) [Закон СССР от 08.12.1961 «Об утверждении Основ гражданского законодательства Союза ССР и союзных республик» (вместе с Основами законодательства)]

31.10.1961 Resolution 22nd Congress KPSS on the charter of the Communist Party of the Soviet Union, Materials of the 22nd Congress KPSS pp. 429-448 [Резолюция XXII съезда КПСС «Об уставе Коммунистической Партий Советского Союза» (Принята едина- гласно 31 октября 1961 года)]'

04.10.1965 Regulations, USSR Council of Ministers, no. 731 of the socialist state production enterprise [Положение СМ СССР от 4.10.1965 «О социалистическом государственном производственном предприятии»]

21.03.1972 Statute of the Ministry of Justice of the USSR, Resolution of the USSR Council of Ministers no. 194 [Положение о Министерстве Юстиции СССР, Постановление Совета Министров СССР от 21 марта 1972 г. № 194]

25.02.1988 Dictionaries of nationalities and languages for responses to questions 7 and 8 of the census form (on nationality, mother tongue and other language of peoples of the USSR), All-union census 1989 [25.02.88 № 5-2-4 Государственный Комитет СССР по Статистике, Словари национальностей и языков для кодирования ответов на 8 и 9 вопросы переписных листов (о национальности, родном языке и другом языке народов СССР) Всесоюзной переписи населения 1989 г].

13.08.1990 Decree, President USSR no. 556 on the restoration of the rights of all victims of political repressions 1920s-1950s [Указ Президента СССР от 13.08.1990 № 556 "О восстановлении прав всех жертв политических репрессий 20—50-х]

Commonwealth of Independent States, Inter-Parliamentary Assembly

29.10.1994 Model Civil Code for states-members of the Commonweallth of Independent States (Part 1) [Модельный Гражданский кодекс от 29.10.1994 для государств—участников Содружества Независимых Государств (часть первая)]

Democratic People's Republic of Korea

Constitution 2012 http://www.kfausa.org/chapter-i-politics/ (accessed 27 September 2016)

United Kingdom

Political Parties, Elections and Referendums Act 2000, 2000 Chapter 41

LEGISLATION OF THE CENTRAL ASIAN REPUBLICS

Russian-language versions of published laws and regulations for each state are available (save where particularly indicated in the table below by *) at one or more of the following online databases or official sites:

Kazakhstan

http://online.zakon.kz/

Kyrgyzstan

https://online.toktom.kg

Tajikistan

http://www.mmk.tj/ru/
http://tj.spinform.ru/

Turkmenistan:

http://www.turkmenistan.gov.tm/?rub=12
http://www.turkmenlegaldatabase.info/ [database maintained by the OSCE; by far the most comprehensive]
http://tm.spinform.ru/

Uzbekistan:

http://www.lex.uz/
http://www.norma.uz/
http://www.pravo.uz/
http://uz.spinform.ru/

1. CONSTITUTIONS AND AMENDMENTS

Kazakhstan

20.04.1978 (1978 Constitution) Constitution (Basic Law) of the Kazakh Soviet Socialist Republic, 20 April 1978 [Конституция (Основной Закон) Казахской Советской Социалистической Республики от 20 апреля 1978]

28.01.1993 Constitution of the Republic of Kazakhstan (1993 Constitution) [Конституции Республики Казахстан от 28 января 1993]

30.08.1995 Constitution of the Republic of Kazakhstan, adopted by referendum (1995 Constitution) [Конституция Республики Казахстан (принята на республиканском референдуме 30 августа 1995]

07.10.1998 Law of the Republic of Kazakhstan no. 284-1 on bringing in amendments and additions to the Constitution of the Republic of Kazakhstan Constitution [Закон Республики Казахстан от 07 10 1998 № 284-1 "О внесении изменений и дополнений в конституцию Республики Каз ахстан"]

21.05.2007 Law of the Republic of Kazakhstan no. 254-III on bringing in amendments and additions to the Constitution of the Republic of Kazakhstan [Закон Республики Казахстан от 21 мая 2007 № 254-III «О внесении изменений и дополнений в Конституцию Республики Казахстан»]

Kyrygyzstan

05.05.1993 Constitution of the Kyrgyz Republic (1993 Constitution), entered into force by the 05.05.1993 Law of the Kyrgyz Republic no. N-1186-XII [Конституция Кыргызской Республики введена в действие Законом Кыргызской Республики от 5 мая 1993 № 1186-XII]

16.02.1996 Law of the Kyrgyz Republic on bringing in amendments and additions to the Constitution of the Kyrgyz Republic, adopted by referendum 10.02.1996 [Закон Кыргызской Республики "О внесении изменений и дополнений в Конституцию Кыргызской Республики" от 16 февраля 1996, принят референдумом 10 февраля 1996]

15.01.1997 Law of the Kyrgyz Republic no. 2 on the new edition of the Constitution of the Kyrgyz Republic [Закон Кыргызской Республики от 15 января 2007 № 2 «О новой редакции Конституции Кыргызской Республики»]

21.10.1998 Law of the Kyrgyz Republic on bringing in amendments and additions to the Constitution of the Kyrgyz Republic, adopted by referendum 17.10.1998 [Закон Кыргызской Республики "О внесении изменений и дополнений в Конституцию Кыргызской Республики" от 21 октября 1998, принятый референдумом 17 октября 1998]

09.11.2006 Law of the Kyrgyz Republic no. 180 on the new edition of the Constitution of the Kyrgyz Republic [Закон Кыргызской Республики от 9 ноября 2006 № 180 «О новой редакции Конституции Кыргызской Респ ублики»]

23.10.2007 Law of the Kyrgyz Republic no. 157 on the new edition of the Constitution of the Kyrgyz Republic [Закон Кыргызской Республики от 23 октября 2007 № 157 О новой редакции Конституции Кыргызской Респ ублики]

27.06.2010 Constitution of the Kyrgyz Republic (2010 Constitution), adopted by referendum 27.06.2010, entered into force by the 27.06.2010 Law of the Kyrgyz Republic [Конституция Кыргызской Республики Принята референдумом (всенародным голосованием) 27 июня 2010 (введена в действие Законом Кыргызской Республики от 27 июня 2010)]

Tajikistan

06.11.1994 Constitution of the Republic of Tajikistan [Конституция Республики Таджикистан от 6 ноября 1994]

30.06.1999 Resolution, Majlisi Oli of the Republic of Tajikistan no. 816 on the proposals of the President of the Republic of Tajikistan for amendments and additions to the Constitution of the Republic of Tajikistan [Постановление Маджлиси Оли Республики Тадж-икистан от 30 июня 1999, № 816 "О предложениях Президента Республики Таджикистан по изменению и дополнению в Конституцию Республики Таджикистан"]

22.06.2003 Amendments and additions to the Constitution of the Republic of Tajikistan adopted by referendum [Изменения и дополнения в конституц ию Республики Таджикистан, принятые на референдуме 22 июня 2003]

Turkmenistan

18.05.1992 Constitution of Turkmenistan, 18 May 1992 no.691-XII [Конституция Туркменистана от 18 мая 1992 №691-XII]

27.12.1995 Constitutional Law of Turkmenistan bringing in amendments and additions to the Constitution of Turkmenistan [Конституционный Закон Туркменистана от 27 декабря 1995 «О внесении изменений и дополнений в Конституцию Туркменистана»]

29.12.1999 Constitutional Law of Turkmenistan bringing in amendments and additions to the Constitution of Turkmenistan

[Конституционный Закон Туркменистана от 29 декабря 1999 «О внесении изменений и дополнений в Конституцию Туркменистана»]

15.08.2003 Constitutional Law of Turkmenistan on the Halk Maslahaty of Turkmenistan (invalidated in 2008) [Конституционный Закон Туркменистана от 15 августа 2003 «О Халк Маслахаты Туркменистана»]

15.08.2003 Constitutional Law of Turkmenistan bringing in amendments and additions to the Constitution of Turkmenistan [Конституционный Закон Туркменистана от 15 августа 2003 «О внесении изменений и дополнений в Конституцию Туркменистана»]

26.12.2006 Constitutional Law of Turkmenistan bringing in amendments and additions to the Constitution of Turkmenistan [Конституционный Закон Туркменистана от 26 декабря 2006 «О внесении изменений и дополнений в Конституцию Туркменистана»]

26.09.2008 Constitutional Law of Turkmenistan no. TKK 13 bringing in amendments and additions to the Constitution of Turkmenistan [Конституционный Закон Туркменистана от 26 сентября 2008 № ТКК-13]

Uzbekistan

08.12.1992 Constitution of the Republic of Uzbekistan [Конституция Республики Узбекистан от 8 декабря 1992]

09.04.1993 Constitution of the Republic of Karakalpakstan, adopted at the 12th session of the Supreme Soviet of the Republic of Karakalpakstan, 12th convocation [Конституция Республики Каракалпакстан (принята 9 апреля 1993 на двенадцатой сессии Верховного Совета Республики Каракалпакстан двенадцатого созыва)]

18.04.2011 Law of the Republic of Uzbekistan bringing in amendments and additions to discrete articles of the Constitution of the Republic of Uzbekistan (articles 78, 80, 93, 96 and 98), Collected legislation of the Republic of Uzbekistan 2011 no. 16, p 159 [Закон Республики Узбекистан «О внесении изменений и дополнений в отдельные статьи конституции Республики Узбекистан (статьи 78, 80, 93, 96 и 98)», Собрание законодательства Республики Узбекистан, 2011, № 16, ст. 159)]

24.04.2003 Law of the Republic of Uzbekistan bringing in amendments and additions to the Constitution of the Republic of Uzbekistan no. 3-4, p. 27 [Закон Республики Узбекистан «О внесении изменений и дополнений в Конституцию Республики Узбекистан», Ведомости Олий Мажлиса Республики Узбекистан, 2003, № 3-4, ст. 27)]

2. CONSTITUTIONAL LAWS, CODICES, OTHER FUNDAMENTAL LEGISLATION

Kazakhstan

16.12.1991 Constitutional Law of the Republic of Kazakhstan no. 1007-XII on the state independence of the Republic of Kazakhstan [Конституционный Закон Республики Казахстан от 16 декабря 1991 № 1007-XII «О государственной независимости Республики Казахстан»]

27.12.1994 Civil Code (General Part) of the Republic of Kazakhstan [Гражд анский кодекс Республики Казахстан (общая часть) от 27 декабря 1994]

28.09.1995 Constitutional Law of the Republic of Kazakhstan no. 2464 on elections in the Republic of Kazakhstan [Конституционный закон Республики Казахстан от 28 сентября 1995 № 2464 «О выборах в Республике Казахстан»]

16.10.1995 Constitutional Law of the Republic of Kazakhstan no. 229 on Parliament of the Republic of Kazakhstan and the status of deputies [Конституционный Закон Республики Казахстан от 16 октября 1995 № 2529 «О Парламенте Республики Казахстан и статусе его депутатов»]

18.12.1995 Constitutional Law of the Republic of Kazakhstan on the Government of the Republic of Kazakhstan [Конституционный Закон Республики Казахстан от 18 декабря 1995 № 2688 «О Правительстве Республики Казахстан»]

26.12.1995 Constitutional Law of the Republic of Kazakhstan n. 2733 on the President of the Republic of Kazakhstan [Конституционный закон «о Президенте Республики Казахстанн» от 26 декабря 1995 № 2733]

29.12.1995 Constitutional Law of the Republic of Kazakhstan no. 2737 on the Constitutional Council of the Republic of Kazakhstan [Конституционный закон Республики Казахстан от 29 декабря 1995 года № 2737 «О Конституционном Совете Республики Казахстан»]

13.12.1997 Criminal Enforcement Code of the Republic of Kazakhstan n. 208-I [Уголовно-исполнительный кодекс Республики Казахстан от 13 декабря 1997 №208-I]

24.03.1998 Law of the Republic of Kazakhstan no. 213-I on normative legal acts [Закон Республики Казахстан от 24 марта 1998 №213-I «О норматив ных правовых актах»]

01.07.1999 Civil Code (Special Part) of the Republic of Kazakhstan n. 409-I of the Republic of Kazakhstan [Гражданский кодекс Республики Казахстан (особенная часть) от 1 июля 1999 №409-I]

13.07.1999 Civil Procedure Code of the Republic of Kazakhstan no. 411-1 of the Republic of Kazakhstan [Гражданский процессуальный кодекс Республики Казахстан от 13 июля 1999 №411-I]

20.07.2000 Constitutional Law of the Republic of Kazakhstan n. 83-II on the first President of the Republic of Kazakhstan —Leader of the nation [Конституционный закон Республики Казахстан «О Первом Президенте Республики Казахстан—Лидере Наций» от 20 июля 2000 № 83-II]

25.12.2000 Constitutional Law of the Republic of Kazakhstan n. 132-II on the judicial system and the status of judges of the Republic of Kazakhstan [Конституционный закон Республики Казахстан от 25 декабря 2000 № 132-II «О судебной системе и статусе судей Республики Казахстан»]

30.01.2001 Administrative Violations Code of the Republic of Kazakhstan no. 155-II [Кодекс Республики Казахстан «об административных правонарушениях» от 30 января 2001 №155-II

26.12.2011 Code of the Republic of Kazakhstan n. 518-IV on marriage (matrimony) and family [Кодекс Республики Казахстан от 26 декабря 2011 года № 518-IV «О браке (супружестве) и семье»]

03.07.2014 Criminal Code of the Republic of Kazakhstan no. 226-V [Уголовный кодекс Республики Казахстан от 3 июля 2014 года № 226-V]

04.07.2014 Criminal Procedure Code of the Republic of Kazakhstan no. 231-V Уголовно-процессуальный кодекс Республики Казахстан от 4 июля 2014 года № 231-V [valid from 01.01.2015]

Kyrygyzstan

08.05.1996 Civil Code of the Kyrgyz Republic no. 15, Part 1 (Civil Code) [Гражданский кодекс Кыргызской Республики от 8 мая 1996 № 15. Часть I]

01.10.1997 Criminal Code of the Kyrgyz Republic, no. 68 [Уголовный кодекс Кыргызской Республики от 1 октября 1997 № 68]

05.01.1998 Civil Code of the Kyrgyz Republic no. 1, Part 2 (Civil Code II) [Гражданский кодекс Кыргызской Республики от 5 января 1998 № 1. Часть II]

04.08.1998 Administrative Violations Code of the Kyrgyz Republic, no. 114 [Кодекс об административной ответственности Кыргызской Республики от 4 августа 1998 № 114]

30.06.1999 Criminal Procedure Code of the Kyrgyz Republic [Уголовно-процессуальный кодекс Кыргызской Республики от 30 июня 1999 № 62]

11.11.1999 Criminal Enfocement Code of the Kyrgyz Republic [Уголовно-Исполнительный Кодекс Кыргызской Республики от 11 ноября 1999]

29.12.1999 Civil Procedure Code of the Kyrgyz Republic no. 146 [Гражданс кий процессуальный кодекс Кыргызской Республики от 29 декабря 1999 № 146]

04.08.2004, Labour Code of the Kyrgyz Republic, Law no. 107 [Трудовой Кодекс Кыргызской Республики от 4 августа 2004 № 107]

09.07.2008 Constitutional Law of the Kyrgyz Republic no. 141 on the status of judges of the Kyrgyz Republic [Конституционный Закон Кыргызской Республики от 9 июля 2008 № 141 «О статусе судей Кыргызской Респу блики»]

20.07.2009 Law of the Kyrgyz Republic no. 241 on normative legal acts of the Kyrgyz Republic [Закон Кыргызской Республики от 20 июля 2009 № 241 «О нормативных правовых актах Кыргызской Республики»]

02.06.2011 Constitutional Law of the Kyrgyz Republic no. 68 on election of the President of the Kyrgyz Republic [Конституционный Закон Кыргызской Республики от 2 июля 2011 № 68 «О выборах Президента Кыргызской Республики и депутатов Жогорку Кенеша Кыргызской Республики»]

13.06.2011 Constitutional Law of the Kyrgyz Republic no. 37 on the Constitutional chamber of the Supreme Court [Конституционный Закон Кыргызской Республики от 13 июня 2011 № 37 «О Конституционной палате Верховного суда Кыргызской Республики»]

18.06.2012 Constitutional Law of the Kyrgyz Republic no. 85 on the Government of the Kyrgyz Republic [Конституционный Закон Кыргызской Республики от 18 июня 2012 № 85 «О Правительстве Кыргызской Республики»]

Tajikistan

21.07.1994 Constitutional Law of the Republic of Tajikistan no. 1042 on elections for the President of the Republic of Tajikistan [Конституционный Закон Республики Таджикистан от 21 июля 1994 № 1042 «О выборах Президента Республики Таджикистан»]

03.11.1995 Constitutional Law of the Republic of Tajikistan no. 84 on the Constitutional Court of the Republic of Tajikistan [Конституционный Закон

Республики Таджикистан от 3 ноября 1995 № 84 «О Конституционном суде Республики Таджикистан»]

04.11.1995 Constitutional Law of the Republic of Tajikistan no. 104 on citizenship of the Republic of Tajikistan [Конституционный Закон Республики Таджикистан от 4 ноября 1995 № 104 «О гражданстве Республики Тадж икистан»]

04.11.1995 Constitutional Law of the Republic of Tajikistan on the resolution of issues of the administrative-territorial organisation of the Republic of Tajikistan [Конституционный Закон Республики Таджикистан от 4 ноября 1995 № 101 «О порядке решения вопросов административно—территориального устройства Республики Таджикистан»]

15.05.1997 Labour Code of the Republic of Tajikistan [Трудовой Кодекс Республики Таджикистан от 15 мая 1997]

21.05.1998 Criminal Code of the Republic of Tajikistan [Уголовный кодекс Республики Таджикистан от 21 мая 1998]

30.06.1999 Civil Code of the Republic of Tajikistan, part 1 [Гражданский кодекс Республики Таджикистан от 30 июня 1999 (часть первая)

10.12.1999 Constitutional Law of the Republic of Tajikistan no. 856 on elections for the Majlisi Oli of the Republic of Tajikistan [Конституционный Закон Республики Таджикистан от 10 декабря 1999 № 856 «О выборах Маджлиси Оли Республики Таджикистан»]

11.12.1999 Civil Code of the Republic of Tajikistan, part 2 Гражданский кодекс Республики Таджикистан от 11 декабря 1999 (часть вторая)]

19.04.2000 Constitutional Law of the Republic of Tajikistan no. 1 on the Majlisi Oli of the Republic of Tajikistan [Конституционный Закон Республики Таджикистан от 19 апреля 2000 № 1 «О Маджлиси Оли Республики Таджикистан»]

12.05.2001 Constitutional Law of the Republic of Tajikistan on the Government of the Republic of Tajikistan [Конституционный Закон Республики Таджикистан от 12 мая 2001 № 28 «О Правительстве Республики Таджи кистан»]

06.08.2001 Constitutional Law of the Republic of Tajikistan no. 30 on courts of the Republic of Tajikistan [Конституционный Закон Республики Таджикистан от 6 августа 2001 № 30 «О судах Республики Таджикистан»]

06.08.2001 Constitutional Law of the Republic of Tajikistan no. 43 on the legal status of a member of the Majlisi Milli and a deputy of the Majlisi Namoyandagon of the Majlisi Oli of the Republic of Tajikistan [Конституционный Закон Республики Таджикистан № 43 от 6 августа 2001 «О правовом статусе члена Маджлиси Милли и депутата Маджлиси Намояндагон Маджлиси Оли Республики Таджикистан»]

06.08.2001 Criminal Penalty Enforcement Code of the Republic of Tajikistan [Кодекс исполнения уголовных наказаний Республики Таджикистан от 6 августа 2001]

08.12.2003 Law of the Republic of Tajikistan on normative legal acts, no. 54 [Закон Республики Таджикистан от 8 декабря 2003 №54 «О нормативных правовых актах»]

17.05.2004 Constitutional Law of the Republic of Tajikistan no. 28 on local bodies of state authority [Конституционный Закон Республики Таджикистан от 17 мая 2004 № 28 «О местных органах государственной власти»]

01.03.2005 Civil Code of the Republic of Tajikistan, part 3 [Гражданский кодекс Республики Таджикистан от 01 марта 2005 (часть третья)]

25.07.2005 Constitutional Law of the Republic of Tajikistan no. 107 on the organs of the Procuracy of the Republic of Tajikistan [Конституционный Закон Республики Таджикистан от 25 июля 2005 № 107 «Об органах прокуратуры Республики Таджикистан»]

30.07.2007 Constitutional Law of the Republic of Tajikistan no. 303 on Gorno-Badakhshan autonomous province [Конституционный Закон Республики Таджикистан от 30 июля 2007 № 303 «О Горно-Бадахшанской автономной области»]

05.01.2008 Economic Procedure Code of the Republic of Tajikistan [Экономический процессуальный кодекс Республики Таджикистан от 5 января 2008]

05.01.2008 Civil Procedure Code of the Republic of Tajikistan [Гражданский процессуальный кодекс Республики Таджикистан от 5 января 2008]

31.12.2008 Code of Administrative Violations of the Republic of Tajikistan [Кодекс Республики Таджикистан об административных правонарушениях от 31 декабря 2008]

03.12.2009 Criminal Procedure Code of the Republic of Tajikistan [Уголовно—процессуальный кодекс Республики Таджикистан от 03 декабря 2009]

15.09.2010 Code of Ethics of the civil servant of the Republic of Tajikistan, no. 932 [Кодекс этики государственного служащего Республики Таджикистан от 15 сентября 2010 № 932]

Uzbekistan

22.09.1994 Criminal Procedure Code of the Republic of Uzbekistan, confirmed by Law of the Republic of Uzbekistan no. 2013-XII [Уголовно-процессуальный кодекс Республики Узбекистан, утвержден Законом Республики Узбекистан от 22 сентября 1994 № 2013-XII]

22.09.1994 Criminal Code of the Republic of Uzbekistan, confirmed by Law of the Republic of Uzbekistan no. 2013-XII [Уголовный Кодекс Республики Узбекистан, утвержден Законом Республики Узбекистан от 22 сентября 1994 № 2013-XII]

22.09.1994 Code of Administrative Liability of the Republic of Uzbekistan, confirmed by Law of the Republic of Uzbekistan no. 2015-XII [Кодекс Республики Узбекистан об административной ответственности, утвержден Законом Республики Узбекистан от 22.09.1994 г. № 2015-XII]

21.12.1995 Civil Code of the Republic of Uzbekistan, Part I, confirmed by Law of the Republic of Uzbekistan no. 163-I [Гражданский Кодекс Республики Узбекистан Часть первая утверждена Законом Республики Узбекистан № 163-I от 21.12.95]

29.08.1996 Civil Code of the Republic of Uzbekistan, Part II confirmed by Law of the Republic of Uzbekistan no. 256-I [Гражданский Кодекс Республики Узбекистан Часть вторая утверждена Законом Республики Узбекистан №256-I от 29 августа 1996]

25.04.1997 Criminal Enforcement Code of the Republic of Uzbekistan, confirmed by Law of the Republic of Uzbekistan № 409-1 [Уголовно-исполнительный кодекс Республики Узбекистан, утвержден Законом Республики Узбекистан от 25.04.1997 № 409-1]

30.08.1997 Civil Procedure Code of the Republic of Uzbekistan, confirmed by Law of the Republic of Uzbekistan n. 477-I [Гражданский процессуальный кодекс Республики Узбекистан, утвержден Законом Республики Узбекистан от 30.08.1997 № 477-I]

14.12.2000 Law of the Republic of Uzbekistan on normative-legal acts, Bulletin of the Olii Majlis of the Republic of Uzbekistan [Закон Республики Узбекистан от 14 декабря 2000 № 160-II «О нормативно-правовых актах»]

12.02.2002 Constitutional Law of the Republic of Uzbekistan on the Legislative chamber of the Olii Majlis of the Republic of Uzbekistan [Конституционный Закон Республики Узбекистан от 12 декабря 2002 О законодательной палате Олий Мажлиса Республики Узбекистан»]

12.02.2002 Constitutional Law of the Republic of Uzbekistan on the Senate of the Olii Majlis of the Republic of Uzbekistan [Конституционный Закон Республики Узбекистан от 12 декабря 2002 "О Сенате Олий Мажлиса Республики Узбекистан»]

04.04.2002 Constitutional Law of the Republic of Uzbekistan no. 350-II on the results of the referendum and the basic principles of the organisation of state authority [Конституционный Закон от 4 апреля 2002 № 350-II "Об итогах референдума и основных принципах организации государственной власти»]

11.04.2007 Constitutional Law of the Republic of Uzbekistan no. 88 on the strengthening of the role of political parties in the renewal and further democratisation of state administration and the modernisation of the country [Конституционный Закон Республики Узбекистан от 11 апреля 2007 № 88 "Об усилении роли политических партий в обновлении и дальнейшей демократизации государственного управления и модернизации страны»]

Turkmenistan

27.10.1991 Constitutional Law of Turkmenistan on independence and the fundamentals of the state organisation of Turkmenistan [Конституционный закон Туркменистана о независимости и основах государственного устройства Туркменистана от 27 октября 1991]

12.12.1995 Constitutional Law of Turkmenistan on the permanent neutrality of Turkmenistan [Конституционный Закон Туркменистана о постоянном нейтралитете Туркменистана]

12.07.1997 Criminal Code of Turkmenistan no.222-I [Уголовный кодекс Туркменистана от 12 июня 1997 №222-I]

17.07.1998 Civil Code of Turkmenistan n. 294-I [Гражданский кодекс Туркменистана от 17 июля 1998 №294-I]

07.12.2005 Law of Turkmenistan no. 31-III on normative legal acts [Закон Туркменистана от 7 декабря 2005 №31-III «О нормативных правовых актах»]

18.04.2009 Criminal Procedure Code of Turkmenistan [Уголовно-процессуальный кодекс Туркменистана от 18 апреля 2009]

25.03.2011 Criminal Enforcement Code of Turkmenistan no. 164-IV [Уголовно-исполнительный кодекс Туркменистана от 25 марта 2011 №164-IV]

19.10.2012 Code of Social Protection of the Population [Кодекс Туркменистана от 19 октября 2012 «О социальной защите населения»

04.05.2013 Elections Code of Turkmenistan [Избирательный кодекс Туркменистана от 4 мая 2013]

12.09.2013 Administrative Violations Code of Turkmenistan Кодекс Туркменистана об административных правонарушениях от 12.09.2013]

3. PRESIDENCY

Kazakhstan

24.04.1990 Law of the Kazakh Soviet Socialist Republic on the establishment of the post of President of the Kazakh SSR and amendments and additions to the Constitution (Basic Law) of the Kazakh SSR [Закон Казахской Советской Социалистической Республики от 24 апреля 1990 «Об учреждении поста Президента Казахской ССР и внесении изменений и дополнений в Конституцию (Основной Закон) Казахской ССР»]

26.12.1995 Constitutional Law of the Republic of Kazakhstan no. 2733 on the President of the Republic of Kazakhstan [Конституционный закон Республики Казахстан от 26 декабря 1995 № 2733 «О Президенте Республики Казахстана»]

20.06.2000 Constitutional Law of the Republic of Kazakhstan 20.06.2000 n. 83-II on the first President of the Republic of Kazakhstan- Leader of the Nation [Конституционный закон Республики Казахстан от 20 июля 2000 № 83-II «О Первом Президенте Республики Казахстан—Лидере Нации»]

11.03.2008 Decree of the President of Kazakhstan no. 552 on the confirmation of the Statute of the Administration of the President of the Republic of Kazakhstan [Указ Президента Республики Казахстан от 11 марта 2008 № 552 «Об утверждении Положения об Администрации Президента Республики Казахстан»]

Kyrygyzstan

24.10.1990 Law of the Kyrgyz Soviet Socialist Republic no. 222-XII on the establishment of the post of President of the Kyrgyz SSR [Закон Кыргызской Советской Социалистической Республики от 24 октября 1990 № 222-XII «Об учреждении поста Президента Кыргызской ССР»]

18.07.2003 Law of the Kyrgyz Republic no. 152 on the guarantees for the activity of the President of the Kyrgyz Republic [Закон Кыргызской Республики от 18 июля 2003 №152 «О гарантиях деятельности Президента Кыргызской Республики»]

20.12.2010 Decree of the President of the Kyrgyz Republic n. 346 on the *Apparat* of the President of the Kyrgyz Republic [Указ Президента Кыргызской Республики от 20 декабря 2010 № 346 «Об Аппарате Президента Кыргызской Республики»]

24.12.2010 Regulations of the *Apparat* of the President of the Kyrgyz Republic, confirmed by Resolution of the Government of the Kyrgyz Republic no. 338 [Положение об Аппарате Правительства Кыргызской Республики утверждено постановлением Правительства Кыргызской Республики от 24 декабря 2010 № 338]

Tajikistan

29.11.1990 Law of the Tajik Soviet Socialist Republic on the establishment of the post of President of the Tajik SSR and the manner of his election [Закон Таджикской ССР от 29 ноября 1990 «Об учреждении поста Президента Таджикской ССР и порядке его избрания»]

17.01.2014 Decree of the President of the Republic of Tajikistan no. 116 on the restructuring of the Executive *Apparat* of the President of the Republic of Tajikistan Указ Президента Республики Таджикистан от 17 января 2014, № 116, «О реструктуризации Исполнительного аппарата Президента Республики Таджикистан»]

Turkmenistan

11.10.1990 Law of the Turkmen Soviet Socialist Republic on the establishment of the presidential form of government in the Turkmen SSR and amendments and additions to the Constitution (Basic Law) of the Turkmen SSR [Закон Туркменской ССР от 11 октября 1990 об учреждении президентской формы правления в Туркменской ССР и внесении изм. и доп. в Конституцию (Основной Закон) Туркменской ССР]

21.05.2011 Law of Turkmenistan no. 192-IV on the President of Turkmenistan [Закон Туркменистана от 21 мая 2011 №192-IV «О Президенте Туркменистана»]

Uzbekistan

24.03.1990 Law of the Uzbek Soviet Socialist Republic on the establishment of the post of President of the Uzbek SSR and amendments and additions to the Constitution (Basic Law) of the Uzbek SSR [Закон Узбекской ССР «Об учреждении поста президента Узбекской ССР и внесении изм. и доп. в Конституцию (Основной Закон) Узбекской ССР».

25.04.2003 Law of the Republic of Uzbekistan no. 480-II on the fundamental guarantees for the activity of the President of the Republic of Uzbekistan [Закон Республики Узбекистан от 25 апреля 2003 № 480-II «Об основных гарантиях деятельности Президента Республики Узбекистан»]

02.04.2005 Decree no. UP-3590 on the creation of the Institute for monitoring legislation in force, attached to the President of the Republic of Uzbekistan [Указ Президента Республики Узбекистан от 2 апреля 2005, № УП-3590 «О создании института мониторинга действующего законодательства при Президенте Республики Узбекистан»]

18.03.2011 Decree of the President of the Republic of Uzbekistan n. UP-4295 on confirming the Statute and structure of the *Apparat* of the President of the Republic of Uzbekistan [Указ Президента Республики Узбекистан от 18 марта 2011 № УП-4295 “Об утверждении Положения и структуры аппарата Президента Республики Узбекистан»] *

4. PARLIAMENT

Kazakhstan

16.10.1995 Constitutional Law of the Republic of Kazakhstan no. 229 on Parliament of the Republic of Kazakhstan and the status of deputies [Конституционный Закон Республики Казахстан от 16 октября 1995 № 2529 «О Парламенте Республики Казахстан и статусе его депутатов»]

08.02.1996 Rules of the Majilis of the Parliament of the Republic of Kazakhstan, Resolution of the Majlis of the Parliament of the Republic of Kazakhstan [Регламент Мажилиса Парламента Республики Казахстан, Постановление Мажилиса Парламента Республики Казахстан от 8 февраля 1996]

08.02.1996 Rules of the Senate of the Parliament of the Republic of Kazakhstan, Resolution of the Senate of the Parliament of the Republic of Kazakhstan [Регламент Сената Парламента Республики Казахстан, Постановление Сената Парламента Республики Казахстан от 8 февраля 1996]

07.05.1997 Law of the Republic of Kazakhstan no. № 101-I on committees and commissions of the Parliament of the Republic of Kazakhstan [Закон Республики Казахстан от 7 мая 1997 года № 101-I «О комитетах и комиссиях Парламента Республики Казахстан»]

Kyrygyzstan

25.11.2011 Law of the Kyrgyz Republic no. 2 on the Regulations of the Jogorku Kenesh of the Kyrgyz Republic [Закон Кыргызской от 25 ноября 2011 года № 223 «О Регламенте Жогорку Кенеша Кыргызской Республ ики»]

Tajikistan

19.04.2000 Constitutional Law of the Republic of Tajikistan no. 1 on the Majlisi Oli of the Republic of Tajikistan [Конституционный Закон Республики Таджикистан от 19 апреля 2000 № 1 «О Маджлиси Оли Республики Таджикистан»]

10.11.2000 Rules of the Majlisi Milli of the Majlisi Oli of the Republic of Tajikistan, Resolution of the Majlisi milli of the Majlisi Oli of the Republic of Tajikistan no. 121 [Регламент Маджлиси милли Маджлиси Оли Республики Таджикистан, Постановление Маджлиси милли Маджлиси Оли Республики Таджикистан от 10 ноября 2000 года №121]

06.08.2001 Constitutional Law of the Republic of Tajikistan no. 43 on the legal status of a member of the Majlisi Milli and a deputy of the Majlisi Namoyandagon of the Majlisi Oli of the Republic of Tajikistan [Конституционный Закон Республики Таджикистан № 43 от 6 августа 2001 «О правовом статусе члена Маджлиси Милли и депутата Маджлиси Намояндагон Маджлиси Оли Республики Таджикистан»]

07.11.2001 Rules of the Majlisi namoyandagon of the Majlisi Oli of the Republic of Tajikistan, Resolution of the Majlisi namoyandagon of the Majlisi Oli of the Republic of Tajikistan [Регламент Маджлиси намояндагон Маджлиси Оли Республики Таджикистан, Постановление Маджлиси намояндагон Маджлиси Оли Республики Таджикистан от 7 ноября 2001 года № 437]

Turkmenistan

09.01.2009 Law of Turkmenistan no. 1-IV on the Mejlis of Turkmenistan [Закон Туркменистана от 9 января 2009 №15-IV «О Меджлисе Туркменистана»]

09.01.2009 Resolution of the Mejlis of Turkmenistan no, 1-IV on confirmation of the Regulations of the Mejlis of Turkmenistan [Постановление Меджлиса Туркменистана от 9 января 2009 №16-IV «Об утверждении Регламента Меджлиса Туркменистана»]

Uzbekistan

12.12.2002 Constitutional Law of the Republic of Uzbekistan no. 434-II on the Legislative chamber of the Olii Majlis of the Republic of Uzbekistan [Конституционный Закон Республики Узбекистан от 12 декабря 2002 № 434-II «О Законодательной палаты Олий Мажлиса Республики Узбекис тан»]

12.12.2002 Constitutional Law of the Republic of Uzbekistan no. 432–II on the Senate of the Olii Majlis of the Republic of Uzbekistan [Конституционный Закон Республики Узбекистан от 12 декабря 2002 № 432–II«О Сенате Олий Мажлиса Республики Узбекистан»]

29.08.2003 Law of the Republic of Uzbekistan no. 522-II on the Regulations of the Legislative Chamber of the Olii Majlis of the Republic of Uzbekistan [Закон Республики Узбекистан от 29 августа 2003 № 522-II «О Регламенте Законодательной Палате Олий Мажлиса Республики Узбекистан»]

29.08.2003 Law of the Republic of Uzbekistan no. 523-II on the Regulations of the Senate of the Olii Majlis of the Republic of Uzbekistan [Закон Республики Узбекистан от 29 августа 2003 № 523-II «О Регламенте Сената Олий Мажлиса Республики Узбекистан»]

5. GOVERNMENT, CIVIL SERVICE, ANTI-CORRUPTION

Kazakhstan

18.12.1995 Constitutional Law no. 2688 on the Government of the Republic of Kazakhstan [Конституционный Закон Республики Казахстан от 18 декабря 1995 № 2688 «О Правительстве Республики Казахстан»]

02.07.1998 Law of the Republic of Kazakhstan no. 267-I on anti-corruption [Закон Республики Казахстан от 2 июля 1998 года № 267-I «О борьбе с коррупцией»]

23.07.1999 Law of the Republic of Kazakhstan no. 453-I on the civil service [Закон Республики Казахстан от 23 июля 1999 года № 453-I «О государственной службе»]

27.11.2000 Law of the Republic of Kazakhstan no. 107-II on administrative procedures [Закон Республики Казахстан от 27 ноября 2000 №107-II «Об административных процедурах»]

03.05.2005 Code of ethics of civil servants of the Republic of Kazakhstan, Decree of the President of Kazakhstan no. 1567 [Кодекс чести государственных служащих Республики Казахстан, Указ Президента Республики Казахстан от 3 мая 2005 года № 1567]

Kyrygyzstan

18.06.2012 Constitutional Law no. 85 on the Government of the Kyrgyz Republic [Конституционный Закон Кыргызской Республики 18 июня 2012 № 85 «О Правительстве Кыргызской Республики»]

08.08.2012 Law of the Kyrgyz Republic no. 153 on anti-corruption [Закон Кыргызской Республики от 8 августа 2012 года № 153 «О противодействии коррупции»]

Tajikistan

13.11.1998 Law of the Republic of Tajikistan on the civil service [Закон Республики Таджикистан от 13 ноября 1998 «О государственной службе»]

25.07.2005 Law of the Republic of Tajikistan no. 100 on anti-corruption [Закон Республики Таджикистан от 25 июля 2005 года № 100 «О борьбе с коррупцией»]

15.09.2010 Code of ethics of the civil servant of the Republic of Tajikistan, no. 932 [Кодекс этики государственного служащего Республики Таджики стан от 15 сентября 2010 № 932]

16.04.2012 Law of the Republic of Tajikistan no. 828 on the system of organs of state management in the Republic of Tajikistan [Закон Республики Тадж икистан от 16 апрели 2012 № 828 «О системе органов государственного управления Республики Таджикистан»]

Turkmenistan

24.11.1995 Law of Turkmenistan no. 82-1 on the Cabinet of Ministers of Turkmenistan [Закон Туркменистана от 24 ноября 1995 № 82-1 «О Кабинете Министров Туркменистана»]

09.08.2002 Law of Turkmenistan on the recruitment to the civil service of Turkmenistan of state managers and officials [Закон Туркменистана от 9 августа 2002 «О подборе государственных руководителей и должностных лиц на государственную службу в Туркменистане»]

Uzbekistan

06.05.1993 Law of the Republic of Uzbekistan no. 818-XII on the Cabinet of Ministers of the Republic of Uzbekistan [Закон Республики Узбекистан от 6 мая 1993 № 818-XII «О Кабинете Министров Республики Узбекистан»]

6. ELECTIONS AND PARTIES

Kazakhstan

28.09.1995 Constitutional Law of the Republic of Kazakhstan no. 2464 on elections in the Republic of Kazakhstan [Конституционный закон Республики Казахстан от 28 сентября 1995 № 2464 «О выборах в Республике Казахстан»]

15.07.2002 Law of the Republic of Kazakhstan no. 344-II on political parties [Закон Республики Казахстан от 15 июля 2002 № 344-II «О политических партиях»]

Kyrygyzstan

12.06.1999 Law of the Kyrgyz Republic no. 50 on political parties [Закон Кыргызской Республики от 12 июня 1999 № 50 «О политических партиях»]

13.06.2011 Regulations of the Central commission for elections and referenda of the Kyrgyz Republic, confirmed by Resolution of the Central commission for elections and referenda of the Kyrgyz Republic no. 16 [Регламент Центр альной комиссии по выборам и проведению референдумов Кыргызской Республики, Постановление Центральной комиссии по выборам и проведению референдумов Кыргызской Республики от 13 июля 2011 № 16]

02.07.2011 Constitutional Law of the Kyrgyz Republic on elections for the President of the Kyrgyz Republic and deputies of the Jogorku Kenesh of the Kyrgyz Republic [Конституционный Закон Кыргызской Республики от 2 июля 2011 № 68 «О выборах Президента Кыргызской Республики и депутатов Жогорку Кенеша Кыргызской Республики»]

Tajikistan

21.07.1994 Constitutional Law of the Republic of Tajikistan no. 1042 on elections for the President of the Republic of Tajikistan [Конституционный Закон Республики Таджикистан от 21 июля 1994 № 1042 «О выборах Президента Республики Таджикистан»]

04.11.1995 Constitutional Law of the Republic of Tajikistan no. 106 on the referendum of the Republic of Tajikistan [Конституционный Закон Республики Таджикистан от 4 ноября 1995 №106 «О референдуме Республики Таджикистан»]

13.11.1998 Law of the Republic of Tajikistan no. 680 on political parties [Закон Республики Таджикистан от 13 ноября 1998 № 680 «О Политических Партиях»]

10.12.1999 Constitutional Law of the Republic of Tajikistan no. 856 on elections for the Majlisi Oli of the Republic of Tajikistan [Конституционный Закон Республики Таджикистан от 10 декабря 1999 № 856 «О выборах Маджлиси Оли Республики Таджикистан»]

10.12.1999 Constitutional Law of the Republic of Tajikistan on elections for deputies to the local majlisi of peoples' deputies [Конституционный Закон Республики Таджикистан от 10 декабря 1999 «О выборах депутатов в местные маджлисы народных депутатов»]

Turkmenistan

10.01.2012 Law of Turkmenistan no. 254-IV on political parties [Закон Туркменистана от 10 января 2012 № 254-IV «О политических партиях»]

04.03.2013 Electoral Code of Turkmenistan [Избирательный кодекс Туркменистана от 4 мая 2013]

Uzbekistan

18.11.1991 Law of the Republic of Uzbekistan on the election of the President of the Republic of Uzbekistan [Закон Республики Узбекистан от 18 ноября 1991 № 414-XII«О выборах Президента Республики Узбекистан»]

28.12.1993 Law of the Republic of Uzbekistan on elections to the Olii Majlis of the Republic of Uzbekistan [Закон Республики Узбекистан от 28 декабря 1993 «О выборах в Олий Мажлис Республики Узбекистан»]

26.12.1996 Law of the Republic of Uzbekistan no. 337-I on political parties [Закон Республики Узбекистан от 26 декабря 1996 № 337–I «О политических партиях»]

30.04.1998 Law of the Republic of Uzbekistan no. 613-I on the Central electoral commission of the Republic of Uzbekistan [Закон Республики Узбекистан от 30 апреля 1998 № 613-I «О Центральной избирательной комиссии Республики Узбекистан»]

30.04.2004 Law of the Republic of Uzbekistan no. 617-II on the financing of political parties [Закон Республики Узбекистан от 30 апреля 2004 «О финансировании политических партий»]

11.04.2007 Constitutional Law of the Republic of Uzbekistan no. 88 on the strengthening of the role of political parties in the renewal and further democratisation of state administration and the modernisation of the country [Конституционный Закон Республики Узбекистан от 11 апреля 2007 № 88 "Об усилении роли политических партий в обновлении и дальнейшей демократизации государственного управления и модернизации страны»]

7. JUDICIARY

Kazakhstan

20.12.1995 Decree of the President of the Republic of Kazakhstan having the force of a Constitutional law no. 2694 on courts and the status of judges in the Republic of Kazakhstan [Указ Президента Республики Казахстан, имеющий силу Конституционного закона, от 20 декабря 1995 № 2694 «О судах и статусе судей в Республике Казахстан»] [invalid]

25.12.2000 Constitutional Law of the Republic of Kazakhstan no. 132-II on the judicial system and the status of judges of the Republic of Kazakhstan [Конституционный закон Республики Казахстан от 25 декабря 2000 № 132-II «О судебной системе и статусе судей Республики Казахстан»]

16.01.2001 Decree of the President of the Republic of Kazakhstan no. 535 on the formation of specialised interdistrict economic courts in Almaty and Karanganda *oblasts* [Указ Президента Республики Казахстан от 16 января 2001 года № 535 «Об образовании в городе Алматы и Карагандинской области»]

16.02.2006 Law of the Republic of Kazakhstan no. 121 on jurors [Закон Республики Казахстан от 16 января 2006 № 121«О присяжных заседателях»]

23.08.2007 Decree of the President of the Republic of Kazakhstan on the formation of specialised inter-district juvenile justice courts [Указ Президента Республики Казахстан от 23 августа 2007 «Об образовании специализированных межрайонных судов по делам несовершеннолетних»]

17.11.2008 Law of the Republic of Kazakhstan no. 9-IV on the Higher Judicial Council of the Republic of Kazakhstan [Закон Республики Казахстан «О Высшем судебном совете Республики Казахстан» 17 ноября 2008 № 79-IV]

03.11.2010 Decree of the President of the Republic of Kazakhstan confirming the Regulations of the Department for the facilitation of judicial operations under the Supreme Court of the Republic of Kazakhstan (Apparat of the Supreme Court of the Republic of Kazakhstan [Указ Президента Республики Казахстан от 3 ноября 2010 года № 1093 «Об утвержден ии Положения о Департаменте по обеспечению деятельности судов при Верховном Суде Республики Казахстан (аппарате Верховного Суда Республики Казахстан)»]

Kyrygyzstan

25.01.1995 Decree of the President of the Kyrgyz Republic no. UP-30, Provisional regulations of the aksakal courts of the Kyrgyz Republic [Указ Президента КР от 25 января 1995 года № УП-30 Временное положение о судах аксакалов Кыргызской Республики]

06.07.2002 Law of the Kyrgyz Republic no. 113 on *aksakal* courts [Закон Кыргызской Республики «О судах аксакалов» от 5 июля 2002 года № 113]

18.07.2003 Law of the Kyrgyz Republic no. 153 on the Supreme Court of the Kyrgyz Republic and local courts [18 июля 2003 № 153 Закон Кыргызской Республики «О Верховном суде Кыргызской Республики и местных судах»]

20.03.2008 Law of the Kyrgyz Republic n. 35 on the organs of judicial self-governance [Закон Кыргызской Республики от 20 марта 2008 № 35 «Об органах судейского самоуправления»]

09.07.2008 Constitutional Law of the Kyrgyz Republic no. 141 on the status of judges of the Kyrgyz Republic [Конституционный Закон Кыргызской Республики от 9 июля 2008 № 141 "О статусе судей Кыргызской Республики"]

15.07.2009 Law of the Kyrgyz Republic no. 215 on jurors in courts of the Kyrgyz Republic [Закон Кыргызской Республики от 15 июля 2009 № 215 «О присяжных заседателях в судах Кыргызской Республики»]

13.06.2011 Constitutional Law of the Kyrgyz Republic n. 37 on the Constitutional Chamber of the Supreme Court of the Kyrgyz Republic [Конституционный Закон Кыргызской Республики от 13 июня 2011 № 37 «О Конституционной палате Верховного суда Кыргызской Республики»]

09.06.2013 Regulations of the Constitutional Chamber of the Supreme Court of the Kyrgyz Republic, Resolution of the Constitutional chamber of the Supreme court of the Kyrgyz Republic no. 1 [Регламент Конституционной палаты Верховного суда Кыргызской Республики, Постановление Конституционной палаты Верховного суда Кыргызской Республики от 9 июля 2013 №1]

Tajikistan

03.11.1995 Constitutional Law of the Republic of Tajikistan no. 84 on the Constitutional Court of the Republic of Tajikistan [Конституционный Закон Республики Таджикистан от 3 ноября 1995 № 84 «О Конституционном суде Республики Таджикистан»]

06.08.2001 Constitutional Law of the Republic of Tajikistan no. 30 on courts of the Republic of Tajikistan [Конституционный Закон Республики Таджикистан от 6 августа 2001 № 30 «О судах Республики Таджикистан»]

14.12.1999 Statute of the Council of Justice of the Republic of Tajikistan, Decree of the President of the Republic of Tajikistan no. 48 [Положение О Совете юстиции Республики Таджикистан, указ Президента Республики Таджикистан от 14 декабря 1999 № 48]

Turkmenistan

29.05.1991 Law of the Turkmen SSR on the organisation of the court and the status of the judge [«О судоустройстве и статусе казы в Туркменистане», принятый Верховным Советом Туркменской ССР 29 мая 1991] [invalid]

14.02.2000 Law of Turkmenistan no. № 16-II on the formation of the Arbitrazh court of Turkmenistan [Закон Туркменистана от 14 февраля 2000 № 16-II «Об образовании Арбитражного суда Туркменистана»]

15.08.2009 Law of Turkmenistan no. 49-IV on the court [Закон Туркменистана от 15 августа 2009 №49-IV «О суде»]

Uzbekistan

02.09.1993 Law of the Republic of Uzbekistan on courts [Закон Республики Узбекистан от 2 сентября 1993 «О судах»]

30.08.1995 Law of the Republic of Uzbekistan n. 103-1 on the Constitutional Court of the Republic of Uzbekistan [Закон Республики Узбекистан 30 августа 1995 № 103-I «О Конституционном суде Республики Узбекист ан"]

29.12.2012 Disposition of the President of the Republic of Uzbekistan № P-3949 on the improvement of the activity of the Higher Qualifications Commission for the selection and recommendation [of candidates] to judgeships under the President of the Republic of Uzbekistan [Распоряжение Президента Республики Узбекистан от 29 декабря 2012 «О совершенствовании деятельности Высшей квалификационной комиссии по отбору и рекомендации на должности судей при Президенте Республики Узбекистан»]

JUSTICE, CRIME, SECURITY

Kazakhstan

15.09.1994 Law of the Republic of Kazakhstan no. 154-XIII on operative-search activity [Закон Республики Казахстан от 15 сентября 1994 года № 154-XIII «Об оперативно-розыскной деятельности»]

21.12.1995 Law of the Republic of Kazakhstan n. 2707 on the organs of internal affairs of the Republic [Закон Республики Казахстан от 21 декабря 1995 №2707 "Об органах внутренних дел Республики Казахстан»]

16.07.1997 Criminal Code of the Republic of Kazakhstan n. 167-I [Уголовный кодекс Республики Казахстан от 16 июля 1997 №167-I]

13.12.1997 Criminal Enforcement Code of the Republic of Kazakhstan n. 208-I [Уголовно-исполнительный кодекс Республики Казахстан от 13 декабря 1997 №208-I]

13.12.1997 Criminal Procedure Code of the Republic of Kazakhstan n. 206-I [Уголовно-процессуальный кодекс Республики Казахстан от 13 декабря 1997 №206-I] [invalid from 01.01.2015]

18.03.2002 Law of the Republic of Kazakhstan n. 304 on the organs of justice [Закон Республики Казахстан от 18 марта 2002 «Об органах юстиции» № 304]

28.10.2004 Statute of the Ministry of Justice of the Republic of Kazakhstan, Resolution of the Government of the Republic of Kazakhstan no.1120 [Положение о Министерстве юстиции Республики Казахстан утверждено постановлением Правительства Республики Казахстан от 28 октября 2004 № 1120]

22.06.2005 Statute of the Ministry of Internal Affairs of the Republic of Kazakhstan, Resolution of the Government of the Republic of Kazakhstan no. 607 [Положение о Министерстве внутренних дел Республики Казахстан, Постановление Правительства Республики Казахстан от 22 июня 2005 № 607]

21.12.2005 Law of the Republic of Kazakhstan n. 2709 on the Procuracy [Закон Республики Казахстан от 21 декабря 1995 №2709 «О Прокуратуре»]

06.01.2012 Law of the Republic of Kazakhstan no. 527-IV on state security of the Republic of Kazakhstan [Закон Республики Казахстан от 6 января 2012 №527-IV «О национальной безопасности Республики Казахстан»]

04.07.2014 Criminal Procedure Code of the Republic of Kazakhstan no. 231-V Уголовно-процессуальный кодекс Республики Казахстан от 4 июля 2014 года № 231-V [valid from 01.01.2015]

Kyrygyzstan

11.01.1994 Law of the Kyrgyz Republic on the organs of internal affairs of the Kyrgyz Republic [Закон Кыргызской Республики от 11 января 1994 № 1360 XII «Об органах внутренних дел Кыргызской Республики»]

11.01.1994 Law of the Kyrgyz Republic no. 1362-XII on the organs of national security of the Kyrgyz Republic [Закон Кыргызской Республики от 11 января 1994 № 1362-XII «Об органах национальной безопасности Кыргызской Республики»]

01.10.1997 Criminal Code of the Kyrgyz Republic, no. 68 [Уголовный кодекс Кыргызской Республики от 1 октября 1997 № 68]

16.10.1998 Law of the Kyrgyz Republic no. 131 on operative-searching activity [Закон Кыргызской Республики «Об оперативно-розыскной деятельности от 16 октября 1998 № 131»]

30.06.1999 Criminal Procedure Code of the Kyrgyz Republic [Уголовно-процессуальный кодекс Кыргызской Республики от 30 июня 1999]

11.11.1999 Criminal Enforcement Code of the Kyrgyz Republic [Уголовно-Исполнительный Кодекс Кыргызской Республики от 11 ноября 1999]

31.10.2002 Law of the Kyrgyz Republic no. 150 on the oder and conditions of detention under guard of persons held on suspicion or accusation of the commission of a crime [Закон Кыргызской Республики от 31 октября 2002 года № 150 «О порядке и условиях содержания под стражей лиц, задержанных по подозрению и обвинению в совершении преступлений»

26.02.2003 Law of the Kyrgyz Republic no. 44 on national security [Закон Кыргызской Республики от 26 февраля 2003 №44 «О национальной безопасности»]

17.07.2009 Law of the Kyrgyz Republic no. 224 on the Procuracy of the Kyrgyz Republic [Закон Кыргызской Республики от 17 июля 2009 №224 «О прокуратуре Кыргызской Республики»]

15.12.2009 Statute of the Ministry of justice of the Kyrgyz Republic, Resolution of the Government of the Kyrgyz Republic no. 764 [Положение о Министерстве юстиции Кыргызской Республики утверждено постановлением Правительства Кыргызской Республики от 15 декабря 2009 № 764]

18.12.2009 Statute of the State Service for the Enforcement of Penalties under the Government of the Kyrgyz Republic, Resolution of the Government of the Kyrgyz Republic no. 775 [Положение о Государственной службе исполнения наказаний при Правительстве Кыргызской Республики, Постановление Правительства Кыргызской Республики от 18 декабря 2009 года № 775]

Tajikistan

21.05.1998 Criminal Code of the Republic of Tajikistan [Уголовный кодекс Республики Таджикистан от 21 мая 1998]

23.05.1998 Law of the Republic of Tajikistan no. 651 on operative-search activity [Закон Республики Таджикистан «Об оперативно-розыскной деятельности» от 23 мая 1998 года №65]

06.08.2001 Criminal Penalty Enforcement Code of the Republic of Tajikistan [Кодекс исполнения уголовных наказаний Республики Таджикистан от 6 августа 2001]

15.07.2004 Law of the Republic of Tajikistan no. 51 on the system for enforcement of criminal penalties [Закон Республики Таджикистан от 15 июля 2004 №51 «О системе исполнения уголовного наказания»]

25.07.2005 Constitutional Law of the Republic of Tajikistan no. 107 on the organs of the Procuracy of the Republic of Tajikistan [Конституционный Закон Республики Таджикистан от 25 июля 2005 № 107 «Об органах про куратуры Республики Таджикистан»]

28.12.2006 Statute of the Ministry of Internal Affairs of the Republic of Tajikistan, Resolution of the Government of Tajikistan no. 592 [Положение о Министерстве внутренних дел Республики Тадж икистан утверждено постановлением Правительства Республики Таджикистан от 28 декабря 2006 №592]

20.03.2008 Law of the Republic of Tajikistan n. 362 on the organs of state security of the Republic of Tajikistan [Закон Республики Таджикистан от 20 марта 2008 №362 «Об органах национальной безопасности Республики Таджикистан»]

01.04.2008 Statute of the Ministry of Justice of the Republic of Tajikistan, Resolution of the Government of Tajikistan no. 176 [Положение Министерства юстиции Республики Таджикистан в редакции Постановления Таджикистан от 1.04.2008 №176]

03.12.2009 Criminal Procedure Code of the Republic of Tajikistan [Уголовно—процессуальный кодекс Республики Таджикистан от 03 декабря 2009]

Turkmenistan

12.07.1997 Criminal Code of Turkmenistan no.222-I [Уголовный кодекс Туркменистана от 12 июня 1997 №222-I]

07.07.2001 Law of Turkmenistan no. 73-II on the police of Turkmenistan [Закон Туркменистана от 7 июля 2001 №73-II «О полиции Туркменистана»]

06.08.2008 Statute of the Ministry of Justice of Turkmenistan, Resolution of the President of Turkmenistan no. 9944 [Положение о Министерстве адалат Туркменистана, Постановление Президента Туркменистана от 6 августа 2008 № 9944]

18.04.2009 Criminal Procedure Code of Turkmenistan [Уголовно-процессуальный кодекс Туркменистана от 18 апреля 2009]

15.08.2009 Law of Turkmenistan no. 50-IV on the Procuracy of Turkmenistan [Закон Туркменистана от 15 августа 2009 №50-IV «О прокуратуре Туркменистана»]

25.03.2011 Criminal Enforcement Code of Turkmenistan no. 164-IV [Уголовно-исполнительный кодекс Туркменистана от 25 марта 2011 №164-IV]

21.05.2011 Law of Turkmenistan no. 195-IV on the organs of internal affairs [Закон Туркменистана от 21 мая 2011 №195-IV «Об органах внутренних дел»]

31.03.2012 Law of Turkmenistan no. 283-IV on the organs of national security of Turkmenistan [Закон Туркменистана от 31 марта 2012 №283-IV «Об органах национальной безопасности Туркменистана»]

Uzbekistan

02.11.1991 Resolution of Cabinet of Ministers under the President of the Republic of Uzbekistan no. 278 on the national security service of the Republic of Uzbekistan [Постановление Кабинета Министров при Президенте Республики Узбекистан №278 от 02.11.1991 «О службе национальной безопасности Республики Узбекистан»]

25.10.1991 Statute of the Ministry of Internal Affairs of the Republic of Uzbekistan, Resolution of the Cabinet of Ministers under the President of the Republic of Uzbekistan no. 270 on the Ministry of Internal Affairs of the Republic of Uzbekistan [Положение о Министерстве внутренних дел Республики Узбекистан, Постановление Кабинета Министров при Президенте Республики Узбекистан от 25 октября 1991 № 270 «О Министерстве Внутренних Дел Республики Узбекистан»]

09.12.1992 Law of the Republic of Uzbekistan no. 746-XII on the Procuracy [Закон Республики Узбекистан от 9 декабря 1992 №746-XII «О Прокуратуре»]

22.09.1994 Criminal Procedure Code of the Republic of Uzbekistan, confirmed by Law of the Republic of Uzbekistan no. 2013-XII [Уголовно-процессуальный кодекс Республики Узбекистан, утвержден Законом Республики Узбекистан от 22 сентября 1994 № 2013-XII]

22.09.1994 Criminal Code of the Republic of Uzbekistan, Law of the Republic of Uzbekistan no. 2013-XII [Уголовный Кодекс Республики Узбекистан, Закон Республики Узбекистан от 22 сентября 1994 № 2013-XII]

25.04.1997 Criminal Enforcement Code of the Republic of Uzbekistan, Law of the Republic of Uzbekistan № 409-1 [Уголовно-исполнительный кодекс Республики Узбекистан, Закон Республики Узбекистан от 25.04.1997 № 409-1]

23.08.2011 Statute of the Ministry of Justice of the Republic of Uzbekistan, Resolution of the President of Uzbekistam on measures for the further improvement of the activity of the Ministry of Justice of the Republic of Uzbekistan [Положение о Министерстве юстиции Республики Таджики стан, Постановление Президента Республики Узбекистан «О мерах по дальнейшему совершенствованию деятельности Министерства юстиции Республики Узбекистан» от 23 августа 2011]

25.12.2012 Law of the Republic of Uzbekistan no. 344 on operative-search activity [Закон Республики Узбекистан от 25 декабря 2012 года № 344 «Об оперативно-розыскной деятельности»]

8. RIGHTS PROTECTION

Kazakhstan

19.11.2002 Decree of the President of the Republic of Kazakhstan no. 947 on the establishment of the post of Plenipotentiary for Human Rights [Указ Президента Республики Казахстан от 19 сентября 2002 № 947«Об учреждении должности Уполномоченного по правам человека»]

10.12.2002 Statute of the National Centre for Human Rights, confirmed by Decree of the Presisdent of the Republic of Kazakhstan no. 992 [Положение о Национальном центре по правам человека утверждено Указом Президента Республики Казахстан от 10 декабря 2002 no. 992]

10.12.2002 Statute of the Plenipotentiary for Human Rights, Decree of the President of the Republic of Kazakhstan no. 992 [Положение об Уполномоченном по правам человека в Республике Казахстан, Указ Президента Республики Казахстан от 10 декабря 2002 № 992]

02.07.2013 Law of the Republic of Kazakhstan no. 111-V on bringing in amendments and additions to certain legislative acts of the Republic of Kazakhstan on issues of the creation of a national preventive mechanism directed to the prevention of torture and other cruel inhuman and degrading methods of treatment and punishment [Закон Республики Казахстан от 2 июля 2013 года № 111-V «О внесении изменений и дополнений в некоторые законодательные акты Республики Казахстан по вопросам создания национального превентивного механизма, направленного на предупреждение пыток и других жестоких, бесчеловечных или унижающих достоинство видов обращения и наказания»]

26.09.2013 Rules for selection of participants in the national preventive mechanism, Disposition of the Plenipotentiary for Human Rights no. 2 [Правила отбора участников национального превентивного механизма Распоряжение Уполномоченного по правам человека от 26 сентября 2013 года № 2]

26.09.2013 Statute of the Coordinating Council under the Plenipotentiary for Human Rights, Disposition of the Plenipotentitary for human rights no. 18 [Положение о Координационном совете при Уполномоченном по правам человека, распоряжение Уполномоченного по правам человека от 26 сентября 2013 № 18]

26.09.2013 Rules for the formation of the group of participants of the national preventive mechanism for preventive visits, Disposition of the Plenipotentitary for Human Rights no. 21 [Правила формирования групп из участников национального превентивного механизма для превентивных посещений, распоряжение Уполномоченного по правам человека от 26 сентября 2013 года № 21]

26.09.2013 Rules of the annual consolidated report on the results of preventive visits, Disposition of the Plenipotentitary for Human Rights no. 22 [Правила подготовки ежегодного консолидированного доклада по итогам превентивных посещений, распоряжение Уполномоченного по правам человека от 26 сентября 2013 года № 22]

Kyrygyzstan

31.06.2002 Law of the Kyrgyz Republic no. 136 on the Ombudsmen (Akyikatchy) [Закон Кыргызской Республики от 31 июля 2002 №136 «Об Омбудсмене (Акыйкатчы) Кыргызской Республики»]

29.09.2010 Statute of a civil society observation council for a state body, Decree of the President of the Kyrgyz Reublic no. 212 [Положение об общественном наблюдательном совете при государственном органе, указ Президента Кыргызской Республики от 29 сентября 2010 № 212]

12.05.2011 Rules, Civil Society Observing Council under the Ministry of Internal Affairs of the Kyrgyz Republic, Decision of Civil society observing council under the Ministry of Internal Affairs of the Kyrgyz Republic, protocol no. 2 [Регламент Общественного наблюдательного совета при Министерстве внутренних дел Кыргызской Республики, Решение Общественного наблюдательно совета при Министерстве внутренних дел Кыргызской Республики от 12 мая 2011 Протокол №2]

25.07.2014 Report of the Ombudsmen (Akyikatchy) of the Kyrgyz Republic on observance of human and citizen rights and freedoms in the Kyrgyz Republic in 2013 [Доклад Акыйкатчы (Омбудсмена) Кыргызской Республики «О соблюдении прав и свобод человека и гражданина в Кыргызской Республике в 2013 году»] http://ombudsman.kg/reports/299-doklad-akyykatchy-ombudsmena-kyrgyzskoy-respubliki-o-soblyudenii-prav-i-svobod-cheloveka-i-grazhdanina-v-kyrgyzskoy-respublike-v-2013-godu-doklad-akyykatchy-ombudsmena-kyrgyzskoy-respubliki.html (accessed 10 October 2014)

Tajikistan

14.12.1996 Law of the Republic of Tajikistan no. 343 on citizens' applications [Закон Республики Таджикистан от 14 декабря 1996 года №343«Об обращениях граждан»]

20.03.2008 Law of the Republic of Tajikistan no. 372 on the Plenipotentiary for Human Rights in the Republic of Tajikistan [Закон Республики Таджик истан «Об уполномоченном по правам человека в Республике Таджикис тан» 20 марта 2008 №372]

Turkmenistan

23.10.1996 Decree of the President of Turkmenistan on the creation of the Turkmen National Institute of Democracu and Human Rights under the President of Turkmenistan [Указ Президента Туркменистана от 23 октября 1996 «О создании Туркменского национального института демократии и прав человека при Президенте Туркменистана»]

19.02.2007 Decree of the President of Turkmenistan on the creation of the State Commission under the President of Turkmenistan for the review of citizens' applications relating to issues of the activity of law enforcement bodies [Указ Президента Туркмнеистана от 19 Февраля 2007 «О создании Государственной комиссии по рассмотрению обращений граждан по вопросам деятельности правоохранительных органов при Президенте Туркменистана»]

Uzbekistan

30.08.1995 Law of the Republic of Uzbekistan no. 108-I on the appeal to court of actions and decisions violating citizens' rights and freedoms [Закон Республики Узбекистан от 30 августа 1995 № 108-I «Об обжаловании в суд действий и решений, нарушающих права и свободы граждан»]

24.04.1997 Law of the Republic of Uzbekistan on the Plenipotentiary for Human Rights (Ombudsman) [Закон Республики Узбекистан от 24 апреля 1997 «Об Уполномоченном Олий Мажлиса по правам человека (омбудсмане)»]

01.08.2005 Decree of the President of the Republic of Uzbekistan on the abolition of capital punishment [Указ Президента Республики Узбекистан «Об отмене смертной казни» от 1 августа 2005]

9. CIVIL, COMMERCIAL, AND ECONOMIC LEGISLATION

Kazakhstan

27.12.1994 Civil Code (General Part) of the Republic of Kazakhstan [Гражд анский кодекс Республики Казахстан (общая часть) от 27 декабря 1994]

23.12.1995 Decree of the President of the Republic of Kazakhstan having the force of law No. 2721 on privatisation [Указ Президента Республики Казахстан, имеющий силу Закона от 23 декабря 1995 года № 2721 «О приватизации»] (annulled)

01.07.1999 Civil Code (Special Part) of the Republic of Kazakhstan n. 409-I of the Republic of Kazakhstan [Гражданский кодекс Республики Казахстан (особенная часть) от 1 июля 1999 №409-I]

13.07.1999 Civil Procedure Code of the Republic of Kazakhstan no. 411-1 of the Republic of Kazakhstan [Гражданский процессуальный кодекс Республики Казахстан от 13 июля 1999 №411-I]

05.08.2002 Statute of the Accounts Committee for control of execution of the republican budget, Decree of the President of Kazkhstan no. 917 [«Положение о Счетном комитете по контролю за исполнением республиканского бюджета», Указ Президента Республики Казахстан от 5 августа 2002 № 917]

08.01.2003 Law of the Republic of Kazakhstan No. 373-II on investments [Закон Республики Казахстан от 8 января 2003 года № 373-II «Об инвестициях»]

Kyrygyzstan

05.01.1998 Civil Code of the Kyrgyz Republic, Part 2 [Гражданский кодекс Кыргызской Республики от 5 января 1998 № 1. Часть II]

08.05.1996 Civil Code of the Kyrgyz Republic, Part 1 (Civil Code) no. 15 [Гр ажданский кодекс Кыргызской Республики от 8 мая 1996 № 15. Часть I]

13.08.2004 Law of the Kyrgyz Republic no. 117 on the Accounts Chamber [Закон Кыргызской Республики от 13 августа 2004 №117 «О Счетной палате»]

27.03.2003 Law of the Kyrgyz Republic no. 66 on foreign investments in the Kyrgyz Republic [Закон Кыргызской Республики от 27 марта 2003 № 66 «Об инвестициях в Кыргызской Республике»]

29.12.1999 Civil Procedure Code of the Kyrgyz Republic [Гражданский процессуальный кодекс Кыргызской Республики от 29 декабря 1999 № 146]

Tajikistan

30.06.1999 Civil Code of the Republic of Tajikistan, part 1 [Гражданский кодекс Республики Таджикистан от 30 июня 1999 (часть первая)]

11.12.1999 Civil Code of the Republic of Tajikistan, part 2 Гражданский кодекс Республики Таджикистан от 11 декабря 1999 (часть вторая)]

01.03.2005 Civil Code of the Republic of Tajikistan, part 3 [Гражданский кодекс Республики Таджикистан от 01 марта 2005 (часть третья)]

12.05.2007 Law of the Republic of Tajikistan no. 260 on investment [Закон Республики Таджикистан от 12 мая 2007 № 260 «Об инвестиции»

05.01.2008 Civil Procedure Code of the Republic of Tajikistan [Гражданский процессуальный кодекс Республики Таджикистан от 5 января 2008]

Uzbekistan

21.12.1995 Civil Code of the Republic of Uzbekistan, Part I, confirmed by Law of the Republic of Uzbekistan no. 163-I [Гражданский Кодекс Республики Узбекистан Часть первая утверждена Законом Республики Узбекистан № 163-I от 21.12.95]

29.08.1996 Civil Code, of the Republic of Uzbekistan, Part II confirmed by Law of the Republic of Uzbekistan no. 256-I [Гражданский Кодекс Республики Узбекистан Часть вторая утверждена Законом Республики Узбекистан №256-I от 29 августа 1996]

30.04.1998 Law of the Republic of Uzbekistan on foreign investments no. 609-I [Закон Республики Узбекистан от 30 апреля 1998 года № 609-I«Об иностранных инвестициях»]

30.08.1997 Civil procedure Code of the Republic of Uzbekistan, confirmed by Law of the Republic of Uzbekistan n. 477-I [Гражданский процессуальный кодекс Республики Узбекистан, утвержден Законом Республики Узбекистан от 30.08.1997 № 477-I]

31.06.2002 Decree of the President of the Republic of Uzbekistan no. 3093 on the completion of the creation of the Accounts chamber of the Republic of Uzbekistan [Указ Президента Республики Узбекистан от 21 июня 2002 года № 3093 «О создании Счетной палаты Республики Узбекистан».]

Turkmenistan

01.10.1993 Law of Turkmenistan no. 858-XII on property [Закон Туркменистана № 858-XII от 1 октября 1993 «О собственности»]

17.07.1998 Civil Code of Turkmenistan [Гражданский кодекс Туркменистана от 17 июля 1998 №294-I]

15.06.2000 Law of Turkmenistan on enterprises [Закон Туркменистана «О предприятиях» от 15 июня 2000]

19.12.2000 *Arbitrazh* Procedure Code of Turkmenistan [Арбитражный процессуальный кодекс Туркменистана от 19 декабря 2000]

03.03.2008 Law of Turkmenistan no. 184-III on foreign investments [Закон Туркменистана № 184-III от 3 марта 2008 «Об иностранных инвестициях»]

18.12.2013 Law of Turkmenistan on denationalisation and privatisation of state property [Закон Туркменистана от 18 декабря 2013 «О разгосударствлении и приватизации государственного имущества»]

10. SOCIAL LEGISLATION

Kazakhstan

25.04.1993 Law of the Republic of Kazakhstan no, 405-II on compulsory social insurance [Закон Республики Казахстан от 25 апреля 2003 № 405-II «Об обязательном социальном страховании»]

15.05.2007 Labour Code of the Republic of Kazakhstan no. 251 [Трудовой кодекс Республики Казахстан Кодекс Республики Казахстан от 15 мая 2007 № 251]

21.06.2013 Law of the Republic of Kazakhstan no. 105-V on pension provision in the Republic of Kazakhstan [Закон Республики Казахстан от 21 июня 2013 № 105-V «О пенсионном обеспечении в Республике Казахс тан»]

Kyrygyzstan

04.08.2004 Labour Code of the Kyrgyz Republic no. 106 [Трудовой кодекс Кыргызской Республики от 4 августа 2004 года № 106]

Tajikistan

15.05.1997 Labour Code of the Republic of Tajikistan no. 417 [Трудовой кодекс Республики Таджикистан от 15 мая 1997 № 417]

Turkmenistan

18.04.2009 Labour Code of Turkmenistan no. 20-IV [Трудовой кодекс Туркменистана от 18 апреля 2009 №30-IV]

19.10.2012 Code of Turkmenistan on the social protection of the population [Кодекс Туркменистана от 19 октября 2012 «О социальной защите насел-ения»]

31.03.2012 Law of Turkmenistan on state pension insurance [Закон Туркменистана от 31 марта 2012 «О государственном пенсионном страх-ованиии»]

04.11.2013 Law of Turkemistan on trade unions, their rights and guarantees of activity [Закон Туркменистана от 04.11.2013 «О профессиональных союзах, их правах и гарантиях деятельности»]

Uzbekistan

03.09.1993 Law of the Republic of Uzbekistan no. №938-XII on the state pension provision of citizens [Закон Республики Узбекистан от 3 сентября 1993 №938-XII «О государственном пенсионном обеспечении граждан»]

12.12.1995 Labour Code of the Republic of Uzbekistan [Трудовой кодекс Республики Узбекистан от 21 декабря 1995]

11. LOCAL GOVERNMENT

Kazakhstan

08.12.1993 Law of the Republic of Kazakhstan no. 2572-XII on the administrative territorial system of the Republic of Kazakhstan [Закон Республики Казахстан от 8 декабря 1993 №2572-XII «Об административно-территориальном устройстве Республики Казахстан»

23.01.2001 Law of the Republic of Kazakhstan no. 148 on local state administration and self-government in the Republic of Kazakhstan [Закон Республики Казахстан» от 23 января 2001 № 148 «О местном государственном управлении и самоуправлении в Республике Казахстан»]

Kyrygyzstan

14.06.2011 Law of the Kyrgyz Republic no. 96 on local state administration [Закон Кыргызской Республики от 14 июля 2011 года N 96 «О местной государственной администрации»]

15.06.2011 Law of the Kyrgyz Republic no. 101 on local self-government [Закон Кыргызской Республики от 15 июля 2011 № 101 «О местном самоуправлении»]

Tajikistan

17.05.2004 Constitutional Law of the Republic of Tajikistan no. 28 on local bodies of state authority [Конституционный Закон Республики Таджикис тан от 17 мая 2004 № 28 «О местных органах государственной власти»]

30.07.2007 Constitutional Law of the Republic of Tajikistan no. 303 on Gorno-Badakhshan autonomous province [Конституционный Закон Республики Таджикистан от 30 июля 2007 № 303 «О Горно-Бадахшанской автономной области»]

Turkmenistan

25.10.2005 Law of the Republic of Turkmenistan on etrap and town halk maslakhaty [Закон Туркменистана от 25 октября 2005 «Об этрапском, городском халк маслахаты»]

01.10.2011 Law of Turkmenistan the representative organs of local authority [Закон Туркменистана от 1 октября 2011 «О представительных органах местной власти»]

Uzbekistan

02.09.1993 Law of the Republic of Uzbekistan no. 915-XII on the organs of citizens' self-government [Закон Республики Узбекистан от 2 сентября 1993 № 915-XII «Об органах самоуправления граждан»]

12. CITIZENSHIP, ASSOCIATION, RELIGION, MEDIA, LANGUAGE, EDUCATION

Kazakhstan

20.12.1991 Law of the Republic of Kazakhstan on citizenship of the Republic of Kazakhstan [Закон Республики Казахстан от 20 декабря 1991 «О гражд анстве Республики Казахстан»]

31.05.1996 Law of the Republic of Kazakhstan no. 3 on social associations [Закон Республики Казахстан от 31 мая 1996 № 3 «Об общественных объединениях»]

23.07.1999 Law no. 451-I on mass media of information [Закон Республики Казахстан от 23 июля 1999 № 451-I «О средствах массовой информации»]

16.01.2001 Law of the Republic of Kazakhstan no. 142-II on noncommercial organisations [Закон Республики Казахстан от 16 января 2001 № 142-II «О некоммерческих организациях»]

18.02.2005 Law of the Republic of Kazakhstan no. 31 on countering terrorism [Закон Республики Казахстан от 18 февраля 2005 № 31«О противодействии экстремизму»]

27.07.2007 Law of the Republic of Kazakhstan no. 319-III on education [Закон Республики Казахстан от 27 июля 2007 № 319-III «Об образовании»]

20.10.2008 Law of the Republic of Kazakhstan on the Assembly of the Peoples of Kazakhstan no. 70-4 [Закон Республики Казахстан от 20.10.2008 N 70-4 «Об Ассамблее народа Казахстана»]

11.10.2011 Law of the Republic of Kazakhstan no. 483-IV on religious activity and religious organisations [Закон Республики Казахстан от 11 октября 2011 № 483-IV О религиозной деятельности и религиозных объединениях]

26.08.2013 Rules for the processing, issue, replacement, surrender, confiscation and destruction of the passport of a citizen of the Republic of Kazakhstan, identity card of a citizen of the Republic of Kazakhstan, residence permit of a foreigner in the Republic of Kazakhstan, stateless document and refugee document, Resolution of the Government of the Republic of Kazakhstan no. 852 [Правила оформления, выдачи, замены, сдачи, изъятия и уничтожения паспорта гражданина Республики Казахстан, удостоверения личности гражданина Республики Казахстан, вида на жительство иностранца в Республике Казахстан, удостоверения лица без гражданства и удостоверения беженца, Постановление Правительства Республики Казахстан от 26 августа 2013 № 852]

Kyrygyzstan

02.07.1992 Law of the Kyrgyz Republic no. 938-XII on media of mass information [Закон Кыргызской Республики от 2 июля 1992 № 938-XII «О средствах массовой информации»]

15.10.1999 Law of the Kyrgyz Republic no. 111 on social associations [Закон Кыргызской Республики от 15 октября 1999 года № 111 «Об общественных объединениях»]

28.12.2006 Law of the Kyrgyz Republic no. 225 on education [Закон Кыргызской Республики от 28 декабря 2006 № 225 «Об образовании»]

21.05.2007 Law of the Kyrgyz Republic no. 70 on citizenship of the Kyrgyz Republic [Закон Кыргызской Республики от 21 мая 2007 № 70 «О гражданстве Кыргызской Республики»]

31.12.2008 Law of the Kyrgyz Republic n. 282 on the freedom of confession and religious organisations in the Kyrgyz Republic [Закон Кыргызской Республики от 31 декабря 2008 № 282 «О свободе вероисповедания и религиозных организациях в Кыргызской Республике»]

31.12.2008 Law of the Kyrgyz Republic no. 282 on the freedom of profession of faith and religious organisations in the Kyrgyz Republic [Закон Кыргызской Республики от 31 декабря 2008 № 282 «О свободе вероисповедания и религиозных организациях в Кыргызской Республике»]

14.07.2011 Law of the Kyrgyz Republic no. 96 on local state administration [Закон Кыргызской Республики от 14 июля 2011 № 96 «О местной государственной администрации»]

15.07.2011 Law of the Kyrgyz Republic no. 101 on local self-government [Закон Кыргызской Республики от 15 июля 2011 № 101 «О местном самоуправлении»]

Tajikistan

04.11.1995 Constitutional Law of the Republic of Tajikistan no. 104 on citizenship of the Republic of Tajikistan [Конституционный Закон Республики Таджикистан от 4 ноября 1995 года №104 «О гражданстве Республики Таджикистан»]

12.05.2007 Law of the Republic of Tajikistan n. 258 on social associations [Закон Республики Таджикистан от 12 мая 2007 года №258 «Об общественных объединениях»]

26.03.2009 Law of the Republic of Tajikistan no. 489 on freedom of conscience and religious associations [Закон Республики Таджикистан от 26 марта 2009 № 489 «О свободе совести и религиозных объединениях»]

19.03.2013 Law of the Republic of Tajikistan no. 961 on the periodic press and other media of mass information [Закон Республики Таджикистан от 19 марта 2013 №961 «О периодической печати и других средствах массовой информации»]

22.07.2013 Law of the Republic of Tajikistan no. 1004 on education [Закон Республики Таджикистан от 22 июля 2013 №1004 «Об образовании»]

Turkmenistan

21.10.2003 Law of Turkmenistan on the freedom of profession of faith and religious organisations [Закон Туркменистана от 21 октября 2003 «О свободе вероисповедания и религиозных организациях»]

15.08.2009 Law of Turkmenistan no. №51-IV on education [Закон Туркменистана от 15 августа 2009 №51-IV «Об образовании»]

22.12.2012 Law of the Republic of Turkmenistan on mass media of information [Закон Республики Туркменистан от 22.12.2012 «О средствах массовой информации»]

22.06.2013 Law of Turkmenistan on citizenship of Turkmenistan [Закон Туркменистана от 22 июня 2013 «О гражданстве Туркменистана»]

03.05.2014 Law of Turkmenistan on social associations [Закон Туркменистана от 3 мая 2014 «Об общественных объединениях»]

Uzbekistan

21.10.1989 Law of the Republic of Uzbekistan no. 3561-XI on the state language [Закон Республики Узбекистан от 21 октября 1989 № 3561-XI «О государственном языке»]

15.02.1991 Law of the Republic of Uzbekistan no. 223-XII on social associations in the Republic of Uzbekistan [Закон Республики Узбекистан от 15 февраля 1991 № 223-XII «Об общественных объединениях в Республике Узбекистан»]

14.06.1991 Law of the Republic of Uzbekistan no. 289-XII on freedom of conscience and religious organisations, [Закон Республики Узбекистан от 14 июня 1991 № 289-XII «О свободе совести и религиозных организациях»]

02.07.1992 Law of the Republic of Uzbekistan № 632-XII [Закон Республики Узбекистан от 2 июля 1992 № 632-XII «О гражданстве Республики Узб екистан»]

29.08.1997 Law of the Republic of Uzbekistan no. 464-I on education [Закон Республики Узбекистан от 29 августа 1997 № 464-I «Об образовании»]

26.12.1997 Law of the Republic of Uzbekistan no. 541-I on mass media of informationЗакон Республики Узбекистан от 26 декабря 1997 № 541-I «О средствах массовой информации»]

21.04.2004 Regulations of the Committee for Religious Affairs under the Cabinet of Ministers of the Republic of Uzbekistan, Resolution the Cabinet of Ministers of the Republic of Uzbekistan no. 196 [Положение о Комитете по делам религий при Кабинете Министров Республики Узбекистан, постановление Кабинета Министров Республики Узбекистан от 23 апреля 2004 года № 196]

WEBSITES OF STATE AUTHORITIES

KAZAKHSTAN

President www.akorda.kz
Parliament www.parlam.kz
Government www.government.kz
Ministry of Justice http://www.adilet.gov.kz/ru
Ministry of Internal Affairs www.mvd.gov.kz
Supreme Court www.sud.gov.kz
Constitutional Council www.ksrk.gov.kz
Plenipotentiary for human rights (Ombudsman) www.ombudsman.kz

KYRGYZSTAN

President www.president.kg/
Parliament www.kenesh.kg
Government www.gov.kg
Constitutional Chamber of Supreme Court http://constpalata.kg/ru/
Ministry of Justice http://minjust.gov.kg/
Ministry of Internal Affairs www.mvd.kg
Supreme Court www.jogorku.sot.kg
Ombudsman www.ombudsman.kg

TAJIKISTAN

President www.prezident.tj
Parliament http://parlament.tj
Ministry of Justice www.minjust.tj
Ministry of Internal Affairs http://www.vkd.tj
Supreme Economic Court www.soi.tj
Constitutional Court www.constcourt.tj
Plenipotentiary for human rights (Ombudsman) www.ombudsman.tj

UZBEKISTAN

President www.gov.uz/ru/president
Parliament www.parliament.gov.uz, www.senat.uz
Government www.gov.uz
Ministry of Justice www.minjust.uz
Ministry of Internal Affairs www.mvd.uz
Supreme Court www.supcourt.uz

Constitutional Court www.ksu.uz
Ombudsman www.ombudsman.gov.uz

TURKMENISTAN

Universal www.turkmenistan.gov.tm

Index